Library of
Davidson College

FUNERAL ORATORY
AND THE CULTURAL IDEALS
OF ITALIAN HUMANISM

John M. McManamon, S.J.

FUNERAL ORATORY

and the CULTURAL

IDEALS *of* ITALIAN

HUMANISM

The University of North Carolina Press

Chapel Hill & London

©1989 The University of North Carolina Press

All rights reserved

Library of Congress Cataloging-in-Publication Data
McManamon, John M.
  Funeral oratory and the cultural ideals of Italian humanism / John M. McManamon.
  p. cm.
  Bibliography: p.
  Includes indexes.
  ISBN 0-8078-1783-X
  1. Speeches, addresses, etc., Latin (Medieval and modern)—History and criticism. 2. Funeral orations—History and criticism. 3. Ethics in literature. 4. Rhetoric—1500–1800. 5. Rhetoric, Medieval. 6. Humanists—Italy. 7. Oratory—Italy. I. Title.
PA8085.M35 1989   88-19840
808.5'1—dc19   CIP

The paper in this book meets the guidelines for permanence and durability of the Committee on Production Guidelines for Book Longevity of the Council on Library Resources.

Printed in the United States of America

93 92 91 90 89 5 4 3 2 1

For my mother and father

CONTENTS

Preface ix

CHAPTER ONE
The Rhetorical Situation 1

CHAPTER TWO
A Humanist Conviction:
"Virtue Increases When Praised" 5

CHAPTER THREE
Bona Externa:
Birthplace, Descent, Education 36

CHAPTER FOUR
Ecclesiastical Ideals:
"As You Did It to Any of the Least" 63

CHAPTER FIVE
Political Ideals:
"Be Merciful to the Submissive, and Crush the Arrogant" 88

CHAPTER SIX
Academic Ideals:
"Perfected in the Arts Appropriate to Humanity" 123

CHAPTER SEVEN
Ethos Enshrined 153

Abbreviations 163

Notes 165

Appendix:
A Short-title Finding List of Funeral Orations
from the Italian Renaissance, ca. 1374–1534   249

Bibliography   293

Index of Manuscripts   321

General Index   325

PREFACE

Some years ago, while rummaging through the catalogues of incunabula in a rather fruitless search for Ash Wednesday sermons from Renaissance Italy, I began to notice how frequently the title "Oratio in funere" recurred among the catalogues' entries. I asked my director at the time, John O'Malley, whether the funeral orations of the Renaissance had ever been studied and if he felt they merited such attention. He answered no to the first question and gave an affirmative response to the second on the basis of his sound scholarly instincts.

A few months later O'Malley introduced me to Paul Oskar Kristeller while we were all attending the annual conference on medieval studies at Western Michigan University. When O'Malley mentioned to Kristeller that I had begun to research the topic of Renaissance funeral oratory, the renowned professor immediately asked me how many orations I had discovered in the course of my research. I had not completed a systematic investigation at that time. I therefore nervously went with an estimate, based upon my impression that there were many speeches, and responded with what seemed to me the enormous total of approximately seventy. Kristeller paused in his tracks, looked at me somewhat perplexed, and assured me on the basis of his vast knowledge of Renaissance sources that there were many more than seventy. He was correct, as a glance at the appendix will demonstrate.

Thus was a project felicitously born, with the encouragement and corrective guidance of two influential scholars whose continued interest over the years has been no less active or appreciated. In fact, I have consistently been fortunate to receive assistance and encouragement from other learned scholars, whom I happily consider friends. I am grateful to Salvatore Camporeale, Arthur Field, Gianfranco Fioravanti, Mark Henninger, Margaret King, Julian Kliemann,

David Marsh, John Monfasani, Helen North, and Charles Rosenberg for reading parts of the study and contributing to its improvement. I wish to thank in a special way the individuals who read and criticized an earlier draft of the entire book: Stephen Baxter, Melissa Bullard, Fred Behrends, George Kennedy, Ann Vasaly, Ronald Witt, and particularly John Headley.

This book interprets a species of oratory practiced in a particular European region over a period of approximately 160 years. I first had to locate the materials relevant to the study. The catalogues of incunabula and the biographical data compiled on Italian humanists in the last hundred years supplied many leads. The single most important resource, however, was the *Iter Italicum* of Paul Oskar Kristeller. An entry-by-entry reading of its three volumes published to date helped me to assemble a list of potentially relevant orations and isolate the more popular ones through their frequency of appearance and diffusion.

Travels to various libraries and archives throughout Italy brought the list into finer focus. I thank the American Academy in Rome, Villa I Tatti in Florence, and the National Endowment for the Humanities for fellowships that financed those travels and permitted me to work in most congenial and supportive scholarly communities. I am also grateful to the many libraries that allowed me to consult their resources firsthand or granted my requests for microfilm. A special word of thanks goes to the prefect and staff of the Vatican Library, whose vast humanist holdings supplied the majority of material for this work.

Lewis Bateman, executive editor of the University of North Carolina Press, has competently guided every stage of production and patiently answered my many queries. I gained much from the careful reading and criticisms of the Press's professional referees and from the diligent work of staff members like Laura Oaks, Sandra Eisdorfer, and Amy Schutz. I especially acknowledge the Press's interest in publishing a work that issues from a rather specialized area of European intellectual history. A generous subvention awarded by Loyola University of Chicago also aided the publication of this book.

I hope to repay the University's confidence by sharing with its students my belief in humanism. Scott Smith of Loyola gave many hours to help me prepare the index.

During the years that I have studied oratory, friends and colleagues have frequently said to me that certain passages and ideas are merely topics. What is important, though, is that orators were fully aware that they were using common ways of thinking and modes of expression in inventing their speeches. In fact, Aristotle had defined the art of rhetoric as the ability to discover the available means of persuasion: one need not persuade to be a good orator; the art lay in choosing from common categories to craft a discourse. Prefaces to scholarly writings often contain acknowledgments like my own. I personally read them as manifestations of the scholar's art of rhetoric and hope that mine are seen to reflect conscious choices and sincere sentiments. Scholarship is much more of a communal venture than it may seem.

In quoting Latin sources, I have decided to standardize orthography and punctuation according to modern criteria. That applies to titles, names, and quotations from the texts themselves. Square brackets indicate material lacking in a source, which I have added. I have not used the recto sign except for references limited to a single folio: e.g., fols. 52–53v, but fol. 52r–v. In notes that involve a series of speeches, the citations are arranged in alphabetical order to facilitate reference to the appendix. I have used vernacular names whenever possible. These steps were taken to assist the reader in entering the peculiar world of celebratory orations so prized by humanists of the Italian Renaissance. If I have misrepresented that world or portrayed it unfairly, the blame is mine alone.

At the conclusion of my sophomore year of high school, I was offered a choice between two curricula. I could pursue a course in Classical Honors, which meant two further years of Latin and two years of Greek, or I could choose Scientific Honors, where French and the physical sciences were emphasized. Though attracted toward science when it was riding the crest of the educational wave, I knew that my parents would insist on the curriculum in classical languages. I therefore decided to contribute to familial harmony for once in my life. I announced my choice for Classical Honors and sensed immediately from my parents' approval that my instincts were correct. I dedicate this book to my mother and father as an expression of affection for two intrepid defenders of the humanist tradition.

FUNERAL ORATORY
AND THE CULTURAL IDEALS
OF ITALIAN HUMANISM

CHAPTER ONE

THE RHETORICAL SITUATION

This book builds upon a scholarly consensus and examines Italian humanism through new sources in a different context. Those who study humanism generally agree with Paul Oskar Kristeller in seeing the movement as a characteristic phase in the rhetorical tradition of Western culture.[1] Rhetoric, as conceptualized by the ancient Greeks, intended to teach students how to invent, organize, stylistically embellish, and deliver a speech. As Cicero stated in the *Orator* (19.61), the essence of oratory lies in artful speaking. Cicero argued that the Greek word *rhetor* should be rendered in Latin by *eloquens*. Rhetoric primarily means speechmaking.[2]

Historians of humanism have focused upon its literary and scholarly concerns and only recently have begun to treat those more directly rhetorical. When discussing Renaissance eloquence, moreover, scholars have directed their energy to technical aspects like the theory and teaching of rhetoric. Little attention has been paid to its practice. Historians have generally ignored or despised the primary products of Renaissance eloquence, the orations composed for occasions like weddings, funerals, the opening of the academic year, and the arrival of political and judicial officials or their departure after a period of service.[3]

This study examines one popular species of oration from the Italian Renaissance: Latin funeral orations delivered in the geographical region now known as Italy, between the time of Petrarch's death in 1374 and the death of Pope Clement VII in 1534. Any chronological definition of the Renaissance is arbitrary. These limits were chosen for the following reasons.

Petrarch died in 1374 at Arquà near Padua. Any study of humanism appropriately begins with Petrarch. A study of funeral oratory confirms the rule in reverse fashion. Petrarch delivered a funeral sermon for Archbishop Giovanni Visconti of Milan in 1354 and was eulogized after his death by a member of his circle, Bonaventura Badoer. Both of these funeral sermons aid our understanding of the evolution of early humanism. They are typically scholastic, not humanist products. Clement VII died in 1534, when new issues of reform and counter-reform had begun to cloud the cultural horizon. The editors of the *Annales ecclesiastici* incorporated into their history a funeral oration written for Cardinal Cajetan in 1534 because of its anti-Lutheran polemics.[4] An era of intellectual tolerance had drawn to a close.

Funeral oratory comprises a species within the genre of epideictic rhetoric. Italian humanists overwhelmingly pursued the eloquence of praise and censure and used that genre in typical fashion to deepen values or to change attitudes. It is a rhetoric prone to portray things as they should be.[5] One of the first humanists to practice classicizing oratory defined a proper funeral speech. In 1426 Poggio Bracciolini rebuked Francesco da Vellate for his incompetence in writing a funeral oration on Jean de Broniac, the papal vice-chancellor. Poggio's criticisms betray his conception of the "ideal funeral oration."[6]

In his attack on Francesco, Poggio upheld two traditional virtues of style. First, any funeral oration should be delivered in correct Latin, but Francesco did not speak or write Latin correctly. Secondly, his grammatical errors and frequent use of circumlocutions and superlatives obfuscated the sense of his discourse. Poggio thus advocated clarity in public speaking. Further, with regard to invention, Poggio derided Francesco for failing to adduce historical deeds as proof for the virtues of de Broniac: he had merely listed virtues without substantiating them. Worse yet, Francesco admitted in a letter to Poggio that he had affirmed things that were less than true and amplified others on the basis of hearsay. Poggio cited Cicero (*De or.* 2.85.345) and Quintilian (3.7.4) to defend his position that all authorities on rhetoric have taught that an orator who praises must prove his assertions by referring to historical deeds. An epideictic orator should proceed as Cicero had in the *De lege Manilia*, when he described actions that Pompey had performed in order to demonstrate his virtues.

Humanists felt that panegyrists should amplify historical deeds in order to reaffirm values or to convince the audience of their necessity. Orators shirked their duty when they lied or expatiated on deeds unfamiliar to them. The orations supplied norms for future conduct and advocated ideals in an important social moment. Death easily suggested an examination of values, and Renaissance Italians developed a variety of commemorative exercises.[7] Funeral eulogies were unique among those forms because they were delivered publicly.

Who constituted a humanist's public? The question is difficult to answer. Often we have only a humanist's own assessment of his success in persuading those present. State funerals attracted large audiences throughout the peninsula. They were an elaborate and solemn public ritual. Would those huge crowds understand a eulogy delivered in classicizing Latin? In Leonardo Bruni's estimation, the question required a double response. One had to distinguish the majority of the audience from the ruling class. The illiterate masses would comprehend the ceremony and its oration much as they understood the Latin spoken during the Mass. Governors would bring a more refined comprehension to the rite. Bruni admitted that he addressed his message primarily to civic authorities. He felt confident that humanist orators successfully communicated their message because they put into words what people saw.[8]

The various elements in the speech act—speaker, speech, audience, occasion—guide the investigation of Italian humanism that follows. Though state funerals attracted large crowds, they were primarily an exercise among society's elite. Humanists principally directed their funeral eulogies to the rulers, bureaucrats, lawyers, doctors, and merchants of their day—and to fellow humanists as well. They focused their attention on those who wielded power in society. Their speeches sought to propagate or reinforce values by presenting historical deeds in vivid terms. They felt that they could convince people by making them see those values portrayed in real life.

Only an orator trained in classical rhetoric could craft such a speech. If humanists persuaded their audiences, they would prove the value of a humanist education. That education fostered concern for the common good. In their public activities, humanists revealed themselves as idealists and as social reformers whose program fundamentally derived from the Roman notion of ethos as a mode of persuasion. Like the Romans, they insisted that the orator combine virtues with gifts of speech (Quintilian 1.Pr.9).

This book seeks to filter out ideals that were shared by humanists in various Italian states. It would be impossible here to supply a detailed analysis of the more than five hundred speeches examined, and their individual contexts. The appendix is offered to assist future scholars who may wish to analyze a particular speech more closely. Here, however, the ideals are presented synthetically. They should enrich the spirit of any commonwealth no matter what its constitutional form. We shall see the public world of the humanists as they desired it to be.

CHAPTER TWO

A HUMANIST CONVICTION
"Virtue Increases When Praised"

"Farewell, my dog, and may you gain the immortality to which your virtue aspires!"[1] With this dramatic apostrophe Leon Battista Alberti concluded a witty eulogy written on a hot summer's night in the mid-Quattrocento to honor his canine companion. Data supplied in the speech lead one to infer that Alberti's dog was prodigious and shared many interests with distinguished persons of his era. Descended from a long line of noble, courageous, and loyal animals, the wily pet renounced a career in combat at a young age in order to devote himself to the liberal arts. Alberti marveled at his friend's speed in mastering literary studies. His dog learned Greek, Latin, and Tuscan in less than three years. Moreover, since his companion spurned wealth in favor of learning and lived a life of self-control, to which a single suit of clothing and no shoes attested, Alberti could adduce him as an exemplar of "moral living."[2]

Alberti's satiric purpose is apparent and effective. That he could present a parody of humanist funeral oratory in the middle of the Quattrocento demonstrates how well entrenched that species had become. Funeral orations provided worthy grist for his satirizing mill.[3] Renaissance humanists had fastened on funeral oratory in part because it had been developed and practiced by their classical forebears. In the exordium of his eulogy, Alberti himself alluded to classical precedents, stressing that the Athenians had invented panegyric and that the Romans had extended the practice beyond public heroes to private individuals and family members. He therefore pressed on to commend his dog.[4] Certainly Italian humanists attempted to imitate ancient practice by delivering funeral eulogies.

But in the half-century between the emergence of classicizing funeral oratory in Renaissance Italy and the composition of Alberti's satire, a creative transformation had occurred.

One can only appreciate the creative contribution of the humanists against the background of the history of the funeral eulogy as a species of epideictic oration. That history, however, defies simple summation for several reasons. The *epitaphios logos* first appeared, in all likelihood, at Athens in the fifth century B.C. and consisted of a collective commemoration of all those who had died in the military campaigns of the previous year. The tradition of commemorative speeches continued into the Hellenistic period.[5] Funeral orators in ancient Greece primarily eulogized war casualties and only rarely and uncharacteristically restricted their focus to important individuals. Scholars therefore tend to agree that the *laudatio funebris* for an individual constitutes an autochthonous Roman oratorical species, perhaps the only major type of epideictic oratory not borrowed from the Greeks.[6]

Whereas the Greek *epitaphios logos* was much more concerned with celebrating the state and its ideology, the Roman *laudatio funebris* focused on the historical person and his or her virtuous actions. Originally a private practice whereby the orator was frequently the deceased's closest relative, the *laudatio* became part of a public ceremony late in the Republican period. The species served the purposes of the ruling elite in Rome, for eulogies generally underlined the nobility and prowess of the governing aristocracy.

Though a Roman creation, the funeral *laudatio* received scant or no attention whatsoever in the Latin technical treatises on rhetoric. The explanation is simple. The Greek treatises, on which the Roman works were modeled, completely ignored such a form. Cicero himself even disparaged the oratorical possibilities of the funeral oration, observing that a funeral speech "is by no means a suitable occasion for parading one's distinction in rhetoric" (*De or.* 2.84.341).[7]

Because the funeral oration received no explicit treatment in Roman technical treatises, orators had two ways to learn to deliver such a speech. They could follow the general prescriptions for an encomium in the compositional exercises known as *progymnasmata*, taught in the grammatical schools and repeated in almost identical terms in rhetorical treatises like the *Rhetorica ad Herennium* (3.6.10–8.15).[8] Or they could learn from the living tradition, imitating the methods and style of other orators accomplished in actual delivery.

Explicit instructions for the composition of a funeral oration only appeared for the first time in Menander Rhetor's *Peri epideiktikōn* (late third century).[9] By that time, the Roman practice of celebrating the virtuous deeds of an individual had made its influence felt on Greek orators. Sophists of the Roman imperial period like Dio Chrysostom, Aelius Aristides, and Libanius wrote funeral encomia on individual persons.[10] Moreover, leaders of the Christian community, often trained by such sophists, adopted the practice and adapted it to the young community's pastoral needs. In fact, Gregory of Nazianzus' funeral oration for his brother Basil constitutes one of the finest examples of the species that survives from antiquity.[11]

By the fourth or fifth century, panegyrics of living persons had largely supplanted funeral oratory in the Latin West. The tradition of funeral eulogies virtually ceased with the gradual collapse of Roman rule and its replacement by Germanic kingdoms.[12] The Byzantine rhetorical tradition, not the Western one, preserved and developed the legacy of the Second Sophistic. Epideictic oratory dominated rhetorical training and practice throughout the history of the Eastern Empire.[13] Rhetoric in the medieval West, in contrast, focused on the technical side of the classical heritage and its application to literary forms like letter-writing (*dictamen*) and poetry (*ars poetriae*).[14] Preaching was the single major form of oral discourse practiced continuously in the medieval West. From the thirteenth century on, sermons fell under the sway of scholasticism and its logical propensities. Preaching manuals known as the *artes praedicandi* prescribed the use of scholastic logic in inventing sermons.[15]

The results of these developments are critical for an appreciation of the Renaissance achievement. The living tradition of funeral oratory had vanished in the West. In addition, no examples of funeral orations were preserved from ancient Rome.[16] Funeral oratory did continue to be popular and to be practiced in the Byzantine East. These three factors all played an important role in the humanist revival of classicizing panegyric during the Renaissance.

When communes were established in many cities of central and northern Italy from the eleventh century on, a civic context again existed in which certain types of classical oratory could be utilized. The funeral oration figured among those oratorical species.[17] Beginning in the thirteenth century, rules for its delivery together with sample orations appear in the manuals written for the instruction of the *podestà*.[18] These sample orations were extremely brief, stressed consolatory topics, and reflected the influence of the dictaminal tradition upon oratory. Like letters written according to the rules of *dictamen*, these orations do not strictly follow classical style. They ignore the chief topoi of a classicizing panegyric: the historical deeds of the person eulogized.[19] Because no orations delivered in imitation of these models survive, it is impossible to evaluate the practice of such oratory. The communal period influenced the subsequent history of oratory in Italy primarily by specifying the occasions on which orations were delivered.

The theory of preaching elaborated in the *artes praedicandi* had more direct influence upon funeral speeches in late medieval Italy. Funerals were celebrated as a religious rite during which thematic sermons were preached. Such sermons were expositions of a verse from Scripture accomplished through a series of divisions and subdivisions, each of which tended to become a separate unit. The Dominicans apparently enjoyed special prominence among Italian funeral preachers of the Duecento and Trecento. The funeral sermons of Remigio de' Girolami, a member of the Order of Preachers, are the earliest yet encountered from Italy.[20] There are reliable indications that the Dominicans were granted a virtual monopoly over funeral sermons at the papal court at the time of its residence in Avignon and that this monopoly lasted until the pontificate of Nicholas V.[21]

That speeches at funerals had become thematic sermons led to the suppression of a vital aspect of the classical precedent, the emphasis on "history." The topics of a classical encomium practically dictated that the speech be a chronological summary of the deceased's life.

Thematic funeral sermons, on the other hand, tended to prove general propositions and to accumulate expressions of admiration for the subject with minimal reference to the deeds of the historical personality. The eulogy of Pierre Roger for Napoleone Orsini at Avignon in 1342, for example, contained vague statements of approbation for the cardinal but made little or no direct reference to his activities. Roger structured the second half of the sermon as a scholastic *quaestio* designed to refute the thesis that death had somehow triumphed over Orsini.[22] Thematic funeral sermons gravitated towards philosophical and theological lectures on issues suggested by the scriptural theme and only remotely touched upon the life of the person eulogized.

Renaissance humanists, when they spoke at funerals, rejected the model proposed by the *artes praedicandi* and sought their inspiration in classical precepts for invention and style. Here in oratory, as in the visual arts, the Italians manifested an explicit sense of disjunction.[23] They perceived that the sermons preached at funerals differed dramatically from ancient oratory. Ancient practice must now be restored. The desire to imitate ancient models already constituted a cornerstone of Petrarch's literary program. Neither he nor the members of his immediate circle, however, broke with the form of the scholastic sermon in their public oratory in general or in their funeral speeches.[24]

Petrarch preached a funeral sermon for Archbishop Giovanni Visconti at Milan in 1354. The speech's fundamental inspiration and spirit were thematic. The oration has come down to us in an Italian translation and consists of two parts.[25] In the first portion of the sermon, the theme (Vulgate Psalm 37:10) was subdivided into its three constituent phrases. Petrarch attempted to demonstrate that the phrases fit Visconti's life. He developed the other major part of the sermon, a consolatory appeal, without reference to the theme. He closed the sermon by urging Milan's citizens to obey the new Visconti lords.

Petrarch's own funeral at Arquà in 1374 provided the setting for a thematic sermon preached by a member of his literary circle, Bonaventura Badoer, O.E.S.A. A good disciple of his master, Badoer used the same verse from Psalm 37 for his theme that Petrarch had selected twenty years earlier when preaching on the death of the Visconti archbishop. The sermon barely adverted to Petrarch's literary and humanist pursuits. Rather, it presented the "father of humanism" in hagiographical terms, underlining his piety by comparing him to David and to Saint Paul. The sermon is filled, moreover, with frequent citations from Scripture that give it a choppy, disjointed quality.[26]

Present evidence indicates that Pier Paolo Vergerio (the elder) first called attention to the disjunction between rhetoric in his day and rhetoric in antiquity.[27] Vergerio articulated this insight in a discussion of rhetoric in his treatise on education, *De ingenuis moribus et liberalibus studiis adulescentiae* (ca. 1402). In that passage he noted with regret that orators no longer gave judicial and deliberative speeches. Only epideictic oratory was still widely practiced though not, in his estimation, according to the right method. True eloquence had been suppressed in the preparation of speeches for ceremonial occasions by the use of the arts opposed to it. Vergerio almost certainly meant the arts of the scholastic tradition, which dominated public speaking. Orators delivered thematic sermons on all occasions. He urged a straightforward remedy: make the rules of classical rhetoric for the invention, disposition, and stylistic embellishment of all types of speeches the basis for rhetorical education and for oratorical practice.

Vergerio also composed the earliest funeral oration yet found among Renaissance exemplars that follow classical norms for oratory. He wrote the speech to commemorate Francesco il Vecchio da Carrara, the lord of Padua, who died in a Visconti prison in 1393. Vergerio's innovative approach emerges when one compares his speech to two others delivered at Francesco's obsequies, by Giovanni Ludovico de' Lambertazzi and Francesco Zabarella. Lambertazzi and Zabarella preached thematic sermons that were simply extended syllogisms organized in the following manner: the outstanding prince, mentioned in the thematic verse in generic terms, must possess certain qualities; Francesco possessed these, and therefore he could be called an outstanding prince. Vergerio's classicizing panegyric provides a stark contrast. He devoted the heart of his oration to a review of Francesco's virtuous actions in private and public life. In this eulogy Vergerio slavishly imitated ancient rhetorical canons.[28]

One can trace the progress of the classicizing funeral oration as it took root in Italy during the first decades of the Quattrocento.[29] Milan held a great public funeral for Giangaleazzo Visconti in 1402. The speech delivered during the funeral by an Augustinian friar, Pietro Castelleto, conformed to the principles of scholastic preaching. However, orations delivered by Gasparino Barzizza and Andrea Biglia, an Augustinian like Castelleto, to commemorate anniversaries of Giangaleazzo's death follow classical norms. By the second decade of the Quattrocento, the classicizing funeral panegyric had achieved great popularity. Orations by Barzizza on Iacopo da Forlì (1414), Andrea Giuliano on Manuel Chrysoloras (1415), and Leonardo Giustiniani on Carlo Zeno (1418) circulated widely.[30] They indicate a growing humanist penchant for the species, and they served as models for future orators.

This classicizing form, preferred almost exclusively in Italy by the second decade of the fifteenth century, made its international debut during the Council of Constance (1414–18). When the famous canonist Francesco Zabarella died in 1417, the assembly at Constance rendered him homage by commissioning two orations. The first, delivered by Poggio Bracciolini, exemplified the progress made in appropriating classical norms. Poggio's oration was so focused historically that it has offered material for modern biographies of Zabarella.[31] The second eulogy was delivered five days later by an English cleric named Henry Flemmyng, who observed the rules for a thematic sermon and attempted to prove that Zabarella had defeated the world, the flesh, and the devil. Flemmyng focused on those victories because he had chosen 1 Corinthians 15:54 ("Death is absorbed in victory") as his theme.[32] Closer analysis of the two speeches clarifies the differences that persisted between humanist oratory and thematic preaching.

Poggio was mindful that he addressed a distinguished European audience that had reached a crucial moment in its deliberations. When Zabarella died, in late September 1417, the Council fathers were debating whether to give precedence to the question of reform or to the papal election. By the end of October, they had decided to vote for a pope and elected Oddone Colonna (Martin V) on 11 November 1417. Poggio's audience would have vivid memories of Francesco Zabarella, who had helped lead the conciliarist party at the Council. Moreover, Poggio himself had recently harangued them with an oration sharply critical of the clergy's vices.[33] Now he summoned them to hear a similar message, pronounced in epideictic's opposite key. From berating clerics for their evil ways, he shifted to praise a virtuous churchman.

Poggio's product is typical of humanist funeral oratory of the Italian Renaissance. He composed and delivered it in classicizing Latin, he gave it the three parts (exordium, praise, peroration) specified for panegyric in classical handbooks, and he varied the style according to the emotional rhythm that the three parts created for the speech. The exordium mixed elements of plain and grand style, the body of the speech was enunciated in a simple narrative, and climactic moments toward the end of the narration and in the peroration were highlighted by use of grand style.

The oration had a brief exordium, whose tone and focus were established in the first few words of the initial dependent clause, "Although I am impeded." Poggio drew his exordium from his own person and from the subject matter of his discourse, topics specified in handbooks as closely related. Personal grief and the breadth of subject matter led him, he said, to wonder whether he could fulfill the demands placed upon him. Though not without reservation, he had accepted the task out of a sense of private devotion and public duty. He concluded the exordium by stating the two major divisions of his speech, the life and good morals of Zabarella. In the exordium, the medium had already become a message: private devotion is commendable but insufficient for the humanist unless coupled with a commitment to public service. Virtues are best illuminated against the background of a person's historical deeds.

In the first part of his praise, Poggio treated Zabarella's life in chronological fashion, beginning with passing mention of his birthplace (Padua) and of his parents. These are what rhetoricians called "external goods," and Poggio's brief note of them implied his preference for the goods of character that follow. He devoted increasingly lengthier treatment to Zabarella's education, his teaching career, and his ecclesiastical service as archbishop of Florence and cardinal. Within that chronological framework, he wove certain crucial themes that comprised the basic message of his discourse.

He repeatedly emphasized the public benefits of Zabarella's careers as professor of law and as churchman. He also underscored that Zabarella had backed his lectures and exhortations with the convincing testimony of virtuous conduct. The two major divisions within the body of Poggio's oration are thus somewhat fluid.

The narration contained personal details gathered from the friendship between the two men. Poggio noted that Zabarella liked to relax by enjoying good jokes and observed that the learned prelate generally avoided any physical exercise except for an occasional bout of wrestling. This first section of praise built to a crescendo when he subsumed his treatment of Zabarella's career as a cardinal under his activities at the Council of Constance. Zabarella's untiring efforts to find a remedy for the schism had reflected his sense of public commitment; had the cardinal lived longer, he surely would have been chosen pope. The message was carefully crafted to appeal to an assembly about to elect a new pope as a means to reunite Christendom: the electors would do their job properly by choosing an individual of ethos like Zabarella.

Poggio next examined Zabarella's morals, which were sifted out from the data supplied by his actions. This part of the speech had two subdivisions. First, he praised Zabarella for his intellectual virtues (wisdom and prudence) and then for his active virtues (justice, generosity, modesty, courage, and so forth). Again the medium constituted a typically humanist message, arguing for a life that conjoined scholarship with engagement in public activities. Zabarella had revealed his intellectual virtue in the breadth of his learning, which combined a solid basis in humanist disciplines like grammar, rhetoric, poetry, and history with proficiency in logic, philosophy, and theology. All of those studies prepared him for his primary academic pursuit, the study and teaching of law. That focus afforded Poggio an opportunity to digress and commend the value of law for creating the bonds of civil society.

When Poggio discussed his subject's active virtues, he made his oration a litany of praise for Zabarella's generosity and assistance to the poor, the oppressed, and those in need, as well as a denunciation of avarice (Poggio's own lifelong gripe). The body of the oration reached an emotional and stylistic climax when he concluded his treatment of the active virtues. He portrayed Zabarella's determined spirit by evoking memories of his recent speech to the assembled representatives of Christendom. The use of vivid description at this moment in the speech accorded well with rhetorical theory and with Poggio's conviction that men are best persuaded by what they see.[34]

Poggio literally summoned his audience to "re-view" the elderly cardinal as he stepped before the assembly and uttered an emotional plea to end the dissension within Latin Christianity, a plea grounded in his own unselfish willingness to sacrifice his life in order to achieve that lofty goal. The oration then shifted from narrative to direct address to Zabarella, as the orator attempted to enhance the emotional appeal of his discourse by using figures of speech like apostrophe and anaphora. The hall at Constance resounded with sentences that began "You . . . You . . . You . . . ." Poggio concluded the body of the oration with a purportedly tearful account of Zabarella's death while laboring for Church unity. Who could doubt the cardinal's ethos?

Poggio opened the peroration by deploring the loss of so great a man and by reflecting on the place of grief in human existence. He changed the mood from mourning to celebration by recalling that God had promised eternal reward to those who live selflessly. He then advocated further forms of commemoration. The Council should sponsor a tomb bearing an inscription that recorded Zabarella's exemplary deeds for Christendom. Those present should imitate Zabarella and conserve his memory perpetually.

When the international crowd of clerics and diplomats assembled the next time to continue their tribute to Zabarella, they heard a different form of oratorical invention, Flemmyng's thematic sermon on 1 Corinthians 15:54, "Death is absorbed in victory." Flemmyng used Latin words unknown in antiquity, frequently marshaled citations from authorities, and attempted at every turn to establish logical grounds for believing that Zabarella's death had been absorbed in a true, Christian victory.

Flemmyng organized his speech according to a different schema. It too had three parts, but these derived from the scriptural theme. His conclusion was extremely brief, encapsulated within a restatement of the theme and a Christological doxology. What had served as the emotional high point of Poggio's discourse became in Flemmyng's sermon a brief recapitulation of what he had proven.

Flemmyng used his exordium to introduce the theme by confronting it with a citation from Petrarch, who had once accused the gods for the loss of a distinguished individual. He then turned to Augustine and Ambrose to clarify his sense of "victory," identifying it with victory over the traditional enemies of the good Christian: the world, the flesh, and the devil. He concluded his introduction with further distinctions that demonstrated how victory over each of these enemies constituted grounds for solace. These subdivisions were again constructed on the basis of citations from authorities and expressed in strictly parallel language.

The body of the sermon consisted of two major divisions that Flemmyng drew from Aristotelian categories. He first defined Christian victory over the flesh as the transition to a more certain life when we shed our bodies. In his own words, this portion of the speech treated "universal matters in a speculative way" (*universalia in speculabilibus*). The logical proof for this contention was developed on the basis of propositions like "daily we are dying" and "the truly wise person contemns life here on earth." He regularly cited passages from Scripture and authorities like Ambrose, Augustine, Peter Damian, Quintilian, Seneca, and "Mercury" Trismegistus. He recapitulated his discussion of speculative issues by quoting Lactantius, who argued that the way we live on earth must be subordinated to our final goal of reaching a better and more certain life after death.

With the major proposition established, Flemmyng next turned to a discussion of "particular matters in the moral sphere" (*in moralibus particularia*). He divided this portion of the sermon into the four ways that Zabarella's life had illuminated his world: by his virtues, learning, reputation, and praises. The section on virtues was the most elaborate and repeated in microcosm the general organizational pattern of the entire sermon. Each virtue was defined by appeal to authorities. Flemmyng then proved, by adducing qualities and activities of his subject's life, that Zabarella had possessed that virtue. The individual sections and the entire oration unwound as syllogisms.

Up to this point, Flemmyng had only dealt with the first of the great victories, that over the flesh. Nevertheless, he brought his sermon to a hurried and characteristically authority-filled conclusion. Preliminary citations argued for consolation from "the tragedies of Troy" and from Paul's first letter to the Thessalonians (4:13). He then restated the trio of victories achieved by Zabarella and deduced that his death had been absorbed in victory.[35] The sermon was an exercise in proof. Zabarella's death represented a clear victory over the restrictions and pitfalls of existence in the flesh. Poggio's oration, by contrast, was an exercise in celebration of historical deeds, deeds that epitomized the proper conduct of a teacher and churchman and should be imitated.

There are indications that the humanists' use of a classicizing form eventually had concrete effects on Church ritual. Funeral preaching at the papal court changed during the fifteenth century. Paris de Grassis, the master of ceremonies in the early sixteenth century and a reliable source for liturgical history, credited Pope Nicholas V with extensive reform of the funeral ceremony.[36] According to de Grassis, Nicholas authorized that an oration after the completion of the funeral liturgy be substituted for a sermon during its celebration. Renaissance practice moved from *sermo* to *oratio* even within Christendom's most sensitive bastion.

Various factors led the humanists to adopt classical standards for funeral orations. The entire humanist endeavor was fueled by a desire to imitate ancient practice. From their acquaintance with ancient history, those scholars knew that funeral orations formed a part of private and public ritual in classical times. In fact, the exordia of many humanist orations alluded to classical precedent in order to corroborate the value of the speeches they introduced.[37]

As early as 1416, Francesco Barbaro pointed out in his eulogy for Giovanni Corradini that he was following ancient custom in delivering such an oration, though he correctly noted that the speaker in Roman times was usually a relative of the deceased. Historical knowledge increased with time and research. In 1428 Leonardo Bruni applauded Solon for legislating that a public funeral and oration be awarded to those who had died in service to the state. This information was readily available to Bruni in works by Cicero.[38] Giannozzo Manetti in turn offered a lengthy justification for joining a funeral eulogy with a posthumous crowning with the laurel wreath—as he was about to place a crown on the corpse of Bruni. Pomponio Leto confessed that he did not know the precise origins of funeral oratory, though he ascribed the custom with certainty to the Romans, who taught it to the Athenians; in this chronology he apparently followed Dionysius of Halicarnassus. In the early sixteenth century, Tommaso Inghirami and Paris de Grassis said that the Egyptians had established the custom. They based their conclusion on a passage in Diodorus Siculus.[39]

In the latter half of the Quattrocento, Renaissance humanists began to present in their funeral speeches lists of Roman precedents, which were derived in large part from Greek and Roman historians. In a eulogy for Leonardo Mansueti, a master general of the Dominicans who died in 1480, Francesco Maturanzio named Romans who had praised close relatives after their death. His list included Quintus Catulus on his mother Popilia, Quintus Metellus on his father Lucius Metellus, Julius Caesar on his wife Cornelia, and Mark Anthony on his uncle Julius Caesar. He went on to applaud the fact that because Lucius Sulla could not be eulogized by a member of his family, as his son was too young to speak publicly, Roman officials had selected the most eloquent orator available. Although Maturanzio basically emphasized the salutary nature of Roman custom in having a family member be the eulogist, he probably referred to the case of Sulla to suggest his own eloquence by unstated analogy.[40]

In a funeral oration in 1483 for Cardinal Ferry de Clugny, Giovanni Antonio Sangiorgi provided another list of Roman orations, which included Publius Valerius Publicola on his fellow consul Lucius Brutus, Quintus Fabius Maximus for his son, Marcus Marcellus for his father Quintus Claudius Marcellus, Julius Caesar for "Ania," and Tiberius for his stepfather Augustus. When combined the two lists demonstrate that Renaissance orators were familiar with approximately one-third of the Roman funeral orations mentioned in a variety of ancient literary sources. Sangiorgi further adduced biblical and patristic examples of written eulogies, like Jeremiah's lament for Josiah and Ambrose's *epitaphius* for the emperor Theodosius.[41] The conjunction of examples from classical and Christian history is instructive. Funeral oratory among Italian humanists illustrates their conviction that pagan and Christian cultures were compatible.[42]

Renaissance orators at times asserted that both cultures responded to a common natural impulse in celebrating the funeral of beloved persons. A public celebration was all the more appropriate for those who gave their lives in service to others. The *res publica* of Greco-Roman antiquity had evolved by the Renaissance into a *res publica Christiana*.[43] All Renaissance commemorative oratory shared a fundamental premise, harmonizing the orator's ideal of public service with the Christian gospels' stress on charitable activities. Scholars like Charles Trinkaus and John O'Malley have aptly described this ethic as "rhetorical," or even better "oratorical."[44]

Funeral orators acknowledged their debt to classical precedent for the ritual they celebrated and the ideals they advocated. In fact, key Church officials like Paris de Grassis admitted that Christian funerary ritual borrowed heavily from pagan antecedents. De Grassis even used pagan precedent to justify norms for the funeral rites at the papal court. Just as the Roman *pontifices maximi* had been forbidden by law to attend or even observe a funeral procession, so it was inappropriate that the pope attend any funeral except the anniversary liturgies for his immediate predecessor.[45] Certain orators likened the pagan request to the Muses for inspiration to their own prayers for divine assistance at the outset of eulogies.[46]

The great examples used to justify the delivery of a funeral oration were almost invariably derived from classical antiquity. Christian precedents were not lacking. De Grassis himself adverted to a tradition that Saint Peter had eulogized the Virgin Mary at her funeral. His source was the *Divine Names* of pseudo-Dionysius. No funeral orator, however, alluded to this tradition during the Renaissance.[47] Moreover, the Latin funeral speeches of Ambrose were rarely referred to as models to be imitated.

In elaborating the content of a eulogy, humanist orators consistently posited a fundamental harmony between Cicero's assertion that those who gave their lives in service to the state were rewarded with beatitude in the afterlife (*Rep.* 6.13.13) and the ideal of self-effacing love and its promise of heavenly reward that Jesus had preached and lived. They stressed that Cicero had correctly identified public service as the activity most cherished by the world's divine ruler,[48] and easily applied that maxim to ecclesiastics who had died during special missions for the Church. For example, Poggio commemorated that the cardinals Francesco Zabarella and Giuliano Cesarini had given their lives for the Christian *res publica*.[49] Eulogists likewise did not hesitate to apply the maxim to bureaucrats like Giannicola Salerno, generals like Sigismondo d'Este, lawyers like Antonio Roselli and Giasone del Maino, and humanist educators like Guarino.[50] Like Plato and like Jesus, humanist funeral orators stressed the excellence of altruism.[51]

They were not oblivious, however, to differences between their Christian culture and the traditions of their ancient counterparts. There was no question, moreover, of the superiority of the Christian message. Occasionally a speaker indulged in rather crude expression of that superiority. The anonymous panegyrist of Giangaleazzo Visconti, for example, rejoiced that Renaissance heroes would enjoy eternal beatitude, whereas the pagans commemorated in eulogies were necessarily consigned to damnation.[52] Such a radical juxtaposition was not typical of the general attitude of Renaissance orators and occurred only very early in the period under investigation. More characteristically, humanist eulogists used *a fortiori* logic in this context. The formula—"how much the more"—proved an adept tool, for it revealed the harmony between pagan and Christian cultures and defended the superiority of the latter. In 1405 Leonardo Bruni observed that the gifts given by God were of greater value than the gifts of fortune that Plato and the Greeks had prized. Pomponio Leto and Baldassare Rasini characterized their eulogies as efforts by Christians to outdo their pagan predecessors in paying tribute to those who had offered their lives for the common welfare.[53] The orators sought to propagate a Christian spirituality that was civic and oratorical.

Renaissance funeral orators knew from historical and literary sources that the classical world had embellished public funerals with speeches in praise of the deceased. As humanists, they sought to imitate that ancient practice. Yet no significant examples of Roman funeral eulogies survived in their day. Nor was there a living tradition of such oratory in Trecento Italy. Funerals were then adorned with scholastic sermons, invented by using arts that were, in Vergerio's words, opposed to the classical art of eloquence. Orators could not usefully consult Roman technical treatises, for those gave no specific instruction on the funeral speech.

Early orators like Vergerio were compelled under the circumstances to follow the prescriptions for panegyric in the Ciceronian treatises that they studied, the *Rhetorica ad Herennium* and the *De inventione*. They were convinced that they would imitate what classical orators had done by proceeding in this way. Such adherence to basic prescriptions yielded a standardized form that persisted throughout the Italian Renaissance. Renaissance speeches frequently repeated the schema for an encomium given in the *Rhetorica ad Herennium* (3.6.10–8.15). After a brief exordium, the oration treated the praise of an individual in chronological fashion, focusing on external goods (birthplace, family, education), goods of the body (strength, beauty), and especially goods of the soul (virtues). In classical handbooks, the cardinal virtues were prudence, justice, courage, and temperance. Their possession was established by appeal to the subject's deeds.[54]

Poggio's oration for Francesco Zabarella illustrates how a Renaissance orator adapted this basic scheme. Poggio severely reduced treatment of external goods and only emphasized the importance of education. He ignored the goods of the body and separated the treatment of Zabarella's life from that of his good morals. Moreover, he expanded his treatment of virtue beyond the cardinal four and used the lesser categories of intellectual and active in that portion of his speech. That funeral orations quickly assumed and thereafter retained a fixed form led earlier historians of Italian Renaissance oratory to minimize their historical value.[55] It also made them ready prey for the wit of Alberti and other satirists.

The use of handbooks to invent panegyric had a further implication: "A panegyric is not the same thing as history." This famous statement by Leonardo Bruni, uttered in defense of his panegyric of Florence and inspired by remarks in Cicero's *De oratore* (2.15.62), yields one interpretation when read backwards through historicist eyes: history and panegyric are seen as polar opposites. The historical worth of humanist panegyric and its relation to humanist histories differ, however, when viewed in the context of the history of public oratory. By rejecting the thematic sermon and returning to classical forms of panegyric, humanists assured that the heart of their funeral orations focused upon the deeds of their subjects, often disposed in chronological order. The entire oration in fact acquired a "historical" character. Various eulogists felt justified in suggesting that their tributes were biographies on a more selective scale. The orations have frequently been read by modern interpreters for factual data of this sort.

Much of humanist historiography shared a didactic purpose with laudatory oratory. That approach rested upon solid classical foundations. In the *Orator* (11.37) Cicero did not oppose history to panegyric but described them both as species of epideictic oratory. Towards the end of the fifteenth century, Girolamo Gioia reversed Bruni's position and stated that "a funeral oration ought to be history."[56]

When they sought to revive the species, Renaissance orators initially had no contact with a living or textual tradition of funeral eulogy. That situation changed when they met Byzantine orators and discussed rhetoric with them. Byzantine rhetoric had inherited the emphases of the Second Sophistic and faithfully maintained those emphases throughout its millenium of existence. Epideictic forms like the funeral oration constituted the characteristic products of the rhetoric of the Eastern Empire. Epideictic orations comprised the vast majority of speeches from the Italian Renaissance as well. Renewed contact with Byzantium spurred the practice of epideictic forms already in use in Italy.[57]

The *Lives* of Plutarch played a role in the initial development of Renaissance panegyric, though they are admittedly not a product of primary rhetoric. Manuel Chrysoloras used Plutarch's *Lives* as a basic textbook for his Greek lessons, and he encouraged their translation into Latin. His pedagogy generated enthusiasm for these moralizing biographies early in the Italian Renaissance.[58] Epideictic norms had guided Plutarch in the composition of his biographies. His works sought to demonstrate the effects of virtue and vice upon human history. In addition, Plutarch wrote with a conscious didactic scope. As he stated in the preface to his life of Pericles, he narrated virtuous actions to move his reader to imitate moral exemplars.[59]

Renaissance translators of Plutarch's *Lives* adduced the same motives for their work.[60] They made Plutarch available in Latin to provide examples of excellence. Contemporaries should echo that excellence in their own actions. Renaissance orators produced identical reasons to defend the importance of their funeral eulogies. Moreover, many of the translators of Plutarch—Vergerio, Bruni, Guarino, Francesco Barbaro, Leonardo Giustiniani, Poggio, and Filelfo—were among the first to deliver classicizing funeral orations. The two efforts were part of a single educational project that looked to the moral improvement of society.

Direct contact with the technical tradition of Byzantine rhetoric also contributed, in all likelihood, to the progress of epideictic oratory in Quattrocento Italy. Chrysoloras again played a fundamental role, for he introduced his students to the *progymnasmata* of Hermogenes, preliminary exercises in composition that included encomium and ecphrasis. Although Priscian had made a free Latin translation of the *progymnasmata* in the sixth century, the exercises had never had the formative influence on oratory and literature in the West that they had in the East for one thousand years.[61] The entire rhetorical corpus of Hermogenes was reintroduced in Italy through the efforts of George of Trebizond.[62] In addition, a codex from the fifteenth century now in the Biblioteca Comunale Augusta of Perugia contains a Latin translation of Menander Rhetor's chapter on the monody, a type of funeral oration that gives large play to expressions of grief.[63] These technical works ultimately served to reinforce the teaching found in Latin manuals like the *Rhetorica ad Herennium*.[64] Contact with Byzantium also permitted Italian orators to rediscover the historical and living tradition of Greek panegyric.

Hans Baron has demonstrated the influence of Greek panegyrical oratory on the formulation of republican ideology for Florence in the speeches and writings of Leonardo Bruni. Bruni's panegyric of the city on the Arno (ca. 1403–4) was inspired according to the author's own admission by the *Panathenaicus* of Aelius Aristides. When Bruni wrote a funeral tribute for Nanni Strozzi in 1428, he drew heavily upon the funeral speech of Pericles as recorded by Thucydides. Later orators also stressed that they were following ancient custom in their orations and adduced Pericles as their model.[65]

Panegyric and funeral orations figured among the Greek works translated during the Renaissance. Xenophon's panegyric for Agesilaus, mentioned in a well-known passage in Cicero's *De oratore* (2.84.341), was translated by Francesco Filelfo.[66] Manuscripts now in Italian libraries contain translations of the "funeral orations" attributed to Demosthenes, Lysias, and Isocrates.[67] Through the efforts of Ambrogio Traversari and George of Trebizond, the funeral orations of the Greek fathers Gregory of Nazianzus and Gregory of Nyssa became available in Latin for the first time since their composition in the fourth century.[68]

Finally, Italian orators heard and read funeral orations delivered by their Greek contemporaries. In 1409 the emperor Manuel II Palaeologus composed a funeral oration for delivery at a ceremony marking the second anniversary of his brother Theodore's death and went to great lengths to circulate his work in the Latin West.[69] He sent a copy of the speech to his ambassador, Manuel Chrysoloras, who was then traveling among Western courts. Chrysoloras, in turn, wrote a detailed commentary in praise of the oration (it has recently been rediscovered),[70] which indicates his interest in such oratory and his knowledge of the history of the species. It is not improbable that the Greek master encouraged the practice of this oratory during his career in Italy. The emperor sent another copy of the oration to Guarino in 1417 with the request that Guarino translate it into Latin.

Many of the Greeks who came to the West were accomplished funeral speakers. The Platonic philosopher Gemisthos Plethon delivered several funeral eulogies for members of the Byzantine imperial dynasty.[71] Cardinal Bessarion wrote a lament for the death of Manuel II in 1419 that was translated into Latin in 1471 by Bessarion's disciple Niccolò Perotti.[72] Italians also heard orations that Byzantine exiles delivered. George of Trebizond, for example, spoke in Latin at the funeral of Fantino Michiel in 1437 at Venice. Bessarion's death was commemorated by a Latin oration at his funeral in Rome delivered by Niccolò Capranica, and also by a Greek monody written on the island of Crete by Michael Apostolis, a refugee whom Bessarion patronized.[73] The panegyrical oratory of the Italian Renaissance provides another instance, neglected till now, of the influence of Byzantine culture on humanism and Renaissance thought.

The importance attached to funeral orations in the Renaissance can be established by several measures. Such orations appear frequently in humanist miscellanies. Funeral orations were widely diffused, and some of them became models in their own time.[74] The speeches for which at least ten manuscript copies exist in Italian libraries alone are listed below in chronological order.

1405 Leonardo Bruni on Otto Cavalcanti (10 MSS)
1414 Gasparino Barzizza on Iacopo da Forlì (13)
1415 Andrea Giuliano on Manuel Chrysoloras (18)
1417 Poggio Bracciolini on Francesco Zabarella (14)
1418 Leonardo Giustiniani on Carlo Zeno (46)
1426 Guarino Guarini on Giannicola Salerno (15)
1428 Leonardo Bruni on Nanni Strozzi (24)
1443 Giovanni Pontano on Gattamelata (10)
1478 Cristoforo Landino on Donato Acciaiuoli (15)

With the advent of printing, funeral orations were quickly made available to the lettered public. At least thirty-five funeral orations had appeared in print by 1500. Speeches like those of Francesco da Toledo for Leonardo della Rovere and Niccolò da Modrussa for Pietro Riario were published several times in the fifteenth century.[75] By the sixteenth century, collections of funeral orations were printed in Italy and elsewhere.

Humanists customarily exchanged copies of their eulogies or those of their students. They would then evaluate each other's oratorical abilities. Guarino liked the oration that his Venetian pupil Andrea Giuliano composed for a memorial celebration of Manuel Chrysoloras, and he sent a copy of the work to Poggio. Though satisfied with the overall treatment, the ever-fastidious Poggio did find grounds to criticize Giuliano's oration, especially for failing to treat Chrysoloras' honesty at greater length.[76]

Most of the leading advocates of Italian humanism delivered funeral orations that have survived for our perusal. In his classic essay on the Renaissance, Jacob Burckhardt correctly observed that social position in no way affected an orator's selection.[77] What was sought was the most cultivated humanist talent. Thus laypersons delivered eulogies from the sanctuaries of churches, and clerics celebrated civic heroes in the major squares of Italian cities.

The choice of an orator and his actions during the speech did occasionally create problems. Johann Burchard and Paris de Grassis expressed misgivings during their tenure as masters of ceremonies when lay orators like Pomponio Leto and Jakob Questenberg refused to dress in the cape prescribed for a funeral eulogist by rubrics at the papal court. Though not dressed properly, the humanists were still permitted to deliver their orations.[78] The final evaluation of their oratory was left to what they said, not to their dressing in street clothes for the occasion.

Occasionally an orator called attention to the anomaly of his commission to deliver a particular eulogy. Alberto da Castelfranco wondered why he had been chosen to honor a Franciscan like Urbano Bolzanio, as he himself was not a member of a religious order. He assured his audience that he had accepted the delegation only as a way of expressing his affection for his former tutor. He also sought to invert the question by observing that his oratory should inflame his Franciscan listeners to pursue virtue and eloquence. In the future, presumably, there would then be a pool of Franciscans capable of eulogizing their own.

The criteria for the choice of the proper eulogist supplied by Renaissance authors again indicates that they harmonized classical and Christian cultures. In a letter to Manuel Chrysoloras describing the funeral of Pope Innocent VII (d. 1406), Iacopo Angeli da Scarperia argued that the eulogist for a pope should be *bonus, sanctus,* and *dicendi peritus.* In this he canonized Cato's perfect orator (Sen. *Contr.* 1.Pr.9; Quint. 12.1.1).[79] Paris de Grassis manifested much more practical concerns as a master of ceremonies. He recommended that an eloquent member of a cardinal's household be selected to eulogize his patron. Such an orator could then be ready on short notice. De Grassis chronicled with ill-concealed annoyance that he had been forced at times to postpone funeral liturgies because the orator had been notified too late and was unprepared to speak at the appointed time.[80]

Certain orators appear to have achieved exceptional popularity. Giovanni Battista Egnazio, for example, delivered more than sixty funeral orations at Venice. Giovacchino Castiglioni told his audience that his eulogy for Isabella di Chiaramonte was the sixty-fifth such discourse he had pronounced since returning to Milan eleven years earlier. Castiglioni capitalized on his frequent selection to capture the goodwill of the audience in his exordia. He once claimed to have written an oration while riding to the funeral because he had received short notice and had little time free from preaching obligations.[81]

Age does not appear to have affected the selection of an orator. Francesco Diedo alleged that, though little more than fourteen years old, Bartolomeo Pagliarini had impressed his listeners by eloquently praising Girolamo Gualdi. Battista Casali reminded his Roman audience that his eulogy for Domenico Grimani marked his return to public speaking after retiring from its rigors; he was fifty years old at the time and died less than two years later. During a speech for Niccolò Piccinino, the Franciscan Antonio da Rho asked his Milanese audience for pardon because he had abandoned his customary methods: because of illness and old age, he sat and read the oration.[82]

Evidence from the papal court indicates that a eulogist's task was not without its financial rewards. Paris de Grassis fixed a fee of fifteen to twenty-five golden ducats for those who spoke at a cardinal's funeral and four ducats for that of a lesser prelate. Paolo Giovio posited a direct correlation between the decline of eloquent oratory at the papal court in the sixteenth century and the prohibitive fees demanded by the better orators; the court simply could not afford them.[83] We also know that the Florentine Signoria assigned large amounts of money to finance the funerals of humanist bureaucrats. The eulogist on those occasions was probably well remunerated.[84]

Speakers earned their pay when the preparation and delivery of a particular oration presented formidable challenges. George of Trebizond recounted that he had only learned of his selection to eulogize Fantino Michiel the night before the funeral. When Francesco Padovano claimed to be speaking extemporaneously at the funeral of Pietro Naldi, his claim for once may have been more than formulaic, as he had eulogized Leonardo Savelli before a similar audience at the papal court the preceding day. The pressures of time constraints are shown by Alamanno Rinuccini's oration for Matteo Palmieri in 1475; the version delivered at the actual funeral on two days' notice is less polished than the one he reworked for circulation.[85]

Difficult circumstances, like short notice, complicated the orator's task. Modern theorists of rhetoric have justly called attention to the peculiar exigencies of each rhetorical situation. Members of the Giustiniani family at Venice were commissioned to speak in delicate situations. Leonardo Giustiniani was called upon to praise Carlo Zeno, one of the Serenissima's most capable admirals but a man who had been condemned for accepting payment from a foreign prince in the course of his career. If the popularity of a speech is a valid indication of its merit, Leonardo proved more than equal to the challenge: no other oration from the Italian Renaissance was so widely copied. At another awkward juncture Leonardo's son Bernardo was selected to praise Francesco Foscari, who had been deposed as doge only days before his death in 1457. Bernardo quickly warmed to his task and spoke for four hours without pause. Those present reported that the audience listened attentively to the entire speech. There is still room for skepticism about that.[86]

Modern rhetoric might well profit by adopting a Renaissance custom regarding an oration's length. In a eulogy for Julius II, Tommaso Inghirami told his audience that he had only one-half hour for his oration and claimed that he could see a water-clock (*clepsydra*) that measured out his time.[87] Vigilant masters of ceremonies at the papal court occasionally acted to enforce time limits. Johann Burchard admitted that he had conspicuously signaled an overly loquacious orator to halt his oration. The chastened preacher cut off his speech and slunk from the pulpit. Other orators never had a chance to exceed their limits. Paris de Grassis recalled that a Dominican named Martino Berna had been physically dragged from the pulpit when his fellow friars learned of his apparently apostate tendencies.[88]

Some orators left concrete evidence of the esteem they had for their own work. Niccolò Palmeri, a member of the Augustinian order, was so enamored of passages in the exordium of his oration for Cardinal Domenico Capranica that he repeated them verbatim in an oration for Cardinal Prospero Colonna five years later.[89] Other orators were apparently less satisfied with the fruits of their labor or intimidated by the circumstances in which they had to work. Pleading illness, Ludovico Bruno failed to appear for an oration at a memorial service for Isabella of Castile held at the papal court in 1505. Both Burchard and de Grassis attributed his absence to a loss of nerve.[90] Bruno did publish the oration shortly thereafter.

Funeral orations occupied a place of importance within an elaborate public ritual.[91] Renaissance society created a variety of honors to commemorate an individual's contribution to the public utility. Processions, banners, wax displays, mourning clothes, honorary titles, epitaphs, a laurel crowning, and tombs were all possible awards for civic heroes. Political authorities manipulated these honors to invest each funeral with a particular symbolic character. For example, the republic of Venice used public funerals as part of a system of rewards designed to convince her condottieri of the respect in which they were held and thereby solidify their loyalty to Venice. Similarly, the ceremonies associated with the funeral and coronation of the doge were used in Cinquecento Venice to forestall the aggrandizing tendencies of ducal families.[92]

Perhaps the case of Niccolò di Leonello d'Este, a nephew of Duke Ercole I, supplies the most telling testimony for the symbolic importance of a public funeral in the Italian Renaissance. He was buried with full civic honors at Ferrara in 1476. As the legitimate son of Leonello, Niccolò had posed a serious challenge to Ercole's assumption of authority in 1471. It was the second time that one of Leonello's brothers had beaten Niccolò to the throne. Ercole had inherited the duchy from his brother Borso and spent his first years in office legitimating his rule. To assure his succession, he had married Eleanor of Aragon in 1473, and she gave birth to a male heir in the summer of 1476. At that moment, spurred by his Gonzaga protectors in Mantua, Niccolò decided to move against his uncle. While Ercole was away from Ferrara in August 1476, Niccolò and his supporters forcibly entered the city. His efforts to incite a popular rebellion failed, and Niccolò and his fellow conspirators were captured by troops loyal to Ercole. Many of Niccolò's supporters were hanged publicly from the windows of the Palazzo della Ragione or from the battlements of the Castello. In deference to Niccolò's lineage, Ercole had him beheaded in a private ceremony. Ercole's sense of honor went further. He organized a public funeral for his nephew and ordered that Niccolò's head be sewn back onto the corpse. The ceremonies then went off with great pomp amidst large crowds.[93]

Other factors confirm that funerals were popular entertainment during the Renaissance. A declaration of public mourning often meant that the population did not have to work. An anonymous eulogist for Leonardo Bruni recounted that such huge crowds thronged the processional route for the deceased chancellor that Florentine officials had to use clubs to clear a path. The presence of large crowds repaid the investment that Florence's government made for funerals of its humanist employees. In life and in death, a humanist of Bruni's renown should enhance the prestige of his state.[94]

Italian humanists logically took advantage of the opportunity offered by funeral obsequies to press their program and their social ideals. They contributed to funeral commemorations through a variety of literary genres. For example, they composed epitaphs, which stressed that a hero's deeds were publicly honored. The wording of the epitaphs imitated that on ancient inscriptions, which humanists were then discovering. They also wrote letters of consolation to the bereaved, who were usually powerful and wealthy patrons. They composed celebrative elegies and epigrams, often competing with each other for poetic supremacy. Commemorative writings could be gathered into a single volume and presented to the family of the deceased.[95] Funeral orations were unique among these genres because they were delivered before a large audience that included civic and religious dignitaries.

The reasons adduced to this point for the importance of funeral orations depend upon external factors like manuscript and printing history or the ritual setting. However, in the exordia of their eulogies humanist orators often supplied their own justification for the importance of their actions. To explain their purpose, they consistently posited an analogy between oratory and the visual arts. Their eulogies sought to be so vivid and descriptive as to engender an image of the deceased. From classical times theorists of rhetoric had compared oratory to the visual arts. They saw an intimate rapport between epideictic oratory and arts like painting and sculpture.[96] The method for achieving "vivid description," known technically as ecphrasis, was set forth in one of the *progymnasmata*. Latin rhetorical manuals treated ecphrasis as a method of amplification or as a figure of thought.[97] During Rome's imperial period, ecphrasis had heavily influenced the composition of panegyrics.[98]

The first lengthy description of Roman funerals had indeed suggested that ancient funeral orators used ecphrasis: the historian Polybius commented on the orator's ability to recall the deeds of the deceased to mind and bring them before the eyes of the audience. The image should occur even for those in the audience who had no direct knowledge of the deceased's life.[99] "To place before the eyes" summarizes the task that Italian Renaissance orators set for themselves.[100] Ludovico Carbone assured his audience that they would be consoled by seeing how honestly Giacomo Dal Lino had conducted himself;

they should then realize that Giacomo lacked nothing necessary for "good and holy living."[101]

The persuasive power of the visual image made it very attractive to humanist orators. Paintings in antiquity had affected the course of events and motivated heroes to great deeds.[102] Paris de Grassis urged that the ancient practice of providing painted scenes of the deceased's actions be revived for funerals of cardinals. Funerary art and oratory could be combined as part of a program to present exemplars.[103] Giannozzo Manetti recalled that the constant sight of a portrait of Petrarch had first inflamed Leonardo Bruni to devote himself to the humanities.[104] Eulogists even cited skill in ecphrasis as evidence of a deceased subject's eloquence.[105]

Renaissance funeral orators did not hesitate to describe themselves as painters. As Cicero had sought to do in the *Orator* (1.7), they attempted to depict an image in words.[106] Their comparisons were even more explicit. Niccolò Capranica recalled a painter's ability to condense a mass of data into a representation on a small canvas. Baldassare Rasini referred to the painter's skill in dealing with perspective. He could create open spaces within the confines of a frame.[107] The orator, like the painter, must select and distill a slice of reality and present it colorfully.

Renaissance orators felt an even closer communion with the sculptor's art, for they were aware that orations and monuments often comprised parts of a single tribute to ancient heroes.[108] Orators recalled the legation of Lucius Roscius and his companions to Fidenae; those loyal servants of Rome were slaughtered in the course of their mission, and the Republic had rewarded their patriotism with a state funeral and statues in the Forum.[109] Poggio concluded his orations for Francesco Zabarella and Giuliano Cesarini by suggesting that public monuments be dedicated to their memory. The Venetian general Gattamelata was awarded such a combined tribute. He was celebrated in two well-known eulogies and immortalized in Donatello's equestrian statue. Gattamelata's relatives apparently financed the statue, but the Venetian government at least sanctioned the project.[110]

Ultimately, the analogy between a funeral oration and the visual arts dramatized the orator's duty to design his oration carefully, to synthesize the wealth of historical data available, and to color his speech subtly and appropriately. The analogy also pointed to the orator's fundamental task. Humanist orators sought to create an image that would impel the audience to imitate a person's excellence.

Not even a statue could compete with a laudatory oration in its efficacy to persuade to imitation.[111] Petrarch argued that although a statue better expressed physical form, a rhetorical *exemplum* proposed virtue itself for imitation. He was repeating sentiments first expressed by Isocrates and Cicero.[112] In the words of Bernardo Giustiniani, "praise is a certain innate stimulus to virtue."[113] Humanist orators therefore liked to specify a dual function for the funeral eulogy in the exordium: they celebrated virtue to render honor to the deceased, but also to inflame those listening to imitation. They felt that by so speaking they would revive ancient practice.[114] In a similar way, they often concluded their orations with an emotional appeal for imitation.[115] Through prosopopoeia, Ludovico Carbone summoned Guarino back from the dead to deliver an appeal for moral living.[116]

The effort to stir imitation moves funeral oratory closer to the persuasional purpose of deliberative oratory. Modern historians of rhetoric have noted the tendency for epideictic and deliberative oratory to overlap.[117] Guarino posited close bonds between the two oratorical genres in the Renaissance.[118] This scope of presenting exemplars links funeral oratory to the educational program of humanism, which sought a truth relevant to the conduct of life. Orators consistently emphasized that the deeds of their subjects exemplified life's crucial art, the Ciceronian art of good and holy living.[119] Poggio and Niccolò Palmeri noted the didactic quality of their eulogies: they were a form of instruction (*doctrina*) that would breed learning (*cognitio*) for the audience.[120]

Classical discussion of epideictic rhetoric had also noted its potential for inspiration. Style made the exemplar attractive, the audience's admiration was aroused, and the orator easily finished by appealing for imitation.[121] Authorities like Polybius (6.53–54), Cicero (*Part. or.* 21.70–71), and Dionysius of Halicarnassus (*A.R.* 5.17.2–6) described the purpose of panegyric in those terms. The Roman historian Sallust provided concrete evidence that examples persuaded when he narrated that the funeral images of deceased ancestors inflamed Quintus Fabius Maximus and Publius Scipio to equal their fame by performing great deeds.[122]

The ultimate beneficiary of such unabashed moralizing should be society. Humanists reasoned that any commonwealth necessarily improved as its citizens were made better. In the peroration to his eulogy for Leonardo Bruni, Poggio exhorted his Florentine listeners to model themselves on Bruni, who had placed his knowledge of letters and his virtue at the service of the state.[123]

Paul Oskar Kristeller once suggested that the concept of stylistic disjunction be applied to Renaissance intellectual history as it had been applied to the history of Renaissance art. There are at least three instances of disjunction between funeral oratory in the Italian Renaissance and antecedent practice.

First, the orations of the humanists differed in significant ways from general late medieval practice. Funerals in Europe in the fourteenth century were occasions for preaching thematic sermons, commentaries on a verse from Scripture designed to prove a particular proposition.[124] Even in Italy, where a tradition of secular funeral oratory had existed in the thirteenth century, the thematic sermon held sway. Such sermons marshaled quotations from authorities to defend an interpretation and made only marginal reference to the deeds of the individual being honored. They had little overall unity and sparse stylistic embellishment. In Renaissance Italy, by contrast, public obsequies became occasions to deliver orations modeled upon classical norms for the epideictic genre. Humanist orators sought to depict an inspirational image of the deceased. Speakers therefore concerned themselves above all with historical deeds. They at times left precise indications of their research into the deceased's life.[125] Deeds were prized for their ability to exemplify virtue. The more visual the image, the more persuasive it would be.

The classicizing methods of invention used for funeral orations led to a second instance of disjunction. The humanism of Petrarch differed from that of Vergerio, Bruni, and Guarino. Italian humanism evolved from its first to its third generation. Petrarch and his immediate followers devoted themselves primarily to reviving the activities and procedures of the *grammaticus* of antiquity. These "grammatical humanists" searched for classical texts, collated various manuscripts, and interpreted classical authors philologically or, if necessary, allegorically. There is no denying the creative quality of Petrarchan humanism. Among his other innovations, Petrarch poured out his personal feelings in his private correspondence in imitation of Cicero's letters to Atticus, thereby opening to later humanists the fertile possibilities of that literary form. Yet his appropriation of the classical tradition failed to penetrate his public life. His orations, consequently, were thematic.[126] However, with Vergerio first and with Bruni and others immediately thereafter, Italian humanism extended its concern to rhetoric's primary matter, oratory. As Vergerio observed, epideictic oratory dominated public speaking in the late Trecento and early Quattrocento. Vergerio objected to the intrusion of scholastic methods in public discourse. Humanists shunned the theory of preaching articulated in the *artes praedicandi* and studied classical norms for oratory in the Ciceronian manuals. The appropriation of classical rhetoric generated a related interest in the moral quality of society. Humanism penetrated the public sphere. Oratorical humanists adapted a phrase of Ovid and asserted that they pursued epideictic rhetoric because "virtue increased with praise."[127]

The third and somewhat ironic instance of disjunction occurred between oratory in the Italian Renaissance and its classical precedents. Rhetorical theory in antiquity focused primarily on judicial oratory. Deliberative oratory ranked next in the hierarchy for its importance in political decisions. The least valued and least practiced of the three oratorical genres was epideictic. Moreover, though funeral orations were the single autochthonous form of Roman oratory, no significant examples had survived from Roman days. Cicero himself, the unquestioned master of Latin eloquence, had once disparaged the rhetorical potential of funeral oratory. In contrast, epideictic oratory constituted the leading genre throughout the Italian Renaissance, and its popularity was never seriously challenged. Similarly, orators in the Renaissance practiced funeral oratory more extensively than their ancient predecessors ever did. Humanists exploited the possibilities of a form that Cicero had belittled. They did so at the beginning by following verbatim the prescriptions for epideictic oratory in the Latin rhetorical handbooks. Once contact was established with Byzantine culture at the end of the Trecento, the living tradition of panegyric among the Greeks spurred the development of that oratory in Italy.

Funeral commendations forced orators to reassess their culture in historical terms. No longer did Renaissance authors need to look solely to antiquity for *exempla*, as Petrarch had advocated. Contemporaries themselves functioned as mirrors of virtue and permitted Italians of the Renaissance to boast of parity between antique culture and their own.[128] The character of funeral oratory in Renaissance Italy demonstrates, first of all, that there was a renaissance in oratory. From Vergerio on, humanists rejected the thematic sermon and invented their orations according to the ancient topics for an encomium. That character suggests differences between the grammatical humanism of Petrarch and the rhetorical humanism of practicing orators like Vergerio and Bruni. That character demonstrates, finally, that Byzantine culture influenced the oratory of the Italian Renaissance as well as its philological methods and its philosophical interests.

What remains to be seen is how humanists assessed their society in the orations. They were presenting their world as it should be. Though under no illusions about their ability to perfect the commonwealth, they did constantly try to make its citizens better. They praised virtue so that it might increase.

CHAPTER THREE

BONA EXTERNA
Birthplace, Descent, Education

"There is nothing so impossible that it cannot be made possible by divine will."[1] With that bald assertion Raffaele Brandolini introduced his account of the way in which Mariano da Genazzano had received his education and thereby set out on the path that would make him one of Italy's most popular preachers in the late Quattrocento.[2] Brandolini discerned the hand of divine providence at work in the complicated sequence of events that helped Mariano obtain a patron for his training. Although Mariano's mother, guided by maternal intuition, had correctly recognized her son's native genius and yearned to see it nurtured, she was too poor to achieve her goal. At that crucial moment, in Brandolini's telling, God intervened through the person of Cardinal Angelo Capranica.

It just so happened one day that the cardinal decided to go to his villa in Capranica Prenestina. No one knew exactly why Capranica made the trip. Perhaps he left Rome to refresh his wearied body or preoccupied soul. Perhaps, like many residents of the eternal city through the ages, he simply wished to flee his business there for a time. It also happened that Mariano's grandmother had nursed Angelo. When the elderly woman heard that Capranica had arrived at his country home, she went with her daughter and little Mariano to greet her former nursling and present appropriate gifts.

Brandolini then narrated the interaction among the four that moved quickly toward resolving the question of the child's education. The cardinal gratefully accepted the elderly woman's gifts, and he fondly embraced her grandson. The child's limpid eyes and rapid tongue caught his interest. When the child's mother bemoaned her poverty, he immediately offered to see to the boy's education. Brandolini speculated on the motives for the cardinal's generous offer. Perhaps he had sympathized with the mother's lament or had so admired Mariano's nascent talent that he wished to see it developed. However, the orator clearly wished that his audience ascribe ultimate causality to the action of God's providence.[3] The encounter assured a humanist education for Mariano that equipped him with skills and virtues beneficial for his service to the believing community.

Brandolini's narrative comprised the central moment in the part of his speech dedicated to the praise of "external goods." The young humanist wove into this narrative topics specified for such praise by the handbooks. These topics included applause for the role of one's parents, the mention of divine omens or interventions that occurred at birth or during childhood, and a person's education. Brandolini may have included a portrait of Capranica's generosity to Mariano out of enlightened self-interest. He himself was desperately searching for a cardinal-patron in the late 1490s to assure a fixed income and alleviate his indigence. Perhaps he hoped that Cardinal Lorenzo Pucci, to whom he dedicated the speech, would take a promising young preacher into his care as Angelo Capranica had done for Mariano da Genazzano.

The earliest treatment of external goods in Roman funeral oratory was restricted, in all likelihood, to the praise of ancestry. Polybius' description suggests that Roman eulogists first praised the deceased and then shifted to the praise of the deceased's ancestors. That order was followed in at least one funeral oration from the early Renaissance.[4] Late in the Republican period the Romans inverted the schema and put the praise of ancestry before that of the deceased. The change generated a stricter chronology and is evinced in the instructions for a panegyric in the *Rhetorica ad Herennium*.[5]

Renaissance funeral orators concentrated their treatment of external goods on three particular topics: the city in which a person was born, his ancestry and parents, and the education he received as a youth. Topics like omens at a person's birth, or his wealth, occurred with less consistency. The three main topics—homeland, ancestry, and education—shared concerns with other humanist endeavors.

Praise for an individual's birthplace stimulated the same sort of research that humanist histories or eulogies of city-states compelled. Humanists used that praise to foster civic myths. In their treatment of ancestry, orators often assumed a position on the nature of true nobility. Worth, not birth, generally triumphed for orators committed to fostering virtue. The topic of education let them illustrate the value of an education in the humanities for the individual and for society.

Praise of the fatherland occupied a central place in Athenian funeral oratory. That topic often received more extensive treatment than the anonymous victims of the war for whom the oration was given.[6] Place of birth was classified under the topos of *genos* in the discussion of encomium in the *progymnasmata* of Greek authors like Theon and Hermogenes.[7] Quintilian was the first Roman rhetorician to treat the praise of birthplace.[8] Priscian's free translation of the *progymnasmata* of Hermogenes, the *Praeexercitamina* (ca. 500), also discussed the topic, and it figured in an anonymous technical treatise from late antiquity published in the nineteenth century by Karl Halm in *Rhetores latini minores*.[9]

In the early Middle Ages, Latin poetry *in laudem civitatis* had a decidedly ecclesiastical focus, stressing the protective presence of martyrs' relics within a city.[10] Communes emerged in Italy in the eleventh century, and those new urban republics had to defend their autonomy before bishop and emperor. Gina Fasoli has suggested that the twelfth-century *Liber pergaminus* of Mosè del Brolo marked a turning point for the communes of the Po valley with regard to ecclesiastical authority.[11] In that work civic consciousness was severed from identification with the episcopal throne. By the fourteenth century, panegyrics of Italian cities were written by professionals, less committed to communal ideals. Fasoli interprets this change as a premonition of the political evolution toward *signori*. Benzo d'Alessandria's encyclopedic work on northern Italian cities probably functioned as a key source for professional panegyrists.[12]

Italian humanists grappled with this issue for several reasons. Often encouraged or commissioned to write histories as part of their chancery service, humanists had to evaluate the communal myths associated with their place of employ. Frequently they incorporated elements of a particular myth into their histories. Pier Paolo Vergerio's *De republica veneta* (ca. 1400–1403?) represents one of the first efforts by a humanist to deal critically with the myth of Venice.[13] Panegyrics of a city-state also served propagandistic purposes in the ideological battles spurred by the wars of the early Quattrocento. Leonardo Bruni's famous panegyric of Florence (ca. 1403–4) moved a step beyond Vergerio's work. It was the first to utilize political notions found in Athenian panegyric. Pier Candido Decembrio countered Bruni's propaganda with a panegyric of Milan, written in 1436 after tensions had revived between the two states.[14]

Though potentially useful to all orators, the topic was most fully exploited by orators from the two great Renaissance republics, Venice and Florence. Orators praising Venice consistently commemorated the Serenissima's peculiarity as a city built upon the sea.[15] That location was unique and appropriate.[16] Leonardo Giustiniani contended that nature herself ceded to the divine will by permitting that a city rise on the water. Venetians protected the natural beauty of their city and enhanced its aesthetic appeal by designing their buildings to harmonize with the setting.[17] Antonio Maggi argued that Venice's climate helped produce a race of men who were learned and eloquent.[18] The characteristics of Venice that orators mention allude to passages from Cicero and suggest that Venice succeeded Athens and Rome as the center of Western culture.

As for the city's appropriate location, in rhetorical terms Venice possessed "decorum." Founded originally as a refuge for Christians fleeing from the barbarian invasions, the city had remained a haven throughout her history because she was so easily defended. Venetian eulogists applied Rome's epithet, *patria communis*, to their city on the lagoon.[19] Venice's location had spurred her development as an international emporium and a matrix for cultural exchange. East and West met at Venice, and both profited. Africa and Asia mixed with Europe along the Serenissima's canals.[20] Finally, it was intimated that the position of Venice practically compelled her to expand.

Orators portrayed the creation of an empire in terms most favorable to Venice. Though hesitant to become involved in wars, Vene-

tians were forced to defend themselves against aggression. The republic had expanded only because her citizens courageously answered all military and commercial threats. In his delicate eulogy for Francesco Foscari (1457), the deposed doge who had led Venice to expand on the mainland, Bernardo Giustiniani labeled Filippo Maria Visconti the aggressor.[21] In a panegyric for Pietro Foscari three years earlier, Ognibene Bonisoli had pushed his analysis of Venetian imperialism back in history, stigmatizing Byzantium, Padua, and Verona as the powers that first drove Venice onto the peninsula.[22] Venetians had used their virtue (*virtus*) in moments of favorable fortune (*fortuna*) to build an empire, and they maintained it by moderate rule and the arm of diplomacy.[23]

Humanist eulogists rationalized a foreign policy of expansion by arguing that Venice had acquired an empire abroad only to protect her liberty at home. Giacomo Boldù rejoiced in a funeral oration for Tommaso Donato in 1504 that Venetian liberty had survived for 1,083 years. (His mathematics yield the legendary date of 421 for the city's founding.)[24] Funeral orators often served as apologists for a foreign policy that had proved increasingly unpopular and dangerous over time. Just four years after Boldù's celebration of the defense of liberty, Venice faced an alliance of Europe's greatest powers, organized by Pope Julius II to regain Church territories in the Romagna that Venice had seized.

According to orators like Bonisoli and Bernardo Giustiniani, Venice's political stability was assured by a constitution that embodied Plato's conception of the ideal republic.[25] Giustiniani explicitly praised the complicated methods used to select a doge, noting that they were designed to prevent the election of a candidate who was overly powerful or incompetent.[26] Funeral orators commended Venice's wide system of consultation and her just laws, which made her "a most serene commonwealth."[27] The praise accorded Venice by her orators suggested issues that were developed in later tracts by authors like Gasparo Contarini.

Besides defending their own political liberty, Venetians remembered their many efforts to assure the liberty of the Church. Eusebio Priuli recalled that Venice had been founded as a Christian commonwealth.[28] Her elaborate ceremonies, distinguished bishops, priceless relics, and beautiful churches all testified to the religious commitment of her citizens. Venice had proved her worth to Christianity by acting for centuries as a bulwark in defense of ecclesiastical liberty. Pietro Contarini adduced three historical proofs of that assistance: the Venetians had attacked "Syria" to regain possession of Jesus' tomb, they defended Pope Alexander III from the aggression of Emperor Frederick Barbarossa, and they had recently waged a ten-year war to stem the advance of the Turks.[29]

Venice therefore deserved to be ranked with history's greatest commonwealths. Orators especially tried to show that Venice had inherited the mantle of Rome: she was an *urbs aeterna*, a *patria communis*, the center of Christendom, and ruler of a vast empire. Pietro Marcello conceded that the Roman Empire and the territories ruled by the Turk were larger than those ruled by Venice. Yet neither Rome nor the infidel had administered so vast an empire for so long a time as Venice had. Bernardo Giustiniani gave reasons why Venice surpassed many of antiquity's famous cities. Venice had a marketplace superior to Tyre, a maritime empire superior to Athens, a land empire superior to Sparta, civic concord greater than Rome (which had been plagued by class struggle), and a religious dedication that set her apart from all other cities.[30]

Funeral orators in the service of Florence generally traced the origins of the city to a colony established by Sulla, an interpretation first offered by Coluccio Salutati.[31] In his eulogy for Nanni Strozzi, Leonardo Bruni emphasized the Etruscan and Roman legacy of the Florentines, maintaining that the Etruscans had first introduced the cult of the immortal gods and the study of letters to the peninsula.[32] Occasionally an orator like Aurelio Bienato alluded to the refounding of the city by Charlemagne, an episode whose authenticity Bruni himself had denied. Bienato raised this theme at a memorial service for Lorenzo de' Medici at Naples in 1492, in the charged political atmosphere of a possible French invasion of Italy. As such, it was probably not his most deft piece of invention.[33]

In his eulogy for Giuliano de' Medici, the duke of Nemours, Marcello Adriani ascribed a particular spirit of determination to the Florentines. They had ingeniously tapped the resources their environment offered, no matter how arduous the task. Adriani noted the manner in which they had exploited the fields that surrounded the city. Those to the west and south were quite fertile and were used for food production. Those to the north and east, however, had little topsoil and challenged Tuscan resourcefulness. The industrious Florentines met the challenge by clearing the *pietra serena* from those fields and using the stone to decorate their buildings.[34]

Eulogists also emphasized the genius of Florentines in drafting political structures. Leonardo Bruni affirmed that the city's residents passed laws to assure that a tyrant or oligarchy could not seize the reins of power. They were convinced that a popular republic constituted the highest form of government. Orators emphasized that Florence opened her offices to all who had the necessary virtue. This political system stimulated Florentines to compete with each other to prove their civic virtue.[35] Bruni first created this image for Florence in 1428, and Marcello Adriani used the idea in 1516 to explain with unintended irony how the Medici had acquired increasing influence within the republic.[36] Like Venetian orators, eulogists who spoke in Florence celebrated the growth of the republic's empire and attributed that growth to a Roman combination of arms and virtue.[37]

Stately, wealthy, physically beautiful,[38] Florence could take pride above all, her panegyrists affirmed, in the rebirth of letters her citizens had effected in that era. Leonardo Bruni contrasted the studies that Florentines had revived to more mundane programs of education that frequently emphasized commerce. Literary studies were more refined. *Elegantia*, a quality of oratory, Bruni also transferred to Florentine education. Florentines had restored Latin letters, the pursuit of eloquence, and the study of Greek. Thanks to Florence, the *studia humanitatis* were taking root again throughout Italy.[39] Poggio Bracciolini labeled his adopted city the common homeland of the good arts and a workshop of eloquence (Cicero *Brut.* 8.32). In his estimation, Florence surpassed even the great urban centers of antiquity in a crucial aspect of its patronage for learning: unlike Athens and Rome, Florence supported those like Bruni, Carlo Marsuppini, and Poggio himself who wrote her history.[40] In 1492 Aurelio Bienato produced a list of eminent Florentines who had contributed to a rebirth of the liberal and visual arts.[41]

Other orators used similar approaches in praising smaller city-states, whose mythology was generally less developed. It was important to establish that a city was founded in antiquity. Funeral speakers in Padua repeated the legend of the city's founding by the Trojan Antenor.[42] Eulogists in Verona pointed to visible Roman ruins like the arena and theater as proof of the city's former glory.[43] Giovanni Cattanei emphasized that Mantua had existed before Rome.[44]

Humanist funeral orators also used the topos to spur the revival of education in their day. University centers like Perugia and Salerno were justly renowned for their faculties of law and medicine. Even Viterbo had emerged as a place where the "good arts" flourished.[45] Padua had produced Livy in Roman times and could boast of a university with eminent faculties of medicine, law, and theology in the fifteenth century.[46] Verona had also begun to produce literary masters, as it had in antiquity. Guarino symbolized the revival of humanist learning in that city, where Roman writers like Catullus, Macer, and both the elder and the younger Pliny were born.[47]

Thus the use of the topos of birthplace stimulated research into the history of the peninsula's cities and promoted a consciousness of their contribution to the renaissance of learning. Orators created pivotal roles for small centers. In a eulogy for Antonio Roselli, for example, Pietro Barozzi stressed the Etruscan origins of the town of Arezzo. Etruscans there had left a rich legacy. They had produced good letters, their linguistic elegance had helped to create Italy's vernacular, and they had settled in an area with a temperate climate that produced rich crops. In addition, Barozzi noted that the Etruscans had offered unflagging resistance to Roman conquest.[48]

Barozzi found one aspect of Arezzo's Etruscan heritage of particular relevance. Residents of the city had always been unique, he claimed, for combining religious devotion with hunger for learning. He lamented a tendency among the pious to spurn culture and to remain practically illiterate. They would do much better to imitate the Aretines and combine the two.

In a eulogy for Leonardo Bruni, Poggio emphasized that Arezzo's citizens had given vital assistance to the Roman Republic. He pointed to Livy's account of the numbers of Aretines who volunteered for Scipio's African expedition during the Second Punic War. And even now Arezzo was renowned for producing brave soldiers and men outstanding in learning and eloquence. Poggio named Petrarch as an example of one born at Arezzo and endowed with eloquence and learning.[49] Barozzi began his list of learned and devout Aretines with Leonardo Bruni and added Giovanni Tortelli, Carlo Marsuppini, and Francesco d'Arezzo.[50]

Italian orators also discussed foreign reigns. For example, they applauded changes in the intellectual tradition of the French kingdom. Though acknowledging that France was long renowned for the theological faculty at Paris, they commended Frenchmen of their day for developing an interest in literary and rhetorical studies and uniting that interest with their traditional emphasis on theology. By the early sixteenth century, the transalpine kingdom could be labeled a worthy competitor with Italy in the race to excel in the liberal arts.[51]

Marcantonio Magno posited close ties between Italians and Spaniards on the basis of their Mediterranean setting and Roman heritage. He recalled that Julius Caesar had selected Spaniards as his bodyguards, because of their courage; had his protectors not been compelled to wait outside the Senate, Caesar would never have been assassinated.[52] Magno presented Caesar as a murdered hero and commended an Italian-Spanish axis in a Naples ruled by the Spanish king.

The topic of birthplace thus pushed orators to strengthen their consciousness of Italy's cultural heritage and its important position on the European chessboard. Humanist funeral orators were enthusiastic advocates for the revival of letters, for which they took credit. They also proclaimed a cultural hegemony for Italy as the vanguard in such a renaissance. Eulogists attributed special honor to Florence as the driving force behind the movement to revive humanist studies.[53] Italian funeral orations often express an appreciation for the aesthetic component of life. Beautiful natural settings were to be protected and enhanced by the concomitant beauty of human edifices. Italian city-states were portrayed as leaders in their world, set apart culturally and consciously set up as standards against which other European states should measure themselves. Cultural and educational concerns superseded matters of ideology.

The topic stirred consciousness of the various cultural strands in antiquity that had helped to mold the civilization of the present. Tuscan orators appreciated the Etruscan legacy; audiences in the Po valley heard acclaim of their heritage as Gauls. In the final analysis, the Roman connection mattered most. Cities sought to weave particular aspects of the myth of Rome into their own civic legends, claiming at times to be eternal or to be a common homeland like the venerable city on the Tiber. All wished to assume Rome's mantle.[54]

Renaissance Rome itself was presented in divergent ways in funeral orations of the period. When its citizens were eulogized, the city too received an orator's accolades. Poggio spoke of the greatness of the city and its empire in antiquity and claimed that Giuliano Cesarini had renewed the reputation of the *civis Romanus* by his probity and learning. Administrators of the modern city might second Iacopo Zeno's observation that it was "indomitable," shifting the focus, however, from external attack to internal administration.[55] At other times, Rome was the object of an equally forceful invective. The city was charged with symbolic significance and offered eulogists a chance to make their subjects look very good. They often compared Rome's sad state at the inception of the Renaissance to its former glory. Once the *caput orbis terrarum*, Rome had become filthy. This insistence on a pattern of decline from former greatness set up praise for those who worked to remedy Rome's plight. Eulogists extolled persons like the della Rovere popes, who helped to restore the city's appearance and its prestige.[56]

Civic concerns dominate the humanist approach. Italian funeral orators tried to vindicate the genius of a particular commonwealth's laws and encourage its support for their educational program. The orators saw no contradiction between their praise for a commonwealth's liberty and its successful domination of other states. Scipio's dream had suggested that the best politicians were those who protected and enlarged the commonwealth. Italian eulogists agreed.

The second major topic among external goods, ancestry, offered funeral orators an occasion to apply their skills in historical and etymological criticism to family names and traditions. They wished to prove the antiquity and importance of an individual's family. Roman funeral orators had an advantage in this regard, for Roman practice prescribed that the memorial eulogy be given by a relative. In a famous eulogy for his aunt Julia, Julius Caesar had traced the descent of his family back to its divine founder, Venus.[57] Renaissance eulogists stopped short of claiming divine descent for anyone, but they did use various measures to corroborate the dignity of their subjects' lineage.

At times, eulogists traced a family's origins back to famous Roman families. Venetians who eulogized members of the Corner family consistently ascribed their descent to the Roman *gens Cornelia* and likened their public contribution to the great deeds of the various Scipios.[58] As the Romans claimed to derive from the Trojans, so Milanese eulogists for the Visconti sought to legitimize that ruling family by identifying Anglus, the African son of Aeneas, as its progenitor.[59] The etymological origins of a family name were presented as charged with significance.[60] A coat of arms gave visual expression to that worth. Orators at times explained the historical justification for the colors and symbols that appeared on a given shield.[61]

Factors like legendary origins, the etymology of a family's name, and a coat of arms constituted static symbols of prestige. They indicated nobility of birth. But humanist orators more frequently used the topic of ancestry to praise the deeds of illustrious ancestors of the deceased. Two eras from the past stand out in those presentations: the epoch of Charlemagne and the epoch of the crusades. The former signaled the end of the cultural chaos engendered by the barbarian invasions.[62] The latter had an acute relevance of its own. George of Trebizond claimed that Domenico Michiel had helped to recapture Jerusalem in the twelfth century. A Byzantine exile, Trebizond probably mentioned the episode because he wanted Venetians to heed calls for another crusade.[63]

Humanists at times revealed that they had perused family archives. Pietro Barozzi identified a lost ancestor of Antonio Roselli, Abavo, who had studied under Accorso at Bologna. Barozzi claimed to have seen a letter from Accorso inviting Abavo to teach at Bologna.[64] Barozzi thus presented Roselli as coming from a distinguished family of jurists, and the rest of his panegyric proved that Roselli maintained family traditions in his illustrious legal career.

The remote past did not exercise a monopoly on *exempla* for humanist eulogists. Illustrious contemporaries related to the deceased were also summoned forth. The anonymous preacher of a eulogy for Louise of Savoy recalled for the papal court that her ancestor, Amadeus VIII, had been elected pope by the Council of Basel. Not reticent to name an antipope in papal Rome, the same speaker praised Amadeus' magnanimous decision to abdicate the papal throne in order to reestablish unity in the Church.[65] Speakers did not pass up an opportunity to extol powerful living members of the family in attendance at the obsequies. Francesco da Toledo paid special homage to Cardinal Giuliano della Rovere in his discourse for Giuliano's cousin, Leonardo.[66]

Renaissance orators demonstrate in their use of the topic of ancestry their firm belief in the power of moral exemplars. The more visible the exemplar, the more persuasive it was. In a eulogy for Doge Leonardo Loredan, Andrea Navagero recalled that famous relatives tended to inspire their descendants: they were like a torch that illumines souls, inflaming them to perform deeds worthy of their parentage.[67] Pietro del Monte compared the inspiration that Francesco and Bartolomeo Zabarella gave to Giovanni Zabarella to that which the Roman heroes Quintus Fabius Maximus and Publius Scipio received from images of their ancestors. He also recalled that paintings of the deeds of Alexander the Great had prompted Julius Caesar to seek equal fame. Del Monte was citing passages from Sallust and Livy that were popular with Italian humanists.[68] His first comparison recalled that Romans had used the masks of ancestors in their funeral processions, thereby creating a visual equivalent for the praise of ancestors in the *laudatio funebris*.

The topic of ancestry also served ideological purposes. Orators introduced historical persons and events to shape contemporary attitudes. For instance, Battista Casali presented the battle between Boniface VIII and members of the Colonna family as a testimony to the Colonnas' greatness under fire. Though he assigned partial blame to Sciarra Colonna, the real villain was Boniface: because Boniface had seized the pontificate in criminal fashion and had administered it without any care for the norms of sanctity, he received due punishment from God when humiliated at Anagni.

Casali's presentation suggested a comparison with actions of Giovanni Colonna, the oration's subject. Apparently Giovanni had been simply maintaining the virtuous traditions of his forebears when he refused to bend to the unjust demands of popes Sixtus IV and Alexander VI, even at the cost of imprisonment and exile. Casali also took this opportunity to commend Pope Julius II for his efforts to restore Rome and pacify Italy. Those were policies originally drafted for the papacy by another of Giovanni's relatives, Pope Martin V.[69] Renaissance funeral orators presented their own times in the mirror of the past.

In cases where the family praised was a ruling dynasty, this topic acquired even stronger ideological overtones. In an anniversary eulogy for Giangaleazzo Visconti, Andrea Biglia adduced three reasons why the Visconti deserved the love and respect of their subjects. First, the family had unified various political entities into a territorial state. No longer did the will of the stronger prevail in a multiplicity of jurisdictions, but political chaos had been reduced to an order where right (*ius*) and equity (*aequitas*) prevailed. Secondly, the Visconti had supplied a single ruler for this state. Finally, the Visconti had helped assure liberty for all of Italy. The presence of a sub-Alpine state had effectively terminated the pattern of invasions across the Alps and spurred the levy of native armies.[70]

Like most humanist praise, Biglia's was conceived as a two-edged sword. It obviously flattered the ruling family; few Renaissance orators risked impairing the source of their sustenance. But it also delineated guidelines for a ruling family's conduct. Biglia created an expectation in his audience that the Visconti would respect equity and right and defend Italian security from foreign aggression.

Biglia's use of this topic also indicates that orators adapted the form of their speeches to particular exigencies. Milanese eulogists under the Visconti and Sforza, for example, made extensive use of the topic of ancestry; it helped to legitimize rule by those families. In contrast, they generally ignored the topic of birthplace. Milanese political prestige derived from its ruling dynasty, not from any mythical founding.

Orators at Florence during the greater part of the Quattrocento made the opposite choice, even though the regimes at Florence and Milan were not as antithetical as Florentine propagandists claimed. Leonardo Bruni was the first to exploit the ideological potential of the topic of birthplace, and he made it the focus of his panegyrical writings. He assimilated the Athenian tradition of praise for the fatherland, and he used its principles to construct propaganda for republican Florence.[71] Florentine humanists continued to emphasize republican values during the Medici regime. Cosimo himself was praised as a republican hero. Moreover, Cosimo and his immediate Medici successors, aware of the explosive symbolic possibilities of a state funeral, left specific instructions prohibiting public honors lest their control of Florence's government be openly celebrated. The topic of ancestry would have suggested just that sort of celebration.

The changes in the Florentine social and political context by 1513 were mirrored in the funerals for the Medici. With a Medici pope and with hegemony reestablished in Florence, both Giuliano, the duke of Nemours, and Lorenzo, the duke of Urbino, received state funerals, which openly celebrated the Medici family. Those funerals were conscious imitations of Pope Leo X's triumphal entry into Florence in 1515.[72] Medici dominance was also acknowledged in the funeral orations delivered during those ceremonies. For the first time in Florence, humanist orators used the topic of ancestry when eulogizing a Medici. In fact, they praised the Medici so effusively that by 1520 no other Italian family could claim a mythical prestige equal to that of Florence's leaders. Nor was any member of that family celebrated as extensively as Cosimo di Giovanni Bicci.

Cosimo had already achieved peculiar prestige when the Florentine government voted him the title *pater patriae* shortly after his death in 1464.[73] Cinquecento eulogists built on Cosimo's reputation for civic service to propagate a rationale for Medici rule in Florence. Battista Casali commended Cosimo's parents for selecting a name that intimated that their son would achieve fame not only in Florence and Italy but throughout the "cosmos." Orators particularly praised Cosimo's political activities, both in domestic and foreign policy. By public consent, Casali observed, the Medici banker was granted powers beyond any other private citizen.[74] Cosimo employed those powers, Marcello Adriani affirmed, for public protection and for charitable purposes. He never used them for gain or pleasure.[75]

In foreign policy Cosimo was portrayed as the architect of a balance-of-power strategy designed to assure Italy's liberty and protect her security.[76] He had realized his purpose by various means: he had contributed advice in debates on foreign policy in government councils, offered financial support for the republic's endeavors, and supported recourse to arms as a last resort. Adriani contrasted this vigorous activity to the delaying tactics used so successfully by Quintus Fabius Maximus. The statesman Cosimo's policy had benefited his homeland, the Church, the kingdom of Naples, and Sforza Milan. In light of the invasions in their lifetime, sixteenth-century eulogists seemed to long for the vanished period of relative stability after the peace of Lodi in 1454.

Cosimo was finally celebrated for his patronage. Though he possessed immense wealth, the banker should not therefore be censured; that wealth was divinely granted for benefaction and was always so employed.[77] Casali specifically cited Cosimo's contribution to churches as far away as Jerusalem, and Adriani noted his support for the liberal arts and for building. A dedicated public servant in all actions, especially in defending Florence from foreign aggression, Cosimo truly deserved the honorary title, *pater patriae*, awarded to Cicero centuries before.[78]

The myth of Lorenzo de' Medici, whose content crystalized in the title "the Magnificent," had also begun to be propagated by the second decade of the sixteenth century. Battista Casali commended Lorenzo's behavior during the Pazzi conspiracy. The plot, known and abetted by Sixtus IV in Casali's account, forced Florence into an unwanted war. At that critical juncture, Lorenzo had risked his life to assure the safety of the state. He secretly traveled to Naples and dissuaded Ferrante I from further support for Florence's enemies. Casali reckoned the moral of this tale in typically humanist fashion: those events demonstrated that patriotism, eloquence, and prudence furnish greater protection for the state than arms.[79]

Casali also recognized Lorenzo's contribution to the rebirth of culture, and his patronage of that rebirth. Lorenzo had earned fame among those who composed in the *volgare*. Moreover, he had supported the liberal arts in such a way, Casali exclaimed, that Athens itself had migrated to Florence in Lorenzo's time.[80] In a funeral oration delivered in Rome for another Medici, Pope Clement VII, Lorenzo Grana called the family the primary impetus behind the revival of Greek and Latin letters. He especially commended Lorenzo's son Giovanni (who became Leo X) for supporting letters during his reign. Marcello Adriani portrayed Pope Leo as one determined to use the resources at his disposal in order to bring the "insanity of war" to an end.[81]

How did the Medici improve their world? Politically, Andrea Alamanno asserted, the family had assured justice and equity for all by their example. They crushed revolts against the republic, curbed the power of civic factions, and gave funding and advice in times of war. The Medici were a force for public order. To prove that Florentines consistently rewarded virtue, Marcello Adriani noted that the Medici were considered "leading citizens" (*principes*) from Cosimo on. The word probably rang true to Medici supporters and opponents in Adriani's audience.[82] Culturally, the Medici formed the vanguard of forces working to reanimate the study of the liberal arts. Religiously, the family showed a sincere dedication; they promoted piety and paid to build and remodel churches.[83]

The development of the myth of the Medici can be partially traced in the use of the topic of descent in funeral orations for family members. In political matters, one can observe a change from the guarded ways in which contemporaries had praised Cosimo. Cinquecento eulogists did not hesitate to describe the Medici as *principes*.[84] The shield of a Medici pope may well have permitted orators to cast aside their traditional caution. Eulogists continued to encourage Medici patronage for culture, as they had when Cosimo was alive. Such praise was intended to spur the revival of the arts and probably to assure financial support for impoverished orators.

Classical handbooks specified that panegyrics mention any omens of future greatness that took place at an individual's birth or during his childhood. Italian Renaissance orators tended to shy away from the topic, perhaps because of its close associations with Greco-Roman religious beliefs. When employed, such events were usually baptized into a Christian context. Prophetic pronouncements were ascribed to the inspiration of the Holy Spirit, and extraordinary events were interpreted as manifestations of divine providence. Like the human persons eulogized, God too was expected to perform good deeds.

Raffaele Brandolini drew such a picture of God working to assure a humanist education for Mariano da Genazzano. Brandolini used the topic again in his funeral eulogy for Lorenzo Cibò, reporting that a miter had appeared miraculously over Lorenzo's head when he was still a child. He contrasted this omen to one in the life of Lucius Cornelius Sulla and used the contrast to emphasize fundamental differences in the roles of leaders from classical and Christian cultures. Whereas Sulla had earned his fame through slaughter and rebellion, Cibò was destined to play a constructive role as pastor.[85] Brandolini spoke in Rome in 1504, and his words may have been an implicit warning to the new pope, Julius II. Julius should be a Cibò for his flock, not a Sulla.

Giannantonio Campano referred to disastrous events in the lives of individuals he eulogized to prove that they had enjoyed special divine protection. Young Enea Silvio Piccolomini, the future Pius II, survived a dangerous fall and a potentially fatal goring by a bull. Even more dramatically, little Alessandro Oliva fell into a well at age three and died before help reached him. His frantic mother carried her child's lifeless body into the local church and implored the Virgin's assistance. Miraculously, the boy revived. When he noticed the Virgin's image sewn into a vestment worn by a deacon, he informed his astonished mother that the woman depicted on the dalmatic was the one who had come to his aid. A chapel was built on the spot, and the young boy entered the Augustinian order two years later.[86] Important vocations for key social actors were assured by such extraordinary interventions.

One last topic within the category of external goods had peculiar relevance for humanist eulogists. Before discussing a person's virtuous deeds, orators praised his education. Education and virtue were closely joined. Italian humanists prized their educational program because it sought to form character. Those eulogized functioned as empirical proofs for the value of the humanities.[87] Funerals and their attendant orations offered Italian humanists an effective forum to show the value of their educational program. Praise for the parents of the deceased often served as a transition from the topic of ancestry to that of education. Parents could do nothing better than create a home environment conducive to a life of virtue and insure a proper education for their child.[88]

Specific stages in the educational process had begun to be defined. Grammar, strictly speaking, tended to be separated from the other disciplines of the *studia humanitatis* and to be approached as rudimentary training in Latin language and composition.[89] Parents themselves could supply elementary grammatical instruction in the home. Formal tutors were subsequently employed for training in syntax, prosody, metrics, and composition. Orators considered even these earliest lessons in their development of the topic of education. Guarino noted, for example, that Vittorino da Feltre had taught Margherita Gonzaga the fundamentals of Latin grammar by using the Vulgate Psalms as his first text and then advancing to Virgil. Vittorino was an acknowledged innovator among Renaissance educators for teaching grammar directly from ancient texts.[90] Humanist orators often conjoined grammar with poetry, as classical theorists of education had done.[91]

Orators then traced a person's progress from grammatical studies to the humanities. The terminology used to define the humanities, and the disciplines included under that rubric, were fluid. At times humanists spoke of *litterae* or the *studia litterarum*, using synecdoche to underline the literary matrix of their program, whose texts were the great books of Greco-Roman antiquity.[92] At times they accentuated the nature of their disciplines as *artes*, matters that can be taught to persons with basic talent. When humanist eulogists described the arts as *bonae* or *honestae*, they did so in the sense of an Aristotelian final cause. Those who pursue the good arts should become better persons.[93] Finally, humanists qualified the character of their studies by the term *humanitatis*, emphasizing that those studies assured the best preparation for the committed human life they so valued. For this insistence Italian Renaissance rhetoricians eventually earned the nickname *humanista*, by which they have continued to be known to this day.[94]

The most comprehensive statement of the disciplines that formed the Renaissance program for education in the humanities is found in the library canon drafted for Cosimo de' Medici by Tommaso Parentucelli, later Pope Nicholas V, which listed grammar, poetry, history, rhetoric, and moral philosophy as the *studia humanitatis*.[95] Though no eulogist repeated the canon exactly, practically all of them manifested a predilection for a portion of that curriculum. The orations delivered by Guarino and by his students demonstrate the ways in which the humanities were approached in one of the Quattrocento's renowned schools.

In 1415 a Venetian student of Guarino, Andrea Giuliano, was chosen to commemorate Manuel Chrysoloras at a memorial service in Venice. Giuliano described Chrysoloras' fundamental learning as embracing "philosophy" and the "liberal sciences"; he later learned Latin by listening to matters discussed by philosophers as well as the orators and teachers of the liberal arts. The oration suggested a tie between the humanities and philosophy.[96] Pietro del Monte, another of Guarino's students, praised Giovanni Zabarella for pursuing the liberal arts, which he defined as studies that lead to "good and holy living." He quoted Cicero, who asserted that the arts of virtue best protect human persons.[97] In these early discourses (ca. 1415–35) Guarino's students did not describe the humanist curriculum in detail. They simply stressed a conjunction between the arts (eloquence) and philosophy (wisdom), and the goal of moral living.

Guarino himself gave more concrete definition to humanist education in a eulogy for his friend and student Giannicola Salerno. He generally praised Salerno for assimilating those disciplines that yielded a good and prudent citizen. Rhetoric, history, and poetry received special commendation. Poetry provided a hermeneutic for interpreting arcane senses and a guide to style. History's function was illustrative; it provided great examples to be imitated. Rhetoric taught a student how to achieve eloquence, which in combination with prudence made one useful to the commonwealth.[98]

In his eulogy for Margherita Gonzaga, Guarino had occasion to praise the program of studies taught by Vittorino da Feltre. The elegance of Margherita's correspondence attested to Vittorino's ability to teach eloquence. So comprehensive was the young woman's knowledge of history that she had even read *The Jewish War* by Flavius Josephus. Guarino noted that Vittorino had included sacred letters in his curriculum. He introduced his students to Scripture and the "patristic humanists," Jerome and Lactantius.[99] Vittorino was known to contemporaries as the "Christian Socrates."

Ludovico Carbone, who delivered the eulogy for Guarino himself at Ferrara in December 1460, repeatedly emphasized Guarino's training in "classical letters."[100] Guarino's parents had cared that he be instructed in letters (*litteris*), and the boy's talent convinced contemporaries that he would shed needed light upon the study of good literature (*bonae litterae*). At age twenty-five, Guarino had traveled to Constantinople, a city flourishing in the study of letters (*studia litterarum*). He went there to learn, believing that he could perfect his knowledge of Latin literature by mastering Greek. He achieved his goal under the tutelage of Manuel Chrysoloras, master of Greek letters (*litterae*).

Carbone also presented a picture of Guarino's lengthy teaching career, focusing on his years at the Estense court in Ferrara. Niccolò III d'Este wanted his son's tutor to be a *grammaticus*, *rhetor*, and *poeta*. He had selected Guarino because Guarino was such a complete humanist. Carbone alleged that good letters had fallen into disuse prior to Guarino's arrival. Ferrara had no one capable of speaking with gravity and elegance, because no one had learned even the basic principles and interpretational skills communicated in the first years of grammatical training.[101] Guarino stepped into the breach and spurred an educational renaissance for Ferrara's rulers and citizens. Carbone described his teacher's curriculum and his textbooks. Guarino first used a short grammar, which he himself had written, to communicate the rudiments of Latin. He then had his pupils study a series of excerpts from the Roman grammarian Servius. Composition was taught through exercises in letter-writing. Students then learned the art of public speaking by studying the precepts in the manuals and by seeing their application in model speeches from each of the rhetorical genres. This method of teaching rhetoric led Carbone to compare Guarino to Quintilian. The course of studies concluded with instruction in interpreting the poets.[102]

Guarino's pedagogy evidently transformed the bleak learning situation in Ferrara. The rhetoric of praise constantly suggested to orators a pattern of rebirth. By 1460, Carbone claimed, Ferrarese students were equipped with a new culture and a new handwriting. Guarino was the ideal humanist master, for he taught his pupils correct grammar and good morals, reviving ancient practice. They became well-spoken (*diserti*), learned (*eruditi*), polished (*limati*), and pleasant (*suaves*).[103]

Eulogies from the school of Guarino thus indicate the humanist concern for breadth in learning and the humanist penchant to emphasize learning's product, the virtuous citizen. Guarino properly focused his education upon the excellence of his pupils' lives. The principal areas of study described in the eulogies—poetry, history, rhetoric—accord well with the more systematic treatment of humanist education provided by Guarino's son Battista in the *De ordine docendi et studendi* (1459). Battista claimed that his father first instructed students in Latin and Greek grammar. Principles of syntax and meter were illustrated from the classical poets and practiced in written exercises. Students then advanced to the study of prose, using Latin historians like Livy, Sallust, and Tacitus as primary texts. The training culminated with rhetoric, based almost exclusively on Ciceronian precepts and examples.[104]

Florentine eulogies reflect the same sort of flexible approach to the definition of the humanities. Antonio Pacini described those studies in a generic way in his oration for Lorenzo de' Medici (d. 1440),

Cosimo's brother. He commended Lorenzo for deciding late in life to take up the dual discipline of the *studia humanitatis*, training in how to speak well and live well. Though generic, the description epitomized the value humanists assigned their program. It would produce the ideal Roman orator, a good person who was skilled in public speaking.

In 1444 Giannozzo Manetti stressed that knowledge of Greek had enriched Leonardo Bruni's culture. He also emphasized the extent of Bruni's learning, explicitly mentioning his mastery of the poets, his knowledge of history, his ability to interpret words and to handle Greek and Latin letters, his eloquence in all genres of rhetoric, and his familiarity with moral philosophy. In effect Manetti took the library canon of his friend Tommaso Parentucelli, written in 1437 for Cosimo, and used it to organize his speech for Bruni seven years later. He publicly proclaimed that the humanities consisted of the five disciplines named in the canon: grammar, poetry, history, rhetoric, and moral philosophy. The epitaph on Bruni's tomb provided a constant visual reminder of the general contents of a humanist education.[105] According to the inscription, history, eloquence, and the Muses of Greece and Rome collectively mourned Bruni's death.

Other humanist educators reveal their approach to the liberal arts in their funeral oratory. Francesco Maturanzio, who wrote a handbook on rhetoric and taught rhetoric and poetry at the University of Perugia late in the Quattrocento, emphasized the complementary character of the disciplines of history and moral philosophy. History instructed the soul in all ways of life; moral philosophy instructed it in affections and deeds. The former offered advice for oneself and for the state; the latter shed light upon matters to be avoided. Both supplied a vast number of examples to be imitated. History, moral philosophy, and eloquence were the three disciplines that Pier Paolo Vergerio specified as particularly useful for public service. They continued to be prized by funeral orators throughout the Renaissance.[106]

Humanists also labeled other disciplines as good arts. Venetian orators like Leonardo Giustiniani and Sabellico classified music as one of those arts. The eulogists esteemed music less for its mathematical qualities than for its sense of harmony and concord. It possessed the precise virtues that orators desired for their society. Like oratory, music also made for good entertainment.[107] Ludovico Carbone believed that painting should be removed from the Aristotelian category of a mechanical art and placed among those considered liberal. His contention represents part of a Renaissance effort to grant greater cultural status to the visual arts.[108] Andrea Navagero echoed practical concerns when he lamented that Venice no longer required that her sons be trained in the art of sailing.[109]

The orators provided only passing suggestions on educational methods. They repeated the three elements that ancient theoreticians of rhetoric had elaborated: nature, training, and practice. One's native genius was to be developed by instruction in the principles of an art and by assiduous practice.[110] Particular emphasis was given to speaking and listening. Andrea Alamanno related that Giovanni de' Medici went to hear the famous Florentine orators and poets and in that way acquired his facility in Latin. Battista Casali cited a saying of Demades that listening to good orators supplied the soundest instruction in eloquence.[111]

The master, by his instruction and example, played the key role in communicating the good arts. According to Poggio, Niccolò Niccoli chose to study under Luigi Marsili because the Augustinian taught clearly and lived morally.[112] Various orators celebrated that Manuel Chrysoloras had reawakened interest in Greek. It was calculated that Italians had not pursued Greek learning for seven hundred years. Giannozzo Manetti attested to Chrysoloras' eloquence when he noted that Leonardo Bruni had abandoned his law studies to pursue Greek after he heard Chrysoloras lecturing.[113]

Renaissance humanists consistently applauded a teacher's character—in rhetorical terms, his "ethos." Niccolò Capranica contended that Bessarion had cherished his teacher Ignazio Cortasmeno, the metropolitan of Selimbria, because he had imparted instruction in philosophy and letters and supplied precepts for moral living. Giovanni de' Medici was inspired, by the exhortations and example of Carlo Marsuppini, to avoid the vices of adolescence. Ognibene Bonisoli educated his distinguished pupil, Francesco Gonzaga, in letters and in morals. Guarino captured this emphasis on a teacher's ethos when he described Vittorino da Feltre as "most irreproachable in his life and morals and outstanding in his knowledge of every genre of literature, Greek and Latin."[114]

Humanists rarely criticized the universities in their orations. Rather than censure the Aristotelian curriculum, humanist funeral orators simply charted their subjects' progress from the humanities to philosophy and then to professional studies. They suggested compatibility between the humanities and the university curriculum and presented the humanist disciplines as ideal preparation for any specialized studies. They also seized the opportunity to present the professional studies of the university in a humanist light.

When discussing their subjects' legal education, eulogists stressed the civic value of law.[115] They borrowed their highest compliment for lawyers from Cicero: the best were those like Quintus Scaevola and Lucius Crassus, who were "the most eloquent of those skilled in law and the most skilled in law of the eloquent."[116] Eloquence and jurisprudence were to be combined in public service. Similar efforts were made to show that the humanities prepared one for further studies in medicine and theology. Whether doctor, lawyer, or theologian, every university graduate should be eloquent.[117]

Though convinced of the fundamental worth of their own program, humanists had always allowed room for choice in education. In the first treatise on a liberal education, Pier Paolo Vergerio discussed disciplines besides grammar, rhetoric, poetry, history, and moral philosophy. Students were encouraged to select the liberal arts that best suited their temperaments. Funeral orations reflect this tolerance and apparent love for abundance in learning. Francesco Maturanzio applauded the Dominican Leonardo Mansueti for mastering dialectic, natural and moral philosophy, the mathematical arts of the quadrivium, and theology, the queen of all branches of learning. Mansueti accomplished this feat in the very capital of the new learning, Florence.

To provide a rationale for his praise of breadth in learning, Maturanzio quoted *"the* orator," Cicero. In defending the poet Archias (1.2), Cicero had asserted that "a subtle bond of a mutual relationship links together all arts which have any bearing upon the common life of humankind (*ad humanitatem*)."[118] Humanists sought in their oratory to foster that mutual relationship and avoided open controversy with their professional rivals. They used their eulogies to emphasize the humane aspects of learning in general.

Italian humanists prized their own program, most of all, for the persons it produced. Those persons should be learned and eloquent. Humanists proposed clear skills to be mastered and chose texts that exemplified those skills.[119] Their education was oriented not toward discovery and research, but toward recovery and imitation. Their students should be conversant with the literature of antiquity, they should commit to memory the great deeds and exemplars of history, and they should internalize the precepts of moral philosophy. The recipient of an education in the *studia humanitatis* should also possess eloquence in all forms of communication. True eloquence was harmonious, persuasive, and full of wisdom.

Renaissance funeral orators openly rejected the magniloquence or garrulousness of sophistry.[120] One's eloquence should perforce be substantive, as it flowed from proper foundations in classical learning. In fact, Renaissance eulogists preferred to combine the terms, praising their subjects for a "learned eloquence." Eloquence should then be utilized in a variety of contexts. Public speaking was the most important, for rhetoric in its primary sense meant speechmaking. In his eulogy for Guid'Ubaldo I of Urbino, Ludovico Odassi attempted to establish the duke's proficiency in the three genres of oratory: judicial, deliberative, and epideictic. Giordano Orsini singled out Giovanni Pontano's skill in epideictic rhetoric and adduced Pontano's popular funeral oration for Gattamelata as proof.[121]

In the humanist conception, literary products were also valid testimonies of eloquence. Guarino thus numbered the letters of Margherita Gonzaga as witnesses to her style. The anonymous author of a funeral oration for Leonardo Bruni stressed the social service Bruni had performed in translating Greek texts into Latin and justified the need for such translations by observing that no translations of authors like Plato and Aristotle had hitherto existed that manifested the proper elegance.[122]

Those who mastered the humanities should be eloquent and virtuous. Their studies impelled them toward activity in the public domain. Good arts produced good persons. Humanists were not concerned with the pursuit of knowledge for its own sake but insisted that truth be related to conduct. The liberal arts inflamed the soul to pursue virtue and helped young persons (*adolescentes*) to develop character.[123] These convictions about a humanist education depended upon a particular anthropology with strong classical roots. Aristotle and Cicero had agreed that libidinous desire (*libido*) was the fundamental passion of adolescence. Humanist funeral orators repeatedly sought to demonstrate that the *studia humanitatis* functioned as a healthy corrective to adolescent *libido*.[124]

All of the liberal arts, therefore, were valuable in helping one to practice life's principal art, that of good and holy living.[125] The virtuous product of an education in the humanities should, finally, contribute to the construction of a better society. Humanist orators repeatedly emphasized that their subjects did not acquire learning for egoistic motives but in order to be useful to others. Plato and Cicero were right to assert that no one is born for himself alone.[126] Like their teachers, students of the humanities had to exemplify the virtues that they advocated.[127] A Roman sense of the persuasive power of ethos sustains this axiom once again.

If an education in the humanities prepared one for service to friends and homeland, there was no more noble vocation than politics, the art of creating and governing a commonwealth.[128] Those committed to the culture of the orator coherently sought to bestir a sense of public involvement. Eloquence civilized. Humanists were convinced that their education sensitized persons to the welfare of the state.

The remainder of discussion in this book flows naturally from the emphasis on the humanities as a preparation for public service. Renaissance orators used their funeral eulogies to show that individuals contributed to bettering their Church, their states, and their world of learning. They implicitly suggested ways in which their audience should likewise participate in a great project of reform.

Italian orators often concluded their praise of external goods with the observation that praise was truly owed to the virtuous deeds of the deceased, not to extraneous circumstances. Cristoforo Landino spoke for his age by citing Cicero's position that virtue alone was to be sought in and for itself. Nobility was not a quality of birth, Poggio argued, but of virtue and good deeds.[129] Their continual praise of certain good deeds demonstrates the deeds that humanists wished to see done. By reviewing their subjects' actions, humanists could evaluate the state of their Church, their political institutions, and their world of learning.

CHAPTER FOUR

ECCLESIASTICAL IDEALS
"As You Did It to Any of the Least"

When members of the papal curia gathered at Santa Maria in Aracoeli on 1 March 1505 for the funeral of Pietro Menzi da Vicenza, they selected Tommaso Inghirami of Volterra, one of Menzi's former students, to deliver the eulogy. Menzi had been general auditor of the Apostolic Camera and bishop of Cesena.[1] Inghirami faced a difficult rhetorical situation. Menzi had been imprisoned in Castel Sant'Angelo for over six months in 1503 on suspicion of having embezzled funds from the papal treasury. According to the Venetian ambassador Antonio Giustiniani, that arrest had sent shockwaves through the curia of Alexander VI.[2] Menzi's request to be buried in Aracoeli was originally overruled because he had died of the plague. Now, six months later, that wish was being fulfilled.[3]

Inghirami's strategy under the circumstances was bold and direct. He lashed out at Menzi's detractors and at the corruption that he perceived as endemic to the curia. He promised to follow Athenian custom in his panegyrical oration, contrasting his approach to the common practice at the court, where fawning orators rarely hesitated to lie and to praise individuals steeped in vice.[4] He denounced Menzi's enemies and praised his patron as their virtuous antithesis.

Inghirami portrayed Menzi as one who had protected his integrity as a judge on one of the Church's major tribunals. Other judges openly accepted bribes and rendered decisions favorable to those who paid them off.[5] Menzi had cherished Rome and sought to improve the moral quality of life in the city. Corrupt Rome, however, had rejected his sage counsel. Inghirami explained that the bishop's efforts to uncover the names of those who had stolen grain during a recent famine had incurred the wrath of powerful factions in the city and led to his disgrace. Like another Marius, Menzi bravely rode out the storm.[6]

Inghirami unleashed the full force of his invective when analyzing the pyschological motives that led to the persecution of his mentor. Many members of the papal court had become so corrupt and decadent that they recoiled before virtue. Their sole defense lay in carping at the minor faults that afflict even the most virtuous human beings.[7] Moreover, Inghirami noted, human nature generally shrinks before severity and discipline even in the rare cases where one recognizes the need for them. Nevertheless, because criminal activity was widespread in Rome, Menzi had felt that only a rigorous application of the laws could remedy the situation. His powerful enemies, enmeshed in a network of crime, could ill afford to allow a committed judge free rein.[8]

Inghirami concluded his discourse with biting irony. He affirmed that Menzi's worst vice and the cause of his demise was personal integrity. He was simply too good, too inexperienced in corruption, too opposed to its practice, and too foolish not to keep silent. Menzi had no chance of escaping harm in the Rome of his day.[9] Inghirami's discourse paints a vivid picture of corruption within the papal court at the beginning of the sixteenth century. Only fawning agreement assured safety and success. Members of the court would even resort to crass injustice to undermine reformers like Pietro Menzi.

The orator's primary purpose is obvious: he was seeking to clear his deceased patron's name by condemning those who had arranged his imprisonment two years earlier. In this he benefited from a new climate in Rome. Alexander VI had died in the summer of 1503, and Julius II, Alexander's bitter foe, had been elected pope. Inghirami could therefore vilify those within the curia who had been associated with one of the final actions of Alexander's papacy.

The oration for Pietro Menzi da Vicenza represents an extreme form of humanist panegyrical oratory in an ecclesiastical context. Humanists did not always resort to such explicit contrast and to the use of praise and invective in their funeral oratory. Although they made no concerted effort to hide the Church's faults, they generally preferred to make their criticisms implicitly through praise. For example, the accumulated weight of insistent praise for churchmen who were not avaricious became a way to sensitize the audience to the gravity of that vice. As Peter Brown has argued regarding the cult of the saints, "the virtues which count most for us are those we do not possess."[10] Praise is an indication of what should be and, often, of what is missing.

This study treats funeral oratory from the death of Petrarch in 1374. The period begins ecclesiastically near the end of the pope's residence at Avignon and shortly before the beginning of the Great Western Schism (1378–1417). That schism badly damaged the reputation of the Western Church. Division festered among believers for almost forty years while a succession of popes at Rome and Avignon clung to their respective claims of authority. The Renaissance Church was born with an obsession for reform, an obsession that lasted right into the sixteenth century.

Humanists shared a general concern for Church reform and spelled out their particular vision in funeral orations for Church leaders. Their approach was intimately tied to their vocation as rhetors. Humanists did not diagnose the cause of the Church's affliction as institutional or doctrinal. In simplest terms the real affliction was ethical: Church leaders and ministers did not practice what they preached. Because their lives were bad, they had lost credibility with their audience of believers. Reform was therefore a question of reforming individual morals. This vision was enunciated by Poggio Bracciolini, who decried the vices of the clergy before Church leaders gathered in the summer or autumn of 1417 at the Council of Constance to resolve the schism.[11]

Immoral behavior by the Church's ministers had disastrous consequences, Poggio claimed, for people are more convinced by what they see than by anything they hear. The vices of the clergy drained their preaching of evangelizing force. It became empty rhetoric. Poggio identified preaching in his day with thematic sermons. He noted that sermons typically began with a quotation (*sententia*). The body of the sermon followed immediately and simply piled up the opinions of learned men. The sermon then closed with an exhortation to practice virtue and avoid vice. Bad persons using bad rhetoric led to a woeful condition for the believing community. Who would heed the exhortations of those who constantly sought their own advantage and ignored the common good?[12]

The Church would begin to free itself from its affliction when its ministers reacquired the persuasive force of ethos. People needed to hear exhortations to virtue and to see virtue lived. "To look upon the life of a good man, to see his morals, to ponder a norm of living, that is by far and away the greatest incitement to imitate excellence."[13] When Francesco Zabarella died at the Council of Constance in September 1417, humanists like Poggio, Pier Paolo Vergerio, and Pietro Donato seized the opportunity to commend an ethical churchman.[14] In the process, they created a Zabarella who reflected their peculiar approach to Christian spirituality.

Issues raised in those panegyrical works of 1417 recur time and again over the course of the next hundred years. Humanists noted that Zabarella had mastered the liberal arts and the professional studies of law and theology. They emphasized that he had sought for twenty years to assist the common utility by educating students.[15] A proper humanist pedagogue, Zabarella had abilities that went beyond mastery of jurisprudence. Though his knowledge was extensive, his success was also due to the moral way he lived. Humanists posited a tie between an education in the *studia humanitatis* and the Christian religion. Given its moral propensities, teaching the humanities became a religious act and required a person of ethos to impart those arts.[16]

Funeral orators also commemorated Zabarella for other actions in service to the public welfare. Pietro Donato celebrated his ability to end civic strife, reminding his listeners that Zabarella had exerted his calming influence through a persuasive *humanitas*. Powerful rulers of the era had sought his advice and used his eloquence for important diplomatic embassies.[17] Zabarella had further contributed to the common good by his generosity to all in need. Donato remarked that the educator was especially generous to indigent students, often taking them into his home and paying their expenses.[18] Humanist spirituality emphasized action and commitment in the public sphere according to the virtues of generosity and beneficence.

Zabarella's commitment to service climaxed with his appointment to important ecclesiastical offices, first as archbishop of Florence and then as a cardinal. His eulogists were quick to point out that his selection had nothing to do with support for a particular papal contender. He stood above such crude politicking. Nor could one ascribe his choice to ambition, to entreaties or bribery, to the influence of his family, or to connections with powerful rulers. In this man the Roman Church had received that of which it had greatest need: a leader selected for his virtues, his wisdom, and his holiness. Zabarella had accepted the summons only because he was convinced that he could help end the schism from a position of influence.[19]

The results of his appointment were propitious. Poggio first emphasized that nothing changed in Zabarella's basic attitude. Rejecting any sense of superiority, he had maintained his integrity and increased his humanity and generosity. Poggio affirmed from personal experience that the learned could approach the high-minded prelate without anxiety about their reception.[20] He used the cardinal to castigate clericalism within the Church and to symbolize that the Church (Zabarella) should welcome humanist learning (Poggio).

Zabarella had consummated his commitment to the Christian republic at the Council of Constance, where he labored to resolve the schism. He had kept his fundamental objective in mind: to end discord among believers and bring peace and unity to the Church.[21] His humanist education proved its worth in dramatic fashion in his last speech to the assembled council fathers, one worthy of Cicero himself. It was an oration characterized by "fullness of expression" (Poggio) and by "great force of words and ideas" (Donato).[22] Zabarella's death shortly after the speech intensified its persuasive ethos.[23] He represented a humanist ethic of self-sacrifice in the name of unity and peace. Had he lived longer, his panegyrists claimed, he surely would have been elected pope. Those about to proceed with a papal election should take note.[24]

In delineating a portrait of the ideal prelate, funeral orators for Zabarella were guided by the appropriation of classical rhetoric. That prelate should be a product, at least in significant part, of a humanist education, which combined knowledge of classical letters and facility in eloquence with a life of virtue that enhanced the appeal of his oratory. That prelate should be committed to the public welfare. He must use his resources for charitable ends and patronage, and labor to end strife and foster holy living. That prelate, finally, should never buy his office or acquire it through powerful connections. He must earn it by the quality of his life.

Humanist orators therefore cast Francesco Zabarella in their own image and likeness. Modern historians since Pastor have studied Zabarella as a canonist of conciliarist convictions. Poggio, Vergerio, and Donato transformed him, from a friend of the humanists whose own culture remained little influenced by humanism, to an exemplar of its value for the Church.[25] Zabarella the institutional reformer of Church structures became Zabarella the humanist reformer of individual morals. The Council of Constance was an important event for humanism. Poggio's two orations to the Council represent the first occasions on which an Italian humanist addressed an international forum using the new rhetoric based upon classical canons.

Humanist orators continued to emphasize certain traits for churchmen. How one obtained a position of authority in the ecclesiastical community remained a primary concern. Eulogists were quick to point out why their subjects did not receive mandates. Such indications comprised implicit and, at times, explicit censure of abuses like simony and nepotism. Good churchmen were those who did not buy their offices or receive them from relatives.

The theory of epideictic oratory supplied the basic categories for this analysis. Selection for ecclesiastical office should not be motivated by external circumstances (*bona externa*) but by qualities of character (*bona animi*). Giordano Orsini used biblical allusions to argue that an individual should not be considered a candidate for the papacy on the basis of family connections.[26] Ministry in the Christian Church was no longer a question of tribal membership (*de semine Aaron*) but of one's intrinsic worth (*secundum ordinem Melchisedech*). It was equally wrong, Orsini maintained, to choose a candidate for his wealth, as the rich are surrounded by temptation.[27]

The orators also urged that those who chose or elected Church officers should never be swayed by the intercession of powerful patrons. Battista Casali, for instance, commended Julius II for rejecting the nominations for cardinals advanced by princes and for promoting worthy individuals like Robert Vitrè.[28] Though among the most controversial of the Renaissance popes, Julius was not a notorious nepotist. Ecclesiastical legislation forbade the buying or selling of offices. Eulogists argued that appointments should be free of even the suspicion of simony.[29] They emphasized above all that their subjects had in no way sought the positions to which they had been appointed or elected.[30] Conradus Vegerius recorded the genuine surprise of Adrian of Utrecht when he learned of his election to the chair of Peter, an election that surprised most of Christendom. Vegerius also noted Adrian's difficulties in adjusting to the honors that came with the Church's supreme office.[31] Poggio overtly contrasted the attitude of Niccolò Albergati to that of the majority of churchmen of that day. Albergati had no ambition for ecclesiastical promotion, though others used every means at their disposal to attain a position and haughtily paraded their authority once in office.[32]

Orators even created a topic whereby holy men actually rejected ecclesiastical promotion in order to serve God better. Through the rhetorical figure of prosopopoeia, Girolamo Gioia introduced the recently deceased Benedetto Rugio, who explained his reasons for turning down positions offered to him in gratitude by the king of Naples. Rugio cited the precedent of holy men like Basil, Gregory of Nazianzus, Peter Damian, Pope Celestine V, and Jerome to support his remaining a monk and to defend his conviction that high office in this life conduces little in the quest for eternal life.[33]

A proper candidate for ecclesiastical office in the Renaissance, in sum, never sought his position. Renaissance orators also stressed the rarity of that phenomenon. Like Poggio, Gaspare Sighicelli adduced Niccolò Albergati as the exception to the immoral rule, an individual who never pursued the offices he received. In fact, Niccolò's selection as bishop of Bologna was a spontaneous act by the Council of Six Hundred, who compelled the cathedral canons, Pope Martin V, and Niccolò himself to accede to their wishes.[34]

Virtue constituted the best cause for advancement, though virtue combined with humanist learning made for a more qualified candidate.[35] Lorenzo Grana applauded Leo X's selection of Giles of Viterbo for a cardinal's hat, and he interpreted that choice as proof that Leo wished to reverse a trend among princes of that day. Many rulers cherished the learned, Grana admitted, but they hesitated to give them positions of importance. Funeral eulogists consistently argued that the Church would profit if its offices were filled by those versed in letters and eloquence. At times they openly protested the appointment of persons without proper cultural formation.[36] The practical consideration of proven administrative ability should also be weighed.[37]

The same point was made by inverting the object of praise. Eulogists also commended those who appointed suitably learned and virtuous candidates. Raffaele Brandolini, for instance, applauded Sixtus IV for making Guillaume Pérès an auditor of the Rota, characterizing the della Rovere pope as "one who rewards letters and virtue." This contention hardly fit one who had appointed several relatives to important positions. Giannantonio Campano noted that Alessandro Oliva had been voted prior general of the Augustinian hermits after he had warned the chapter in unambiguous terms that reform of the order would be his priority and that their vices would come in for severe censure were he called to the governing office.[38]

Tommaso Inghirami recapitulated many convictions about ecclesiastical office in his eulogy for Ludovico Podocataro. In an excursus he described the two ways in which one might become a cardinal. There was a rapid way, whereby one was promoted without previous indication. Though ostensibly positive, Inghirami's description of this way has subtle overtones of sarcasm. Too often cardinals promoted without previous cause were relatives of wealthy supporters of the pope. When Inghirami described the slow way to advancement, his censure became explicit. He spoke in that case of a type of ecclesiastical *cursus honorum*. Because of the love for gossip at the papal court, that path was strewn with hazards. Few reputations, Inghirami observed, survived such close and unfair scrutiny over a long period. As in his eulogy for Pietro Menzi, he did not mince words when he described the sad state of the curia. Nonetheless, he remarked, those who proved themselves to be men of integrity through the rigorous testing eventually rose like cream to the heights of ecclesiastical authority.

Inghirami then provided a list of cardinals in the Church's history who exemplified its finest talent. Few would quibble with him for naming Domenico Capranica and James of Portugal as worthy cardinals, but his list could spark controversy, for it also included Hildebrand, Gil Albornoz, and Giovanni Vitelleschi. By naming these latter, Inghirami tended to endorse Julius II's policy of vindicating control over the Papal State. He concluded by awarding Podocataro a place among that select group who reached the dignity of cardinal the hard way.[39]

No Church office had greater prestige for Renaissance eulogists or greater importance for the welfare of Church and society than the papacy. In a carefully crafted peroration to his popular eulogy for Pope Innocent VIII (1492), Leonello Chiericati stated in succinct terms the rationale that led humanist orators to attach much importance to the papacy.[40] That portion of his speech comprised a theoretical "mirror of the popes," derived in typical humanist fashion from a combination of pagan and Christian sources.

Chiericati used Cicero's *De legibus* to support his basic political principle that any change in behavior on the part of the ruler is mirrored in the wider body politic. He next depicted the qualities necessary in a proper candidate for Peter's chair, citing Plato and Leo the Great as his authorities. Plato rightly contended that the proper candidate for a governing office must be one proven in virtue and one who has always striven to do what conduces to the common good. Leo had argued for a candidate experienced in ecclesiastical administration and promoted in the past for his morals and actions. Chiericati closed with a biblical example that should dissuade any elector from campaigning for the papacy: he proposed a causal connection between the ambition of the Israelite judge Abimelech and the turbulence of his rule and eventual assassination.[41]

Funeral orators upheld the importance of the papacy through another popular topos. They sought to increase admiration for their subjects by asserting that they surely would have been elected pope. Four different eulogists made such a claim for Francesco Zabarella. The Greek cardinal Bessarion constituted an even more dramatic case. Niccolò Capranica swore that Bessarion had actually been elected pope during an evening session of the conclave summoned to choose a successor to Nicholas V (d. 1455). The cardinals, however, had decided to withhold news of the election until the following morning in order to prevent rioting. That decision proved to be fateful, because the cardinals changed their minds overnight. The next morning they overturned Bessarion's election and chose Alfonso Borgia, thereby ending Bessarion's pontificate before it began.[42]

Angelo Gabrielli alleged that the Roman people had rejoiced when Battista Zeno was named a cardinal, for they assumed that Zeno would be their next bishop and pope. Their hopes were crushed, however, by Zeno's sudden death. To be considered worthy of the papacy in the Renaissance carried prestige, but it was also a reputation with inherent risks. In the conclave of 1447, Cardinal Prospero Colonna was the betting favorite. When he emerged to announce the results of the election, the Roman populace immediately assumed that their suspicions had been correct—and joyfully dispersed on their traditional mission of sacking the new pope's former palace. Colonna never had a chance to announce that Tommaso Parentucelli, not he, had won the election.[43]

Since appointment or election was ideally earned by virtue and learning, humanists proposed a simple criterion for evaluating a candidate's performance in office: his behavior should not change once he assumed a new position. Orators felt constrained to observe, however, that few ecclesiastics did not change for the worse when elevated to positions of authority.[44] The dissatisfaction of humanists may be ascribed in part to a spirit of anticlericalism. It also stemmed from their conception of Church office, which emphasized, not the power carried by those positions, but rather the responsibilities of pastoral service they implied. When Niccolò Albergati set as one of the conditions for his accepting election as bishop of Bologna that funds generally paid for the sake of his episcopal confirmation be used instead to assist the poor of the diocese, he was already delineating the proper pastoral tenor for his term in office.[45]

This vision of pastoral service had support in key passages from Scripture. Jesus had reproached the religious authorities of his day, who lorded it over the people, and cast his own mission in terms of service (*diakonia*), using the image of a slave who waits at table. Scripture expressed the same ideal through the metaphor of a "good shepherd" who labors to assure that his flock live in harmony and peace. Giacomo da Alessandria depicted Fantino Valaresso as a good shepherd, filled with paternal affection for a flock on the island of Crete that included Latin and Greek Christians as well as Jews. Valaresso manifested his care in a brief catechism written for the instruction of the clergy and people. The pastoral scope and reforming intentions of the work assured its continued use after the bishop's death. Giacomo emphasized that all bishops, including the bishop of Rome, could learn from Valaresso's example.[46]

The monarchical structure of Church government was never questioned by Renaissance eulogists. They used their praise for members of the hierarchy to push their specific ideals. For example, humanist orators accepted that the papacy was the Church's highest office. The pope's standing meant that his behavior had positive or negative effects upon Church and society. They therefore supported the authority of the papacy not in legal terms but in moral terms as a "mirror of good living." Their praise of the popes emphasized the character of stewardship inherent in that office. A pope betrayed that stewardship, explained Niccolò Palmeri, if he used his talents to acquire the adulation of his contemporaries and not in service to his flock.

In this eulogy for Nicholas V, Palmeri resorted to an *ubi sunt* passage to counteract tendencies to exaggerate the honor owed to the papacy. He imagined that the dead Nicholas had returned to address the prelates assembled at his funeral. Nicholas warned that death had stripped away the outward trappings of his office: "Behold this miserable and fetid corpse! Where now are those who would kiss my feet or genuflect before me and acclaim me with the title 'most blessed father,' which they often used with feigned adulation?"[47] Thus although Italian eulogists ascribed a crucial ministry to the papacy, they circumscribed that ministry within pastoral guidelines and deemphasized the external grandeur of the office.

Orators also emphasized the pastoral role of cardinals and their character as complements to the pope, who headed the hierarchy. Two eulogies present proofs for the divine institution of the cardinal's office. Both are unconvincing and seem bizarre efforts at philological criticism.[48] Most orators were content to stress a cardinal's responsibility to advise the pope in the apostolic senate. Funeral eulogists praised cardinals who had had the courage to follow their conscience when counseling the pope and who did not capitulate to his pressure.[49] Cardinals were right to refuse support for mistaken papal policies. Saint Paul had done likewise with Saint Peter on the crucial issue of the circumcision of the gentiles.[50] Cardinals had a further responsibility as papal electors, and the orators again urged them to fulfill that duty according to personal conscience.[51] If humanist panegyrists viewed the Church in monarchical terms, they nonetheless suggested a curb on unlimited papal authority, in the conscientious advice of the pope's cardinals.

Ecclesiastical office brought with it no magical assurance of success. Rather, the office placed its holder in a visible position from which his colleagues and fellow citizens could readily judge his character on the basis of his actions.[52] If virtue and learning were the requisite qualities to be sought when selecting a candidate, those same qualities should inform an officeholder's deeds. Niccolò Capranica listed the exemplary activities of Bessarion, which he reminded his listeners they had seen. The list summarized the ecclesiastical concerns of humanist eulogists: Bessarion was committed to the cause of letters and patronized the learned; he aided and defended the oppressed; he generously supported church building and remodeling; and he labored to defend the liberty of the Church.[53] Deeds like these proved a person's virtue and learning and Christian faith.

Humanist orators carefully carved a niche for their program within the ecclesiastical edifice. They introduced eloquence as an art of assistance to the apostolic see in its diplomatic missions and its work of evangelization. Papal and curial letters were depicted as effective means to persuade princes to peace and concord and to offer useful advice in religious matters.[54] Moreover, the diplomacy that popes exercised through legates was presented as achieving impressive results due to the eloquence of churchmen. When the king of France heard Bessarion speak, Niccolò Capranica declared, he was genuinely moved and felt that the Greek cardinal had superhuman powers.[55]

Diplomatic missions were not without their hazards, and to create a mystique of heroism for servants of the Church, orators often reminded their listeners of the perils that papal legates faced. Giannantonio Campano narrated how Enea Silvio Piccolomini (later Pope Pius II) was driven off course to Norway while sailing on a mission to Scotland; although he contracted a painful foot disease in Scandinavia, he pressed on and managed to fulfill his assignment. Campano especially commended him for earning the respect of barbarians like the Scots, so removed from Mediterranean *humanitas*. Nicholas V sent Bessarion to quell a rebellion in Bologna but received an added bonus: Bessarion had succeeded in pacifying the city and in stirring enthusiasm for the liberal arts.[56]

Preaching represented another activity where humanist learning could have an impact upon ecclesiastical culture. Early humanists like Vergerio and Poggio explicitly criticized thematic preaching. Other funeral orators claimed that preaching was renewed in their era through the appropriation of classical rhetoric. The learned preaching of mendicants like Ludovico da Ferrara, O.P., and Mariano da Genazzano, O.E.S.A., was singled out for commendation.[57] Such statements represent the ideals of humanist orators. Ludovico's surviving sermons indicate that in fact he mixed elements of thematic preaching and classicizing oratory. Mariano is an even more instructive case; admired by humanists like Giovanni Pontano and Poliziano, he was reputed to have imbibed humanist ways so thoroughly that he mined classical sources and cited them frequently in his sermons. His sermons that survive do not entirely bear out this reputation. Even in panegyrics, he retained aspects of the thematic form.[58]

Humanists essentially presented preachers as they wished them to be. They typically applauded those who spoke through vivid images. Funeral orations offered examples of preachers who were successful in the humanists' own preferred genre of praise and blame. Reform was advancing within the papal curia and within religious orders because forthright preachers did not hesitate to reproach moral profligacy and endorse virtue. Even the anger of a pope like Nicholas V could be defended on those grounds, for it supplied emotional force to his invective. Humanist eulogists wanted their audiences to see that epideictic rhetoric worked in promoting reform.[59]

Eloquence served above all to promote the key art prized by humanists, the art of good and holy living.[60] To promote the art one had to practice it. Funeral orators called upon ecclesiastics to be pillars of virtue. Their orations suggested specific areas where virtue was typically lacking. One might infer, for example, that ecclesiastical trials were easily manipulated, because Antonio Maggi decided to emphasize that Cardinal Marco Corner could acquit an individual whom he despised or condemn one whom he loved.[61] The demands of justice alone should determine a verdict. Judicial problems were further complicated by sexual promiscuity. Raffaele Brandolini recalled that the cardinal Lorenzo Cibò had refused the advances of a lovely young woman sent by her mother in an effort to have the charge of parricide dismissed against her son.[62]

Orators at times took sides in controversies over the propriety of activities by churchmen. At least three panegyrists defended cardinals for participating in the hunt. They built their case upon hunting's value for maintaining physical condition and upon classical precedents.[63] Battista Casali pointed out that hunting had been practiced by the ancients and that it symbolized a past golden age. Who could therefore criticize a cardinal like Aloysius of Aragon for spending his leisure in that activity? The issue appropriately came up in a eulogy for Aloysius, who regularly organized hunting parties for Pope Leo X at Magliana.[64]

To understand how Renaissance humanists adapted Cicero's art for a Christian context, it is necessary to filter out the causes promoted, and goals achieved, that humanists regularly praised. Those activities proved that an ecclesiastic practiced Cicero's art. As orators, humanists tended to reject a conception of the ontological worth of an action. They praised deeds as the proper response to particular historical exigencies. This difference may be clarified in terminology used by Lorenzo Valla. Humanist funeral orators focused not so much on whether a person did a good thing (*agere bonum*), as on whether, under the circumstances, that person acted well (*agere bene*). The art was a way of life.

The Renaissance had opened for the Church with the scandal of the schism. Funeral orators consistently applauded efforts by churchmen to assure unity within the believing community. Internal discipline was essential, whereas schism and heresy were to be combated. Poggio commended Giuliano Cesarini for withdrawing his support from the Council of Basel once he understood its schismatic intentions. He then berated ecclesiastics who had persisted in schism, as well as the princes of his day who abetted them. Cesarini had in fact been slower to act than Poggio would have his audience believe, but the memorial service in his honor in 1445 gave the humanist secretary a chance to chide persons like Emperor Frederick III who persisted in backing the antipope Amadeus of Savoy.[65]

When internal discipline and doctrinal conformity were at stake, some orators recommended stiff punishment as the means to restore order. Our post-Enlightenment mentality justly recoils before the congratulations that eulogists like Cristoforo Barzizza, Borgognone d'Asti, and Niccolò Palmeri awarded churchmen for consigning heretics to be burned at the stake by secular authorities.[66] The refusal of the Jews to accept Jesus as Messiah troubled other orators. Paolo Veneto and Giles of Viterbo were commended for composing works designed to convince the Jews of the truth of the Christian message. Lorenzo Grana felt that Giles's work would be especially effective, as the cardinal had studied Jewish mystical writings.[67]

Despite these issues, the Italian Renaissance manifested an incipient approach toward more humane treatment of religious nonconformity. Iacopo Zeno, for instance, praised Giuliano Cesarini for abandoning the idea of a crusade against the Hussites and for inviting their representatives to the Council of Basel, where he had used rhetorical methods—warning, disputing, teaching, persuading, delighting—to convince them of their errors.[68] Zeno's contention that Cesarini had abhorred violence from his youngest days is another case of epideictic license. Cesarini had in fact preached a crusade against the Hussites at the Diet of Nuremberg in 1431 and accompanied the crusading army into Bohemia, where it was roundly defeated at the battle of Tau. The cardinal had had to sneak back into Germany disguised as a soldier.

Cesarini did, however, welcome the arrival of Hussite delegates to the Council of Basel in 1433 with a conciliatory discourse. The Hussites abandoned the Council before any final agreement was reached on doctrinal disputes. Zeno consciously chose to praise Cesarini's behavior in this latter instance as the way that the Church should approach doctrinal divisions. His speech suggests that principles from rhetorical culture helped pave the way for the idea of religious tolerance. Rhetors seek to persuade, not to compel. They deal with probable truths, not certainties.[69]

Issues of discipline, unity, and protection are closely allied to another great deed of the era. Consciously evoking memories of the period of Pope Gregory VII's reform, Italian orators applauded churchmen for defending their institution's liberty. That liberty was occasionally specified in terms of the clergy's immunities. Pietro Barozzi recalled that his uncle Giovanni resisted the Venetian government when it tried to tax the clergy in order to fund a crusade.[70] More frequently, the liberty of the Church was used in a reductionist sense to mean the vindication of papal control over the Papal State in central Italy. The orators' ideals in part reflected economic realities. Revenues from that state were increasingly essential to the papacy during the Renaissance.

No commendation for the defense of the liberty of the Church can compare in drama to Tommaso Inghirami's funeral oration for Julius II (d. 1513).[71] Inghirami opened his discussion of Julius' pontificate by taking his listeners on a journey through the Papal State, painting in vivid terms its implacable character.[72] The journey began in Rome and its environs, where many important families had been driven from their rightful possessions. Next pictured were Tuscany in arms, the city-states of Umbria rent by dissension or oppressed by tyranny, and the Marches divided among rebellious factions. Hatred and discord were everywhere. The inhabitants of the new pope's domain mocked their lord even as they prepared to render him homage.

The picture that Inghirami offered of the Papal State at the conclusion of Julius' reign left no doubt about the efficacy of the pope's ways. The Church had now entered upon a golden age. Julius had left the treasury full of gold, silver, and gems. He had expanded the territory under papal control and left it pacified and obedient. Ecclesiastical authority, formerly an object of contempt, had been restored. The peoples who lived under papal rule were united to their sovereign by love and devotion. Inghirami directly confronted the controversial issue of Julius' method. He offered a defense of the pope's recourse to arms as a last resort and as consistent with historical precedent.[73]

Inghirami's eulogy for Julius employed the often-used oratorical theme of rebirth. During the Roman Empire, panegyrists similarly had painted a bleak picture of the state of affairs at an emperor's accession in order to heighten the sense of his achievement. The imperial metaphor was widespread during Julius' pontificate.[74] Its political reference, however, was not to world rule but to control of the Papal State.

Popes were not the only persons praised for activities along these lines. Gaspare Sighicelli used an implicit framework of rebirth in his eulogy for Niccolò Albergati, to remind his Bolognese audience how much better the city had fared once it submitted to its papal vicar.[75] Albergati had set as his first condition for accepting the bishopric that the commune restore the castles seized from the Church. His subsequent reform efforts were accomplished for believers who recognized Church overlordship. After years of decline, reflected in its university's loss of prestige, Bologna regained its vitality under Albergati's guidance. Who, Gaspare wondered, would now assure the cause of the needy or the support of students?

When orators shifted their gaze from ecclesiastical discipline to the condition of society, they held that peace and concord among believers were essential. In blunt terms Marcello Adriani claimed that Giovanni de' Medici had struggled as pope to put an end to the insanity of war.[76] The obligation to promote concord had special significance for anyone who held office in Christ's Church, for Christ's own legacy, as humanist eulogists repeatedly emphasized, was peace (John 14:27). That obligation weighed heavily upon those who claimed to be Christ's vicar. Funeral orators for the popes commended their subjects for leaving believers in unity and peace.[77] Papal legates were praised as prominent actors in a vast crusade for peace.[78] War among Christians constituted an execrable evil that weakened Christian ethos.

The imperative for peace in the Italian Renaissance extended only to the Christian community and had direct relevance for the epoch's just war. Rather than scandalously fighting each other, Christian princes and kings should settle their rivalries and unite in a common crusade against the Turk.[79] The advance of the Turks in the Quattrocento was interpreted as proof of Christian immorality. War against the Turk was justified as a last resort. Renaissance orators envisioned Christian and Muslim civilizations locked in mortal combat. Christendom had already lost vast possessions, and only a crusade could stem the Turkish advance.

Church leaders thus exercised the art of good and holy living when they made the Church's authority an object of respect and when they used the Church's influence to foster peace among Christians and to organize a crusade against the infidels. Humanists reminded their audiences that churchmen could also practice that art through their patronage. They sought the support of wealthy clerics for their program of learning and for building and remodeling sacred edifices. This investigation of ecclesiastical ideals began chronologically with the death of Francesco Zabarella in 1417, which afforded humanists the opportunity to celebrate a famous churchman who was sympathetic to their cause and committed to Church reform. The death of Pope Nicholas V in 1455 marked a similar watershed. Now the papacy itself, the heart of Church activity, could be shown to have committed its prestige and resources to the cause of cultural and moral renewal.

Humanists like Ludovico Carbone and clerics like Jean Jouffroy and Niccolò Palmeri celebrated Nicholas's support for the revival of learning and for the rebuilding of Rome. Carbone commented that Nicholas had promoted the rebirth of classical studies throughout his life and lamented that the supportive pope had not lived longer. Orators specified Nicholas's contribution in terms most appropriate for a former librarian. They applauded him for his efforts to recover codices and to assure the translation of Greek works. He was depicted digging through old chests in the hopes of finding lost works.[80]

The patronage of Nicholas V extended to the rebuilding of Rome, his episcopal see. What monastery or church in this city, asked Jean Jouffroy, did not reap benefits from the pope's generosity? As witnesses he cited the churches in Rome that Nicholas had patronized: San Pietro, San Paolo, Santo Stefano Rotondo, San Teodoro, the Pantheon, and Santa Maria in Trastevere. He characterized Nicholas as an honorary founder of the city, who should be linked historically with Romulus for his efforts to fortify Rome, and with Augustus for his repair of public buildings.[81]

Recent scholarship has shown that the basic themes of this myth of Pope Nicholas were traced in his lifetime and celebrated after his death.[82] Humanists took full advantage of the propaganda offered to their cause when a friend became pope, and by their praise they encouraged ecclesiastics to continue Nicholas's patronage. Support for the humanities could be most palpably expressed by sponsoring men of letters. Addressing himself directly to Julius II during a eulogy for Gabriello Gabrielli, Battista Casali claimed that Julius' patronage for the liberal arts would be remembered as a deed even greater than his ambitious building program or his crusade to expel tyrants from Italy.[83]

Eulogists applauded the ways in which ecclesiastics sought to improve the state of clerical learning. By endowing schools and creating libraries for those studying for the priesthood, concerned churchmen virtually assured the renewal of the Church's ministry. Such efforts were taking place throughout the Italian peninsula. Domenico Capranica, Niccolò Forteguerri, and Branda Castiglioni, who had founded colleges in Rome, Pistoia, and Pavia respectively, were presented as especially concerned to assist poor students.[84]

A cardinal's household could also play a decisive role in this regard. Orators continually praised cardinals for welcoming the company of the learned. Niccolò Perotti compared Pietro Riario's home to a residence for the Muses. Painters, sculptors, orators, poets, teachers of the liberal arts, mathematicians, and all persons of virtue experienced the owner's munificence.[85] In an intense, two-year period as cardinal, Riario had used his court to sponsor a number of sumptuous and controversial public festivals that advertised his pretensions to control Roman politics during his uncle's papacy. Just a few months before Riario's death, Niccolò da Modrussa, a member of his household and one of his funeral eulogists, had obliquely referred to his patron as a latter-day Caligula.[86]

Humanists' praise for a cardinal's patronage sometimes suggested limits of decorum. Their descriptions of ideal meals within a cardinal's home exemplify this tendency. John O'Malley has identified a "godly feast" topos in Renaissance funeral oratory that Erasmus artfully developed in his colloquy. Meals were to be sparse, elegantly served, and provide a forum for learned discussion of a passage from ancient sources, especially Scripture. They should mirror the decorous habits of ancient Romans like Cicero's friend Atticus or the emperor Hadrian. Humanists applauded such meals to assure their place at table, to promote learned conversation, and to rein in tendencies toward a lavish and less godly feast.[87]

Leading churchmen also did well when they used their resources to endow libraries. Cardinal Pietro Riario is again a case in point. Niccolò Perotti avoided mention of the festivals Riario organized and adverted instead to his plans to found a library. Riario had commissioned Giannandrea Bussi to collect books, and his efforts may have slowed the development of the pope's own library. After Riario's death in 1474, his uncle Sixtus IV moved vigorously to build up a library for the Vatican, entrusting its direction to Platina.[88]

Similarly Battista Casali recounted that the Venetian cardinal Domenico Grimani had liked to collect books. He had sold his silver vases and some valuable items of furniture in order to buy the writings of Pico della Mirandola. The cardinal eventually split this collection, purportedly more than fifteen thousand volumes, between the convent of Sant'Antonio in Venice and his nephew Marino.[89]

Virtually all Renaissance funeral orators commended ecclesiastics for building or rebuilding churches and other sacred edifices, categorizing such endeavors as acts of piety (*religio*). The aesthetic renewal of the Church formed part of the art of good and holy living because it bore fruit for others.[90] Humanist eulogists applauded the fact that the artists and architects of their age were commissioned to use their talent to decorate churches. Their rationale for such praise is based on two key premises.

The first premise also supported their preference for epideictic oratory: the visible convinces. Poggio had enunciated that conviction before the Council of Constance. Believers needed to see their leaders live the ideals that the Christian faith propagated. Christendom's leaders must be persons of ethos. When attempting to characterize the malaise of Christianity, humanists frequently expressed their conviction that religion had "collapsed"—and needed to be rebuilt. The aesthetic dimension of renewal should symbolize and spur the moral reform that was the heart of their program.[91]

This first premise has two important corollaries. First, although church building everywhere deserved praise, projects undertaken at Rome possessed a special significance. Rome was the Church's capital, its administrative and spiritual center. It had always possessed a particular symbolic meaning, which Renaissance orators exploited. Niccolò da Modrussa called attention to Rome's magnetism as a mecca for pilgrims and urged that its palaces, churches, and entire urban fabric provide a fittingly magnificent reception for all of its distinguished visitors. Marco Vigerio had Rome itself commend Sixtus IV for restoring its physical appearance as the emperor Augustus had done centuries before.[92] In their campaign for church reform, Italian humanists gambled heavily on the potency of Rome as symbol, and of Saint Peter's as its most sacred edifice.

The conviction that visible images best persuade had a second corollary. Ecclesiastical wealth per se was not evil. In fact, the expectation that cardinals' households be foci of culture created heavy financial burdens. Wealth was not evil, but avarice was. At times eulogists defended their deceased subjects from the accusation of avarice, using patronage for building projects as primary evidence. They also condemned the hypocrisy of the mendicants, who had publicly vowed poverty and then accumulated material comforts; such actions again violated the code of ethos. In general humanists agreed with Cicero that riches should be devoted to acts of beneficence.[93]

Cicero's opinion leads us to the second major premise that supported the value of rebuilding and patronage. Renaissance funeral orators urged that God be admired and venerated for generosity, largesse, and kindness. His salvific deeds brought those qualities into light. Grace was given abundantly. Could those who proclaim to believe in God behave any differently?

The art of good and holy living culminated with charity. Though many virtues were singled out for praise, none had greater significance for humanist orators, who often placed charity last in the list of their subjects' qualities, to emphasize its comprehensive character. Using the biblical categories of the poor, widows, and orphans, they applauded churchmen for assisting the underprivileged and needy of their society. The munificence of ecclesiastics mirrored that of their God, who so generously assists humankind.[94]

For exemplary worth, no charitable deed could compare to the sacrifice of one's life for others. With clear reference to the tenth chapter of the Gospel of John, the anonymous eulogist of Bernardo Eroli emphasized that an ecclesiastical officeholder ought to be a pastor, not a hireling. That pastor could give no greater proof of his love than to lay down his life for the flock. Poggio extolled Cardinal Giuliano Cesarini as a martyr because he was killed in the battle against Turkish forces at Varna in 1444. Cesarini had contemned death to assist Christ's flock. Poggio wished to exploit Cesarini's worth as an example: here at last was a churchman willing to give the ultimate proof of charity and lay down his life for his friends (John 15:13).[95] (The actual circumstances of Cesarini's death have not been clarified to the satisfaction of all. Some historians argue that he was not killed by the Turks but by the crusading troops who blamed him for their defeat.)

Funeral eulogists provided one further spur to ecclesiastics to reform their lives. They praised the piety of important lay contemporaries and used that praise to create a foil. Laypersons often demonstrated a deeper commitment to religion than the officially religious or the ecclesiastically powerful. Renaissance orators even adduced soldiers like Pandolfo II Malatesta, Gattamelata, and Francesco Sforza as paradigms of piety who had surpassed the priests and religious of their day in devotion and charity. In his oration on Barbara Gonzaga, Giovanni Cattanei had a group of nuns confess their embarrassment after realizing that the noblewoman had demonstrated greater willingness than they to perform the most humble services.[96]

The use of laypersons as foils led to an anomaly: only they were consistently commended for performing the traditional acts of piety and asceticism associated with clerical and religious life. Guarino said that Leonello d'Este had celebrated the divine office in his home with as great a devotion and regularity as any priest or monk, so that his home seemed more like a bishop's household than a castle. Battista Mantovano repeated a rumor that Eleanor of Aragon had confessed and received communion once a month; Battista Guarini asserted without condition that Eleanor had indeed received communion on so regular a basis.[97] Noble men and women were also commended for wearing ascetic undergarments and for having fasted willingly and practiced flagellation for pious purposes.[98] Orators similarly praised their subjects' temperance and continence. These pious persons only ate food and drank wine for purposes of sustenance and only engaged in sexual intercourse to fulfill their marriage duty.[99]

Comparisons between laypersons and their religious counterparts did not exhaust the picture of their piety. Like their ecclesiastical contemporaries, laypersons were praised for their charitable services. The specific actions adduced as proof are identical to those praised in clerics. There was, first of all, generous aid to those in need, the biblical poor, widows, and orphans. Anonymous almsgiving, proper care and feeding of prisoners, donations for dowries, and other actions helped to address the needs of the neediest.[100] Laypersons were also commemorated for sponsoring the rebuilding or construction of churches. Funeral orators delivered a clear message to the audiences: let your generosity be seen.[101]

Praise of lay piety also echoed concern for the effects of violence and war. Guarino claimed that Leonello d'Este had best revealed his religious convictions by keeping Ferrara out of the wars then raging in Italy. The type of believer cherished by funeral eulogists was one, in Battista Casali's words, who always integrated his convictions with his religious belief and who never shrank before his civic responsibilities.[102] Agostino Dati restated the same ideal in significant terminology when he affirmed that Bartolo Bandini had conjoined contemplation with action. Through this vision of dual piety orators were able to harmonize styles of life that would seem antithetical to many observers today.[103]

It is now possible to summarize the ideal Church proposed by Italian humanist funeral orators. They filtered their ideal of the Christian life through their commitment as orators. *Religio* was defined in terms of munificence and compassion, generosity and assistance. In the words of Poggio, charity was the parent of all virtues.[104] Their ideal fused the orator's commitment to public service, with the Christian imperative to act on behalf of those most in need. Antonio Solerio tied Cicero's affirmation, that men most nearly resembled the gods when they helped others, to a verse from the letter of James, which prescribed that true piety impelled one to assist orphans and widows in their tribulation. Other eulogists fastened upon the Last Judgment scene in Matthew (25:31–46) as their primary Christian source and commended their subjects for unselfish assistance to "the least of their brethren."[105]

If this ideal were to be realized, it was essential, according to these orators, that humanist learning penetrate the structures of the Church. Church officeholders should be products and patrons of the humanities. Those who lived the ideal would participate in a great project of renewal for Church and society by assisting society's poorest members, by rebuilding or embellishing the physical structures of the institution, and by ending violence, civil strife, and war.

This humanist ideal opened up new frontiers for holiness. No longer did one need to flee the city in order to serve God. Action in the forum was as valid a pursuit of holiness as the more traditional way of contemplation. Nor must one be a priest or vowed religious to live the imperatives of the Christian gospel. Laypersons were often better exemplars of spirituality. Their fervent commitment to charitable service and to pious practices should shame the clergy and religious into acknowledging their failings and seeking reform.

Italian humanists never questioned the validity of the Church as an institution, but their belief in the institution did not blind them to the fact that many of the Church's officeholders were less than paragons of virtue. This disjunction had crucial consequences. Only an individual of integrity could convincingly advocate the lofty ideals of the Christian gospel. Without virtue, as Raffaele Brandolini proclaimed, one could not practice the art of good and holy living or receive eternal beatitude.[106]

The spirituality of Renaissance funeral orators was, appropriately, oratorical. Consistent with their Christian vocation and their avocation as orators, they encouraged heroic actions by believers in the city and its forum. They fused pagan and Christian ideals into an ethic of public service. Consequently, the world of politics assumed a special importance. Humanist orators scrutinized that world with care.

CHAPTER FIVE

POLITICAL IDEALS
*"Be Merciful to the Submissive,
and Crush the Arrogant"*

In 1418 the Venetian admiral Carlo Zeno died at the age of eighty-four, after an eventful life in the service of the Serenissima and of other city-states in northern Italy.[1] He had contributed memorably to the defense of Venice during the War of Chioggia (1378–81), the fourth campaign pitting Venice against her maritime rival, Genoa. For eight months during 1379 he had commanded a Venetian fleet that successfully raided Genoese shipping in the Mediterranean. Furthermore, he had returned to Venice with his squadron of galleys at a crucial moment in the war's evolution and helped Venice recapture Chioggia. That act broke Genoa's crippling blockade of the island republic.

Twenty-five years later, Zeno fell from grace. Ironically, his military leadership for Venice in her campaign to crush the Carrara in Padua caused him serious troubles. The secret account books of the Carrara listed him as one who had received their funds. Because Venetian law forbade any patrician to accept salary or gifts from the Signore of Carrara, Zeno's action was judged by the Council of Ten. He was found guilty and ordered to resign all offices and to serve a year in prison. In model patrician fashion he humbly submitted. When he died, the rulers of the republic did not forget his heroic contributions and ordered a state funeral at Santa Maria Celeste. Doge Tommaso Mocenigo and many senators honored his memory by attending the ceremony.

A young Venetian patrician, Leonardo Giustiniani, was chosen to deliver the commemorative eulogy. The choice proved felicitous. Under such delicate circumstances, Giustiniani gave an oration that became a bestseller.[2] Various reasons may account for the eulogy's extraordinary success. First of all, he devised his oration to invest Zeno with qualities of renowned warrior-statesmen from antiquity. Zeno was said to have surpassed the Athenian admiral Themistocles, for example, because he did not waste his free time as a youth but devoted his leisure to physical exercise and to music; he learned to play the lyre, something his Athenian counterpart could not do. This superiority might seem trivial at first glance, but, like much good humanist oratory, it had hidden implications. Cicero and Quintilian had both cited Themistocles' refusing requests to play the lyre at banquets as evidence of insufficient training: he was less than learned (*indoctior*). Giustiniani hence acclaimed Venice, whose liberal education was broader than that offered at Athens. He reminded his audience that Cicero had described Athens as the inventor of all learned disciplines (*De or.* 1.4.13).

The Ciceronian matrix of Giustiniani's presentation had further importance. Cicero several times had referred to Themistocles as one unjustly exiled by Athens.[3] He had also censured Themistocles, who reacted by betraying Athens and joining her Persian enemies. By comparing Zeno to Themistocles, Giustiniani implied that Venice had acted ungratefully toward her war hero in the punishment meted out by the Council of Ten. Zeno, however, had rightly submitted to the sentence, thereby protecting the spirit of cohesion (*unanimitas*) so vital to the republic. Giustiniani also suggested that Quattrocento Venice, like fifth-century Athens, had entered a period of brilliant cultural development.

He went on to claim that Zeno's clemency was superior to that of Julius Caesar, alluding to Cicero's portrait of Caesar in the *Pro Marcello*. Caesar had merely permitted some of the Roman Republic's most deserving citizens to return from exile without granting them any real liberty. Zeno had given life and liberty to a scoundrel like Apulus, who deserved no benefits from the republic.[4] Giustiniani finally maintained that Zeno had derived his successful strategy for defeating Genoa from the tactics of Scipio Africanus. For the first time since the Second Punic War, a general had carried the attack to the gates of the enemy's city when his own city seemed ready to surrender.[5]

Giustiniani's eulogy also provided a typical representation of the ideal statesman in humanist terms. He praised Zeno for his genius and virtues in public service. The oration at times conveys the impression of a rather unusual admiral. Zeno developed his native talent through a liberal education that emphasized letters. Like the great philosophers of antiquity, he enriched his knowledge of human nature by traveling in the Mediterranean world. Those travels also gave him experience in ships and sailing.[6]

Zeno's commitment to learning persevered throughout his life. He devoted his leisure to literature, not to games or festivals. He cherished the company of the learned, generously patronizing gifted masters like Antonio del Massa and Guarino. He concentrated upon the disciplines of philosophy and oratory, which contribute most effectively "to good and holy living and to the public utility." In a passage reminiscent in technique of Cicero's praise for Pompey in the *De lege Manilia*, Giustiniani listed places that could testify to Zeno's prominence in philosophy and eloquence.[7]

When Giustiniani extolled Zeno's virtues, he emphasized those exercised in service to the republic. Not surprisingly, the admiral's military victories supplied the primary material. The orator began with Zeno's contribution to the Venetian victory during the War of Chioggia and concluded by recalling his assistance to the king of Cyprus at an advanced age. He dedicated the heart of his list, however, to celebrating a new sort of victory that Zeno had won for Giangaleazzo Visconti. The ruler of Milan had dispatched him with a small band of soldiers to pacify a settlement of Alpine folk, who had driven off previous Visconti expeditions. Zeno won the battle without using arms. In this he exploited the skills of the orator: "authority, humanity, clemency, affability, civility, eloquence."[8]

Giustiniani's panegyric presented Zeno as an ideal warrior-statesman, conversant with the liberal arts and equipped with an eloquence sufficiently persuasive that it tamed the ferocious temperament of mountain men. Zeno was a Scipio, a Julius Caesar, and especially a Themistocles *redevivus*. Cicero had applauded Themistocles for combining practical wisdom and eloquence (*Brut.* 7.28) and argued that Themistocles acquired important political responsibilities at Athens because he possessed the twofold wisdom of speaking and acting (*De or.* 3.16.59). Like Themistocles, Zeno was an individual of ethos.

Giustiniani's funeral oration for Zeno recalls the political matrix of epideictic oratory from its inception in antiquity. Eloquence should be a civilizing force in human society. As adherents of eloquence, Italian humanists looked to the arena of politics as a fundamental concern. The first models written for funeral oratory after ancient times were incorporated in the manuals of instruction for the *podestà*, the chief officer of medieval Italian communes. Speeches at funerals were then part of a politician's duties.

Those speeches continued to be delivered when the political context changed from communes to principalities. In fact, the ceremonies organized to commemorate the death of rulers at the northern courts became more elaborate in the second half of the Trecento. Some years ago Benjamin Kohl coined the term "subdital humanism" to characterize the political thought of Italian humanists employed at those courts. Early funeral sermons share a common purpose with the formal tracts on monarchy and the biographies of rulers written by subdital humanists. All three sought to legitimize monarchy by emphasizing its benefits for the subjects (*subditi*).[9]

Orators commended monarchs for ending the factional violence that had afflicted communes throughout their existence. Petrarch stressed that benefit in his eulogy for Giovanni Visconti at Milan in 1354. He addressed himself directly to the crowd of Milanese mourners and reminded them that "all live in peace and justice under our lord."

Early Renaissance funeral preaching sought to foster an artificial loyalty, to create a sense of a wealth that was common. For example, Petrarch was concerned to assure the fidelity of Milan's populace to its Visconti lords. Continued loyalty to the dynasty would guarantee civic harmony. Petrarch's oration for Archbishop Giovanni concluded on an optimistic note by recalling that one Visconti ruler had been succeeded by three: Matteo, Galeazzo, and Bernabò. Grief should give way to joy at this multiplication of benefits on high.[10]

The first fully classicizing funeral oration from the Renaissance was written by Pier Paolo Vergerio (the elder) and reflected the culture of subdital humanism. Vergerio commemorated the good deeds done by Francesco il Vecchio da Carrara for his subjects at Padua. When he shifted the medium from thematic sermon to classicizing oration, he also created new emphases for the message: the benefits of monarchical rule could be proven by appeal to historical deeds and to visual evidence.

Vergerio described the crowd of mourners who assembled to pay final tribute to Francesco. Their presence at the funeral visibly manifested the state. He then moved outward from the ruling family to name the clergy, patricians, advisors, soldiers, teachers of the good arts, and their wives. All segments of the dominant class were represented. The legates of Padua's allies, who attended the ceremony, reminded everyone of the principality's place in a larger system of states.

Vergerio likewise used visible evidence to prove the benefits of Francesco's rule. In matters of war, there were the fortifications built for the city, as well as the churches and monuments erected to commemorate Francesco's triumphs. In peacetime Francesco had made his concern visible by financing private and public buildings. Homes were restored, churches decorated, and the liberal arts thrived. "I have no need to dwell on these accomplishments," Vergerio observed, "since you have all seen them." Padua's welfare was assured by the succession of Francesco's son, Francesco Novello, to whom Vergerio addressed a concluding exhortation.[11]

By the end of the fourteenth century, court humanists had outlined their political ideals and adopted a new rhetoric to propagate them. Government existed for the sake of the governed. Humanist eulogists sought to bestir a sense of public loyalty and commitment. Quality government depended upon the good behavior of the governors and the governed. Governors must be imbued with a sense of public service and act morally; the governed should cooperate by placing the public good before personal questions of ambition or vendetta. Rulers attained legitimacy through the benefits that they conferred on their subjects. By strict enforcement of justice, monarchs rid their states of factional violence. By their building and patronage, they made their concern visible and their protection real. The aesthetic dimension chiefly demonstrated the benefits of good government.

The political context for panegyrical oratory changed toward the end of the Trecento. Until that time, issues of legitimation and consolidation of control had preoccupied humanist propagandists at the northern courts. From 1400 to 1454, the primary question for Renaissance states became survival. They had to define their position against other states. The aggrandizing wars of rulers like Giangaleazzo Visconti and Ladislas of Naples raised the possibility of a unified Italy in the first quarter of the Quattrocento. Subsequently, a series of wars that involved the peninsula's major powers forced each state to determine how much space any other could occupy without threatening its own existence.

As the propagandists of the dominant class, humanist funeral orators grappled with the consequences of the new situation. The wars of the first half of the Quattrocento were a political crisis akin to the Great Western Schism in the religious sphere.[12] During this second stage of political development, panegyrical oratory acquired a more ideological tone as the peninsula's states defined themselves in opposition to rivals. The new context created a second challenge for humanist orators. War characterized the first half of the Quattrocento and cut in opposite directions socially and politically. War was a primary means to mobilize public support and assure survival. On the other hand, constant warfare threatened the hegemony of a state's ruling class. War generated spiraling costs, endemic violence, and persons of authority who could challenge rulers. Humanists were called upon to celebrate military heroes. The panegyrical oratory from the first half of the Quattrocento reveals a softening of their ideological positions as their ambivalence toward warfare increased.

Hans Baron has long argued for Leonardo Bruni's central role in using panegyrical oratory to elaborate republican propaganda for

Florence. Bruni's panegyric of his adopted city (ca. 1403–4) and his funeral oration for Nanni Strozzi (1428) constituted powerful salvos in a battle for public support during Florence's wars against Milan. They idealized Florence as the unwavering opponent of tyranny and defender of republican liberty. Bruni's panegyric of Florence opened with a vivid description of the city and its surroundings. The humanist felt that an ecphrasis would best ground his praise for Florentine achievements. Once persons have actually seen the city, he affirmed, "their amazement at its great accomplishments ceases." To use Burckhardt's terms, Bruni presented the Florentine state as a work of art.[13]

Bruni assisted the spectator in understanding the political realities behind the physical sight. Florentines had judiciously set the city into its physical environment. Topographical elements like the surrounding hills and the Arno River played an aesthetic and a utilitarian role. The city's buildings were also well ordered and aesthetically pleasing. Indeed Bruni first called the viewer's attention to Florence's churches. His ecphrasis implied that republican government had achieved harmony and concord. He invested that government with a quasi-sacral character.

The final part of Bruni's description assumed explicit political overtones. He directed his audience's gaze to the Palazzo Vecchio, prime symbol of the city's government, then invited them to look outward from that towering palazzo to the walls and, beyond them, to the castles and villas scattered throughout the countryside. Thus evoked, the landscape suggested consciousness of the symbiotic rapport between Florence and its *contado*. Florentine rule justly spread beyond the walls. The same description ended on an overtly imperialist note. As Rome's successor, Bruni argued, Florence was worthy of world dominion. He reinforced this idea in the second part of the panegyric, when he traced the founding of Florence to the final years of the Roman Republic, years when Rome's hegemony extended throughout the Mediterranean world under the direction of a "popular government."[14]

Bruni's subsequent praise for the Florentine constitution built upon the basic qualities suggested in his ecphrasis. The constitution enshrined the ideals of a state that was harmonious, sacral, and imperialist. Bruni characterized a republic as a society composed of economic classes from wealthy to poor. Class differences created advantages and disadvantages; the wealthy perforce had greater means to exercise influence and defend their cause. Bruni therefore posited that government existed primarily to protect society's less powerful members against a powerful elite. As long as the state performed its role of protection (*custodiam civium*), its authority was legitimate. The state forfeited that legitimacy when it exercised despotic rule (*tyrannidem*) over its citizens.

Bruni emphasized that Florence had adopted specific measures to protect its vulnerable citizens. Strict enforcement of the law, and punishments meted out with severity proportionate to social standing, would overcome the inequities that economic classes created. He envisaged a state where the most vulnerable received the greatest protection, and advocated such equity for Florence at the beginning of the Quattrocento.[15] Those who participated in government were expected to abide by the code of justice and were frequently rotated in and out of office. This ideal had a lasting impact upon Florentine thought. Panegyrists for Lorenzo de' Medici pointed out in 1440 that Cosimo's brother had acted as a model magistrate, using his position to enforce justice on behalf of the lower class (*ordo popularis*). By not rebelling at the time of Cosimo's imprisonment, Lorenzo had placed public order before family interests. He had accepted exile with his brother in 1433.[16]

Bruni's oration for Nanni Strozzi in 1428 developed his ideal of republican government.[17] He distinguished popular rule from oligarchy and monarchy, attacking with special verve the inadequacies of the latter. The form that government assumed should encourage the pursuit of virtue. According to Bruni, monarchs were suspicious of good men and frightened by virtue, which was alien to their nature. Citizens in a republic, by contrast, feared no injury and had equal access to public office. Hence virtue flourished in a republican setting, where the possibility of winning public office spurred all to its practice. Bruni here defined equity in terms of basic rights and equal access to public office.

The panegyric for Nanni Strozzi was composed shortly after Bruni became chancellor of Florence and during the negotiations to end the city's war with Filippo Maria Visconti.[18] He used the panegyric to strip monarchy of its monopoly on the high moral ground in questions of government. For centuries the mirror-of-princes literature had emphasized that the exemplary behavior of a monarch produced virtue in a state. Bruni now posited that virtue was inimical to monarchs and natural to a republic. This tie between virtue and a republican constitution also permitted him to assign Florence the leading role in the revival of the liberal arts. The good arts logically flourished in a state that opened its government to the virtuous. And, conversely, a humanist education provided the ideal preparation for future Florentine magistrates, because it sought to instill virtue.

Bruni used both of these orations to justify Florence's engagement in conflicts against the Visconti regime. The wars were justified as a defense of liberty against Milanese aggression. In both instances Bruni harkened back to past Florentine victories and used them to rally support for the state.[19] Soldiers like Nanni Strozzi had succeeded in battle because of their reliability and sense of honor (*fides*). They maintained promises even to the enemy and never resorted to deception.[20]

Bruni's funeral oration for Strozzi celebrated the virtues of a citizen-soldier who was the son of Florentines in exile at Ferrara. The need to assure fidelity to pacts entered by mercenaries was a practical matter for Florence. Shortly after the outbreak of war against Filippo Maria Visconti in 1424, Niccolò Piccinino, a leading condottiere, had broken his contract with Florence and signed one with Milan. Bruni cast Strozzi as a countertype to the treacherous Piccinino—as a servant of Florence who had defended the state out of personal loyalty.[21]

The spirit of patriotism and pride engendered by past Florentine victories could be fed into civic support for Florence's own wars of aggression. Arms and martial virtue would assure victory for the republic as they had for Rome. Bruni's panegyric of Florence was probably written after Giangaleazzo's death in 1402 and shortly before Florence's conquest of Pisa in 1405. He celebrated the conquest of Pisa and other neighboring cities in his funeral oration for Strozzi, at a moment when Florentine rulers were considering the conquest of Lucca (1428–29). Florence was realizing the imperial aspects of her Roman inheritance at the same time that she battled to save Italian liberty from Visconti aggrandizement.[22] Bruni and his fellow Florentine orators used panegyric to further both causes.

Authorities in Milan acknowledged the efficacy of political propaganda that humanists were supplying for Florence. Giangaleazzo Visconti, Florence's great antagonist, supposedly said that Coluccio Salutati's public letters were more effective weapons than a troop of horses. Bruni's panegyrics stirred similar admiration. In 1429 Archbishop Bartolomeo della Capra of Milan wrote to the Visconti secretaries to alert them that Bruni's funeral oration for Strozzi made for effective propaganda. The Milanese chancery began to search abroad for humanists capable of presenting a case for Filippo Maria Visconti.[23]

Initially Milanese humanists did not counter Florentine propaganda by praising their city, as Bruni had done, but by celebrating the Visconti dynasty. The duchy sponsored public festivities to commemorate the anniversaries of the deaths of Giangaleazzo Visconti and his wife Caterina. For these occasions humanists with ties to the regime, like Gasparino Barzizza and Andrea Biglia, were summoned to deliver panegyrics. Only in 1436, during the competition among Italian cities for the right to host the Council of Basel, did Pier Candido Decembrio write a panegyric of Milan itself to counter Bruni's for Florence.[24]

Like Florentine humanists, those at Milan adduced visible proofs to demonstrate that the Visconti were concerned for the welfare of their subjects. Visconti magnificence exceeded that defined by Aristotle, for Giangaleazzo patronized both civic and Christian edifices. Praise for the building or rebuilding of churches here again was used to invest the regime with a sacral character. Giangaleazzo had provided the greatest testimony when he financed the construction of a Certosa at Pavia. The building symbolized the ruler's religious commitment through support for Christianity's strictest religious order. Gasparino Barzizza asserted that Giangaleazzo had actually intended to abdicate his position and retire to a life of prayer in the monastery.[25] The Milanese orators likewise sought to create a sense of government's protection, by pointing to the walls with which Giangaleazzo's father, Galeazzo Visconti, had surrounded his capital.[26]

They also tied the form of government to its benevolent purpose, emphasizing that the creation of a duchy in the Lombard plain had moved that region from political chaos to order and tranquility. The entire region had been welded into a single state ruled by a duke, who assured that right and equity prevailed. Ducal rule comprised a mean between the political extremes of tyranny, where arrogance had free rein, and the inherent anarchy of a republic. Pier Candido Decembrio classified the duchy as a Platonic timocracy, where those who govern seek honor alone.[27] The true duke must fear God, the eternal *dux*, and love justice (cf. Wisdom 1:1); his subjects had rights that even he must respect.[28] The good order that now prevailed, panegyrists affirmed, was assured by the continuation of the dynasty. Giangaleazzo's greatest gifts to his populace were his sons.[29]

Milanese humanists mixed classical and biblical precedents to ground their ducal ideology. Andrea Biglia noted that all the great regimes in ancient times had achieved their greatness under the leadership of dukes. He used the title ambiguously and included a variety of "leaders" in his historical survey. The Thebans under Epaminondas, the Spartans under Leonidas, the Athenians under Codrus and Themistocles, the Corinthians, Syracusans, Carthaginians, and even the Romans were all peoples led to greatness by *duces*. God himself had entrusted the direction of the Chosen People to Moses and Joshua, dukes who had earned his confidence. By presenting the Visconti as successors to the biblical heroes, Biglia reinforced the sacral character of ducal rule at Milan. His use of classical models inspired his reading of Scripture. Both were joined to form an ideology for the duchy.[30] The reference to Joshua, who successfully led God's people in the conquest of the Promised Land, provided a precedent for Milanese imperialism in the first half of the Quattrocento.

Eulogists affirmed that the Visconti sought by expansion to spread the benefits of ducal role throughout the peninsula. The Milanese waged war only to free Italy from tyranny and provide an effective defense against foreign intervention across the Alps. An anonymous panegyrist of Giangaleazzo Visconti suggested that a united Italy under Visconti protection would recreate the glorious days of Rome. Pier Candido Decembrio insisted that Milan was the only true successor to Rome, for Roman emperors had been invested there with the crown and insignia of office. The descriptions of Milanese leadership in protecting Italy from the barbarians were also consciously designed to recall the exploits of the Lombard League against the emperor Frederick I Barbarossa. Giangaleazzo was hailed as a conqueror, carrying on the traditions of Darius, Cyrus, Alexander the Great, and Julius Caesar.[31]

To counter Florentine propaganda, Milanese panegyrists also sketched an idealized portrait of Giangaleazzo's conduct in war. He was trustworthy and faithful to the soldier's code of honor, even though his enemies frequently did not reciprocate. His clemency toward the conquered induced many cities to accept his rule voluntarily. Panegyrists stressed that Giangaleazzo's son Filippo Maria imitated his father's example, engaging in war only to achieve peace and never causing undue harm. Filippo's chief condottiere, Niccolò Piccinino, had three times saved Lucca from enslavement to Florence. Milan, therefore, not Florence, fought wars for liberty with virtue.[32] In the absence of natural borders, panegyrists for the Visconti disguised wars of aggression as just wars of defense.[33]

Venice, the third major power involved in the peninsula's wars, employed her orators to celebrate the merits of her political system and justify her entry into conflicts on the mainland. They contended that Venice's reputation as "most serene" pointed to her success in creating a regime of patricians, who were willing to sacrifice personal ambitions in the name of public utility. Venice had realized the constitutional ideals that eminent Greeks like Solon, Lycurgus, and Plato had only been able to imagine. She had rendered those ideals visible. George of Trebizond made Venice synonymous with liberty. He praised young patricians like Fantino Michiel for devoting their youth to studies that prepared them to defend this ideal. Leonardo Giustiniani attributed Venetian concord to the fact that all were consulted and cared for. These orations adumbrated the basic arguments of Gasparo Contarini's treatise on the Venetian republic, composed a century thereafter.[34]

Bernardo Giustiniani's funeral oration for Francesco Foscari in 1457 summarized the evolution of Venetian political ideals in the first half of the fifteenth century.[35] The peculiar nature of the office of doge led Bernardo to speak on the genius of Venice's constitution. One was elected to the republic's highest office only after proving a sense of commitment to the public good through a lengthy series of offices, a *cursus honorum*.[36] That series culminated in two positions, which institutionalized the highest impulses of humanist political ideals. First, the office of public attorney (*avogador di comun*) empowered its holders to assure that government officials followed the law. After service as public attorney, worthy patricians passed to the office of procurator of San Marco, which manifested the government's beneficence. Bernardo applauded Venice for incorporating the fundamental and rather dialectical virtues of justice and clemency into her machinery of government. The procedures for electing a doge were designed, moreover, to prevent the selection of an incompetent or ambitious candidate. A lengthy period of testing in public offices and complicated voting procedures assured that a committed public servant filled Venice's highest office.[37]

Once elected as doge, Francesco Foscari had continued to pursue the political virtues of justice and generosity. Giustiniani symbolically awarded him a place of honor between pope and emperor when he recalled the diplomatic mission that Foscari had successfully sponsored to make peace between Emperor Sigismund and Pope Eugene IV. He commemorated this achievement to evoke memories of Venice's golden moment, when peace had been established between Pope Alexander III and Emperor Frederick I Barbarossa— an event ritually celebrated in the wedding of Venice and the sea. The doge's ambassadors had thus assumed their proper role as arbiters between the two most potent symbols of authority in Latin Christendom.[38]

Francesco's tenure as doge had coincided with Venice's involvement in the wars of the early Quattrocento and her territorial expansion on the Italian mainland. In fact, Venice had become the linchpin in the emerging system of Italian states. Giustiniani stressed that Foscari's policy of expansion continued policies initiated by his immediate predecessors. Venice had always acted to protect her liberty and dignity, whether against Francesco Novello da Carrara at Padua, against King Sigismund of Hungary in Friuli, or against Filippo Maria Visconti in the Po valley. The wars were once again justified as defensive measures to protect the safety of Venice and her allies. They inspired Venetians to heroism.[39] For example, Paolo da Lion had left his sickbed to assist the Venetian army in its war against Hungary.[40] Giustiniani praised Foscari for expanding Venetian rule on land and sea.[41]

The funeral speeches delivered during the first half of the fifteenth century are unique in Italian Renaissance history for two reasons. First, their content is more ideological than those that preceded or followed. Much of this oratory was conditioned by Leonardo Bruni's creative efforts for Florence. After Bruni, panegyrists elsewhere attempted to define the worth of a regime in constitutional terms and in explicit contrast to other political systems. Issues of internal legitimation no longer monopolized the orators' consciousness. Instead they praised their own cities' forms of government and ruling classes as better than those of their direct antagonists.

Secondly, orations from the period focused on great deeds accomplished in warfare. The field of battle became the preeminent field of virtue. Military heroes stepped into the spotlight of commemoration throughout the peninsula. The use of funeral oratory for admirals and generals permitted humanist orators to advance virtuous ideals for soldiers and to grapple with issues related to the conduct of war. Leonardo Giustiniani's popular portrait of Carlo Zeno, described at the beginning of this chapter, typified their ideals in this delicate area. Humanist eulogists sought to instill a sense of *humanitas* in an activity that was seldom humane.

Commemorations for soldiers took a variety of forms. Victories were celebrated in public triumphs honored by a humanist oration, equestrian statues were erected for the first time since antiquity, works of art with subtle ideological overtones were commissioned, and biographies of famous mercenary soldiers were written.[42] State funerals and their orations formed a chorus in this overture of praise. All of these forms of commemoration were manipulated to serve a variety of meanings. Governments used public funerals to tie condottieri more intimately to their service. Mercenaries were given concrete assurance of the state's appreciation for their loyalty. These funerals also served propagandistic purposes for the regimes under whose auspices great victories had been won. We are here concerned specifically with the way that humanists praised soldiers and the relationship between that praise and humanist ideals.

Speakers ascribed a legendary quality to particular accomplishments. Venice's effort to annex and defend Brescia against Filippo Maria Visconti was one such accomplishment. George of Trebizond contended that the capture of the city in 1426 by forces under the operational control of Fantino Michiel, Leonardo Mocenigo, and Pietro Loredan had surpassed the victories of the Athenian general Miltiades at Marathon and the Roman commander Lucullus over the Parthians. Later eulogists commemorated the heroism of Gattamelata, who had led Venetian forces on retreat from Brescia and then returned with a fleet of galleys to battle Milanese forces on Lago di Garda (1439–40). Assisted by Francesco Sforza, Gattamelata had finally succeeded in breaking the Milanese siege. The two generals were compared to Hannibal and Scipio Africanus for the rigors of their journey, and to Jason and the Argonauts for carrying their fleet overland.[43] Venice's opponent, Niccolò Piccinino, was also deemed another Hannibal for his own strategy during the campaign.[44]

Such generals were models because they willingly risked their lives for the state. The ideal military leader had to be virtuous. As humanists of this period attempted to define martial virtue, ideals that were to characterize the administration of the state were similarly carried over to the field of battle. Generals thus fulfilled their obligations when they showed mercy to defeated opponents and when they strictly enforced discipline among their own troops. They were also to practice the virtues of justice and clemency.[45] Above all, military leaders had to be persons of integrity. Only by exemplifying courage and patriotism could they ask and expect sacrifices from their troops.⁴⁶ Humanists urged that soldiers have ethos. Ethical generals would correct problems created by the mercenary system.

Soldiers would thus profit from a humanist education. They should especially pursue history. One could garner information on strategy by studying past military successes. Alexander the Great, Pompey, and Julius Caesar had all gained vital tactical information in that way. A humanist education would also supply eloquence, which helped to instill courage in troops prior to battle and to congratulate and instruct them at battle's end. Following ancient models, funeral orators recreated famous speeches of military leaders.⁴⁷ They advocated that the example of Carlo Zeno, who had surpassed ancient heroes like Themistocles in his zeal for the liberal arts, be imitated.

Humanists hoped that humane military commanders would change the way that war was conducted. Several orators praised their subjects because they had renounced the sacking, pillaging, and raping that made warfare morally dissolute. An anonymous eulogist of Bartolomeo Padovano emphasized the contrast between his subject and other leaders of his day; Bartolomeo did not allow his troops to pillage churches. Orators like Leonardo Bruni evoked the quasi-sacral character of a soldier's pledge to serve the commonwealth. Nanni Strozzi had properly discharged his commission with virtue and never by fraud. Bruni implicitly censured the shifting allegiances and open treachery that too often settled wars in his day. The same point was made when orators railed against those who murdered soldiers in an ambush.⁴⁸ In an age when mercenaries were hired to do much of the fighting, eulogists supplied a practical moral counsel when they stressed that their subjects had not been motivated by avarice. Italian humanists concurred with Sallust, who had asserted that ambition and avarice were the roots of all evil in military matters.⁴⁹

Warfare was a risky enterprise for any state. As the fifteenth century progressed and one war followed upon another, Italian eulogists openly admitted their ambivalence about war. Bruni's praise for Nanni Strozzi as a citizen-soldier indicates the trend. Bruni had to turn Strozzi, the son of a Florentine exile raised in Ferrara, into a patriotic hero who had defended Florentine liberty. If warfare helped to define the state and focus the allegiance of citizens, it lost much of that value if mercenaries, not citizens, did the fighting. Moreover, it became an increasing drain on the republic's treasury. Bruni wrote his tribute for Strozzi less than a year after the imposition of an income tax (*catasto*) in 1427.[50]

Similar ambivalence toward warfare was expressed by funeral orators in Milan and Venice. After granting Giangaleazzo Visconti a place among history's greatest conquerors, Gasparino Barzizza immediately added that the slightest action of virtue was of greater benefit for the state than any territorial conquest. Collective exhaustion with war in Milan was also indicated by Filippo Maria's scruple in 1446. Stung by remorse for the heavy taxes that his wars had forced, he asked Giovanni Lampugnano to gather a group of theologians and assess his possibilities for salvation. The duke admitted that he could not repay the exactions and wondered if there were any other way to make amends. The theologians debated at length before responding to their lord's query. They urged Filippo to make total restitution in keeping with Church teaching on theft. However, they suggested a series of great benefits that Filippo might perform in lieu of restitution. He would have to remove new *gabelle* imposed during the wars, change his personal habits, care for Church reform, assure justice for the people, end spending for luxuries at court, and see that Italy at last enjoy peace. They felt that Filippo could do nothing better for his people and for all Italy than to end the warfare that had continued almost unabated during his reign.[51]

In his eulogy for Francesco Foscari, Bernardo Giustiniani betrayed similar ambivalence toward Venetian involvement in the *terra firma* wars. Delivered shortly after the doge's deposition and public disgrace in 1457, the oration confronted charges that Venice had consciously embarked on an imperialist policy. The orator claimed that Venice had been compelled by divine providence to defend the liberty of Italy against the aggrandizing designs of Filippo Maria Visconti. He cited Venice's decision not to annex Bologna as evidence that it had no overarching imperial objective. Consequently, war should always be seen as a divinely dictated initiative to dramatize how preferable peace is. The Venetian victories admittedly produced growth in her empire. They also cost a heavy human price. Venice had accepted the call to defend Italian liberty and was vindicated in its struggle by divine justice.

Giustiniani's eulogy also reflected the less glorious side of Foscari's wars, a factor often advanced by historians to explain the doge's deposition. Giustiniani sought to mute stress on the efficacy of war by positing that Francesco had achieved even greater victories through diplomacy. He claimed that the Spartans, antiquity's fabled warriors, had rated the victories won by "kindness and persuasion" a greater gift from the gods than victories on the battlefield. The doge had obtained more lasting and beneficial results through persuasion than by relying on battles. Though naturally inclined toward peace, Foscari had been forced to oppose Milan. His most important bequest was not the land empire but a "golden age" of peace.[52] Amidst the ambivalent strains of the patrician's eulogy, one intuits a war-weary Venice.

War created ambivalence for humanists because they were proponents of rhetorical culture. In the *Brutus* (12.45), Cicero had argued that eloquence was properly the companion of peace and of a settled society.[53] Though eloquence thrived in periods of civic concord, it was swept away by the passions of war. Cicero's violent death during Rome's civil wars supplied tragic proof for his assertion. Sensitive to this contention, humanist orators consistently tempered their praise for heroics in war and attempted to delineate the circumstances that would justify a state's recourse to war. War should be avoided at all costs and should only be undertaken as a last resort. No war could be justly waged unless, paradoxically, peace were the final goal. When Andrea Biglia affirmed that governments too frequently waged war for base motives, he challenged his audience to acknowledge that not all of the wars of the early fifteenth century had been just.[54] Like their hero Cicero, humanist orators of the Renaissance viewed eloquence as the ally of peace and concord. They used their public speaking to move contemporaries away from easy reliance on belligerency in matters of foreign policy.

Rulers best served their people by not engaging in war. Guarino felt that Leonello d'Este had acted most beneficently by doing just that for his subjects at Ferrara. He offered theoretical support for this judgment. Rulers were to be imitators of God and were placed in their positions of authority to act morally. As Seneca had observed, political authorities should abstain from shedding human blood. Savagery denigrated human dignity, reducing human beings to conduct typical of wild beasts. Clemency enriched that dignity.[55]

In the *De officiis* (1.11.34–35) Cicero had described two ways to settle a dispute: by using physical force like wild animals, or through discussion, an innately human method. The only possible excuse for war, Cicero argued, is that we may live in peace. In light of their commitment to the rhetor's culture, their particular vision of Christianity, and their experience of wars in Italy for more than fifty years, Italian humanists celebrated the peace of Lodi in 1454 as a watershed.

All of the protagonists who contributed to the diplomatic agreement were singled out for praise. In 1465 the Florentine government posthumously awarded Cosimo de' Medici the title *pater patriae*, "father of the fatherland." In the oration for that occasion, Donato Acciaiuoli cited Cosimo's part in arranging the peace settlement as a principal reason for the honor.[56] Francesco Filelfo affirmed that Francesco Sforza had so desired peace for Milan that he made extreme concessions to Venice in the settlement. His legacy to his citizens was that of a true follower of Christ, peace. Venetian orators spoke of a "golden age" ushered in by Doge Francesco Foscari and her chief condottiere, Bartolomeo Colleoni. Colleoni's final shift from Milanese to Venetian employ and his control over the territory in and around Bergamo did constitute one of the pieces in the diplomatic puzzle of Lodi.[57]

The last and most reluctant ruler to adhere to the settlement, Alfonso I of Naples, was described by his panegyrist Adamo di Montaldo as the moving force behind its organization and success. Writing from Naples, Giannozzo Manetti credited the Florentine ambassador Giannozzo Pandolfini with wearing down Neapolitan resistance to the agreement. That the peace was arranged during the pontificate of Nicholas V and arbitrated by him in important ways contributed greatly to Nicholas's prestige among humanists.[58]

The years 1453–54 were critical for humanist political ideals for a further reason. In 1453 Constantinople fell to the Turks. The capital of the Byzantine empire and symbol of Christian presence in the eastern Mediterranean now belonged to the infidels. Humanist orators seized upon the catastrophe to dramatize the threat posed by the Turks. They advocated a crusade to stem their advance, as *the* just war for the epoch. If the rulers of their age needed to prove their military prowess, let them do it on the battlefields of the Levant in defense of Christian liberty. Otherwise, let the "domestic war" of the hunt suffice.[59] All other wars should cease.

Humanists considered the half-century that followed the peace of Lodi halcyon years. They used their orations after 1454 to promote projects deemed of special importance for the "protection of citizens." Justice and clemency were to be artfully combined in an ongoing struggle against civic discord. Governments should employ eloquent diplomats to help maintain peace. Whenever wars flared up, humanists dutifully defended their outbreak but warmly applauded their conclusion. Government should act on behalf of its most vulnerable citizens and make its concern visible through building. Most of all, humanists sought to enhance the prestige of their learning by celebrating the prestige they themselves brought to the peninsula's states.

To promote civic concord, funeral orators continued to emphasize loyalty to a ruling dynasty. The dynastic principle was intimately connected to the success of Lodi, which had turned on the acceptance of Francesco Sforza as successor to the Visconti in Milan. The physical link between those families was Francesco's wife, Bianca Maria Visconti, the daughter of Filippo Maria. In an anniversary eulogy for Filippo Maria, Giovanni Montano recalled the violence that had ensued after the duke's death and depicted Bianca Maria as a savior sent from heaven. Montano congratulated Bianca Maria on the birth of her first son, Galeazzo Maria, and exhorted her to continue to produce offspring.[60]

Milanese orators for Francesco Sforza also sought to reinforce loyalty to the new ruling family and to blunt insurrection. Francesco Filelfo alleged that the citizens of Milan would thereby continue Sforza's salutary domestic policy, designed to eliminate residual resentment. Filelfo shared with his audience Sforza's response to the suggestion that he enter Milan in triumph. Sforza had rejected the advice precisely because he feared that a triumphal entrance would fan the flames of factional enmity. Filelfo presented a leader disposed to forgive all previous injuries in order to achieve civic concord.[61]

Sforza rule had had healthy effects for the state. Filelfo adduced as proof of Sforza's lofty moral standards his summary execution of one of his soldiers for callously raping a young woman who had taken sanctuary in a church. Baldassare Rasini contrasted the duke's deportment with that of Julius Caesar: Caesar, once he had consolidated power, began to despise divine and human law, but Sforza had retained a rigorous sense of justice and equity throughout his reign. Filelfo saw the Castello raised by Sforza at Milan as visible proof of the value of his rule. It deserved a place among the world's wonders.[62]

Filelfo's contention reminds one of the precarious position of monarchs in Renaissance Italy. By stressing the building's technical and architectural achievement, the humanist orator attempted to transform a visual symbol of the duke's dominance and vulnerability into a symbol of his protection. The moment of a ruler's funeral was also the delicate moment of succession. Humanist eulogies at that critical point cut in two directions. Orators did their part as courtiers to marshal support for the dynasty. They also traced activities and programs for the new ruler.

Orators at minor courts in Italy emphasized that a monarch's authority rid the state of internal discord and factionalism. Funeral orations for the Baglioni of Perugia illustrate this approach. Giannantonio Campano revealed that the pope himself had wept at the news of Nello Baglioni's death, defending his show of grief by asserting that Nello alone could repress uprisings in Perugia and guarantee its tranquility. Campano had rushed back to Perugia from Rome to deliver the oration for his friend Nello at a moment of tension in the city. Nello's sons Pandolfo and Galeotto had withheld news of their father's death for two days, fearing that their cousin Braccio might revolt against them.[63]

The humanist bishop structured his eulogy for Nello to forestall violence against Nello's heirs. He highlighted a fundamental change in Nello's conduct as lord of the city. After his father was assassinated and he was driven from Perugia as a boy, Nello had desired to avenge his father's murder. With the assistance of Braccio Fortebracci, the Baglioni had retaken the city. Nello then realized his vengeance by slaughtering those who had murdered his father. Afterwards he had repented of his vengeful actions and became a model of honest living. Campano claimed that Nello had acted humbly in contrast to the ostentation and immorality of other leading citizens.[64] His later conduct was that worthy of imitation.

Campano's depiction of this conversion and his underlying argument in favor of civic order probably helped avert an uprising in the wake of Nello's death. However, Braccio Baglioni did move against his cousins three years later; he organized and, in all likelihood, materially participated in their assassination. When he was reproached by his friend Campano, he did public penance and was granted a pontifical absolution. The incident proved to be an occasion on which Perugia's rival factions were reconciled for a time under Braccio's leadership. The city enjoyed a period of stability and cultural efflorescence.

Francesco Maturanzio applauded the epoch of calm under Braccio in his funeral eulogy. Quick to block the formation of factions and crush plots against his authority, Braccio had worked to consolidate public support by making Perugia an amenable place to live. He sponsored games to entertain the populace and built gardens, villas, residences, and churches throughout the small principality. Braccio earned a reputation as "Il Magnifico," like his more famous neighbor to the north. Maturanzio alleged that Braccio was so effective in engendering civic concord that neighboring towns frequently requested his assistance to settle disputes.[65]

Humanist orators wished to see civic concord spread everywhere. During the first half of the fifteenth century, eulogists had celebrated the conquests of their states. Orators now sought to illuminate the benefits of imperialism for newly acquired territories. They presented the victors as bringing civic concord in their wake. Order and security were values in the monarchical and republican contexts. Statebuilding had begun in earnest, and it brought humanist skills into the limelight.

Orators portrayed provincial governors with admirable powers of persuasion. Florentine humanists had quelled tumults during their tenure as provincial administrators. Venetian patricians had performed the same service. Girolamo della Torre had fostered unanimity and charity among the various magistrates at Padua. This internal unity among the governors supposedly spread outward to the governed, engendering tranquility for that vexatious region of the *terra firma* empire.[66]

To assure domestic harmony in any state, panegyrical orators consistently recommended the virtues of justice and clemency.[67] Orators appealed to the deeds of ancient political leaders to prove the value of those virtues. Aristides at Athens and Lucius Iunius Brutus at Rome had shown that justice meant strict and impartial enforcement of the laws of the commonwealth. Brutus gave the ultimate proof of impartiality when he ordered the execution of his sons. Julius Caesar epitomized clemency—the imaginary Caesar that Cicero had created in his *Pro Marcello*. That Caesar was disposed to pardon his political opponents for the unity of the state.

In addition to these examples, humanists were inspired by the ideal of political rule presented in Virgil's *Aeneid* (6.853). The passage narrates Aeneas' vision of his descendant Augustus. As under Augustus, so with the settlement reached in 1454 the world of the humanists was at peace. They urged that the moment be used to imprint civilized order on the peninsula's various states. It was a moment to exercise the art of government "by being merciful to the submissive and by crushing the arrogant." Romans had prided themselves for introducing a moral standard into government. Humanists advocated that the best of Roman political civilization be recreated in their era.

Panegyrists offered examples of rulers who had exercised the dual art of good government. Adamo di Montaldo singled out two "good deeds" (*beneficia*) that made Alfonso I of Naples unique. First, Alfonso had displayed his generosity (*liberalitas*) in the festivities and contests that he held to entertain the emperor Frederick III during his sojourn at Naples. Such public festivities were presented by orators as visible proof of government's largesse. Adamo thus sought to enhance Alfonso's reputation as "magnanimous."[68] Secondly, the king had acted justly. Adamo recalled the case of a woman whose husband had been condemned to death for robbery. When she approached her husband's judge to beg for his life, the magistrate promised to release him if she consented to sexual relations; out of desperation, the woman committed adultery. Assuming that she would never dare to reveal her action, the cynical judge had her husband executed. But the judge had underestimated the woman's sense of equity. Determined to obtain justice even at the cost of her own reputation, she cast herself at the feet of the king, recounted the sexual extortion and deception, and begged for vindication. Adamo observed that the corps of Neapolitan jurists had rated Alfonso's decision in the case a singular example of impartial justice. The king had first ordered the judicial magistrate to marry the poor woman and then had him beheaded.[69] The kingdom of Naples was in the hands of a ruler who knew how to be kind to the submissive and to punish the arrogant.

The same virtues were to inform the political life of the peninsula's republics. As noted earlier, Venice prided herself on building the practice of clemency and justice into the fabric of her institutions.[70] Public attorneys investigated allegations of impropriety by government officials. Justice was a potent symbol in Venice and informed much public architecture, particularly in the ducal palace. The state also practiced public beneficence through the procurators of San Marco, who collected funds willed to the state and distributed them to those in need. This was the second most powerful office in the republic and that from which all doges were chosen.

Eulogists for the Renaissance doges remarked that they acted with justice and clemency. Doges thereby realized their role as symbol of the spirit of the island republic. Pietro Marcello, for example, recounted that Doge Andrea Vendramin had used clemency with an enemy who publicly insulted him. The unnamed offender had been condemned to death by the Council of Ten for the crime of lesemajesty. Vendramin asked the council to reduce the punishment to exile in Dalmatia, and they abided by his request. Nevertheless he had imposed the letter of the law when his own son was exiled from

Venice. He refused to reduce the term of punishment and saw that a new law was passed, which forbade the return of exiles under any circumstances. Marcello made the obvious comparison to Lucius Iunius Brutus.[71]

The same political ideals appear frequently in humanist oratory from the court of the Este in Ferrara. From the death of Leonello in 1450 to that of Alfonso I in 1534, orators commemorated the many actions of those rulers "for the good of our city."[72] Celio Calcagnini stated that Alfonso I had been primarily concerned to treat his subjects with equity. Estense rulers did take a direct interest in the effective functioning of the judicial system at Ferrara.

Eulogists for the Este also enumerated the achievements of their reigns in order to present a government that wedded the Roman and Christian ideals of clemency and charity. Guarino sought to instill that spirit in his pupil Leonello and to assure its appeal among future rulers from the family by celebrating it at Leonello's funeral. Descriptions of the family's charity to a certain extent reflect life in Renaissance Ferrara. Activities like flood control, land reclamation, careful attention to the food supply, and direct philanthropy were cornerstones of Estense policy and explain in part the regime's stability.[73]

Funeral orators reminded their audience that this spirit of government had been rendered visible. Borso d'Este was celebrated for patronizing the construction of a Certosa for Ferrara, the centerpiece of a program of support for religious orders.[74] Borso's successor, Ercole I, used rituals of charity to express the goals of his rule. He daily distributed food to a dozen paupers, he annually solicited gifts of food for poor relief on the feast of the Epiphany, and he sponsored a banquet for the poor on Holy Thursday, which included a ritual washing of feet in imitation of Jesus' gesture.

Visitors to Ferrara and citizens of the duchy should recognize the general success of Estense government in Ercole's addition to the city. Filled with magnificent civic and religious edifices, it was a lasting tribute to the *magnificentia* of the ruling family.[75] The Ercolean addition still functions as a visible expression of many humanist political ideals. In sharp contrast to medieval Ferrara, the new quarter evokes the spirit of order and expansion celebrated by humanists from the time of Leonardo Bruni.

In all of his activities Ercole had the assistance of his talented wife, Eleanor of Aragon.[76] Battista Guarini and Battista Mantovano emphasized that Eleanor possessed traditional feminine virtues like modesty (*pudicitia*) and public virtues like practical wisdom (*prudentia*). Ercole could confidently entrust the administration of Ferrara to Eleanor when he had to be away.[77] Funeral orators noted that Eleanor had properly governed on those occasions, enforcing Ferrara's laws with equity and compassionately assisting the poor.

Such praise by humanist orators implied that women were capable of a governing role. In addition to the traditional activities of bearing and raising children, women were praised in Renaissance funeral orations for their actions as regents for their husbands or sons.[78] Eleanor of Aragon constitutes a relevant example where panegyric for once reflects reality. She was almost assuredly more capable than Ercole in matters of government.

Humanist eulogists made the same point by praising women for acquiring eloquence, the art essential to public service. Elisabetta Malatesta earned the admiration of the senate of Pesaro for smoothly delivering weighty opinions. Guarino noted that Margherita Gonzaga's humanist education helped her to write eloquent letters. Giannantonio Campano characterized Battista Sforza as a prodigy in the art of speaking. At age four, Battista had pronounced a Latin oration that led her eulogist to wonder if she had imbibed eloquence with her mother's milk. The learned woman later delivered an oration that Pius II commended for seriousness and stylistic polish.[79]

To praise women in this way marked a change in humanist thinking. Following Aristotle, in his treatise on the study of letters written for Battista Malatesta da Montefeltro sometime between 1422 and 1429, Leonardo Bruni had declared that women should avoid public life. He wondered why a woman should bother to learn the subtleties of rhetoric when she would never have an opportunity to exercise it. In his eulogy for Battista Sforza, Campano directly confronted opinions like Bruni's, citing instead Pope Pius II, who was convinced that women were unjustly denied an education in humane letters.[80] Their eloquence attested to their capacity to master the humanities and to play a role in the forum.

Humanist orators commended rulers who transferred Christian rituals to a political setting in order to illumine government's scope. For example, rulers were praised for repeating Jesus' gesture of service at the Last Supper when they washed the feet of the poor during Holy Week. Orators extolled that act in the hope that something of its spirit of service might inform government.[81]

Among the various institutions of Renaissance Italy, perhaps none embodied that spirit more palpably than the hospital. Hospitals occupied large pieces of land within cities and performed a variety of social services as poorhouse, asylum, and medical center. The facade of the Hospital of the Ceppo in Pistoia presents the institution as an expression of the evangelical ideal of service. Santi Buglioni decorated it with representations of the corporal works of mercy from the Gospel of Matthew.[82]

Much fine contemporary scholarship on the hospital in the Renaissance has debated whether those institutions reveal the secularization of charity or its resacralization. It is a distinction that humanist orators would probably not understand. They preferred to see ideals from classical culture and Scripture as mutually reinforcing. Charity must inform the world of politics. One of the central scenes in Buglioni's series, the welcoming of strangers, includes a representation of the washing of feet.

Humanist ideals were in part a reaction to social developments, especially developments that sharpened economic differentiation within society. The gap between wealthy and poor was to be bridged by a magnanimous civic spirit. Greed was reprehensible, but wealth was neutral. In Venice, wealth was celebrated as a means to express public commitment. Ludovico Strassoldo mentioned that when friends of Francesco Corner had berated him for giving away so much money, the Venetian administrator had responded that it would be unjust and inhumane not to do so. Strassoldo called upon the poor, orphans, the church of Santo Stefano, and the Christian religion in general to attest to Corner's generosity.

Future generations of the same family carried on Francesco's habit of generosity. Pietro Contarini stated that Marco Corner had acquired his fortune honestly and used it to aid the underprivileged. If Marco was the first to lobby for taxes, he was also the first to turn them over to an exhausted public treasury. In the sixteenth century, Carlo Cappello described Giorgio Corner's successful effort to rebuild the family fortune, which had been depleted by his sister's dowry of one hundred thousand gold ducats, and argued that Giorgio's actions had a civic reference. In order to show his belief that his wealth was for the utility of the state, he had spent large sums to restore the family palace. Giorgio had performed his greatest service to the state, however, by convincing his sister Caterina to will her kingdom of Cyprus to the Serenissima, thus supplying Venice with grain and income.[83]

Humanists wanted rulers to practice a magnificence beyond that defined by Aristotle, because it was motivated by Christian charity.[84] Pietro Marsi's funeral oration for Girolamo Riario in 1488 illustrates the extent to which these ideals applied in all circumstances. Riario had agitated Italian politics when he tried to carve out a state in the Romagna in the 1470s and 1480s.[85] Historians like Ludwig Pastor have characterized him as vile, ruthless, and an indefatigable intriguer. Riario earned this reputation in large part during the reign of his uncle, Pope Sixtus IV. His cruelty and his role in the Pazzi conspiracy against Lorenzo de' Medici proved his unscrupulous ways. After the death of Sixtus in 1484, however, Riario's politics changed. The new pope, Innocent VIII, and Lorenzo de' Medici both had designs upon his principality in the Romagna. Like many of his predecessors, Innocent planned to use his papacy to establish his family in a territorial state. Riario's possessions in the Romagna seemed the only realistic possibility. Lorenzo de' Medici saw Imola as vital to the security of Florence. To pry it free from Riario's control would also provide a measure of revenge for his brother Giuliano's murder and the attempt on his own life. Without the protection of his uncle, Riario sought to win the favor of the residents of Imola, Forlì, and Forlimpopoli through a politics of largesse. His efforts backfired when spending for public works forced him to rescind important tax immunities. Leading noble families, goaded on by Medici agents, assassinated him in his castle at Forlì on 14 April 1488.

Pietro Marsi was chosen to commemorate the slain count in the turbulent days immediately following the assassination. He claimed that Riario had remodeled Imola into a city that attracted visitors from all over Italy. He also credited Riario with an instinctive distaste for war even in conditions that might justify it. "We are born for peace and concord," asserted Marsi, stressing ideals that functioned as an indictment of much of Riario's career. They also condemned the insurrection by his citizens.[86]

Marsi discussed the rebellion itself later in the speech. He imagined Riario delivering an exhortation to his son Ottaviano and to the cities of his tiny state. In keeping with Roman ideals, Riario exhorted his son not to seek revenge indiscriminately. Only after careful investigation should Ottaviano proceed to punish those proven guilty of complicity in the crime. He should treat the innocent with clemency and assure reconciliation to the family by his magnanimity.[87] The revenant Riario then summoned the populace to recover a spirit of Roman *humanitas*, so contrary to the plotting and deceit that had characterized their rapport with recent papal vicars. Even in cases of an arrogant lord (presumably one like Riario himself), the populace should react with patience and not rebel. Marsi then contended that the Italian race historically had proven its superiority in humanity. He urged the citizens of Imola, Forlì, and Forlimpopoli to care for the public good as true Roman progeny.[88]

Marsi's speech pleads for the principal political ideals of humanist orators: for impartial justice, for generous clemency, for order within the state, for peace and concord throughout the peninsula, for *humanitas* as the informing spirit of governors and the governed. Although he urged the citizens of the Romagna to endure a domineering ruler, he did not attempt to conceal that Girolamo had unduly burdened his subjects. The speech is a call for reform to citizens and ruler alike and yet a rejection of revolution. It is also a reminder that the "golden age" that followed the peace of Lodi was not without violence.

With the invasions that began in 1494, Italy became Europe's battlefield. Humanist funeral eulogists were again called upon to celebrate military deeds. They did not focus upon the survival of the state they served, but on the defense of the peninsula's state system against foreign invasion. They used funeral orations to repeat their preference for peace over war.

Francesco Vigilio provided a vivid description of Francesco II Gonzaga's inspirational leadership of the Italian armies that claimed to have defeated Charles VIII of France at the battle of Fornovo in 1495. Vigilio stressed that the situation had become desperate for Gonzaga. Milan's forces refused to assist him and many other members of the alliance were considering flight. At that dramatic moment, Gonzaga exhorted all who wished to save Italy to follow him.[89] He threw himself against the French lines and had his horse shot from under him. His courageous example inspired his tentative allies to fight on and turned the tide against the French.

Vigilio described the battle of Fornovo to highlight the heroics of Francesco Gonzaga. He also attempted to convey a sense of war's less pleasant realities by recreating the sights and sounds of conflict: the clash of arms, the moans of the wounded, the explosions of artillery, and the River Taro that ran red with blood. Humanist ambivalence toward the "glory" of warfare never abated. Vigilio continued his speech by detailing actions of Gonzaga's that had demonstrated his charity toward his Mantuan subjects. He had assured adequate supplies of grain during periods of famine, had personally assisted them during an outbreak of the plague, and had worked to assure a network of alliances to free his people from the devastation of warfare. Vigilio ranked peace, not military victory, as Gonzaga's sublime accomplishment.[90] In that conviction he continued emphases of his Quattrocento forebears.

To convey the proper spirit of government, humanist funeral orators censured certain activities and praised others. They condemned politicians who sacrificed their integrity to greed or personal ambition. These criticisms were often made indirectly. George of Trebizond praised the integrity of a public servant like Fantino Michiel, who had accepted government office only to be useful to the commonwealth: he had not wished to acquire profit and proved his integrity by resigning an office when his work was accomplished or when his assistance was no longer needed.[91] Humanists censured politicians who embezzled public funds or accepted bribes. Bribery was especially grievous when it compromised the exercise of justice. No government could claim legitimacy unless it were free from such taint.

Eulogists also censured politicians for placing personal or factional interests before the common good. They rated factional violence a blight upon their epoch.[92] The ideal spirit of governing was public: one who administered a principality or a republic should be concerned with the protection of all citizens and with a wealth that was common. Humanists looked above all to a change in the attitude of governors and governed, and not to changes in institutional structures to achieve reform. Politicians passed a humanist's test when they were loved rather than feared.[93]

The title *pater patriae* reflects a paternalistic ideal of government. It appealed to humanists as a revival of Roman practice. They also liked the title because it was supra-ideological. Camillus and Cicero had received the title as heroes of the Roman Republic. Julius Caesar and Augustus were given the same award after Rome reverted to monarchical rule. In the *De clementia* (1.14.2) Seneca had recapitulated the abiding Roman sense of the honor: "To the 'Father of his Country' we have given the name in order that he may know that he has been entrusted with a father's power, which is most forbearing in its care for the interests of his children and subordinates his own to theirs."[94]

A sampling of the politicians who were celebrated in funeral orations as the "fathers of their country" reads like a diachronic summary of the political ideals advanced in the orations. In 1403 Francesco Zabarella thus praised Arcoano Buzzacarini for his heroic defense of Padua. In 1440 Antonio Pacini emphasized that Lorenzo de' Medici and his brother Cosimo deserved the honor for using their wealth to assist Florence against foreign aggression. Twenty-five years later Cosimo was officially honored with the title by vote of the Signoria. Donato Acciaiuoli delivered a public oration to announce the award and expressly commended Cosimo's role in negotiating peace in Italy in 1454. Humanists shifted from honoring warriors to honoring diplomats.[95]

Despite family rivalries, Nello and Braccio Baglioni were considered fathers of the Perugian state for their success in ending factional strife and for ushering in an era of magnificence. Lazzaro Becci was so honored in San Gimignano for a piety that expressed itself civically in patronage for rebuilding. In the sixteenth century Celio Calcagnini praised Alfonso d'Este's fatherly concern to fortify Ferrara and supply it with food, also claiming that Alfonso had judiciously kept Ferrara out of the peninsula's wars. The various "fathers of their country" stood out in the later period for their largesse and for their success in avoiding involvement in war.[96]

From the period of Milanese wars that helped to define the peninsula's states, to the golden era of peace and consolidation, and again during the era of foreign invasions, Italy's true civic heroes in the estimation of humanist orators were those who served the interests of all citizens, including humanists. The orators portrayed a symbiotic rapport between the state and their educational program. A humanist education instilled a sense of public concern and supplied training in eloquence, which set human beings apart from wild beasts and civilized them. Rulers therefore did well to patronize the humanities. Moreover, the presence of humanists in government was bandied about to enhance the prestige of republics and principalities. Humanists acclaimed patronage for orators and poets because it revived one of antiquity's laudable customs.[97]

In a eulogy for Ludovico Casella (d. 1469), Battista Guarini offered visible proof that Estense government supported the humanities. Casella had effectively served as Borso d'Este's prime minister in Ferrara. Guarini recalled that Casella had publicly demonstrated his affection for Battista's father, Guarino, by helping to carry his bier during the state funeral. The orator created a verbal tableau to convince his audience that the state of Ferrara supported humanists.[98]

The symbiotic rapport between government and the humanities reached maximal potential when rulers and administrators practiced what they patronized. Leonello d'Este, Federigo da Montefeltro, and

Lorenzo de' Medici had generously supported the humanities and mastered the literary and rhetorical arts.[99] Beatrice of Aragon had exported the best of humanist learning to Hungary and helped to civilize her husband Mattia Corvino and his barbarian realm.[100] Florence especially had sought to exploit the prestige that humanist administrators brought to a state by sponsoring elaborate public funerals for them. The humanists selected to deliver orations at funerals seized the opportunity to present a manifesto for uniting humanism and public service.[101]

In the years prior to 1454 orators at Florence praised fellow humanists for their activities as secretaries and for the advice they offered in the councils of state. Special commendation was given to activities that had fostered the Florentine war effort. Giannozzo Manetti, for example, applauded Leonardo Bruni's participation on the special wartime *balia* of the Ten. Those were the appropriate fora in which a humanist could use eloquence for the common good.[102]

Manetti also recalled that Bruni had succeeded in calming an enraged Pope Martin V, who was upset by a mocking jingle that Florentine urchins liked to sing below his window. Bruni reminded Martin of Florence's good services to him and the benefits that had occurred while he was living in the city (1419–20). The account functions as a paradigm of the political value of eloquence. Bruni's speech to Martin resolved acrimony and cemented harmony between the republic and one of its important neighbors.[103]

After the peace of Lodi, Florentine humanists were commended for their administration of the state and their success as diplomats. Men of integrity, Matteo Palmieri and Donato Acciaiuoli could not be bribed from executing the requirements of justice. Acciaiuoli had skillfully reconciled the factious citizens of Pistoia to Florentine overlordship. Cristoforo Landino judged that Acciaiuoli lived a sincere piety, as he had always sought to engender peace and concord.[104]

Landino built his eulogy to an emotional climax when he narrated that Acciaiuoli had died on a diplomatic mission for Florence, a faithful public servant who had given the ultimate proof of his dedication. The summer of 1478 was a propitious moment to commend such a demonstration of loyalty. Just a few months earlier, Lorenzo de' Medici had been wounded and his brother Giuliano killed in a plot to overthrow the Medici regime. Landino used the eulogy for Acciaiuoli as a plea to rally behind Medici leadership. He reinforced that appeal through a vivid description of Giuliano's assassination in the Duomo, tying the sacrifice of his innocent life to the liturgical rite during which it occurred.[105]

Such deeds proved that Florence's humanists were men of public virtue. Alamanno Rinuccini summarized the humanist art of government when he asserted that Matteo Palmieri had adjusted his actions to the necessity of the moment. Like oratory, government required a developed sense of decorum. Palmieri could be kind or severe. Good persons welcomed his company, but the depraved feared his presence in office.[106]

The art of government required one to practice virtues and harmonize actions at opposite ends of an epideictic spectrum. Governors properly treated the good in a different manner than the wicked. Epideictic orators likewise praised the former and censured the latter. The professional commitments of humanists in government required them to combine pursuits that were not easily combined. They had to be activists and scholars at the same time.[107]

Their virtuous deeds flowed from their training in the humanities. In the first half of the fifteenth century, Florentine eulogists emphasized that humanist employees of the republic were "wise and eloquent." The description was Ciceronian, and humanists used it to blunt criticism of their eloquence as mere sophistry.[108] In the second half of the century, eulogists emphasized that their subjects combined the active and contemplative lives. When describing speculative learning, Cristoforo Landino included training in philosophy from logic to physics to metaphysics.[109]

Although this manner of praise reflected changes in the Florentine cultural scene, the basic message did not change. In simplest terms, Renaissance humanists were convinced that neither the unexamined nor the uncommitted life was worth leading. Once individuals like Salutati and Bruni had established the credibility of eloquence, humanists accepted coexistence with the formal philosophical currents of pedagogues like Argyropulos and Ficino. They predicated their acceptance on one condition. As Poggio stated in his eulogy for Bruni, learning must never be used for purely personal ends or to harm the state. It was better to be unlearned than to be without virtue.[110]

The pursuit of virtue pulled the human person beyond himself and directed him toward the common good. Stated concisely, humanist eulogists everywhere during the Italian Renaissance related truth to the conduct of life.[111] That conception of truth made the humanist program of education vital for society. Humanists proclaimed the value of their learning when they eulogized deceased teachers of the humanities.

CHAPTER SIX

ACADEMIC IDEALS
*"Perfected in the Arts
Appropriate to Humanity"*

In 1416 Guarino da Verona proudly began to write to his humanist friends to praise a funeral eulogy delivered by his student Andrea Giuliano. At times he sent along a copy of the speech to prove its excellence.[1] Guarino had selected Giuliano to commemorate Manuel Chrysoloras during a memorial ceremony held at Venice shortly after Chrysoloras' death at the Council of Constance in April 1415. Giuliano, a young Venetian patrician, readily acknowledged his debt to Guarino. He speculated that Guarino had chosen him for the task because Guarino had shared with him the many reasons for which he admired Chrysoloras.[2] Giuliano's eulogy gave teacher and student an opportunity to pat each other on the back.

The eulogy also represents the first classicizing panegyric from the Italian Renaissance for a person who taught the humanities. Form affected content. When Bonaventura Badoer eulogized Petrarch at Arquà some forty years earlier, he had followed the tenets of scholastic preaching and portrayed Petrarch in hagiographical terms, virtually ignoring his literary and scholarly achievements.[3] Giuliano learned the principles for panegyric from classical handbooks, which Guarino had taught him. He used them to construct an influential image of Chrysoloras as humanist and public servant.

Giuliano enunciated the substance of that image in the speech's exordium when he described Manuel as "a most noble man and most distinguished philosopher."[4] The speech turned on the poles of nobility and philosophy. Giuliano divided the body of the work into two parts, which treated the morals (*mores*) of Chrysoloras and his native genius (*ingenium*). Although speaking to patricians in Venice, he still characterized nobility primarily as a function of virtue expressed in public commitment. He used the section on morals to depict Roman qualities of Chrysoloras, deriving his notions largely from Cicero's *De senectute* and *De amicitia*. When he presented the philosophic side of his subject's genius, he emphasized the Greek heritage. Chrysoloras had incarnated in the fifteenth century the talents of famous philosophers and orators from ancient Athens. The two currents, nobility and philosophy, morals and genius, Roman and Greek, had fused in his career as a humanist educator.

The Venetian orator reminded his audience that they had gathered to honor a public hero. Antiquity would have considered Chrysoloras worthy of a state funeral and a place among the blessed. He had died while attending the Council of Constance. He had faced the hazards of the journey there in order to do all that he could to heal the schism within the Latin Church and that between Latins and Greeks. He had given his life for typical humanist values of unity, harmony, and reform. His death was the culmination of a life dedicated to public service.[5] Giuliano's portrait of Chrysoloras advocated many of humanism's religious and political ideals.

Giuliano asserted that Chrysoloras was incorruptible and without avarice. When sent by the Byzantine emperor to raise funds for the defense of Constantinople, he had persuaded Western rulers to donate and scrupulously handed over their contributions. Moreover, he had rejected lucrative offers to serve other governments. Chrysoloras also embodied the clemency and humanity required of a good official. Rather than seek revenge on jealous courtiers who had slandered him before the emperor, he had protected them from punishment. He had lived the virtues of generosity, loyalty, mercy, and love with Platonic altruism because he assisted family, friends, and fellow citizens.[6]

Chrysoloras had committed himself to learn in order to develop his native genius. Giuliano presented him as the ideal product of an education in "the liberal arts and philosophy." He had mastered natural philosophy, metaphysics, and sacred letters. He had also acquired eloquence. The garden in his home at Constantinople testified to his knowledge of agriculture, which Cato had described as the ideal pursuit of a wise man. Giuliano summarized the breadth of Chrysoloras' learning by suggesting that his death might well end the tradition of Greek philosophy. Chrysoloras "re-presented" the wisdom of Socrates, the divine genius of Plato, the passionate curiosity of Aristotle, and the eloquence of Demosthenes.[7]

Chrysoloras' dedication to learning as an adolescent led Giuliano to affirm that his life had been a mirror of good and holy living.[8] With apparently no knowledge of Chrysoloras' adolescence, the orator created it on the basis of passages in Cicero's *De senectute*. Cato had emphasized in that dialogue that he admired an old person, who had developed moral habits during adolescence. Cato reminded his Roman audience that unrestrained desire was the chief vice of adolescence. Giuliano claimed that Chrysoloras had struggled as an adolescent against libidinous desires and avarice, the unrestrained passions of body and soul. His learning and way of living had made him a philosopher at an earlier age than Plato or Aristotle.[9]

This solid grounding had carried over into Chrysoloras' career as an educator. His sense of service drove him to learn Latin as an adult. Only through knowledge of that language could he impart his native culture to the Latin world. Chrysoloras taught Greek letters to clarify Latin literature and to save Greek culture from extinction, to which the indifference of the Greeks and the advance of the Turks had apparently doomed it.[10] The words that Giuliano chose to describe this achievement reveal a number of suppositions held by humanist educators.

By teaching Greek, Chrysoloras had sought to enlarge (*propaganda*) and conserve (*conservanda*) culture. Greek learning was a worthy complement to the literature of Roman antiquity. Knowledge expanded through its recovery. The emphasis upon recovery and conservation reveals the classicist strain within the culture of humanism. The great thoughts had been thought. They came to life in the great deeds recorded by authors like Plato, Plutarch, and Demosthenes.[11]

Finally, Giuliano's language showed that humanists set as their goal the formation of character. Chrysoloras had taught good letters, the best arts, and virtues. Guarino, his student and Giuliano's mentor, had acquired from Chrysoloras learning (*doctrina*) and good morals (*mores*). Generally characterizing Chrysoloras' students, Giuliano described them as learned (*periti*) and good (*boni*).¹² The Greek pedagogue had trained many orators who met the standards proposed by Cato. That seems appropriate given that Cato was the protagonist of the *De senectute*, the dialogue that inspired much of Giuliano's speech.

Important strands come together in Giuliano's portrait of Chrysoloras. The learned Greek had served his Byzantine homeland and worked to reform the Church. Basic concerns of Italian humanists had merged in the life of this man, their first master of Greek. Much of humanist public oratory advertised a program of learning in the humanities. Orators fastened on the praise of humanist educators to accomplish that purpose.

The perception of Chrysoloras' impact upon humanism grew during the Quattrocento. Forty years later Guarino began to collect an anthology of works as a memorial tribute to the Byzantine instructor. He wrote to Poggio Bracciolini to request that Poggio send him a copy of his funeral oration for Chrysoloras.¹³ Poggio responded that he had intended to write a panegyric for Chrysoloras but had been stopped by Cencio Rustici, a Roman humanist. He admitted that he would have preferred to praise Chrysoloras rather than Cardinal Francesco Zabarella and outlined for Guarino the possibilities that the funeral eulogy offered.

Because Chrysoloras was a Greek from Constantinople, the topos of birthplace could be developed in many ways. For the main theme, Poggio proposed the classic conjunction of the subject's learning (*doctrina*) with his virtue (*virtus*), honest morals (*mores probatissimi*), and chaste life (*castissima vita*). He should be portrayed as a humanist educator, who had a positive effect (*utilitas*) upon learning. Before his arrival Latin letters were mute and enfeebled and Greek letters unknown. Poggio would have shown that Chrysoloras had changed that situation by his eloquence.¹⁴ Humanists wanted letters to speak again. Poggio's imagined oration indicates that themes originally stated by Giuliano remained popular among Quattrocento humanists.

Chrysoloras' teaching in Italy affected the practice of oratory. Humanists publicized their program by taking advantage of the renaissance that Greek learning represented. The career and funeral of Leonardo Bruni demonstrate that humanists transformed oratory and that they used Greek culture as the primary symbol of a renaissance.

When Florence was threatened by Giangaleazzo Visconti, Bruni used his knowledge of Greek to craft a panegyric of Florence modeled upon the *Panathenaicus* of Aelius Aristides. His studies with Chrysoloras had equipped him with facility in epideictic oratory and familiarized him with new sources. He had adapted the Athenian political ideals presented in epideictic orations to fit the historical situation in Florence. Humanists practiced imitation creatively.[15]

After Giangaleazzo's sudden death in 1402, Bruni's primary concerns began to shift away from politics to the cultural program of humanism and to stable employment. When humanism was attacked by clerics like Giovanni da San Miniato and Giovanni Dominici, he translated the letter of Saint Basil in favor of pagan learning. He dedicated the translation to Coluccio Salutati, the object of Dominici's censure. Salutati, now late in life, had apparently become more apprehensive about the merits of studying pagan authors. Bruni showed no such hesitation and openly stated the apologetic character of his translation. Basil's letter would serve the cause of the humanities by revealing the ignorance and perversity of their detractors.[16]

Bruni also translated Plato's *Phaedo* at that time and dedicated the translation to Pope Innocent VII; he hoped to win employment in the papal chancery. If the letter of Basil defended the worth of pagan learning for believers, the *Phaedo*, according to Bruni a dialogue on "the immortality of the soul," went a step further. Bruni explained to Innocent, the chief pastor of souls, that Plato's dialogue confirmed the teaching of the true faith. Using technical language derived from Cicero, he noted the accord (*convenientia*) between Greek and Christian doctrine on crucial issues like the soul's immortality.[17] In this Bruni typified the mentality of Italian humanists. They sought to recover lost sources—Latin, Greek, Hermetic, Jewish—and to show the convergence between those recovered doctrines and the Christian faith. Harmony and order should reign in the academic world as in society.

Bruni made his message public in what was apparently the first speech he actually delivered. He gave a funeral oration for Otto Cavalcanti, a nephew of Cardinal Angelo Acciaiuoli, before the papal court at Viterbo in 1405. The oration was brief, roughly composed, and had an abrupt ending, but it became quite popular.[18] Bruni structured the heart of the oration as an *a fortiori* argument. He granted that Otto had possessed good health, beauty, and riches, which he honestly inherited from his family. He noted that Plato had agreed with earlier thinkers who had characterized these as the highest human goods, in their banquet poems. However, Bruni himself ranked the gifts of virtue that God had bestowed on Otto higher on his scale.[19]

Bruni wondered whether the Greeks had mistakenly evaluated human goods because they drank too much wine at their banquets. The short oration offered humanists a strategy for confronting objections to their program of learning. By using *a fortiori* logic, they could affirm the value of pagan learning and protect the superiority of the Christian. Bruni brought that conviction before the Church's leadership at a moment when humanism was under attack by respected clerics. The teaching of Manuel Chrysoloras had opened new fields to humanists, and they welcomed a challenge to defend their acquisitions before hesitant contemporaries.

Bruni's own funeral in 1444 provides evidence of Chrysoloras' lasting place in humanist propaganda for the humanities. Funeral eulogists filled in a picture of Bruni's life that he himself had sketched in his "journal" on his times. Bruni revealed that Petrarch had first kindled his interest in the humanities. The sight of Petrarch's portrait in the castle of Quarrata had inflamed him with love for literary studies.[20] His conversion, however, was not yet complete. Only under the influence of Manuel Chrysoloras had he abandoned the study of law to pursue the humanities.

The genealogy makes good sense. Many humanists of the Quattrocento traced the revival of learning in their day to Petrarch.[21]

What is somewhat surprising is that this chain of learning omits any mention of Coluccio Salutati. Neither Bruni nor his eulogists adverted to Salutati's role in inspiring a circle of Florentine scholars to pursue the humanities. Chrysoloras received full credit for turning Bruni's interest from law to letters.[22]

In fact, Salutati is only mentioned prominently in the oration that Poggio wrote for Niccolò Niccoli. Poggio described Salutati as a person of integrity and learning, who joined with Niccoli to sponsor Chrysoloras' teaching in Florence. Even Poggio tended to reappraise Salutati's role: he had helped to inspire learning in Florence, but only after Luigi Marsili had begun the rebirth. Moreover, Poggio gave Niccoli ultimate credit for leading Greek letters back to Italy, because he had paid the lion's share of the bills.[23]

By 1440, humanist funeral orators assigned Salutati a reduced role in the revival of learning. The Florentine intellectual context may have influenced this stance. Bruni had composed his memoirs while a council met at Florence and succeeded briefly in reuniting the Latin and Greek churches. He died just a few years after the council ended. Enthusiasm for Greek letters, first stirred by Chrysoloras some forty years before, flourished again in Italy under the impact of the council and the Byzantine scholars who came in its wake. In addition, the Greek language and its literature provided a basis for humanist claims that their learning was reborn after centuries of neglect. Funeral eulogists designed their praise of Bruni and Chrysoloras to demonstrate their roles in that rebirth.

Poggio declared that thanks to Chrysoloras "those ancient times in which eloquence flourished in conjunction with wisdom seem to be renewed in our era." Chrysoloras had logically spurred a rebirth because, Poggio claimed, he surpassed all the Greeks in wisdom and eloquence.[24] Florentine eulogists tended to reduce Greek learning to Ciceronian ideals. Though humanists paid lip service to all Greek learning, they focused particularly upon its rhetorical side.

If Chrysoloras had stirred the revival of eloquence and wisdom, Bruni assured that it continued. An anonymous orator attributed four significant revivals to Bruni's scholarship. First, through translations of Greek works on ethics, Bruni had revitalized the central discipline of philosophy. Secondly, he had reawakened appreciation among Florentines for their own history through his research and writings. And, in a dual achievement, he had contributed to the recovery of Greek letters and Latin eloquence, which had vanished during the barbarian invasions some eight hundred years earlier.[25] Ethics, history, and eloquence prospered once again.

Bruni's scholarly achievements were legendary in their own time. Renaissance funeral orators structured their praise for his writings to uphold the worth of the *studia humanitatis*. Their portrayals suggested the comprehensive nature of his scholarship and of the program of learning that had inspired him. Giannozzo Manetti alleged that Bruni had accomplished more in history than Livy and more in oratory than Cicero. The golden age of Latin culture lived again on the Arno's banks. Poggio classified Bruni's *Dialogi ad Petrum Histrum* as a piece of epideictic prose in praise of Dante, Petrarch, and Boccaccio and explained the criticism of those poets in Book 1, so puzzling to interpreters, as simply a means to heighten the panegyric of Book 2.[26]

Orators also sought to demonstrate the creative character of Bruni's translations from the Greek.[27] All three of his eulogists emphasized the works that he had chosen to translate, his motives, and the rebirth they effected. They propagated a special myth related to Bruni's translations of Aristotle. The anonymous orator remarked that all the works that Bruni had translated from Greek had dealt with ethics, the humanist branch of philosophy.[28] Manetti and Poggio specifically named Aristotle's *Ethics, Politics,* and *Economics,* his civic corpus.

The orators still needed to explain why Bruni had bothered to translate works that had already been translated. His eulogists berated medieval translators for stripping the texts of Aristotle of the eloquence they had originally possessed.[29] Bruni's translations restored that eloquence. Renaissance scholars could now understand why Cicero had spoken of the Stagirite's artful prose. By combining philological and rhetorical skills, Bruni had succeeded where others had failed. Humanists advertised their translations as products of scholarship and eloquence.[30]

A conscious sense of rebirth was not the only construct that informed eulogies for Bruni. His anonymous panegyrist used four categories to present Bruni's writings. The first group were works that introduced the liberal arts and delineated proper conduct. Into this prescriptive category the eulogist placed writings like the *De interpretatione recta* and the *Isagogicon moralis disciplinae*. The second cluster was historical. Those writings assured that posterity would have examples of moral living in addition to rules. Bruni's oratorical works as chancellor of Florence comprised a third major category. The works that were left were lumped by the eulogist into an eclectic grouping that he called "domestic."[31]

The first three of these categories paralleled the three disciplines—ethics, history, and eloquence—that Pier Paolo Vergerio (the elder) had called essential to an education for public service. This subcurriculum among the liberal arts is recognized as one of the creative features of Vergerio's treatise, the *De ingenuis moribus* (ca. 1402). Bruni's eulogist organized his praise of Bruni's writings to press the study of those same disciplines. Early in the sixteenth century the Venetian orator Giovanni Quirini repeated that history and moral philosophy were essential for liberal minds engaged in public affairs.[32] Humanists hammered away at the need to relate education to public service.

In the arc of time from Petrarch's death to that of Leonardo Bruni, humanist eulogists noted that teachers dedicated to the humanities had raised key educational questions and provided alternatives to the existing curricula. They articulated a clear vision of the product of their education, an individual of excellent character. They insisted upon a tie between the learner and his life. Knowledge should not be pursued for its own sake but must be relevant to the art of good and holy living. Irenic ideals encouraged humanists to investigate sources from all ancient cultures. A classicist mentality dictated that truth be recovered, not discovered. Though humanists acknowledged that many arts were liberal, they especially valued disciplines useful in public life.

In essence humanists proposed a vision of education that was total and integrating. They presented that vision in further eulogies for humanists by celebrating the quality of their teaching, the number and skills of their students, and their contributions to textual scholarship. They suggested an educative function for environments other than the school, and they consistently emphasized the moral import of all of this activity. The orators believed that humanist education served the commonwealth because it fostered an attitude of public commitment. Humanists praised teachers who sought to aid the common utility.[33]

In an oration for Gasparino Barzizza written in 1430, Cabrino Cabrini assembled a group of authorities to demonstrate the public value of a humanist education. Cabrini mixed passages from the biblical books of Ecclesiasticus (10:3) and Proverbs (11:10) with citations from Cassiodorus and the code of Justinian. The authors of those works shared a conviction that city-states grow and prosper under the guidance of the righteous.[34] Cabrini, a young student at the time, had progressed little beyond standard medieval authorities, but he did prize the art of governing and tied it to a program of education that produced good persons.

Later Renaissance eulogists adopted Roman positions to define the social utility of a liberal education. They argued that humanist educators reincarnated the essence of Roman orators, who were no less teachers of life than authorities in speaking. Their successful students would be learned in speaking and virtuous, like the ideal Roman orator.[35] Among the primary manifestations of virtue should be a concern for the effect that oratory had upon an audience. Like Cicero, Renaissance orators feared the manipulative potential of oratory. Eulogists emphasized that humanists designed an educational program to develop eloquence and wisdom.[36]

The orators argued that the eloquence, which they taught, would be a civilizing force that knit society together. They took Cicero seriously when he said that eloquence should function as an ally of peace and a building block in the construction of a harmonious commonwealth.[37] Eloquence had the power to persuade. Orators believed that their eulogies would win students to the humanities. They remembered Chrysoloras, who had convinced Bruni to abandon law.

By insisting that their education inculcate a skill, eloquence, humanists tied their grand vision to earth. Clear speaking promoted clear thinking. Several orators attributed a metaphorical "river of eloquence" to their subjects, borrowing a phrase that Cicero coined to evoke the force of artful speech. Poggio extolled Francesco Zabarella, who combined copiousness with serious opinions even when he spoke extemporaneously.[38] Historians today would probably agree that much oratory from the Italian Renaissance was distinguished for "abundance of words." By insisting that *copia* be joined with *gravitas*, eulogists indicated their concern for how a speech was stylistically embellished and for what it argued.

Italian humanists betrayed their appropriation of classical rhetoric in the ways that they described a subject's eloquence. Eloquent orators rightly adapted the tone of a speech to its purpose, proving their sense of decorum. For example, Niccolò Lucaro was said to be good-natured (*facilis*) when persuading, generous (*copiosus*) with praise, and bitter (*acerbus*) in his invectives. He also artfully employed each of the three kinds of style—plain, middle, and grand.

Funeral orators tried to evoke images of individuals actually delivering a speech. Their descriptions advocated certain applications of the rules of style. Gian Giacomo Crotti stated that Niccolò Lucaro was skillful in adapting himself to his material, using long periods and arousing various emotions in his listeners. Crotti compared his polished delivery to that of Roman orators like Gaius Gracchus, Lucius Licinius Crassus, and Hortensius. Giasone del Maino maintained in similar fashion that Girolamo Torti had adjusted his style to suit the moment of his discourse, using a plain style in the exordium and grand style in the peroration. Torti's intuitions led him to thunder out when his material called for dramatic pronouncements. He also used lengthy periods that he managed to rattle off in a single breath.

Such oratory supposedly permitted orators to capture the attention of their audiences and hold it for long blocks of time. Giannantonio Campano claimed that his three-hour introductory lecture for a course at the University of Perugia had mesmerized his listeners.

Bernardo Giustiniani went on for four full hours in praise of Doge Francesco Foscari. Even those feats pale before the ability of Giannozzo Manetti, whose oration to Alfonso I of Naples was so eloquent that the king sat through it without bothering to chase away a fly that had landed on his nose.[39]

Humanists praised humanists, furthermore, for the breadth of their oratory, their capacity to use all three kinds of style and to speak in all three rhetorical genres. Such commendation fits the humanist penchant for eclecticism, but it seems to ignore the status of oratory in that era. Pier Paolo Vergerio lamented at the beginning of the Quattrocento that courtroom procedures eliminated the need for judicial oratory. That situation did not change during the Renaissance. Humanists have left very few judicial orations. Deliberative oratory was restricted in practice to diplomacy and colored heavily by epideictic, the Renaissance's leading genre. Vergerio himself observed that oratory in his day was overwhelmingly epideictic.

Practice began to have its effect upon theory. A rhetorical handbook like Lorenzo Traversagni's *Epitome Margaritae eloquentiae* (1478) eliminated all discussion of stasis theory, which defined categories to assist orators when preparing a judicial speech. Another Renaissance treatise on the three rhetorical genres, now preserved in a manuscript at Basel, inverts classical teaching by emphasizing epideictic rhetoric over the other two genres. By the late sixteenth century Marc Antoine Muret, a leading theoretician of rhetoric, complained about the stranglehold that epideictic oratory had exercised over public speaking for so long.

Lorenzo Valla even tied this preference for the genre of praise and blame to an epistemology that emphasized the subjective dimension of truth. He felt that the human person was motivated by a desire to love. Consequently, that type of rhetoric best persuaded, which appealed to the primary human affection.[40] Renaissance orators especially relied upon vivid description to arouse the affections. Funeral orators in turn praised persons who practiced ecphrasis adeptly. Giannantonio Campano recalled that Enea Silvio Piccolomini had sought to gain support for a crusade by providing a dire picture of the consequences of Turkish victory. Convinced that people acted on what they saw, humanists used their rhetoric to exploit the convincing power of the visual.[41]

The orators consistently advocated broad learning across a spectrum of studies, of oratorical genres, or of writings. Celio Calcagnini commended Ercole Strozzi because he had excelled in judicial, deliberative, and epideictic oratory and because he had handled all the genres of poetry with equal ability. From one perspective, his association of oratory with poetry is not surprising. Before the term *humanista* was coined in the Quattrocento, a humanist was normally described as an "orator and poet." Macrobius had described Virgil in that way in his fifth-century commentary (*Saturnalia*), and the combination was used in Italy at least from the time of Petrarch.[42]

From another perspective, however, the joining of orator and poet seems less appropriate. The two vocations were carried on in different settings. To describe his longing for Vaucluse, Petrarch scratched the phrase "my most pleasant solitude" in the margin of a codex of Pliny. He captured the poet's need to work alone in peace.[43] Orators practiced their vocation in the public squares of a city. Typical of their mode of praise, humanists again blended distinct ways of life.

The Florentine government attempted to give a special character to the funerals of its humanist employees by adding a posthumous crowning with laurel. Petrarch had revitalized the award by organizing his own crowning on the Capitoline Hill in 1341. Florentine humanists like Salutati, Bruni, and Palmieri were all crowned at their funerals.[44] The tribute created awkward moments for their eulogists, for those men were not exclusively nor primarily poets. Giannozzo Manetti spoke at length on the historical origins of the custom and its justification in the case of Leonardo Bruni.

At the end of his digression, Manetti admitted that Bruni was more renowned as an orator and historian than a poet. He cited two passages from Cicero's *De oratore* that represented the orator and poet as next of kin. He also contended that Bruni had been preparing to publish his own poetry, as well as commentaries on that of the ancients, just before he died. Manetti then crowned Bruni with laurel, an act immortalized in Rossellino's tomb sculpture.[45] Florence's effort to create a tribute for its humanists, like that of naming a politician "father of the country," stirred little or no enthusiasm outside of Tuscany. Humanists in government had little time or quiet to write verse.

Humanists trained eloquent students. They also sought to develop excellence of character. The virtuous lives of teachers and students of the humanities proved their value. Those persons were good because they had studied the good arts. Virtually every oration for a humanist sought to portray the tie between learning and virtue. Poggio wove the principle through his oration for Niccolò Niccoli. In the exordium he referred to Niccoli's integrity, which had flowed from his study of sacred letters and the humanities.[46] Niccoli had chosen an education in the *studia humanitatis* despite his father's wish that he go into business, believing that literary studies alone indicated the path to virtue and curbed vice.[47]

Good letters had taught Niccoli how to conduct his life. He had sought to conform his behavior to the morals of those whose virtue was praised. He had used every means at his disposal—books, exhortations, money—to foster the pursuit of the new learning, and he had employed the epideictic skills of praise and blame to improve the practice of oratory in his day.[48] The humanist preference for epideictic rhetoric guided Poggio's presentation. He praised Niccoli's humanist learning and virtue to animate his listeners. His praise for Niccoli's virtue should inspire them just as praise had inspired Niccoli.

Orators substantiated the success of the humanist program in several ways. They pointed to the diffusion of their program throughout the peninsula. Humanist grammarians offered a preparatory education to students in many places. Small cities like Lucca and San Gimignano had awarded public funerals and the laurel crown to their local grammarians, Gian Pietro d'Avenza (d. 1457) and Mattia Lupi (d. 1468). Their instruction relied upon unglamorous methods like rote memory and repetition. Still, humanist orators insisted, even such rudimentary training could stir one to practice charity and humanity.[49]

Francesco Cleofilo gave a marked Florentine tone to his eulogy for Antonio Costanzi at Fano in 1502. He celebrated Costanzi's opposition to Malatesta tyranny and his defense of liberty. Cleofilo thus revived ideals first proposed by Leonardo Bruni to rally support against Visconti aggression. He pronounced them for citizens of Fano, a small city within the Papal State, during the pontificate of Alexander VI and may have been criticizing the aggrandizing actions of Alexander's son, Cesare.

In treating his subject's teaching career, Cleofilo emphasized that out of devotion to his homeland Costanzi had spurned lucrative offers to lecture elsewhere. Teachers of any era would probably admire Costanzi's ability to motivate his students. Cleofilo said that they were so eager to learn that they spent their holidays in study. Costanzi first introduced his pupils to Latin grammar, then taught them the poets, historians, and orators, and completed his instruction with Greek, which he viewed as a tool to help them understand Latin literature. Cleofilo noted that Costanzi had conceived the training as preparation for university studies. The curriculum that he taught fits fairly neatly into the generic plan of the *studia humanitatis*, and it reflects the foundational nature of that schooling.[50]

Funeral speakers also pointed to the numbers of learned and good students who issued from the schools of humanist educators. Those educators trained many of society's key public figures, the clerics, lawyers, philosophers, theologians, secretaries, poets, and orators of the state. Ludovico Carbone named many of Guarino's students, who came from all over the world. (His thoroughness has been a help to historians, but one wonders if his Ferrarese audience appreciated it.) Bartolomeo Pagello remarked that Ognibene Bonisoli had taught Latin and Greek letters so effectively that many Greeks came to study their language and Latin under his tutelage.[51] Italians of the Renaissance viewed themselves as exercising a cultural hegemony over Greece that Greece itself had exercised in Roman times.

Such vast numbers of students suggested a comparison to one of antiquity's greatest pedagogues. In the *De oratore* (2.22.94) Cicero had asserted that leaders poured out of the school of Isocrates as they had from the Trojan horse. In a eulogy for the Roman humanist Pomponio Leto, Pietro Marsi attributed great influence to the model of Isocrates. Leto had produced quantities of learned students like Isocrates, and like Isocrates he had taught them to live and speak well. He had worked to rid the Latin language of barbarisms and restore it to its pristine dignity.[52] Leto was thus another Isocrates in his success, his ethical example, and his concern for prose style.

The figure of Isocrates became increasingly important for Italian humanists as his works became known. Whether mediated through Cicero or adopted through direct contact, Isocrates reinforced many of the fundamental ideals of Italian humanism. Isocrates had stressed the importance of ethos, described virtue as humanity's most cherished possession, and fixed right conduct as the goal of education. And he himself had stated that he was the first person to praise a deceased individual in prose.[53]

The parallel spilled over into the political sphere. Although historians have noted that Isocrates did not consistently advocate one form of government, he was more consistent on global issues. He often urged a pan-Hellenic alliance to arrest the advance of the Persians from the East; the scandalous, internecine warfare among Greeks threatened the existence of the civilized world. Italian humanists admired that political stance and adapted it for their own times. They saw a parallel between the situation in their day and that of Isocrates. Barbarian hordes from the East again threatened civilized society. They censured fighting among Christian princes and urged a pan-Christian alliance against the Turks. Italian humanists were cultural elitists like Isocrates, arrogating to themselves the leadership of the civilized world. They shied away from overly defined ideologies.

As proof of their success, humanists adduced the way that they were patronized. These disciples of the Muses rarely missed a chance to remind their Apollos of the services they performed. In a eulogy for Leonello d'Este, Guarino portrayed court patronage as mutually advantageous. Humanists received their livelihood; the prince wisely patronized teachers of a curriculum that incited his citizens to virtue, and he received a pool of talented writers ready to immortalize his great deeds. Humanists at times used the public forum to complain that their salaries did not reflect their social worth. Battista Casali lamented that professors at the Roman *studium* had to battle to obtain a just wage. Payment to those professors was delayed at times because the popes used revenues assigned to the university to cover the building program—which the same humanists frequently praised.[54]

Humanists felt that their schools were important, but they never reduced education to schooling. They related education to the total environment and held that values were best appropriated in good company and conversation. Students and teachers were extolled for their willingness to travel in order to learn.[55] When properly decorated, a humanist's home contributed to the advance of learning. Pietro Marsi spoke of the sober modesty of Pomponio Leto's house in Rome. It visibly contrasted with the ostentation of neighboring palaces and mirrored the modest person who lived there. In fact, Leto's behavior was so temperate as to border on the bizarre. His shabby dress and reclusiveness led contemporaries to nickname him Rome's latest ghost.[56]

Poggio noted that Niccolò Niccoli's house contained many Latin and Greek books, portraits of scholars from antiquity, and a collection of coins. Niccoli had chosen the decorations to incite his visitors to pursue virtue and to master the liberal arts. Battista Casali similarly reminded his Roman audience that Domenico Grimani had collected antique statues and coins and rewarded others who did so. Those artifacts had provided a silent stimulus to the pursuit of virtue, much like the reading of history.[57]

Niccolò Lucaro treated his dinner guests to learned conversations that were stimulated by readings from the wise men of antiquity. Such learned discussions at a humanist's table are reminiscent of the godly feasts so often extolled in eulogies for Renaissance prelates.[58] The refinement of feeling, taste, and intellect in that environment mirrored and fostered the product that a humanist education looked to produce.

The emphasis on the humanist's home functions as a reminder of the institutional matrix of humanism in the Italian Renaissance. Though some obtained university chairs, humanists did not displace the Aristotelian curriculum of the universities in Italy. Many taught in their own homes. They also held classes in religious convents or at the courts, where they sometimes combined secretarial and educational responsibilities. They transformed domestic environments into academies by their learned discussion.[59]

Finally, praise for the humanist contribution to learning in the Renaissance was not restricted to the task of teaching. Orators celebrated the nature and breadth of humanist scholarship and often cited particular writings that showed a scholar's ability in the humanities. Eulogists praised grammatical primers and commentaries on classical texts, works of poetry, histories, and dialogues and treatises related to the conduct of a good and holy life. The list of a subject's works often culminated with praise for his orations and letters, the two humanist products where classical rhetoric exercised most influence. They occupied the highest position in the creative hierarchy and comprise the most numerous works of humanist prose that have survived from the Renaissance.[60]

Alberto da Castelfranco mentioned the Greek grammar that Urbano Bolzanio had written. Anyone who desired to learn Greek, Alberto asserted, need only follow the Franciscan's precepts. Bolzanio was not be faulted for revising his work over the years, for Cicero, Hippocrates, and Augustine had likewise retouched their writings late in life. Grammatical manuals were primary tools of the humanist educator's trade.

Francesco Cleofilo praised Antonio Costanzi for writing a commentary on the *Fasti* of Ovid. Rather than rely on his own conjectures when seeking to explain a difficult passage, Costanzi had consulted the comments of earlier scholars. Cleofilo added a personal anecdote, recalling that Costanzi had written to him once at Rome to ask that he check some sources for him there. Costanzi's letter soliciting assistance represents a scholarly tradition familiar to all who do research in Italy's capital. The anecdote also says much about the nature of the commentary in the Renaissance as a cumulative and rather conservative type of scholarship.[61] Information was collected and stored.

Alamanno Rinuccini praised the overtly Platonizing theme of Matteo Palmieri's poem *La città di vita*, which described the journey made by the soul after it was freed from the weight of its earthly body. The soul wandered to a variety of places until it reached its true home and partook of "beatitude for eternity" (Cic. *Rep.* 6.13.13). Rinuccini's commendation again reveals how irenic humanism tended to be; the poem that he chose to praise publicly had come under suspicion as heretical. Similarly, in order to convince an audience in Ragusa that Ioannes Gotius wrote excellent verse, Elio Lampridio Cerva quoted a letter from Poliziano, who praised that poetry.[62] The republic of letters had spread from Italy to Dalmatia.

Humanists praised the writings of other humanists both as supports for their educational program and as its expressions. Grammatical manuals were essential tools of the trade. Without sound knowledge of the classical languages, one could not study good letters or learn to speak eloquently. Commentaries on texts applied philological and historical criticism to aid understanding. Humanists were aware of the risks in such academic ventures, especially that they become purely academic. Giannozzo Manetti spoke derisively of "the grammarians" who battled endlessly over Seneca's authorship of the *Tragedies*. Scholarship should be relevant to life's pursuits.[63] Ironically, though humanism inculcated appreciation for literature, its adherents produced few great literary works during the Renaissance.

Orators also commemorated all the ways in which humanists recovered learning in their epoch. Funeral orators applauded the search for codices of lost ancient works and the attempt to make those resources available to a wider public. Humanists promoted the expansion of knowledge in the Renaissance. Poggio described Niccolò Niccoli's efforts to acquire codices from all over Europe, as well as his role in inspiring Poggio to undertake the same search. Niccoli criticized persons who hoarded or hid books, because books were written for the common utility.

Eulogists for Nicholas V noted that the former librarian had rummaged through dusty old chests in the hopes of discovering an unknown codex. Nicholas had indeed collected some six hundred tomes of value to scholars in his day—robbing Greece, Niccolò Palmeri confessed, to enrich Italy. Alberto da Castelfranco described the scholarly pilgrimage that Urbano Bolzanio had made to Greece in search of manuscripts, and Battista Casali emphasized that Domenico Grimani had sold some precious possessions in order to purchase the works of Pico della Mirandola.[64]

Italian humanists and patrons of humanism, therefore, performed a vital service by collecting ancient works. As funeral orators pointed out, such persons made an even greater contribution by placing their treasures at the disposition of scholars. Poggio proclaimed that Niccolò Niccoli's bequest of his manuscripts to form the core of a "public library" comprised a new public service, one that continued to assist Florentines even after his death.

Poggio contrasted Niccoli's action to what his learned Florentine predecessors had done.[65] Petrarch's library had been dispersed among many persons after his death. The volumes collected by Boccaccio and Luigi Marsili had been given to the Augustinian library of Santo Spirito for the private use of the friars. Worse yet, the sons of Coluccio Salutati had sold off most of the valuable codices that the chancellor had accumulated during his lifetime. Poggio himself had tried to get his hands on Salutati's books immediately after the chancellor's death. Only Niccoli had consigned his eight hundred volumes for public use. Those eager to learn would always have access to them.

The library functions as a visible symbol of the humanist approach to truth. Humanists sought to recover and collect knowledge. Facts and information were stored for use as ornamentation or as examples to illustrate virtue. Investigations of humanist libraries by contemporary scholars have opened up the world of those learned individuals.[66] Yet the humanist approach to knowledge, that of the collector who preserves, could dull a sense of exploration and discovery in the learning process.

Although humanism represents the most pervasive intellectual movement of the Italian Renaissance, it cannot be equated with the thought of the period. Humanism did not displace Aristotelian currents and methods in the Italian universities of the Quattrocento. Moreover, thinkers like Nicholas of Cusa and Marsilio Ficino promoted a revival of Platonic and Neoplatonic doctrine, which constituted yet a third major thread in the tapestry of Renaissance thought.

Funeral eulogies from the Italian Renaissance reflect the diversity of that scholarly world.

The scholastic logician and theologian Paolo Veneto (d. 1429), medical doctors and professors from the University of Padua like Iacopo da Forlì (d. 1414) and Girolamo della Torre (d. 1506), and the Italian humanist and mathematician Giorgio Valla (d. 1500) all received public funerals.[67] Eulogies for those academics demonstrate an appreciation for their intellectual achievement on its own terms. The orators accordingly paid tribute to scholastic methods of lecturing and disputing and to their concomitant literary genres of the commentary and question.

The same eulogists nevertheless sought to foster influences that humanism might have upon other currents of thought. They invariably adverted to a subject's training in the humanities as a foundation for more specialized studies. They also called attention to new texts, in various disciplines, that had been made available through the recovery of ancient codices and their translation from Greek. They ultimately stressed humanist goals by delineating the ethical responsibilities incumbent upon all the learned. Scholastic methods were tolerated if they led to moral living.

In eulogies for professors of philosophy, the portrait of the subject tended to reflect the emphases of the orator's own training. Cristoforo Barzizza, who had studied philosophy under the Augustinian Paolo Veneto at Padua and later taught medicine in the same university, rated Paolo's writings on dialectic superior to any from antiquity. He further claimed that his mentor's logical *Summa* would have earned him renown even in Ockham's England.[68] He appreciated Paolo's achievements in scholastic learning.

Orators who were practicing humanists portrayed philosophy in ways more consonant with their own program of learning. At times they used *philosophia* in a reductionist sense to mean ethics alone. Like Socrates, humanists felt that they were properly steering philosophy to focus upon human beings and their behavior. Like Cicero, they were eclectic in their approach to philosophy. The Florentine eulogist Francesco Cattani, who sought early in the sixteenth century to harmonize the thought of Plato and Aristotle, was continuing an intellectual tradition that can be traced back at least to the teaching of Giovanni Argyropulos. A faithful disciple of Ficino, however, Cattani sought to subordinate Aristotle to Plato.

When dealing with philosophy, humanist orators consistently sought to invert the educational traditions of their day and make logic subordinate to rhetoric. Truth must be elegant, persuasive, and relevant to the art of good and holy living. To place logic before rhetoric, as scholasticism had, generally led to a truth that was sterile, rigid, and irrelevant.[69]

Funeral eulogies also presented the graduate studies of law, medicine, and theology in two ways: some commended those studies on their own merits, others sought to push them in humanist directions. In eulogies for lawyers, humanists built their case for linking rhetoric and law on solid Ciceronian foundations. Cicero had been the first in educational history to argue that orators must be trained in law (*De or.* 1.36.165–46.203).

In the early Cinquecento, Sebastiano Sapia disagreed with those who argued that the Muses and jurisprudence were incompatible. The career of Giasone del Maino proved that they were wrong, for he had emerged from his studies as a most eloquent lawyer. Paolo Bigolini asserted that Battista Casali had studied jurisprudence only to improve his command of the art of speaking.[70] Dissatisfied that eloquence had been banished from the courtroom, humanist eulogists advocated its return. The general absence of judicial oratory from the period, however, suggests that they largely failed in that campaign.

Humanism was more successful in shaping the approach to legal scholarship and introducing historical philology as a tool in that study. In a eulogy for Antonio Roselli, Pietro Barozzi gave five reasons why the study of jurisprudence was more demanding in his day than it had been in antiquity.[71] First, legal scholars of the fifteenth century possessed the code of Justinian, unavailable to lawyers in Cicero's time. Secondly, a whole new corpus of legal doctrine had been added with the codification of canon law. The successful student in Barozzi's day, in contrast to his ancient predecessor, frequently became a "doctor of two laws." Barozzi's further reasons related to the textual and scholarly side of legal studies. Thirdly, he said, the scholarship of ancient lawyers had often reached Italians of the Quattrocento in a mutilated state. That scholarship, furthermore, was frequently written in a Latin corrupted by accretions from barbarian times. And, lastly, Renaissance students and professors of law had to wade through a mass of contradictory glosses on the canonical codes and assess their worth. Barozzi's five reasons pointed students of jurisprudence to their scholarly tasks. Humanists pressed for scholarship and teaching of law that would eliminate historical inaccuracies, purify the language, and harmonize discordant interpretations.

Eulogists granted that such goals could be achieved by scholastic methods. Giasone del Maino recalled that Girolamo Torti had used dialectic to construct his lectures, thus holding his students' attention as he moved through a series of divisions and distinctions. The material was easily retained due to the rational sequence of delivery, and his lectures helped to disentangle knotty legal problems. Sebastiano Sapia, Maino's eulogist, in turn claimed that Maino could maintain the attention of his students for periods of two hours.[72]

Lawyers were presented as working to achieve consensus in their written commentaries. Sebastiano Sapia complimented Maino for his legal writings because they unlocked seemingly insoluble dilemmas and eliminated the confusion and discord of previous interpreters. They also made for pleasant reading. Maino himself applauded the use of a humanist method of interpretation when he recalled that Girolamo Torti had refused to be satisfied with the literal sense of the legal code and searched diligently for its hidden nucleus. Torti's allegorizing method, Maino observed, contrasted with the general preference for literal interpretation among legal students.[73] Agostino Dati echoed a recurrent humanist theme when he noted that Mariano Sozzini's writings on jurisprudence were learned and urged students "to a virtuous way of life."[74]

The same values of scholarship were projected onto society when eulogists commended lawyers in action. Antonio Solerio described Pietro Canonici as a lover of peace and concord who had always referred the letter of the law to its informing spirit of equity and justice and always preferred to resolve controversies rather than encourage them.[75] Lawyers in the Renaissance were idealized as protectors and patrons of the underprivileged, men of integrity who could not be bribed and who were solely concerned with proving guilt or innocence. Legal training could also assist in settling political disputes. Like eloquence, law was a tool for diplomacy. Antonio Roselli supposedly mediated disputes between Ladislas of Poland and the emperor Sigismund, as well as between Sigismund and Pope Eugene IV. Orators suggested that law might regulate relations between states.[76]

Antonio Solerio paraphrased a popular maxim from Plato when he asserted that Pietro Canonici had moved from the study of letters to law because he believed that men were not born for themselves alone. Many eulogists shared this conception of law's public utility. In a eulogy for Francesco Zabarella in 1417, Poggio digressed from his praise of the cardinal in order to discuss the nature of jurisprudence. Using Cicero as his authority, he defined law as a bond that secures privileges and as the primary foundation of liberty in a commonwealth.[77] Eulogists praised Renaissance lawyers to corroborate that they converted law to society's needs. Law and rhetoric were allies in a campaign to create an ordered society.

In the fourteenth century humanists had debated the appropriateness of a link between rhetoric and medicine. Petrarch had objected when doctors encroached upon eloquence, but Coluccio Salutati had recommended that they pursue the art.[78] Most funeral orators agreed with Salutati. They praised doctors and medical professors who were models for their eloquence and their virtuous behavior.

In 1414 Gasparino Barzizza commended Iacopo da Forlì for using his talent and speaking ability to teach medicine. Two years later, Francesco Barbaro noted how difficult it was to judge whether the physician Giovanni Corradini was more learned in his eloquence or more eloquent in his learning. In the sixteenth century, Cristoforo Sassi maintained that Luca Alberto Podiani had contributed to the welfare of his state through his medical practice and his eloquence and counsel.[79]

To affirm the dignity of medicine, more than one eulogist referred to the myth that the founders of the discipline, Apollo and his son Asclepius, were divine.[80] Eulogists also traced the historical development of the discipline. Its Greek and medieval roots were honored when orators commended teachers for their lectures and disputations and scholars for their commentaries on Galen, Hippocrates, and Avicenna. They also claimed that medical educators in the Renaissance had equaled or surpassed the achievements of their Greek and Muslim forebears. Humanist concerns at times guided an orator's selection of a physician's qualities. Piero Valeriano stressed the humane way in which Girolamo della Torre had taught medicine at Padua, and Pietro Partenio highlighted the wit of the same professor's delivery.[81] Agostino Dati provided a list of erudite professors of medicine that culminated with two of his fellow Sienese, Ugo Benzi and Bartolo Bandini.[82]

In addition to their learning and eloquence, practitioners of medicine were commended for the quality of their lives. Agostino Dati explained to his Sienese audience that Bartolo Bandini felt that a doctor should combine contemplation with action. Proper praise for virtue derived from one's deeds. Elio Lampridio Cerva characterized virtue and wisdom as necessary complements to the medical skills that Andrea da Modena had acquired during his training. Giovanni Tortelli drew a parallel between medicine and moral philosophy. The former taught ways to heal the body; the latter disseminated principles for guiding the soul in the ways of virtue.[83]

Funeral orators also encouraged charitable activity when they described the work of physicians. Francesco Barbaro claimed that Giovanni Corradini had refused payment for his services; he called upon witnesses in Venice and throughout Italy to attest to the doctor's generosity. Ludovico Carbone similarly recounted that Giovanni Ercole had treated the poor without charging them and assumed the cost of their medicine.[84] For twenty years Niccolò Ricoveri had administered the hospital in Siena and used his post, Agostino Dati affirmed, to carry out the corporal works of mercy. Medicine became a prime field in which to practice the activist spirituality advocated by humanist orators. Pietro Partenio recalled that Antonio Fracanziani had sacrificed his own life to cure his mother; he contracted her ailment and died shortly after she recovered.[85]

Funeral orations for the theologians of the Italian Renaissance provide a sampling of the theological currents represented in Italy during the Quattrocento and early Cinquecento. Eulogies for theologians also recall the issues debated at that time and indicate a desire that humanism shape the "queen" of the arts and sciences. Orators were again at their eclectic best in recognizing and commending diverse theological currents.

Funeral speakers commemorated the assistance offered by their subjects in resolving theological controversies. Theologians succeeded when they combined a grasp of the Church's doctrine with eloquence. Niccolò Capranica celebrated Bessarion's efforts to reunite the Greek and Latin Churches at the Council of Florence. By his eloquence and wisdom Bessarion had moved the Greek delegation to accept a document proposed by the Latins as a basis for reconciliation. He had advocated its acceptance, however, only after all errors had been removed. Giacomo da Alessandria claimed that Fantino Valaresso had labored for the same goal of reunion in the field as he preached and disputed with Orthodox clergy during his tenure as archbishop of Crete.[86] Because it had realized ideals of peace and harmony among believers, humanist orators treated the Council of Florence as a paradigmatic event.

Humanists had little sympathy with doctrinal disputes, often taking refuge in a conception of truth as probable. The eloquence of a preacher like Mariano da Genazzano served the cause of conciliation and persuasion. Mariano had also explained obscure or disputed theological issues in his writings. Mariano's eulogist, Raffaele Brandolini, confessed that he could not prove the Augustinian's achievement because his writings had gone down with a ship en route to Naples. Traveling scholars may shudder to see one of their constant fears realized.[87]

The controversies of the sixteenth-century Reformation transformed a climate of relative doctrinal tolerance. The change is apparent in Giovanni Battista Flavi's eulogy of 1534 for the Dominican cardinal Cajetan. Flavi asserted that Cajetan had convinced Julius II to convoke a Church council. The cardinal also was chosen by Leo X to engage Luther in colloquy at Augsburg in 1518. Flavi speculated that Cajetan did not poison Luther on the spot for fear of making the Augustinian friar some sort of martyr and thereby increasing his celebrity. He also maintained that Cajetan himself had been banished to Hungary during the pontificate of Adrian VI because he had pressed for reform of practices like simony, pluralism, and trafficking in indulgences.[88]

Orators applauded the salutary effects that humanism had upon the study of theology in their day, particularly in spurring the development of a "sacred philology." Humanists challenged the monopoly that philosophy exercised over preparatory studies for theology and proposed that solid grounding in the biblical languages served a student of theology just as well.[89] Conradus Vegerius recalled that Adrian of Utrecht, the future Adrian VI, had established a college at Louvain for students who had an interest in "the study of sacred letters." Biblical studies undertaken according to humanism's philological and historical methods prospered at Louvain in the early sixteenth century. Thaddeus of Lyon commended Claude de Seyssel, archbishop of Turin, for acquiring an ancient style of theology based upon the Bible and Christian classics composed by the Latin fathers. Thaddeus complimented the archbishop in an Erasmian way for repudiating the contentious modern brand of theological learning.[90]

Given a context of praise, humanist orators rarely reduced the issue of proper method to rigid alternatives. Though some eulogists expressed a preference for a humanist style of theology, others demonstrated appreciation for aspects of the scholastic enterprise. For instance, they treated elements of Thomism positively. Giovanni Battista Flavi recalled that Cajetan's parents had introduced him as a boy to the clear thinking of Thomas Aquinas. The Dominican's commentaries on Aquinas had been written to demonstrate that Aquinas comprised a font of learning and to rebut his detractors. Humanist orators like Battista Mantovano objected to the overly systematic nature of Aquinas' theological corpus and his presumption of scientific demonstration of doctrine. They were, however, much in accord with the world-affirming character of his thought. Recent research has established that Rome was Europe's leading center for Thomism in the Renaissance.[91]

Funeral eulogists welcomed the introduction of new sources for theology and encouraged familiarity with as many traditional sources as possible. In the sixteenth century the Augustinian Giles of Viterbo created his own eclectic and at times bizarre brand of theology based upon Platonic, Neoplatonic, and Cabalistic sources. Lorenzo Grana noted Giles's propensity to rummage among unstudied source materials, recalling that he had paid dearly to study the Cabala, and claimed that those studies equipped him with arguments to convince the Jews of the truth of Christian doctrine.[92]

Pietro Rossi certainly pursued an eclectic theology. The Sienese professor sought to demonstrate that all of Aristotle's disciplines were found in Scripture. The books of Samuel, for instance, taught rhetoric equally as well as Aristotle's handbook did. In his eulogy, Agostino Dati alleged that Rossi had cited all the patristic and scholastic theologians of merit in his commentaries. He named many of these in his speech: Ambrose, Augustine, Jerome, Gregory the Great, Cyprian, Hilary, Bede, Isidore, and other Latins; Origen, Gregory of Nazianzus, John Chrysostom, pseudo-Dionysius, John of Damascus, and other Greeks; scholastics like Albert the Great, Aquinas, Bonaventure, Alexander of Hales, Franciscus de Mayronis, John Duns Scotus, Egidio Romano, Gregory of Siena, and Gregory of Rimini. Few could fault Rossi for lack of diligence, for Dati also contended that the professor had managed to comment on all the books of Scripture.[93]

By the sixteenth century this tendency to praise copiousness in learning reached new heights. It is as though funeral orators wished to show that their subjects had realized Cicero's ideal for the culture of the orator expressed in the *De oratore*. The scholars whom they eulogized seemed to have made all learning their province. The portrait of the humanist mathematician and natural scientist Giorgio Valla offered by Bartolomeo Zamberti exemplifies the trend toward praise for abundant learning.

Zamberti said that Valla had progressed from the study of the humanities to the disciplines of the quadrivium because he felt that, to be educated, one must know the causes of all things. He accordingly mastered mathematics, physics, and medicine and began a teaching career that took him from Genoa to Milan to Venice. Judging from Zamberti's list of his writings, Valla was prolific. The forty-eight books of his "encyclopedia" prove his concern for breadth. He also translated Greek works from a variety of disciplines. There were medical treatises by Alexander of Aphrodisias and Galen, works on natural science by Aristotle and others, treatises on the astrolabe and on mathematical and astronomical topics, works in a more humanist vein like Aristotle's *Ethics* and *Poetics*, and theological questions written by Eusebius. His endeavor presupposed thorough knowledge of Greek, which Valla had acquired under the tutelage of Constantine Lascaris.

We have come full cycle from our starting point with Manuel Chrysoloras. Greek sources continued to fuel the recovery of classical culture throughout the Italian Renaissance. Giorgio Valla was a teacher like Chrysoloras. He achieved lasting benefits through oratory. Zamberti stated that the Genoese had convinced Valla to teach there by offering him a healthy salary. Valla had succeeded in turning the citizens of Genoa from their obsession with commerce to zeal for the study of letters.[94] Valla had left a record of his humanist instruction when he wrote a handbook on rhetoric.

Funeral orators themselves made their voices heard in the new controversies that sprang up in the early sixteenth century. Celio Calcagnini dominated public oratory in Ferrara at that time. He also wrote treatises against Martin Luther and one that suggested that the earth rotated around the sun. As bishop of Padua, Pietro Barozzi became the center of a controversy about the immortality of the soul, then raging among professors at the university. His eulogist, Cristoforo Marcello, claimed that Barozzi had found enough time free from pastoral and doctrinal concerns to discover a way to square the circle. The danger, of course, from an educational standpoint was that persons who sought such breadth ended up as nothing more than dilettantes.[95]

The funerals of humanists in the Italian Renaissance afforded eulogists an important occasion to celebrate the deeds accomplished by fellow humanists and to promote an education in the humanities. Orators characterized the achievements of humanists according to a favorite construct of epideictic oratory. Humanists had effected a rebirth of the liberal arts, a rebirth of eloquence combined with wisdom, a rebirth of learning that engendered virtue. As the pervasive intellectual movement of its day, humanism was further credited with significant influence upon the nonhumanist disciplines. Social and religious ideals like harmony and concord should inform the entire world of learning.

Funeral orators ultimately directed their audiences' attention to the benefits that a humanist education produced for society. Students of the humanities should mirror the goodness of the arts that they studied. Humanists claimed to instill in their students consciousness of the civic world and a desire to make it better. In the ideal realm portrayed by funeral eulogists of the Italian Renaissance, humanist educators sought to train students who would commit themselves to serve the commonwealth. Those educators had to be persons of ethos. Uncommitted scholars pursuing irrelevant truths had no place in that realm.

CHAPTER SEVEN

ETHOS ENSHRINED

Like all celebratory rhetoric, funeral oratory helps to create and propagate historical myths. Renaissance eulogies confirm that particular personalities and events, many of which continue to be commemorated five centuries later, were famous in their own day. Funeral orators acclaimed Nicholas V as a pope of admirable foresight, who patronized the new learning and began in earnest the rebuilding of Rome, his image-laden see. Eulogists presented Cosimo and his Medici descendants as dedicated public servants and patrons par excellence of the revival of the liberal arts. When Florentine authorities posthumously conferred the title *pater patriae* upon Cosimo, they struck a responsive chord throughout the peninsula. Other Italian cities imitated Florence's example in reviving the Roman tribute. Niccolò Niccoli excited peculiar respect among his fellow citizens for inventing a way to be of service even after death: he left his books to Florence on the condition that they form the nucleus of the first public library.

Humanist funeral orators propagated one myth with greater consistency than any other, a myth that links their celebration of illustrious individuals of their age. They repeatedly emphasized that the study of letters, the study of the liberal arts, the study of the humanities was reborn in that era. They affirmed that this rebirth had animated an educational revival and spurred the physical renewal of the environment and the moral renewal of human activity. Moreover, they gloated over a certain cultural hegemony exercised by "Italians" in their day, noting with pride the incipient spread of the humanities to bastions of theological scholasticism like Paris. Even Greeks emigrated to study their own language and literature under Italian tutelage.

The oratory that Renaissance humanists preferred, the praise and blame of the epideictic genre, constantly proposed to them a heuristic pattern of rebirth and renewal. To heighten the sense of a person's achievements, Renaissance panegyrists, like their classical counterparts, regularly painted a grim picture of circumstances that had prevailed before that individual appeared on the ecclesiastical, political, or academic scene. In this frame, to heighten the sense of their own achievement, humanists depicted the rebirth of eloquence and learning in Italy after a dark age of some seven hundred years. The portion of humanist erudition that funeral orations represent confirms, in significant ways, the validity of those claims for a renaissance. When Vergerio, Bruni, and others adopted classicizing rules for their panegyric and decided not to preach a thematic sermon, they transformed the form and related content of public speaking in their epoch.

The question remains how a study of one species of humanist rhetoric may enhance our understanding of humanism as a characteristic phase in Western rhetorical culture. That study supports a distinction that contemporary scholars have made between two currents—the grammatical and the rhetorical—within humanism's broad cultural stream. Secondly, that study indicates that certain of the five disciplines that comprised the *studia humanitatis* had particular relevance for one or the other current. Grammatical humanists devoted themselves in general to scholarly and literary activities associated with the disciplines of grammar and poetry. They were textual scholars and textual commentators, and they turned to verse composition when they sought to plumb the depths of the "world within." Those learned activities were best carried on far from the madding crowd.

Many of the leading figures whose work has engaged the interest of scholars of Italian humanism—persons like Petrarch, Lorenzo Valla, and Poliziano—were fundamentally grammatical humanists. Their orientation inspired the labors of the greatest of the northern humanists, Desiderius Erasmus, in the sixteenth century. To characterize their erudition as grammatical in no way denigrates their achievement. Most humanist scholars in our own age carry on the traditions of textual analysis and commentary pursued by grammatical humanists of the Italian Renaissance. We are the direct heirs of that approach to scholarship.

At the other pole of humanism's spectrum, easily distinguished from his grammatical counterpart in solitary study, stands the orator of the rhetorical tradition, actively engaged in the affairs of civic life. Rhetorical humanists focused primarily on the disciplines of moral philosophy, history, and rhetoric itself because those disciplines integrally related to their commitment to public service. This subcurriculum within the liberal arts was first conceptualized during the Renaissance. In his *De ingenuis moribus* (ca. 1402) Pier Paolo Vergerio posited those three disciplines as essential preparation for a career in the public domain. It is no accident, therefore, that Vergerio was among the first humanists to adopt a rhetorical orientation in his program of learning and among the first to practice classicizing oratory. He was quickly followed by orators like Bruni, Poggio, Francesco Barbaro, Leonardo Giustiniani, and others who have frequently appeared in these pages.

Few if any humanists practiced a purely grammatical or rhetorical humanism. Virtually all adherents of the new learning appropriated and tested the techniques of both poles at some point in their careers. They liked to be eclectic. It is often possible, however, to place a particular humanist nearer to the grammatical or rhetorical pole on the basis of his scholarship and activities. The more rhetorical a humanist, the less he often wrote, as much of his time was taken up by public responsibilities.

Disciplines like moral philosophy, moreover, were not the exclusive preserve of rhetorical humanists. All humanists from Petrarch on were concerned to improve the quality of behavior in their time. Those committed to a rhetorical brand of humanism prized moral philosophy because of its usefulness to a person actively involved in civic affairs—the rhetor of the classical tradition. They pursued an eloquence that affirmed values.

In fact, the epideictic genre of praise and blame functioned as a matrix that integrated the study of rhetoric, history, and moral philosophy. History was closely tied to epideictic rhetoric, for a person's deeds functioned as proof of his virtue or vice. Moral philosophy impinged directly upon the practice of that oratory, because it looked to supply exemplars of good conduct and censure the bad. General ethical precepts were incarnated in the good life of a praiseworthy person; evil character and actions could be censured through invective.

Emphasis on the rhetorical disciplines affected the character of humanism as an educational program. Rhetorical humanists valued their educational program precisely for its efficacy in producing good citizens. The orientation of that education toward virtue propitiously set an adolescent on the road to moral living in that sensitive moment when the passion of libidinous desire threatened to destroy character. That education also produced an eloquent youth, capable of persuasion and inclined toward engagement in the public sphere. The breadth of learning frequently praised by eulogists suggests that *copia* was just as prized a quality in education as in speech.

The educational program propounded by humanists did not emphasize research and discovery. One learned by studying the recovered letters of antiquity, the classics, and by imitating their exemplary modes of expression and their moral exemplars. One also learned a great deal outside the classroom. Italian humanists never identified education solely with schooling. Rather, they consistently celebrated the educational contribution made by visual images, by shared meals and conversation, and by the physical and natural environment. The virtuous life and good example of the master constituted the crucial factor in their pedagogical program.

Rhetorical humanists shared an epistemology that grounded their convictions about the method and purpose of education. Truth for those humanists related to the conduct of one's life. Life's primary art was that of good and holy living. Given their commitment to rhetoric, humanists rejected the quest for scientific demonstration that was the province of eristic and instead embraced a quest for probable truth, a charge assigned to the orator from Aristotle on. Visual images with their emotional content, not logical concepts, were most persuasive.

Italian humanists were often harmonizers in their praise, willing to blur distinctions. They stated a profound respect for scholars who successfully reconciled discordant opinions. They celebrated individuals who combined seemingly antithetical lifestyles like the active and contemplative. They ignored social distinctions in the oratorical moment, permitting clerics to harangue civic audiences at funerals in public squares, and properly dressed laypersons to speak from the sanctuaries of their most sacred edifices.

The propensity to harmonize was perhaps nowhere more evident than in the manner in which rhetorical humanists fused pagan and Christian ideals to elaborate their ethic of public service. The rhetor's technique of *a fortiori* logic, often expressed in wording like "If the pagans . . . how much more Christians . . . ," afforded Italian humanists a ready means of protecting themselves against the objections of vigilant ecclesiastical censors. Two visions of the afterlife grounded in a special way their advocacy of public service. In the *De republica* (6.13.13), Cicero recounted Scipio's dream, in which those who preserved, aided, and enlarged the state were rewarded with eternal beatitude. Cicero adduced the state as the human creation most cherished by the divine ruler of the world. Similarly, in the twenty-fifth chapter of the Gospel of Matthew, which describes in vivid terms humanity's "last judgment," those who had given assistance to their fellow human beings most in need are invited to share eternal beatitude. The suffering and oppressed are introduced in that passage as the persons most cherished by the divine judge of the world; in fact, the judge identifies his ongoing presence with them. Humanists were convinced that politics represented man's highest calling and was best realized by concrete deeds of mercy.

Two descriptions of the committed human life, again fusing pagan and Christian ideals, reinforced that basic ethic of public service. Cicero had twice quoted Plato's saying that authentic human existence was altruistic (*Off.* 1.7.22; *Fin.* 2.14.45). Not born for himself alone, man realized his potential in ever-expanding circles of relationships from family to friends to the commonwealth. The Roman orator emphasized that one contributed to the common good by acts of kindness. The Christian counterpart to this, as expressed in the first chapter of the letter attributed to the apostle James (1:27), defined "religion" as acts of kindness toward society's vulnerable groups, described in traditional biblical language as orphans and widows.

The rhetor's role in society was further delineated in key passages regularly cited or alluded to in Renaissance funeral orations. Cicero had prescribed that eloquence was to be used for the safety and protection of society (*Off.* 2.14.51). It was perverse to utilize artful speaking in a way damaging to good persons. Jesus had employed a metaphor from his Palestinian culture when he stressed that he had entrusted his flock of believers to the care of selected pastors (John 10:1–30, 21:15–19). Public leaders were to be stewards of a reality much larger than themselves, never corrupted by possibilities of financial gain and never corrupting by their eloquence.

Orators used classical and Christian citations to sketch the proper setting in which rhetoric thrived. Eloquence was the ally of peace, Cicero had asserted (*Brut.* 12.45), and the companion of a settled society. Jesus had defined his legacy as one of peace (John 14:27). To abuse that legacy through civic strife or war constituted a grave violation of the desires of humanity's savior. Humanists supported a social ideal of peace and concord that at times became overt pacifism.

One rhetorical principle underpinned all the others. For a rhetor to be effective, he must live the moral life he advocated. Italian humanist eulogists manifest a vigorous Roman sense of the persuasional power of ethos. That sense received ready reinforcement in the Judaeo-Christian value of religious integrity, a value repeatedly emphasized in the polemic of Jesus against religious hypocrisy.

Cato's ideal orator (Sen. *Contr.* 1.Pr.9; Quint. 12.1.1), a good person skilled in public speaking, pervades all of Renaissance funeral oratory and sustains the vision of reform proposed by rhetorical humanists. Ecclesiastical culture had need of good men in all of its offices. The Church's impact on society was vitiated by leaders who were ambitious or avaricious and who attained their positions of leadership by being powerfully connected or by buying their offices. This ethical problem became particularly acute when it reached the uppermost levels of office: popes should be virtuous individuals who were willing to rid their own administrative organs of unworthy bureaucrats. Renaissance orators acclaimed the value for the ecclesiastical community of prelates like Francesco Zabarella and popes like Nicholas V.

Political culture also had need of good men, for rhetorical humanists postulated that the rapport of government, the creation of a state, existed for the betterment of everyone involved in that rapport. Virtuous leaders were crucial no matter what form government assumed. Excellence was predicated as the implicit criterion for monarchical legitimacy. That offices were open to all citizens in a republic was seen as a forceful spur to virtue; the more virtuous aspirant would logically be selected for any post. Humanist education, therefore, assumed a vital importance for any society. Those trained in the good arts emerged as good persons. Methodologically, the teacher exercised a primary role. Orators celebrated pedagogues from Isocrates to Guarino for combining learning and moral living in their instruction.

Persons skilled in speaking were portrayed as assisting their society in a variety of ways. In ecclesiastical culture eloquence invigorated preaching, aided the work of Church councils, and empowered legates to effect peace and concord. Active service to one's fellow human beings comprised the hallmark of piety for rhetorical humanists. Orators specified that service by encouraging activities like almsgiving, patronage for the new learning, and the rebuilding of collapsed churches, which symbolized a desired moral renewal of the institution. Funeral speakers exhorted the Church to reform.

Political rulers and administrators could avail themselves of the persuasive force of eloquence in their state letters, in the advice offered in state councils, and in diplomatic embassies. Service to the commonwealth was endorsed through praise of a series of activities analogous to those specified for ecclesiastics: honest administration, social assistance, the resolution of urban violence and factionalism, peace among city-states, and building projects that culminated in the fortification of a city, symbolizing the paternal care that government was meant to provide.

The path to success in eloquence began with a humanist education, for that education was designed to communicate the force and style of artful speaking. Orators like Giannantonio Campano engaged in an enlightened polemic for that era by advocating such an education for women as well. Campano's position implied that women could attain proficiency in eloquence and therefore participate fully in public affairs.

The study of a species of humanist oratory sheds light, finally, upon the question that constantly preoccupied adherents of that cultural program. How did they see the human person and define *humanitas*?[1] Celebratory oratory not surprisingly provides ample evidence of a positive vision of humanity. The importance that humanists attached to funeral oratory indicates that they agreed with Ovid, who contended that excellence increases when it is praised. That agreement implies that human nature is disposed toward the pursuit of the good and spurred to that pursuit when good actions receive public commendation. Public honor nourishes the arts, Cicero proclaimed (*Tusc.* 1.2.4), and persons are inspired to act morally when the reward is fame.

Humanists therefore felt that their activity as panegyrists made a significant contribution to the welfare of society. They believed with Cicero that "just as the whole state is habitually corrupted by the evil desires and the vices of prominent men, so it is improved and reformed by self-restraint on their part" (*Leg.* 3.13.30).[2] Rhetorical humanists marshaled the power of their oratorical training to present exemplars of self-restraint in their eulogies.

Three brief scenes from those eulogies help to recapitulate the vision of *humanitas* commended by rhetorical humanists. Bernardo Navagero spoke emphatically of the human person as a doer in his eulogy for Doge Andrea Gritti. The human person comes into existence to act, Navagero affirmed, and sparks of virtue implanted by nature in the human soul are awakened by seeing honest actions.[3] When he recounted the deathbed speech of Giovanni Ercole, Ludovico Carbone upheld that man must be a moral doer. Ercole had exhorted his descendants to concord and consoled them by claiming that he was about to meet his redeemer face to face. In company with Christ, he asserted, he would also find Plato, Aristotle, and Cicero, who had written so well "about the manner of good and holy living."[4] Heaven reserved a place even for pagans who recommended and lived a moral life.

Stefano Sterponi, lastly, narrated that the friends of Alessandro Pucci had criticized him for "too humanely" assisting peasants, artisans, and others from society's lower class. They had failed to understand the imperative of evangelical charity. Sterponi cited three different sayings of Jesus to defend such beneficent actions on behalf of the poor and powerless and concluded with a bold allegation that summed up the ethic urged by rhetorical humanists throughout the Italian Renaissance: "Nothing is so holy, so amiable, so approved before God and men than that one make use of kindness and clemency toward every class of persons and that one manifest toward all that humanity from which we derive the title of our excellence."[5]

ABBREVIATIONS

All funeral orations from the Italian Renaissance are cited according to an abbreviation composed of the author's name and the name of the oration's subject; an alphabetical list with complete bibliographical information on the funeral orations is supplied in the appendix. Abbreviations for classical authors and works are taken from *A Latin Dictionary*, ed. Charlton T. Lewis and Charles Short (New York: Oxford University Press, 1962), pp. vii–xi; and *A Greek-English Lexicon*, ed. Henry George Liddell and Robert Scott (Oxford: Oxford University Press, 1953), pp. xvi–xli. Abbreviations relating to modern sources are limited to the following:

BAV	Vatican City, Biblioteca Apostolica Vaticana
BMC	*A Catalogue of Books Printed in the Fifteenth Century Now in the British Museum*. Edited by R. Proctor and A. W. Pollard. 12 vols. (London: Trustees of the British Museum, 1908–).
Copinger	W. A. Copinger, *Supplement to Hain's Repertorium Bibliographicum*, part 2, *Additions*. 2 vols. (London: H. Sotheran & Co., 1898–1906).
CTC	*Catalogus Translationum et Commentariorum*, ed. P. O. Kristeller and F. Edward Cranz (Washington, D.C.: Catholic University Press, 1960–).
DBI	*Dizionario biografico degli Italiani* (Rome: Istituto della Enciclopedia Italiana, 1960–).
GW	*Gesamtkatalog der Wiegendrucke* (Leipzig: K. Hiersemann, 1925–).
Hain	Ludovicus Hain, *Repertorium Bibliographicum* (Berlin: J. Altmann, 1925).
Iter	Paul Oskar Kristeller, *Iter Italicum*, 3 vols. (Leiden: Brill, 1965–).
Mazzatinti	Giuseppe Mazzatinti et al., *Inventario dei manoscritti delle biblioteche d'Italia*, 97 vols. (Forlì: L. Bordandini, 1891–1911; Florence: L. Olschki, 1912–80).
PG	*Patrologia graeca*, ed. Jacques Paul Migne. Paris.
PL	*Patrologia latina*, ed. Jacques Paul Migne. Paris.

Reichling	Dietericus Reichling, *Appendices ad Hainii-Copingeri Repertorium Bibliographicum* (Munich: J. Rosenthal, 1905–11).
RIS	*Rerum italicarum scriptores*, ed. Ludovico Antonio Muratori (Milan: Typographia Palatina, 1723–51); NS (Città di Castello: S. Lapi, and Bologna: N. Zanichelli, 1900–).
s.a.	sine anno (date of publication unknown)
s.l.	sine loco (place of publication unknown)
s.t.	sine typographo (publisher unknown)

NOTES

CHAPTER ONE

1. Weinstein, "In Whose Image and Likeness?"
2. My understanding of classical rhetoric is deeply indebted to the scholarship of George Kennedy. See his *Persuasion in Greece, Rhetoric in the Roman World, Classical Rhetoric,* and *Greek Rhetoric under Christian Emperors.*
3. See, e.g., the contributions from the Newberry Library Conference published in *Renaissance Eloquence: Studies in the Theory and Practice of Renaissance Rhetoric,* and the review of that volume by John Bateman in *Rhetorica* 2 (1984): 284–92. Paul Oskar Kristeller has insisted throughout his career that humanist oratory deserves study. See his "Humanism and Scholasticism," pp. 94–95, and "Philosophy and Rhetoric: The Renaissance," p. 248.
4. The speech was written by Giovanni Battista Flavi and published in *Annales ecclesiastici post . . . Caesarem Baronium* (Cologne: A. Boëtzerius, 1630), 19:900–909. See, in general, McGinness, "Rhetoric and Counter-Reformation Rome." Galletti, *L'eloquenza,* pp. 520–27, described Petrarch's orations as the least Petrarchan of his works.
5. See my "Ideal Renaissance Pope"; O'Malley, *Praise and Blame*; and Kennedy, *New Testament Interpretation,* pp. 19–20, 73–77.
6. Poggio Bracciolini, *Opera,* ed. Fubini, 3:224–58. Francesco da Vellate's oration is preserved in BAV, MS Vat. lat. 8919, fols. 1–6v. See further Poggio Bracciolini on Leonardo Bruni, p. cxxv: "cum virtutis laus in actione consistat . . ."; and Fubini, "Il 'teatro del mondo,'" pp. 38–40.
7. Kristeller, "Francesco Bandini," pp. 415–22; and McClure, "The Vision of Solace and Tranquillity." The act of consoling comprises a deliberative element in an epideictic speech. For that reason I have chosen not to treat the consolatory topics from funeral orations.
8. Leonardo Bruni, *Epistolarum libri VIII,* ed. Mehus, 2:62–63: "Ego autem non maiora ista puto quam nunc sint Evangelia Missarumque solemnia latine ac litterate in audientium turba pronuntiari. Intelligunt enim homines licet illitterati sint, nec tamen ipsi ita locuntur, nec illo modo loqui scirent, licet intelligant, propterea quod longe facilius est intelligere alienum sermonem, quam proferre. . . . Sed multo magis ad eos qui in rei publicae gubernatione versabantur et quorum intererat quid populus decerneret, orator loquebatur. Praestantes igitur homines oratorem latine litterateque contionan-

tem praeclare intelligebant; pistores vero et lanistae et huiusmodi turba sic intelligebant oratoris verba ut nunc intelligunt Missarum solemnia." Bruni's remarks were made in the context of his debate with Leon Battista Alberti in 1435 concerning the language spoken by the Romans. On a humanist's oratorical public see also Wittschier, *Manetti*, pp. 183–85.

CHAPTER TWO

The quotation in the chapter title is based upon Ovid *Pont.* 4.2.35–36.

1. Leon Battista Alberti on his dog, [fol. 45v]: "Vale igitur, mi canis, atque esto, quantum in me sit, prout tua expetit virtus, immortalis." An Italian translation of the work, entitled *Il cane*, was published by Piero di Marco Parenti (Ancona: Aurelli G. E. Comp., 1847). See now Grayson, "Il *Canis*."

2. Leon Battista Alberti on his dog, [fols. 39v–45]. In Renaissance art, humanists are often pictured at work in their studies accompanied by a dog. See Reuterswärd, "The Dog in the Humanist's Study" (Philipp Fehl gave me this reference).

3. Grayson, "Il *Canis*," p. 195, discusses Alberti's general indebtedness to Lucian in satires of this sort. See further Michel, *Un idéal humain*, pp. 229–55; and Mattioli, *Luciano e l'umanesimo*, pp. 74–100. Laura Cereta parodied the form of the funeral oration, particularly its consolatory topics, in a mock encomium for an ass. Tommaso Sclarici dal Gambaro also published a parody in the sixteenth century. See the appendix for complete references.

4. Leon Battista Alberti on his dog, [fol. 39].

5. On the Greek *epitaphios logos* see Burgess, "Epideictic Literature," pp. 146–57; and Kennedy, *Persuasion in Greece*, pp. 29, 154–66. Modern scholars have focused their investigation of these speeches largely upon their historical accuracy. See, e.g., Strasburger, "Thukydides," pp. 20–28; and Walters, "'We Fought Alone at Marathon.'" The theory and practice of epideictic oratory in antiquity are surveyed by Russell and Wilson in their introduction to *Menander Rhetor*, pp. xi–xxxiv. On the early history of the genre see Buchheit, *Genos Epideiktikon*.

6. The Roman origins of the *laudatio funebris* were posited in antiquity by Dionysius of Halicarnassus, *A.R.* 5.17.2–6. Among modern scholars who concur with this judgment see Vollmer, "Laudationum funebrium Romanorum historia," pp. 450–51; Drury, "Laudatio funebris et rhétorique," pp. 108–10; Kennedy, *Rhetoric in the Roman World*, pp. 21–23; and Kierdorf, *Laudatio Funebris*. Some Italian humanists interpreted Cicero's remarks in the *De or.* 2.84.341 to mean that the Greeks invented written panegyric and the Ro-

mans adapted it to funeral speaking. See, e.g., Giannozzo Manetti, "Praefatio in laudatione Agnetis Numantinae," fols. 2v–3.

7. English translation by E. W. Sutton and H. Rackham, Loeb Library (London: W. Heinemann; Cambridge: Harvard University Press, 1948), p. 457.

8. Drury, "*Laudatio funebris* et rhétorique," pp. 106–8; Kennedy, *Rhetoric in the Roman World*, pp. 22–23; and Russell and Wilson, "Epideictic Practice and Theory," in *Menander Rhetor*, pp. xxii–xxix. A table summarizing the various schemata proposed for an encomium in Latin rhetorical treatises is supplied by Cousin, *Etudes sur Quintilien*, 1:194.

9. *Menander Rhetor*, ed. Russell and Wilson, pp. 170–79. Menander's rules for a consolatory speech (pp. 160–65) and for a monody (pp. 200–207) were also relevant for funeral oratory. Russell and Wilson provide an English translation of a treatise on epideictic oratory mistakenly attributed to Dionysius of Halicarnassus (rules for funeral speeches are on pp. 373–76).

10. Vollmer, "Laudationum funebrium Romanorum historia," pp. 471–72; Kennedy, *Rhetoric in the Roman World*, pp. 553–641; Bowersock, *Greek Sophists in the Roman Empire*; and the further bibliography in *Approaches to the Second Sophistic*, ed. Bowersock, pp. 30–34.

11. See, in general, Kennedy, *Classical Rhetoric*, pp. 140–47. For the funeral orations of the Greek fathers see Ruether, *Gregory of Nazianzus*; Gregg, *Consolation Philosophy*, pp. 62–79, 140–44; and Kennedy, *Greek Rhetoric under Christian Emperors*. The Latin funeral orations of Ambrose are analyzed from various perspectives in Ricci, "Definizione della *prudentia*"; Ruiz, *Investigationes*; and MacCormack, *Art and Ceremony*, pp. 146–50.

12. MacCormack, *Art and Ceremony*, pp. 93–94, observes that the *laudatio funebris* remained a part of public funerals until the second century but never played an important role in the procedures of imperial *consecratio*.

13. Kennedy, *Classical Rhetoric*, pp. 161–72; idem, *Greek Rhetoric under Christian Emperors*; Kustas, "Byzantine Rhetoric"; idem, *Studies in Byzantine Rhetoric*; and Hunger, *Die hochsprachliche profane Literatur der Byzantiner*, vol. 1.

14. Murphy, *Rhetoric in the Middle Ages*; *Medieval Eloquence*, ed. Murphy; and Kristeller, "Philosophy and Rhetoric: The Middle Ages." For further bibliography on individual topics see Murphy, *Medieval Rhetoric*.

15. Murphy, *Rhetoric in the Middle Ages*, pp. 269–355; and Charland, *Artes Praedicandi*.

16. Kristeller, "Francesco Bandini," p. 416.

17. Kristeller has consistently emphasized the existence of secular oratory in medieval Italy. See his "Humanism and Scholasticism," pp. 94–95; and "Philosophy and Rhetoric: The Middle Ages," pp. 237–38. The only attempt at a comprehensive history of oratory in Italy is still Galletti, *L'eloquenza*. On the history of funeral oratory see my "Ideal Renaissance Pope"; and *Leichenpredigten als Quelle historischer Wissenschaften*, ed. Lenz.

18. The earliest of these treatises, the anonymous *Oculus pastoralis* (ca. 1222), was republished by Dora Franceschi in the Memorie dell'Accademia delle scienze di Torino, ser. 4a, no. 11 (1966). Cf. also Ioannes Viterbiensis, *De regimine civitatum*, ed. Salvemini. For discussion of the *podestà* literature see Hertter, *Die Podestàliteratur*; Sorbelli, "I teorici del reggimento comunale"; and Franceschi, "L'*Oculus pastoralis*."

19. For discussion of the differences between dictaminal and classical Latin prose see Kristeller, "Philosophy and Rhetoric: The Middle Ages," pp. 232–36; Hyde, *Padua in the Age of Dante*, pp. 294–95; and esp. Witt, "*Ars dictaminis*." A consolatory letter composed by Pier delle Vigne for the death of Iacopo Baldovini in 1235 is mistakenly called an "Oratio funeralis" in Rome, Bibl. Corsiniana, MS 33 E 27, fols. 126v–27.

20. The sermons of Remigio de' Girolami, a contemporary of Dante, are preserved in Florence, Bibl. Nazionale, MS Conventi soppressi G 4, 936. Excerpts were published in Salvadori and Federici, "I sermoni d'occasione." See Davis, "An Early Florentine Political Theorist"; Panella, "Fra Remigio dei Girolami"; and idem, "Un sermone in morte." Kaeppeli's *Scriptores Ordinis Praedicatorum* lists the following Italian Dominicans who wrote funeral sermons in the thirteenth and fourteenth centuries: Dominicus Nardi de Florentia (d. 1385), 1:331; Fridericus Franconus de Neapoli (d. 14th c.), 1:402–3; Iacobus de S. Andrea (Cini) Senensis (d. 1378), 2:338–39; Ioannes de Opreno (prior of S. Eustorgius in Milan, 1261–65), 2:516; Ioannes de S. Geminiano (d. after 6 May 1333), 2:541–42; Nicolaus Asculanus (14th cent.), 3:145–46; and Philippus de Spoleto (mid-14th cent.), 3:276. None of the sermons *de mortuis* of Ioannes de Opreno, which would antedate those of Remigio de' Girolami, have survived.

21. Paris de Grassis, *Tractatus de funeribus*, fol. 223v.

22. I used the copy of the sermon in Venice, Bibl. Naz. Marciana, MS 2293 (Marc. lat. III 79), fols. 53v–54v. See also G. Mollat, "L'oeuvre oratoire de Clement VI," pp. 268–69.

23. The notion of disjunction, of course, was central to Panofsky's analysis in *Renaissance and Renascences*.

24. Witt, "*Ars dictaminis*," pp. 28–34; and my "Oratory of Vergerio."

25. Petrarch on Giovanni Visconti, pp. 335–40. Further indications of Petrarch's use of the thematic sermon in his public oratory are provided by Godi, "L'orazione del Petrarca per Giovanni il Buono."

26. The extant portions of Badoer's sermon are published in Bucci, *Il Memoriale Quadripartitum*, ed. Curlo, pp. 162–71. See also G. Cracco on Badoer in *DBI*, 5:104; and Arbesmann, *Der Augustinereremitenorden*, pp. 66–69.

27. See my "Oratory of Vergerio," pp. 4–9. In a letter to Giovanni Bartolomei in 1379, Coluccio Salutati lamented that oratory had lost its vigor be-

cause civil questions were treated by lawyers, not by orators. Salutati felt that preachers did exercise such vigor. See his *Epistolario*, ed. Novati, 1:341 (Ronald Witt called my attention to this reference).

28. Kohl, "Political Attitudes," p. 426.

29. For a list of funeral orations delivered in Italy between 1373 and 1420 see my "Oratory of Vergerio," pp. 19–23, 32. The following should be added: Giovanni Capogallo on Giangaleazzo Visconti, Antonio Contarini on Andrea Contarini, Lorenzo de' Monaci on Vitale Lando, and all those by Francesco Zabarella. The sermon of Filippo da Lucca on a Iacoba may also have been delivered before 1420.

30. See my "Oratory of Vergerio," pp. 20–21, 24.

31. Poggio delivered his oration on 27 September 1417. See *Acta Concilii Constanciensis*, ed. Finke et al., 2:516–17; cf. Arendt, *Die Predigten des Konstanzer Konzils*, pp. 106–7. The orations of Poggio and Pietro Donato for Zabarella are frequently cited in Zonta, *Zabarella*.

32. Flemmyng's oration was delivered on 2 October 1417. He had earlier preached a funeral sermon at the council for Robert Halam. See *Acta Concilii Constanciensis*, ed. Finke et al., 2:513, 516–17.

33. Fubini, "Un'orazione di Poggio" and "Il 'teatro del mondo.'" The latter includes an edition of the oration, pp. 103–22.

34. Fubini, "'Il teatro del mondo,'" p. 103: "Permultum quidem animis inhaerent quae ipsis oculis videmus." The implications of Poggio's speech for Church reform are discussed in chapter 4 below.

35. See also my "Ideal Renaissance Pope," pp. 29–32; my "Oratory of Vergerio," pp. 12–19; O'Malley, *Praise and Blame*, pp. 42–44, 50–76; and idem, "Erasmus and the History of Sacred Rhetoric," pp. 4–7, 11–12.

36. Paris de Grassis, *Tractatus de funeribus*, fols. 219v–24v. On fol. 220, he attributes the mistaken practices to two causes: (1) the shallowness of the French and (2) the discords engendered by the Great Schism ("vel licentiosa Gallorum levitas ante corrupisset vel schismaticorum pontificum discordia variasset"). On Paris de Grassis as a liturgical historian see O'Malley, "The Feast of Thomas Aquinas."

37. I list here a sampling of orators who refer to the classical custom to supplement the examples in the text. If the orator refers to a specific ancient oration, I give it in parentheses followed by the source for our knowledge of that oration. Classical sources are drawn from Burgess, "Epideictic Literature," pp. 146–48, and Vollmer, "Laudationum funebrium Romanorum historia," pp. 478–80. Giannantonio Campano on Nello Baglioni, [fol. 104]; Carlo Cappello on Giorgio Corner, pp. 178–79; Ludovico Carbone on Giacomo Dal Lino, fol. 13v (C. Caesar on Julia and on Cornelia in Plut. *Caes.* 5 and in Suet. *Caes.* 6; Q. Lutatius Catulus on Popilia in Cic. *De or.* 2.11.44); Angelo Gabrielli on Battista Zeno, p. 227; Leonardo Giustiniani on Carlo Zeno, p.

141; Battista Guarini on Eleanor of Aragon, [fol. 1]; Tommaso Inghirami on Ludovico Podocataro, p. 291 (Q. Metellus on Scipio Africanus in Val. Max. 4.1.12); Francesco Maturanzio on Francesco da Porto, fols. 76v–77 (Q. Metellus on Scipio Africanus in Val. Max. 4.1.12); Gabriele Mauro on Benedetto Pesaro, [fol. 2] (Pericles on soldiers in Plut. *Per.* 8.6 or in Thuc. 2.35–46); Andrea Navagero on Leonardo Loredan, p. 26; Baldassare Rasini on professors and students (II), fols. 94–95; Ubaldino on Lorenzo Pucci, fol. 23; Piero Valeriano on Girolamo della Torre, [fol. 3] (Pericles on soldiers in Plut. *Per.* 8.6 or in Thuc. 2.35–46); Conradus Vegerius on Pope Adrian VI, [fol. 2].

38. F. Barbaro on Giovanni Corradini, fols. 61v–62; and Leonardo Bruni on Nanni Strozzi, pp. 2–3, referring to Cic. *Leg.* 2.26.65. Ludovico Carbone, in his eulogy for Giacomo Dal Lino, fol. 13v, mentioned Athenian legislation dictating a public funeral and oration annually in honor of those killed while fighting for the homeland. This legislation is recorded in sources like Dem. *Lept.* 141; see Burgess, "Epideictic Literature," p. 147.

39. G. Manetti on Leonardo Bruni, pp. lxxxix, civ–cxiv; P. Leto on Leonardo Grifi, fols. 86v–87, referring to Dionysius of Halicarnassus *A.R.* 5.17.2–6; T. Inghirami on Galeotto Franciotti, pp. 62–64; Paris de Grassis, *Tractatus de funeribus*, fol. 134 (Inghirami and Paris de Grassis refer to Diodorus 1.92.5).

40. Maturanzio on Leonardo Mansueti, fol. 128. The possible sources for each of the funeral orations he noted are:

1. Q. Catulus on Popilia: Cic. *De or.* 2.11.44.
2. Q. Caecilius Metellus on Lucius: Plin. *H.N.* 7.43.139.
3. Julius Caesar on Cornelia: Suet. *Caes.* 6; Plut. *Caes.* 5.
4. Mark Anthony on Julius Caesar: Cic. *Att.* 14.10.1, 15.20.2, *Phil.* 2.36.90; Plut. *Brut.* 20.2, *Ant.* 14.3; Suet. *Caes.* 84; Cass. Dio 44.35–49.
5. Anon. on L. Cornelius Sulla: Appian *Civ.* 1.105.

41. Sangiorgi on Ferry de Clugny, [fol. 1]. His possible sources for the orations are:

1. P. Valerius Publicola on L. Brutus: Dion. Hal. *A.R.* 5.17.2; Plut. *Popl.* 9.7.
2. Q. Fabius Maximus for his son: Cic. *Sen.* 4.12; Plut. *Fab. Max.* 1.5.24.4.
3. M. Marcellus on Q. Claudius Marcellus: Livy 27.27.
4. Julius Caesar on Julia (Sangiorgi's text reads "Ania"): Suet. *Caes.* 6; Plut. *Caes.* 5.
5. Tiberius on Augustus: Suet. *Aug.* 100; Cass. Dio 56.34.

In this context Sangiorgi also adverted to Jacob's *eulogium* for Rachel and the consolatory letters of Jerome on the deaths of Nepotianus and Fabiola. Cf.

also the conjunction by Bernardo Giustiniani of the funeral orations of (1) Mark Anthony for Julius Caesar, (2) Demosthenes for those killed at Chaeroneia, and (3) David for Saul, in his eulogy for Francesco Foscari, p. 21 (ed. Molin).

42. Branca, "Ermolao Barbaro," p. 226, contends that one facet of Petrarch's bequest to Venetian culture was the consciousness "that the Christian message constitutes the harmonious completion of that of antiquity as well as the triumph over it."

43. See, e.g., Gian Francesco Varini on Bartolomeo Cassinari (III), fol. 55v; Conradus Vegerius on Pope Adrian VI, [fol. 2v]; and esp. the anonymous oration on Pandolfo II Malatesta, p. xxiv: "Animadverto ergo, patres, in hoc ipso dicendi genere Graecos Latinosque scriptores tam multa nobis firmissimaque fundamenta iecisse, ut naturam ipsam humanitatis sive fidei lumen sequeremur."

44. Trinkaus, *In Our Image and Likeness*, 1:126–28, 141–42, passim; O'Malley, *Praise and Blame*, pp. 165–94; and idem, "Egidio da Viterbo."

45. Paris de Grassis, *Tractatus de funeribus*, fols. 60–65, 128–30v. Kajanto, "*Pontifex Maximus*," has argued that the title Pontifex Maximus only came to be used consistently to refer to the pope in the Renaissance. There are at least two instances of popes attending a funeral for a cardinal during the Renaissance, both of which are noted by Paris de Grassis, fols. 64v–65. The unusual tribute is also mentioned by the funeral orators. See Poggio Bracciolini on Niccolò Albergati (regarding the presence of Eugene IV), p. 269; Niccolò Capranica on Bessarion (regarding the presence of Sixtus IV), p. 406; and cf. Battisti de' Giudici on Roberto Malatesta (regarding the presence of Sixtus IV), fols. 2–3. Pietro Barozzi, in his eulogy for Giovanni Barozzi, pp. 123–26, included a direct appeal for financial assistance to Pope Paul II.

46. See the anonymous oration on Elisabetta Malatesta, p. xxix (where the prayer is cast in the form of a poem in dactylic hexameter); Giovanni Cattanei on Federigo I Gonzaga, [fols. 25v–26]; and Aurelio Brandolini on Lorenzo Giustini, fols. 216–17.

47. Paris de Grassis, *Tractatus de funeribus*, fol. 62v, referring to pseudo-Dionysius the Areopagite, *D.N.* 3.2 (*PG*, 3:cols. 681–84).

48. On this Ciceronian passage, known as the "Dream of Scipio," see Büchner, *Somnium Scipionis*, and Baron, "Cicero and the Roman Civic Spirit."

49. Poggio Bracciolini on Zabarella, pp. 259–60; and idem on Giuliano Cesarini, pp. 725–26.

50. See Guarino on Giannicola Salerno, col. 482; Pietro Barozzi on Antonio Roselli, pp. 181–82; Gian Luigi Faccino on Sigismondo d'Este, fols. 173v–74v; Andrea Giuliano on Manuel Chrysoloras, p. 27; and Sebastiano Sapia on Giasone del Maino, [fols. 6v–7]. Sapia attributed to Apollonius of Tyana the opinion that those who practiced "good and holy living" achieve heavenly

reward ("Ibi perfectissima requies, ut aiebat Tyanaeus Apollonius, quam qui bene beateque vixerint adipiscuntur," fol. 7). Stefano Sterponi, in his tribute to Alessandro Pucci, fol. 25r–v, conjoined the Ciceronian text with the saying of Jesus that "a man has no greater love than to lay down his life for his friends" (John 15:13). Further references to the dream of Scipio may be found in Battista Mantovano on Ludovico Caccialupi, p. 175; Raffaele Brandolini on Mariano da Genazzano, p. 237; Carlo Curro on Juan of Aragon, fol. 3v; A. Gabrielli on Battista Zeno, pp. 232–33; Sabellico on Zaccaria Barbaro, col. 497A; and Leonardo Giustiniani on Giorgio Loredan, pp. 12–13. The last oration is attributed to Leonardo Giustiniani rather than to Guarino by Sabbadini in his edition of Guarino's *Epistolario*, 3:132–33.

51. Plato's dictum that we are not born for ourselves alone is quoted by Cic. *Off.* 1.7.22 and *Fin.* 2.14.45. See further O'Malley, *Praise and Blame*, pp. 168–70.

52. Anonymous on G. Visconti, fol. 91r–v. Cf. also the remarks of Giovanni Gatti in his eulogy for Cardinal Latino Orsini, fol. 78r–v, where he stresses that the Romans spoke at funerals to cause mourning whereas Christians have the true consolation of the words of Christ. Gatti's eulogy draws heavily upon Jerome's consolatory letters on the death of Blesilla (Epist. 39) and of Nepotianus (Epist. 60).

53. Leonardo Bruni on Otto Cavalcanti, p. 144; Pomponio Leto on Leonardo Grifi, fols. 86v–87; and Baldassare Rasini on professors and students (II), fols. 94–95.

54. See DeNeef, "Epideictic Rhetoric," pp. 208–9. In the *Inquisitio super XI orationes Ciceronis* composed ca. 1393, Antonio Loschi discussed Cicero's use of a three-part schema (*exordium/confirmatio/peroratio*) in the epideictic oration *Pro Marcello*. See the *Inquisitio*, pp. 240–43. Loschi mistakenly thought that Cicero was accommodating his *dispositio* to the circumstances of time, thereby eliminating the *narratio*, *divisio*, and *confutatio*. Roman theory called for only three parts for an epideictic speech. On Loschi's work see Garin, "La cultura milanese," pp. 550–56.

55. Galletti, *L'eloquenza*, pp. 563–69; Santini, *Firenze e i suoi "oratori"*, pp. 236–37; and Rossi, *Il Quattrocento*, p. 153.

56. Bruni's statement (*Epist.*, ed. Mehus, 8:4) is discussed by virtually all of the commentators on his historical writings. See, e.g., Ullman, "Bruni and Historiography." The statement by Girolamo Gioia that "funebris oratio historia esse debet" is found in his eulogy for Benedetto Rugio, [fol. 1v]. See also Battista Casali on Francis of Luxemburg, fol. 38v; Ludovico Odassi on Guid'Ubaldo I, pp. 407–8, 414–20; Pietro Partenio on Girolamo della Torre, [fol. 9v]; Gaspare Sighicelli on Niccolò Albergati, fol. 200r–v; and Mazzuconi, "Dell'epistolario di Gasparino Barzizza," pp. 194–95. Antonio da Rho, in his oration for Niccolò Piccinino, fol. 143v, referred his audience to Pier Candido

Decembrio's "biography" of the condottiere for more details on his life. The tie between history and eloquence in Petrarch's historiographical program is stressed by Kessler in "Petrarch's Contribution to Historiography" and *Petrarca und die Geschichte*. On humanist historiography see Gilbert, *Machiavelli and Guicciardini*, pp. 203–35; and idem, "The Renaissance Interest in History."

57. For the general influence of Byzantine culture on the Italian Renaissance see Setton, "The Byzantine Background"; Geanakoplos, *Interaction of the "Sibling" Cultures*, pp. 172–280; Weiss, *Medieval and Humanist Greek*; Kristeller, "Italian Humanism and Byzantium"; and Pertusi, "L'umanesimo greco." For the rhetorical interaction see Monfasani, "The Byzantine Rhetorical Tradition."

58. For the pedagogy of Chrysoloras see Cammelli, *Crisolora*, pp. 81–98; and Thomson, "Chrysoloras." On the importance of Plutarch's *Lives* in the early Renaissance see Giustiniani, "Sulle traduzioni latine delle 'Vite' "; Witt, "Salutati and Plutarch"; and Weiss, *Medieval and Humanist Greek*, pp. 204–77. Weiss, p. 226, labeled the period of humanism from 1395 to 1405 "l'età plutarchiana." Later humanists attempted to supply a condensed version of Plutarch's *Lives*. See Resta, *Le epitomi di Plutarco*.

59. Wardman, "Plutarch's Methods"; Russell, *Plutarch*; and Giustiniani, "*Homo, Humanus*, and the Meanings of 'Humanism,' " pp. 189–91.

60. See the prefaces of Francesco Barbaro and Leonardo Giustiniani quoted by Pertusi, "L'umanesimo greco," pp. 208–9. Pertusi's comments are appropriate: "Queste traduzioni nascono dunque dal desiderio di presentare degli *exempla* di personaggi illustri che possano essere oggetto di imitazione da parte dei contemporanei; donde anche l'intonazione oratoria dei traduttori." See also Guarino's praise for Leonardo Giustiniani's translation of Plutarch's *Cimon*, quoted in Labalme, *Bernardo Giustiniani*, p. 22. Guarino rejoiced to have biographies of persons from antiquity, which "urge, admonish, and invite us to the imitation of virtue."

61. Baxandall, "Guarino, Pisanello and Chrysoloras," pp. 190–97; and idem, *Giotto and the Orators*, pp. 62–96. On the formative influence of the *progymnasmata* for Byzantine rhetoric and literature see Kustas, "Function and Evolution"; Hunger, *Die hochsprachliche profane Literatur*, 1:92–120; and Jenkins, "The Hellenistic Origins of Byzantine Literature."

62. Patterson, *Hermogenes and the Renaissance*; and Monfasani, *George of Trebizond*.

63. "Ex Menandro Rhetore in secundo divisionis demonstrativi generis capite de oratione funebri caput XIIII.," Perugia, Bibl. Comunale Augusta, MS Fondo Vecchio C 61, fols. 121v–23v. See Kristeller, *Iter*, 2:55, who refers to an epilogue of the translator that is signed "Aurelius tuus Romanus." A 1558 edition of the entire work, *De genere demonstrativo libri duo* . . . , trans. Natale

Conti (Venice: Petrus Bosellus, 1558), is labeled the first such printing in Latin.

64. Monfasani, *George of Trebizond*, p. 280, observes that Trebizond's treatment of epideictic rhetoric in the *Rhetoricorum libri V* is based almost exclusively on the *Rhetorica ad Herennium*. Sabbadini and Pertusi have argued that Guarino's epideictic orations reflect the influence of the *Rhetorica ad Herennium* and the treatise on epideictic forms falsely attributed to Dionysius of Halicarnassus (see n. 8 above). See Sabbadini, *La scuola di Guarino*, pp. 64–71; and Pertusi, "L'umanesimo greco," pp. 198–99.

65. Baron, *Crisis*, rev. ed., pp. 412–39; and idem, *From Petrarch to Leonardo Bruni*, pp. 102–37, 151–71. The latter contains an edition of Bruni's panegyric of Florence, pp. 232–63. An English translation by Benjamin Kohl with an introduction by Ronald Witt appears in *The Earthly Republic*, pp. 119–75. See also O'Malley, *Praise and Blame*, pp. 77–78, who first emphasized the importance of oratorical genre in his discussion of Bruni's *Laudatio*. Among other orators who refer to the oration of Pericles see, e.g., Gabriele Mauro on Benedetto Pesaro, [fol. 2].

66. BAV, MS Chigi. I VI 215, fols. 69–80.

67. Isocrates, ". . . oratio in funere Evagorae regis Cypri," anon. trans. (Guarino?), BAV, MS Chigi. I VI 215, fols. 37–42v. The "funeral oration of Demosthenes," translated by Lapo da Castiglionchio, is found in Florence, Bibl. Riccardiana, MS 149, fols. 40–45v (*Iter*, 1:187). Both Filelfo and Andrea Brenta translated the *oratio funebris* of Lysias. For Filelfo's translation see BAV, MS Vat. lat. 8761, fols. 77–94. Brenta's version is preserved in BAV, MS Vat. lat. 6855 (*Iter*, 2:341). See, in general, Kristeller, "Philosophy and Rhetoric: The Renaissance," pp. 245–47; Monfasani, "The Byzantine Rhetorical Tradition," pp. 177–78; Sabbadini, *Le scoperte dei codici latini e greci*, 1:43–71; and Rosa, *La fede nella "Paideia."*

68. Way, "Gregory Nazianzenus."

69. Manuel's oration is printed in *PG*, 156:cols. 181–308. For the date of its intended delivery and Manuel's efforts to circulate the work see Barker, *Manuel II Palaeologus*, pp. 525–27; and *Letters of Manuel II Palaeologus*, ed. and trans. Dennis, pp. 158–60, 166–69.

70. Patrinelis, "An Unknown Discourse of Chrysoloras."

71. See the funeral orations for Helena and Cleope Palaeologina in *PG*, 160:cols. 939–58; and Hunger, *Die hochsprachliche profane Literatur*, 1:140–42. Runciman, *Mistra*, pp. 111–12, has noted that more manuscript copies of Plethon's obituary encomium for the Despoena Cleope survive than of any other of his works.

72. *PG*, 161:cols. 615–20. Monfasani, "Bessarion Latinus," pp. 176–77, argues for the date 1471. Perotti also translated monodies by Aelius Aristides and Libanius and composed one for the death of his brother Severo. All of

these works are found in BAV, MS Vat. lat. 6835. On Perotti's life and career see Mercati, *Niccolò Perotti*; and the papers from an international conference published in *Res Publica Litterarum: Studies in the Classical Tradition* 4 (1981).

73. See the appendix for the orations. Monfasani, *George of Trebizond*, p. 284, notes that all of George's existing orations are epideictic. The life and career of Apostolis are discussed by Geanakoplos, *Greek Scholars in Venice*, pp. 73–110.

74. See Kristeller, "The Scholar and His Public," p. 11: "Their [humanist orations'] diffusion was dependent on the public success of the oration, which was indeed regarded by the audience as a public entertainment like a theater performance or a concert, as well as on the fame of the speaker."

75. Editions of Francesco da Toledo's eulogy for Leonardo della Rovere (d. 11 November 1475) include:

1. Rome: Stephan Plannck, 1481–87 (Hain 7337)
2. Rome: Ulrich Han, after 11 November 1475 (Hain 7338, 7340)
3. Rome: Bartholomäus Guldinbeck, after 11 November 1475 (Hain 7339)
4. Rome: Eucharius Silber, 1483–90 (Copinger 2575)
5. Rome: Eucharius Silber, 1490–1500 (BMC, 4:121)

The six editions of the oration by Niccolò da Modrussa for Pietro Riario (d. 5 January 1474) are:

1. Rome: Johann Gensberg, not before 18 January 1474 (Hain 11770)
2. Rome: Stephan Plannck, 1481–87 (Hain 11771)
3. Rome: s. t., s. a. (Hain 11772)
4. Rome: Johann Besicken, ca. 1500 (Hain 11773)
5. Padua: Matthaeus Cerdonis, 30 August 1482 (Hain 11774)
6. Rome: In the house of Antonio and Raffaele da Volterra, not before 18 January 1474 (BMC, 4:48)

For the relative predominance of oratorical works among books printed at Rome in the fifteenth century see Lombardi, "Aspetti della produzione e circolazione del libro."

76. See my "Oratory of Vergerio," p. 22n. 2. Debates among humanists about the merits of orations were not uncommon. Guarino's panegyric for Carmagnola, for example, sparked a considerable controversy. See Sabbadini, "Guarino Veronese"; and Monfasani, *George of Trebizond*, pp. 29–32.

77. Burckhardt, *Civilization*, pp. 138–44.

78. Burchard, *Liber Notarum*, ed. Celani, pp. 133, 536; and Paris de Grassis, *Tractatus de funeribus*, fols. 171r–v, 185v–86. The circumstances of Leto's oration for Grifi in 1485 are briefly described by Lee, *Sixtus IV*, p. 65. On Questenberg see Güldner, "Questemberg"; and Mercati, "Questenbergiana."

79. Alberto da Castelfranco on Urbano Bolzanio, [fols. 3–4]. Leonardo

Dati, *Epistolae XXXIII*, ed. Mehus, p. 70: "Inter agendum autem vir quidam inprimis dicendi peritus, sanctus, bonusque pro rostris surgit." Iacopo goes on to contrast the Latin custom, where the orator stands and the audience is seated, with his understanding of Greek practice, where a seated orator addressed a standing audience.

80. Paris de Grassis, *Tractatus de funeribus*, fols. 135v–36. Pietro del Monte and Giordano Orsini were apparently asked to prepare orations for the funeral obsequies of Calixtus III in 1456, when it appeared that the aged and ailing pope would die. However, Calixtus regained his health and outlived del Monte. See Diego Quaglioni's review of my article "The Ideal Renaissance Pope," in *Roma nel Rinascimento* 1 (1984): 18–21, where he corrects my errors in discussing the nature and authorship of these orations.

81. Giovacchino Castiglioni on Rolando Pallavicini, [fol. 1]. See Ross, "Venetian Scholars and Teachers," p. 540 n. 73; and Verani, "Notizie," pp. 80–81.

82. Francesco Diedo, "Laudatio in Bartholomaeum Paierinum," fol. 74; Tournoy, "Francesco Diedo"; Battista Casali on Domenico Grimani, fol. 69r–v; and Antonio da Rho on Niccolò Piccinino, fol. 143.

83. Paris de Grassis, *Tractatus de funeribus*, fols. 181, 209. He also notes, fol. 132v, that under normal circumstances the costs of a cardinal's funeral at the court should be paid from the cardinal's estate. If the bequest was insufficient, money could be assigned by the pope from public funds. Giovio's assessment is quoted by Burckhardt, *Civilization*, p. 144.

84. Martines, *The Social World*, pp. 239–45.

85. Trebizond believed that epideictic oratory required much less time to prepare than either judicial or deliberative. See Monfasani, *George of Trebizond*, p. 27n. 120. Francesco Padovano on Pietro Naldi, fol. 87r–v. For other orators who claimed to be speaking extemporaneously see Giovacchino Castiglioni on Egidio Guidoboni (in Verani, "Notizie," p. 95); Francesco Filelfo on Stefano Federigo Todeschini, fol. 76v; and Marco da Verona on Gil Albornoz, [fol. 2v]. For the preparation of Rinuccini's speech see the remarks of Vito Giustiniani in his introduction to the edition, p. xix. Evidence is conflicting on the question whether the orations that we have represent the speech as it was delivered. Gasparino Barzizza and Bernardo Giustiniani polished orations before circulating them. See Mazzuconi, "Dell'epistolario di Gasparino Barzizza," pp. 185, 195; and Labalme, *Bernardo Giustiniani*, pp. 256–57. According to Kristeller, "The Scholar and His Public," p. 11, Renaissance orators did not usually revise speeches before publishing them.

86. Bitzer, "The Rhetorical Situation"; Oberdorfer, "Di Leonardo Giustiniano," p. 110; Mosto, *I dogi*, p. 208.

87. Inghirami on Julius II, pp. 80–81. Greek and Latin sources frequently mention the custom of limiting a speech to a period of time measured out by

a water clock (*clepsydra*). See, e.g., Aristophanes *V*. 93, 857; Demosthenes 407.17, 1052.21; Cic. *De or*. 3.34.138, *Tusc*. 2.27.67; and Plin. *Ep*. 2.11.14, 6.2.6. Glenn Most called my attention to the practice.

88. Burchard, *Liber Notarum*, p. 153: "In choro ecclesiae conventus Sancti Augustini praedicti habitus est sermo per unum ex fratribus conventus, praeter consuetum et ordinationem meam; qui cum prolixe nimis oraret, dixi ei satis esse dictum, residuum servaret pro alia die. Frater aliquantulum perterritus truncavit orationem, excusavit se, et recessimus." The friar was speaking at the funeral of Bishop Nicola Bucciardi Cibo on 13 July 1499. Paris de Grassis, *Tractatus de funeribus*, fols. 223v–24.

89. The two orations are preserved in the same Vatican codex, MS Vat. lat. 5815. The passages are found on fols. 13–14v (for Capranica) and fols. 119–20 (for Colonna). On Palmeri see O'Malley, *Praise and Blame*, pp. 88–90.

90. Burchard, *Liber Notarum*, p. 472; and Paris de Grassis, *Tractatus de funeribus*, fol. 217. On Bruno's career see *DBI*, 14:669–71. His oration for Isabella was published at Rome by Euch. Silber in 1505. Antonio Lollio, in his exordium to a eulogy for Laudomia Piccolomini, col. 686, narrated the story of Messala, who, though used to public speaking, was so intimidated by the sight of a crowd that he forgot his own name.

91. Beale stresses the importance of the occasion for epideictic oratory in his "Rhetorical Performative Discourse."

92. For the Venetian practices see Mallett and Hale, *Military Organization*, pp. 192–94; and Muir, *Civic Ritual*. Strocchia has analyzed the manipulation of symbolic tributes at Florence in her "Burials in Renaissance Florence, 1350–1500." Cf. also Giesey, *The Royal Funeral Ceremony*. The representation of the figure of death in Renaissance and Baroque tomb sculpture took on an ever more positive, commemorative aspect. See Panofsky, "*Mors vitae testimonium*."

93. These events are described by an anonymous Ferrarese diarist in *RIS*, n.s. 24, no. 7 (fasc. 1), 91–93; and by Zambotti in ibid., (fasc. 5–6), 15–20. See Chiappini, *Gli Estensi*, pp. 144–54; and Gundersheimer, *Ferrara*, pp. 182–83.

94. See anonymous on Leonardo Bruni, pp. 154–55; and Martines, *The Social World*, pp. 239–45.

95. For humanist influence on epitaphs see Kajanto and Nyberg, *Papal Epigraphy*. For the various genres of funerary literature in the Italian Renaissance see Kristeller, "Francesco Bandini," pp. 415–22.

96. Kennedy, *Classical Rhetoric*, pp. 5–6, 120; Austin, "Quintilian on Painting and Statuary"; and Gombrich, "The Debate on Primitivism." MacCormack, "Latin Prose Panegyrics," p. 46n. 76, provides references from Latin rhetorical sources where visual and verbal expression are associated.

97. See Downey, "Ekphrasis"; Hunger, *Die hochsprachliche profane Literatur*, 1:170–88; and Lausberg, *Handbuch*, 1:399–401, 544.

98. MacCormack, "Latin Prose Panegyrics," pp. 46–54; eadem, *Art and Ceremony*, pp. 1–14, 270–71. Ecphrases in Byzantine sermons assisted painters who sought to portray scriptural episodes. See Maguire, *Art and Eloquence*, pp. 22–52.

99. Polybius, *The Histories*, 6.53–54, trans. W. R. Paton, Loeb Library (London: Heinemann; New York: G. P. Putnam's Sons, 1923), 3:389: "or if not [an elder son], some other relative mounts the rostra and discourses on the virtues and successful achievements of the dead. As a consequence the multitude and not only those who had a part in these achievements, but those who had none, when the facts are recalled to their minds and brought before their eyes [*lambanontas hupo tēn opsin*], are moved to such sympathy that the loss seems to be not confined to the mourners, but a public one affecting the whole people." Polybius goes on to describe the practice of using wooden masks at Roman funerals that spur youth to virtue by their sight. On Renaissance translations of Polybius see Lee, *Sixtus IV*, p. 90; and Reynolds, "Bruni and Perotti."

100. See, e.g., Poggio Bracciolini on Leonardo Bruni, p. cxviii; idem on Niccolò Albergati, p. 262; idem on Niccolò Niccoli, p. 277; idem on Giuliano Cesarini, p. 726; Raffaele Brandolini on Mariano da Genazzano, p. 230 (dedicatory letter to Lorenzo Pucci); Battista Casali on Aloysius of Aragon, fol. 40r–v; Agostino Dati on Niccolò Ricoveri, fol. xcvii; Leonardo Giustiniani on Giorgio Loredan, p. 13; Giannozzo Manetti on Giannozzo Pandolfini, fol. 20v; Gabriele Mauro on Benedetto Pesaro, [fol. 2]; and Iacopo Zeno on Giuliano Cesarini, fol. 1. For the use of ecphrasis in Renaissance oratory see my "Oratory of Vergerio," pp. 10–12, 18; O'Malley, *Praise and Blame*, pp. 63–67, 78–79; and Schweyen, *Guarino Veronese*, pp. 177–79. Schweyen notes, p. 109, that Guarino traced the etymology of the word *historia* to the Greek verb *historein*, which he interpreted to mean "seeing." Historians of Renaissance art have also emphasized the connection between visual and verbal expression. See, e.g., Baxandall, *Giotto and the Orators*, pp. 51–120; Spencer, "*Ut rhetorica pictura*"; and Westfall, *In This Most Perfect Paradise*, pp. viii–ix, 42–47, 61.

101. Carbone on Giacomo Dal Lino, fol. 14: "Sed quemadmodum ex indigno Iacobi nostri casu summam suscipimus amaritudinem, ita eam lenire ac mitigare poterimus si eius honestissimum vitae cursum ante oculos posuerimus nihilque ei quod ad bene beateque vivendum desiderari soleat defuisse intelligemus."

102. Julius Caesar was supposedly spurred on to greatness after seeing an image of Alexander the Great at Cadiz (Suet. *Caes.* 7). Sallust (*Iug.* 4.5–6) narrates the effect that images had upon Quintus Fabius Maximus and Scipio. Pier Paolo Vergerio (the elder) cited both cases in his treatise on education *De ingenuis moribus* (ca. 1402; ed. Gnesotto, pp. 102–3); he attributed greater

efficacy to living exemplars of virtue. See also Giovacchino Castiglioni on Rolando Pallavicini, [fol. 3r–v], where Castiglioni described ancient heroes like Caesar, Porcius Cato, and Marcus Brutus who selected great individuals from history (Alexander, Curius, and Iunius Brutus respectively) with whom they competed in the practice of excellence. Castiglioni felt that this effort to surpass heroes explained why such persons were represented in paintings on vases and in statues in fora.

103. Paris de Grassis, *Tractatus de funeribus*, fols. 136–38.

104. Manetti on Bruni, p. xcii: "In eo loco forte Petrarchae poetae, qui et ipse Aretii Florentinis parentibus natus erat, imago pariete egregie depicta cernebatur, quam cum cottidie tantulus puer etiam atque etiam intueretur, vehementissimo quodam, mirabile dictu, studiorum suorum ardore incendebatur. Nam suapte natura disciplinarum amore flagrabat." Bruni's anonymous eulogist also mentioned the incident, p. 150. Bruni himself first told the story in his *Commentarius*, p. 428. Francesco Maturanzio asserted that Orazio I Baglioni was inspired to study military affairs by seeing portraits of outstanding leaders (fol. 54r–v). Maturanzio's first compositions were elegies and inscriptions for portraits of illustrious Perugians in the palace of Braccio I Baglioni. See Vermiglioli, *Memorie*, pp. 12–13; and Bombe, "Der Palast."

105. Giannantonio Campano, [fol. 103r–v], described the ability of Enea Silvio Piccolomini to create visual images in his oratory. Byzantine orators used the same criterion. See, e.g., Bessarion's praise for the eloquence of Emperor Manuel II, *PG*, 161:col. 618.

106. See, e.g., Raffaele Brandolini on Guillaume Pérès, pp. 201–2; Girolamo Crivelli on Bianca Maria Visconti, col. 425C–D; Gerardo da Lucca on Silvestro de' Gigli, fol. 14; Elio Lampridio Cerva on Georgius Crucius, fol. 1r–v; Pietro del Monte on Calixtus III, fol. 41; Sabellico on Benedetto Rugio, col. 498A; Iacopo Sadoleto on Oliviero Carafa, p. 323; and esp. Giasone del Maino on Girolamo Torti, [fol. 2v]: "Nam sicuti in imaginibus et picturis gratiores illae sunt quae cognitos et viventes referunt et effingunt, in quibus rugas et singula oris liniamenta rimari et dignoscere possumus ac, si praesentes, intueremur, ita verbis meis dum hominis huius notam imaginem depingo, non tam recensere quam vobiscum, patres, ut viventem recommemorare videbor."

107. Capranica on Bessarion, p. 405: "permulta pro paucis imitatus eos qui magnum atque immensum orbem brevi admodum tabella depingunt." Rasini on Francesco Sforza, fol. 1v: "Argutissimam pictorum industriam nunc nuper sum imitaturus qui latissimum cum orbem sunt picturi illum brevi tabella mirum in modum sua arte coercent."

108. See, e.g., Giannantonio Campano on Pius II, [fol. 99]; Cleofilo on Antonio Costanzi, [fols. 57v–58v]; Guarino on Teodora Zilioli, col. 1241; Antonio Pacini on Lorenzo de' Medici (the elder), fol. 1r–v; and esp. Donato

Acciaiuoli on Cosimo de' Medici, p. 260: "Nam et in Graecia ab Atheniensibus, Thebanis, Lacedaemoniis, Rhodiis, et in Italia a Romanis hunc morem sic servatum fuisse accepimus, ut frequenter aliis in foro statuas, aliis sepulcra in campis, aliis aliud honoris genus ob bene gestam rem publicam ex senatus populique auctoritate decernerent. Censebant enim nihil in hac vita praeclarius, nihil excellentius, nihil sanctius quam in administranda re publica patriae pietatem officiumque praestare." On this oration and others in praise of Cosimo see Brown, "Humanist Portrait." For the moralizing purpose of monuments in antiquity see Fehl, *The Classical Monument*, pp. 50–69. Leon Battista Alberti conceptualized a civic role for sculpture and stressed the value of tombs in that regard. See Riess, "The Civic View of Sculpture."

109. See, e.g., Niccolò Capranica on Bessarion, p. 413; Giovanni Battista Egnazio on Niccolò Orsini, fol. 65r–v; and Francesco Maturanzio on Orazio I Baglioni, fol. 56v. The account of the statues erected for the legates slain at Fidenae is found in Livy 4.17.6 and Cic. *Phil.* 9.2.4–5. Cicero's ninth Philippic was actually an attempt to convince the Senate that Servius Sulpicius deserved a statue in bronze and public burial. Renaissance orators also mentioned the statue dedicated to Scipio Africanus (Livy 38.56.1–4). See, e.g., Elio Lampridio Cerva on Marinus Gradaeus, fol. 110r–v. Petrarch adduced both examples (Lucius Roscius and Scipio) in his *De remediis utriusque fortunae* 1.40–41 (Latin text and English translation in Baxandall, *Giotto and the Orators*, pp. 55–58, 141–43). However, he contrasted the practice of the ancients, who rewarded public heroes, to wealthy merchants in his day, who commissioned their own likenesses. The social value of a statue was defended by early humanists like Salutati and Vergerio after Carlo Malatesta tore down a statue of Virgil at Mantua in 1397. See Salutati, *Epistolario*, ed. Novati, 3:285–308; Vergerio, *Epistolario*, ed. Smith, pp. 189–202; and Robey, "Virgil's Statue at Mantua."

110. Poggio Bracciolini on Niccolò Niccoli, p. 277; and idem on Giuliano Cesarini, pp. 734–35. See also G. B. Egnazio on Niccolò Orsini, fol. 65r–v; and A. Giuliano on Manuel Chrysoloras, p. 27. The orations for Gattamelata were delivered by Giovanni Pontano and Lauro Quirini. The statue was erected in 1453. See Mallett, "Venice and Its Condottieri," pp. 129–30; and Janson, "The Equestrian Monument."

111. See T. Inghirami on Pietro Menzi, pp. 243–44; L. Giustiniani on Carlo Zeno, p. 146; and Sabellico on Benedetto Rugio, cols. 500B–501A.

112. Petrarch's letter to Giovanni Colonna in *Le familiari*, ed. Rossi, 2:80: "Profecto autem, si statuae illustrium possunt nobiles animos ad imitandi studium accendere, quod Q. Fabium Maximum et P. Cornelium Scipionem dicere solitos Crispus refert, quanto magis ipsa virtus hoc effict, claro dum proponitur non marmore sed exemplo? Corporum nempe liniamenta statuis forsan expressius continentur, rerum vero gestarum morumque notitia atque

habitus animorum haud dubie plenius atque perfectius verbis quam incudibus exprimuntur, nec improprie mihi videor dicturus statuas corporum imagines, exempla virtutum." See Cicero *Arch.* 12.30. Cf. Kessler, *Das Problem,* pp. 165–200; and Raith, *Die Macht des Bildes,* pp. 25–42.

113. Bernardo made the statement in a letter to Ambrogio Traversari regarding the translation of Isocrates' *Ad Nicoclem.* I have quoted the translation of Labalme, *Bernardo Giustiniani,* p. 53. See also the remarks of Coluccio Salutati quoted from his *Epistolario,* ed. Novati, 2:18, in Kessler, *Das Problem,* p. 193n. 37 ("Incitamur enim exemplo et quodam quasi stimulo ad virtutem impellimur, cum aliorum benefacta legimus vel audimus"); and the discussion of praise as the "motor of virtue" in Schweyen, *Guarino,* pp. 183–89.

114. Such purposes for a funeral oration were stated in 1393 by Pier Paolo Vergerio (the elder) in his "De dignissimo funebri apparatu," col. 189A–C. All of the following speakers cite these purposes, and many refer to their imitating ancient practice: Alberto da Castelfranco on Urbano Bolzanio, [fols. 3v–4]; Poggio Bracciolini on Leonardo Bruni, p. cxvi; idem on Niccolò Niccoli, p. 270; idem on Niccolò Albergati, pp. 261–62; L. Bruni on Nanni Strozzi, p. 3; C. Calcagnini on Alfonso I d'Este, pp. 264, 266–67; G. Campano on Giovanni della Ratta, [fol. 114v]; idem on Alessandro Oliva, [fol. 116r–v]; C. Cappello on Giorgio Corner, pp. 178–79; L. Carbone on Guarino, p. 91; G. B. Egnazio on Marco Corner, fol. 1r–v; T. Inghirami on Pietro Menzi, p. 192; G. Marini on Antonio Suriani, [fol. 2]; A. Navagero on Leonardo Loredan, pp. 25–26; L. Quirini on Gattamelata, pp. 348–49; Sabellico on Benedetto Rugio, col. 498A; and esp. George of Trebizond on Fantino Michiel, p. 447: "Quanquam omnes antiquitatis mores plurimum laudare soleo, illustrissime princeps, ille tamen ceteris mihi videtur praestantior quo institutum est clarissimorum virorum vitam ac laudes in funere recenseri. Nam et quam grata in bene meritos universa sit civitas nulla magis quam hac re percipi posse videtur, et ad imitandas virtutes eorum huiuscemodi oratione quicunque audiunt incitantur atque inflammantur." G. A. Sangiorgi, in his oration on Ferry de Clugny, [fol. 1v], derived the same purpose for funeral oratory through a rather tortured exegesis of Genesis 30:37–39.

115. See, e.g., G. Barzizza on Iacopo da Forlì, p. 26; Poggio Bracciolini on Francesco Zabarella, pp. 260–61; idem on Lorenzo de' Medici, p. 285; A. Brandolini on Lorenzo Giustini, fols. 226v–27; R. Brandolini on Guillaume Pérès, pp. 217–18; N. Capranica on Bessarion, p. 414; G. Cattanei on Barbara Gonzaga, [fol. 14]; P. Donato on Francesco Zabarella, p. 148b; A. Giuliano on Manuel Chrysoloras, p. 35; L. Giustiniani on Carlo Zeno, p. 146; Giacomo da Pesaro on Carlo Malatesta, pp. xxxvii–xxxviii (with ancient parallels); T. Inghirami on Ludovico Podocataro, pp. 331–32; C. Landino on Donato Acciaiuoli, fol. 18; P. Marsi on Pomponio Leto, [fol. 4r–v]; F. Maturanzio on Francesco da Porto, fol. 81; G. Mauro on Benedetto Pesaro, [fol. 4v]; G. B. Ramu-

sio on Francesco Fasolo, pp. 392–93; S. Sapia on Giasone del Maino, [fol. 7]; A. Telesio on Giangiacomo Trivulzi, [fol. 7r–v]; and P. Valeriano on Girolamo della Torre, [fol. 8].

116. Ludovico Carbone on Guarino, pp. 104–6, esp. p. 106.

117. Kennedy, *Classical Rhetoric*, pp. 73–75; and Oravec, "'Observation,'" pp. 169–70.

118. See Guarino's conjunction of *collaudatio* (the praise of past deeds) and *cohortatio* (the exhortation to future deeds) in the *Epistolario*, ed. Sabbadini, 1:340–41. Guarino's theory is discussed by Sabbadini, *La scuola di Guarino*, pp. 64–65; and Schweyen, *Guarino*, pp. 184–85.

119. See, e.g., Poggio Bracciolini on Niccolò Niccoli, p. 270; R. Brandolini on Domenico della Rovere, [fols. 2v–3]; G. Cattanei on Barbara Gonzaga, [fol. 14]; C. Cappello on Giorgio Corner, pp. 178–79; L. Carbone on Guarino, p. 99; A. Giuliano on Manuel Chrysoloras, p. 34; L. Giustiniani on Carlo Zeno, p. 143; F. Maturanzio on Leonardo Mansueti, fols. 135v–36; E. Priuli on Pietro Dolfin, [fol. 2r–v]; and L. Rocca on L. Dardani, [fol. 2r–v]. The phrase *ad bene beateque vivendum* and expressions like it are found in Cic. *Off.* 1.6.19, 2.2.6; *Rep.* 4.3.3.; *Tusc.* 5.1.2; *Sen.* 19.70; and *Part. Or.* 21.70. See further O'Malley, *Praise and Blame*, pp. 70–71, 193–94.

120. Poggio Bracciolini on Niccolò Niccoli, p. 270: "Plurimum enim conferre solet ad incitamenta virtutum cognitio earum rerum quas viri excellentissimi nobis suo exemplo reliquerunt." Palmeri on Domenico Capranica, fol. 14v: "cum non ad defunctorum adiutorium sed ad consolationem doctrinamque nostram vitam praeteritam commemorare a sanctis patribus institutum fuisse saepenumero legamus."

121. Hardison, *The Enduring Monument*, pp. 52–56.

122. Sallust *Iug.* 4.5–6, trans. J. C. Rolfe, Loeb Library (London: Heinemann; New York: G. P. Putnam's Sons, 1921), pp. 137–39: "I have often heard that Quintus Maximus, Publius Scipio, and other eminent men of our country were in the habit of declaring that their hearts were set mightily aflame for the pursuit of virtue [*vehementissime sibi animum ad virtutem accendi*] whenever they gazed upon the masks of their ancestors. Of course they did not mean to imply that the wax or the effigy had any such power over them, but rather that it is the memory of great deeds that kindles in the breasts of noble men this flame [*memoria rerum gestarum eam flamimam egregiis viris in pectore crescere*] that cannot be quelled until they by their own prowess have equalled the fame and glory of their forefathers."

123. Poggio Bracciolini on Bruni, pp. cxxv–cxxvi: "Itaque omnes qui viri magni et ceteris praestantiores esse volunt nomenque suum reddere clarum, litterarum studiis et doctrinae exercitia virtutum adiungant eaque ad reipublicae et ad singulorum utilitatem conferant."

124. Kristeller, "Humanism and Scholasticism," p. 86. Adalbert of Prague's sermon for the Emperor Charles IV (d. 1378) is markedly different from the practice of Italian humanists one generation later. See Adalbert of Prague, *Leben und Schriften*, ed. Kadlec, pp. 155–74.

125. Guarino wrote to Iacopo Zilioli requesting information that he could use for his funeral oration for Iacopo's mother, Teodora (*Epistolario*, ed. Sabbadini, 2:65; and Sabbadini, *Il metodo*, pp. 77–79). Pietro Barozzi, in his eulogy for Antonio Roselli, p. 168, described his search for letters related to the history of the Roselli family from the time of Accorso's teaching at Bologna. On the historical orientation of epideictic orations in the Renaissance see Kristeller, "Francesco Bandini," p. 419; idem, "Philosophy and Rhetoric: The Renaissance," p. 248; and O'Malley, *Praise and Blame*, pp. 61–62.

126. Witt, "*Ars dictaminis*," and O'Malley, "Grammar and Rhetoric in Erasmus."

127. The phrase is found in Ovid *Pont.* 4.2.35–36, and it is quoted by Guarino (see Schweyen, *Guarino*, pp. 187–88) and Poggio (see Brown, "Humanist Portrait," p. 204).

128. Petrarch, *Le familiari*, ed. Rossi, 2:78–79. See, e.g., Ermolao Barbaro on Niccolò Marcello, p. 99; Gasparino Barzizza on Giangaleazzo Visconti, fol. 16r-v; and Carlo Cappello on Giorgio Corner, p. 180.

CHAPTER THREE

1. Raffaele Brandolini on Mariano da Genazzano, p. 232: "Verum nihil est tam impossibile quod non divina voluntate fiat possibile." Brandolini is alluding to Luke 1:37. For Brandolini's life and works see G. Ballistreri in *DBI*, 14:40–42.

2. David Gutiérrez, "Testi e note."

3. R. Brandolini on Mariano da Genazzano, p. 232. Mariano's eloquence and learned piety were also praised by humanists like Poliziano and Pico della Mirandola. See Aulo Greco's introduction to his edition of Brandolini's oration, "La *docta pietas*," pp. 210–21.

4. Polybius 6.53–54. See, e.g., Vollmer, "Laudationum funebrium Romanorum historia," pp. 476–77; and Bettini, *Antropologia e cultura romana*, pp. 155–57, 186–93. Ludovico Strassoldo, in a eulogy for Francesco Corner, fols. 91–93v, first praised Francesco and then his father.

5. *Her.* 3.6.10.

6. Burgess, "Epideictic Literature," pp. 146–47; and Kennedy, *Persuasion in Greece*, pp. 154–55.

7. Burgess, "Epideictic Literature," p. 122.
8. See Russell and Wilson's introduction to their text of *Menander Rhetor*, pp. xxiii–xxiv.
9. Both texts are published in *Rhetores latini minores*, ed. Karl Halm (Leipzig: Teubner, 1863). For Priscian's treatment of the *laudes urbium* see p. 557. The anonymous treatise that contains a section entitled "De laudibus urbium" appears on p. 587.
10. Curtius, *European Literature*, pp. 154–59.
11. Fasoli, "La coscienza civica," pp. 307–10.
12. See Fasoli, "La coscienza civica," p. 318; Berrigan, "Benzo d'Alessandria"; and Hyde, "Medieval Descriptions of Cities."
13. Robey and Law, "The Venetian Myth."
14. Baron has stressed the originality of Bruni's *Laudatio* and demonstrated the influence of the *Panathenaicus* of Aristides on the work; see his *From Petrarch to Leonardo Bruni*, pp. 102–37, 151–71, and 232–63 (edition of the text). A modern edition of Decembrio's *Panegyricus* of 1436, by G. Petraglione, appears in *RIS*. For differences between these Renaissance panegyrics and medieval precedents see Stäuble, "Due panegirici"; and O'Malley, *Praise and Blame*, pp. 77–79. Panegyrics of various Italian cities continued to be written during the Renaissance. See, e.g., those on Perugia by Francesco Maturanzio and Cristoforo Sassi in Zappacosta, *Studi e ricerche*, pp. 65–113.
15. See, e.g., Giacomo Boldù on Tommaso Donato, [fol. 2r–v]; Pietro Contarini on Marco Corner, [fol. 2]; Leonardo Giustiniani on Giorgio Loredan, p. 13; L. Giustiniani on Carlo Zeno, p. 141; Antonio Maggi on Marco Corner (the younger), [fol. 3v]; Pietro Marcello on Andrea Vendramin, p. 145; Andrea Navagero on Leonardo Loredan, p. 27; and Giovanni Battista Ramusio on Francesco Fasolo, p. 387. For the myth of Venice see Fasoli, "Nascita di un mito"; Gaeta, "Alcune considerazioni"; and Muir, *Civic Ritual*, pp. 13–61.
16. Both Leonardo Giustiniani in his oration for Carlo Zeno, p. 141, and Pietro Marcello when eulogizing Andrea Vendramin, p. 145, use the phrase "novitas ac situs opportunitas." Cf. Cic. *Rep.* 2.3.5.
17. See, e.g., Giacomo Boldù on Tommaso Donato, [fol. 2v]; Pietro Contarini on Marco Corner, [fol. 2]; Leonardo Giustiniani on Giorgio Loredan, p. 13; Antonio Maggi on Marco Corner (the younger), [fol. 3]; and Pietro Marcello on Andrea Vendramin, p. 145.
18. Maggi on Marco Corner (the younger), [fol. 3]: "Sub caelo enim crassissimo orti pingues et hebetes, sub tenui et salubri acuti et solertes sunt, ferventissimis aestibus obnoxii exustis animorum viribus timidiores fiunt. Qui autem frigidas regiones incolunt, ingenii et artificii minimum habent. Urbs Venetiarum temperato salutarique aere eos educat viros qui et ingenio et doctrina et eloquentia plurimum excellunt." Cicero (*Fat.* 4.7) contrasts the "caelum crassum" of Thebes to the "caelum tenue" of Athens.

19. Leonardo Giustiniani on Giorgio Loredan, pp. 13–14; and Andrea Navagero on Leonardo Loredan, p. 27. See also Giovanni Battista Ramusio on Francesco Fasolo, p. 387. O'Malley, *Praise and Blame*, pp. 208–9n. 49, observes that the phrase "patria communis" was coined by Isocrates and applied to Rome by authors like Cicero (1 *Cat.* 7.17) and Seneca.

20. Giacomo Boldù on Tommaso Donato, [fol. 2v]; Bernardo Giustiniani on Francesco Foscari, pp. 22–23; Sabellico on Benedetto Rugio, col. 498A; and George of Trebizond on Fantino Michiel, p. 448.

21. See Bernardo Giustiniani on Francesco Foscari, pp. 31–32, 41, 44–46, 59; and Labalme, *Bernardo Giustiniani*, pp. 116–18.

22. Bonisoli, untitled panegyric for Pietro Foscari, fol. 50r–v. See also Giovanni Battista Egnazio on Luigi Dardani, [fol. 2v]; Leonardo Giustiniani on Giorgio Loredan, pp. 14–15; Giovanni Marini on Antonio Suriani, [fol. 3]; and Andrea Navagero on Leonardo Loredan, p. 27. For the debate over Venice's imperialist policy in the Quattrocento see Labalme, *Bernardo Giustiniani*, pp. 109–25.

23. Leonardo Giustiniani on Giorgio Loredan, pp. 14–15; and Eusebio Priuli on Pietro Dolfin, [fol. 2v].

24. Giacomo Boldù on Tommaso Donato, [fol. 2v]. The date 25 March 421 for the founding of Venice appeared for the first time in the fourteenth-century chronicle of Iacopo Dondi; see Muir, *Civic Ritual*, pp. 65–74.

25. Bonisoli's panegyric for Pietro Foscari, fol. 50; Bernardo Giustiniani on Francesco Foscari, p. 22; and Muir, *Civic Ritual*, pp. 30–32.

26. Bernardo Giustiniani on Francesco Foscari, fol. 186. The passage is omitted in the printed version of the speech.

27. See, e.g., Giacomo Boldù on Tommaso Donato, [fol. 2v]; Pietro Contarini on Marco Corner, [fol. 2]; and Leonardo Giustiniani on Giorgio Loredan, p. 14.

28. Eusebio Priuli on Pietro Dolfin, [fol. 2v]. See also Carlo Cappello on Giorgio Corner, p. 180; Ermolao Barbaro on Niccolò Marcello, p. 100; Francesco Barbaro on Giovanni Corradini, fol. 62v; and Giovanni Marini on Antonio Suriani, [fol. 3].

29. Pietro Contarini on Marco Corner, [fol. 2r–v]. See also Bernardo Giustiniani on Francesco Foscari, fols. 192–93.

30. Pietro Marcello on Andrea Vendramin, pp. 145–46; and Bernardo Giustiniani on Francesco Foscari, pp. 22–23.

31. See, e.g., Aurelio Bienato on Lorenzo de' Medici, [fol. 1v]; Elio Lampridio Cerva on Niccolò Morelli, fol. 19v; and Giannozzo Manetti on Giannozzo Pandolfini, fols. 1v–2. For Salutati's position on the founding of Florence see Witt, "Coluccio Salutati." In general see Weinstein, "The Myth of Florence."

32. Bruni on Nanni Strozzi, p. 3. On the appreciation for the Etruscan contribution to Florence's cultural heritage see Cipriani, *Il mito etrusco*, pp. 1–

69. Baron discusses Bruni's oration for Nanni in *Crisis*, rev. ed., pp. 412–39.

33. Bienato on Lorenzo de' Medici, [fol. 1v]. Bruni rejected the tradition that Charlemagne had rebuilt Florence in his history of the city, but leading humanists like Manetti, Poggio, Matteo Palmieri, and Donato Acciaiuoli continued to accept it. See Fubini, "Osservazioni," pp. 435–41.

34. Adriani on Giuliano de' Medici, duke of Nemours, fol. 72r–v. Aurelio Bienato, in his eulogy for Lorenzo de' Medici, [fol. 4r–v], also noted that the stonework of Florence contributed to the city's beauty.

35. Bruni on Nanni Strozzi, pp. 3–4, and Baron, *Crisis*, rev. ed., pp. 412–20, who demonstrated that Bruni used the funeral speech of Pericles for his ideological inspiration. An anonymous eulogist for Paolo Tron, fols. 99v–100, contended that the Venetian republican constitution stimulated a similar competition for virtue.

36. Marcello Adriani on Giuliano de' Medici, duke of Nemours, fols. 72v–73; and Aurelio Bienato on Lorenzo de' Medici, [fols. 2–3].

37. See, e.g., Aurelio Bienato on Lorenzo de' Medici, [fol. 2]; Leonardo Bruni on Nanni Strozzi, p. 3; and Cristoforo Landino on Donato Acciaiuoli, fol. 12.

38. See, e.g., Marcello Adriani on Giuliano de' Medici, duke of Nemours, fol. 72; Aurelio Bienato on Lorenzo de' Medici, [fol. 4r–v]; Poggio Bracciolini on Lorenzo de' Medici (the elder), p. 283; and Leonardo Bruni on Otto Cavalcanti, p. 143.

39. Leonardo Bruni on Nanni Strozzi, p. 4. He also (ibid.) compares Florence to Camillus because Florence had "refounded" the Latin language. Bruni had posited a cultural supremacy for Florence in his *Laudatio* (ca. 1403–4); see Baron, *From Petrarch to Leonardo Bruni*, pp. 151–71. In general see Ferguson, *The Renaissance in Historical Thought*, pp. 18–28; and Mazzocco, "Decline and Rebirth."

40. Poggio Bracciolini on Leonardo Bruni, p. cxxiv. Both Bruni and Poggio benefited from generous tax breaks.

41. Bienato on Lorenzo de' Medici, [fols. 3–4]. Bienato named Petrarch, Dante, Boccaccio, Poggio, and Tito Strozzi as Florentines who contributed to the rebirth of letters, and he adduced Giotto and Donatello for the visual arts.

42. See Girolamo Aliotti on Bartolomeo Zabarella, p. 312; Poggio Bracciolini on Francesco Zabarella, p. 252; and Francesco Filelfo on Filippo Borromeo, fol. 75v. The legend is based on Virgil *Aen.* 1.242–49.

43. Ludovico Carbone on Guarino, pp. 91–92; idem on Giovanni Ercole, fol. 169; and Piero Valeriano on Girolamo della Torre, [fol. 2r–v].

44. Giovanni Cattanei on Barbara Gonzaga, [fol. 5]; and idem on Francesco Gonzaga, fol. 15v. For Mantua, cf. also the anonymous oration on Antonio

Gonzaga, fol. 156. For Modena as a Roman colony see Elio Lampridio Cerva on Andrea da Modena, fol. 131.

45. See the anonymous oration on Ioannes Germanicus, fols. 113v–14, for Perugia; Girolamo Gioia on Benedetto Rugio, [fol. 1v], and Sabellico on Benedetto Rugio, col. 498B, for Salerno; and Lorenzo Grana on Giles of Viterbo, p. 296.

46. Pietro Donato on Francesco Zabarella, p. 145b; and Girolamo Aliotti on Bartolomeo Zabarella, p. 312.

47. Ludovico Carbone on Guarino, p. 92; and idem on Giovanni Ercole, fol. 169.

48. Pietro Barozzi on Antonio Roselli, pp. 165–67, esp. p. 165: "Etruriam cum ceterarum provinciarum, tum inprimis Italiae florem esse, partim litterae quibus Romani pueri, ut postea Graecis, ita olim Etruscis vulgo erudiri solebant, partim virorum ingenia et vernaculi sermonis elegantia, partim aëris temperies et regionis situs, partim denique frumenti ac pecoris et omnium copia rerum indicio sunt."

49. Poggio Bracciolini on Leonardo Bruni, p. cxviii (referring to Livy 28.45.16–17) and pp. cviii–cvix, where Poggio described Arezzo as the home of the Muses and a place where the "studia humanitatis et sapientiae" are cultivated. Cf. also Giannozzo Manetti on Leonardo Bruni, p. xc.

50. Pietro Barozzi on Antonio Roselli, p. 167. Barozzi concluded by drawing an analogy between the perfume that is produced in Arabia and the facility with which Arezzo produces men outstanding in religion, eloquence, and the liberal arts.

51. See Vettore Fausto on Francesco Rosso, pp. 471–78, esp. 472–73; and cf. Antonio Lollio on Philibert Hugonet, [fol. 2]; and Pietro Ranzano on Francesco da Toledo, [fol. 2].

52. Marcantonio Magno on Ferdinand of Aragon, [fols. 3v–4], esp. [fol. 4]: "Denique nulla gens similior Italis nostrisque moribus convenientior quam Hispana. Sunt etenim vere Romani, immo servant adhuc Romanorum et spiritus et mores et fere linguam, quandoquidem (ut scriptum reperimus) plurimae sunt a Romanis deductae coloniae in Hispaniam. Vicinitas quasi quaedam et caeli similitudo quae mari tantummodo Mediterraneo dividitur efficit ut idem fere sint Itali atque Hispani." Elio Lampridio Cerva often emphasized the connections between Rome and Dubrovnik (Ragusa). See his orations on Nicolaus Gotius, fols. 84v–85v; on Orsatus Gotius, fols. 88v–89; and on Martullo Zamagna, fols. 114v–16v; and Škunca, *Aelius Lampridius Cervinus*, pp. 167–70. Remo Guidi called my attention to Škunca's work.

53. Baron, *Crisis*, rev. ed., pp. 412–39, argues that Bruni's oration for Nanni Strozzi first presented a relationship between humanism and Florentine political freedom.

54. The Celtic heritage of Milan is mentioned by Francesco Filelfo in his oration for Filippo Borromeo, fol. 75v. On the myth of Rome see O'Malley, *Praise and Blame*, pp. 206–11; Hammer, "The New or Second Rome"; Pratt, "Rome as Eternal"; Gaeta, "Sull'idea di Roma"; and Stinger, "*Roma Triumphans*."

55. Poggio Bracciolini on Giuliano Cesarini, pp. 726–27; and Iacopo Zeno on Giuliano Cesarini, fol. 1v: "Repetebam enim ab initio primum quae urbs illi ex qua originem traheret evenisset, Roma scilicet, terrarum orbis caput et princeps. Qua quidem neque gloria nominis ulla celebrior, neque imperii propagatione potentior, neque virium potestate robustior, neque hominum praestantia dignior, neque bonarum artium disciplinarumque omnium studiosior ulla unquam inter mortales fuit. Urbs quidem et orbis domina cui nulli reges, nulli bellorum duces nec ulli ferocissimi et immanissimi populi satis esse vel pugnando vel vincendo vel regendo et dominando valuere." Cf. also Raffaele Brandolini on Mariano da Genazzano, p. 233; Alessandro Oliva on Ugolino de' Micheli, fol. 38r–v; Francesco Padovano on Leonardo Savelli, fol. 86; and idem on Pietro Naldi, fol. 87v.

56. See in general O'Malley, *Praise and Blame*, pp. 211–16; and my "Ideal Renaissance Pope," pp. 43–46. For the contribution of the della Rovere see Tommaso Inghirami's eulogy for Julius II, pp. 82–83. Ancient panegyric often used the pattern of decline and rebirth to highlight a ruler's efforts to restore culture. See Maguinness, "Some Methods of the Latin Panegyrists"; and Ramage, "Velleius Paterculus 2.126.2–3."

57. The speech is recorded in Suet. *Caes*. 6. See Kennedy, *Rhetoric in the Roman World*, p. 285. Giovanni Gatti, in his eulogy for Latino Orsini, fol. 79, listed persons from antiquity of outstanding lineage. He conjoined classical and Christian precedents: (1) Alexander the Great (father Philip and line traced to Achilles); (2) Julian house (to Aeneas); (3) Plato (from Solon); (4) Aristotle (from Asclepius); (5) Cicero (from King Tullius); and (6) Jesus (son of Mary whose line traced back to kings, prophets, and patriarchs of Israel).

58. See, e.g., Pietro Contarini on Marco Corner, [fol. 2v]; Giovanni Battista Egnazio on Marco Corner (the younger), fols. 2–3; and Antonio Maggi on Marco Corner (the younger), [fol. 4]. Strássoldo's remarks are found in his oration on Francesco Corner, fol. 93. Cf. also anonymous, "Oratio in laudem Thadei Quirino [sic]," fols. 144v–45.

59. See the anonymous oration on Giangaleazzo Visconti, fols. 97v–98v; Giovanni Montano on Filippo Maria Visconti, col. 435D; and Pietro Castelleto on Giangaleazzo Visconti, cols. 1046A-48A. Lorenzo Rocca posited Trojan origins for Luigi Dardani, [fol. 3v], on rather obvious etymological grounds. In his eulogy for Ippolito I d'Este, [fol. 1v], Alessandro Guarini traced the origins of the Este back to "Marthus," one of the seven generals (*duces*) of Antenor. Celio Calcagnini, in his eulogy for Alfonso I d'Este, pp.

267–68, assigned the family's origins to Germans who came to Italy at the time of Charlemagne. See further Gundersheimer, *Ferrara*, pp. 19–20. Calcagnini felt that the Costabili of Ferrara had every right to boast about their Italian origins. See his oration on Antonio, pp. 274–75, esp. p. 275: "Troianos alii, alii Gallos aut Germanos auctores generis iactent, hi vetustatem et incunabula gentis non peregre, sed inter eos ipsos lares in quibus creverunt ostendunt." On the emergence of a sense of *Italianità* during the Renaissance see Ilardi, " 'Italianità.' "

60. The etymologies of family names are discussed by Battista Casali on Giovanni Colonna, fols. 29v–30; Tommaso Inghirami on Pietro Menzi, pp. 193–96; Montorio Mascarelli on Giovan Francesco Capodilista, fols. 71v–72; and Pietro Partenio on Antonio Fracanziani, [fol. 11v]. Cf. also the anonymous oration on Bernardino Marimeni, fol. 42; and Francesco Pucci on Francesco Minutolo, fol. 1v. Orators also proferred etymological explanations for the names of places. See, e.g., Gabriele Bucci on Ludovico I, marchese di Saluzzo (*Il Memoriale Quadripartitum*, p. 183); Francesco Negro on Ercole I d'Este, [fol. 3]; and Ludovico Pontico Virunio on Elisabetta Visdomini, [fols. 5–6v].

61. For discussion of the symbolism of a coat-of-arms see Marcello Adriani? on Cosimo de' Pazzi, [fol. 2]; and Francesco Vigilio on Francesco II Gonzaga, fol. 126r–v. Both examples are from the second decade of the sixteenth century.

62. The Este (Celio Calcagnini on Alfonso I d'Este, pp. 267–68), the Malatesta, the Baglioni, and the Gonzaga (Francesco Vigilio on Francesco II Gonzaga, fol. 126r–v) all supposedly came to Italy during the time of Charlemagne. Vigilio claimed that the last three families were driven out of Germany by Charlemagne and cited Enea Silvio Piccolomini as his source.

63. George of Trebizond on Fantino Michiel, p. 448. See also Francesco Maturanzio on Orazio I Baglioni, fol. 53v; and Marcello Adriani? on Cosimo de' Pazzi, [fols. 2v–3], where the orator narrates the legend that the Pazzi received the sacred fire from the holy sepulcher in Jerusalem for their efforts in recapturing the city.

64. Pietro Barozzi on Antonio Roselli, p. 168.

65. Anonymous on Louise of Savoy, fol. 2r–v: "Tanta in eo Christianae pietatis reverentia enituit ut, cum principes cerneret partim Eugenio deinde Nicolao pontificibus, partim Basiliensi Concilio varias in factiones distractos adhaerere ut [*sic*] omnia in unum redigeret ne tanti indies mali radices diutius alerentur et funesta illa fax quae universam inflammarat Italiam penitus exstingueretur, sciens volensque ultro se pontificatu abdicavit et Nicolaum Romanum pontificem verum Christi vicarium professus est." Bartolomeo Zamberti called Lorenzo Valla the "delitiae Latinae linguae" in his eulogy for Giorgio Valla, p. 305. Pietro Marcello narrated the miraculous recovery of a

silver cross by Andrea Vendramin, the grandfather of Doge Andrea, pp. 146–47. The event was immortalized in Gentile Bellini's painting now in the Accademia in Venice. See also Battista Casali on Francesco Soderini, fol. 292 (for mention of Piero); and Antonio Lollio on Laudomia Piccolomini, cols. 687–88 (for mention of Pius II).

66. Francesco da Toledo on Leonardo della Rovere, [fol. 2v]. Lorenzo Grana appropriately paid tribute to Alessandro Farnese at the funeral of Clement VII (pp. 263–64). Alessandro was elected pope a few days later.

67. Andrea Navagero on Leonardo Loredan, p. 29: "Longe tamen maiores res ab illis geri quos et exspectatio hominum et parentum virtus excitet. Haeret enim eorum animis, quasi fax quaedam, assidua cogitatio quae noctes diesque illos ad egregium agendum aliquid inflammet, quo maiobus [sic] suis digni reperiantur ac patrimonium gloriae sibi ab illis relictum et tueri et augere possint." Cf. also Piero Valeriano on Girolamo della Torre, [fol. 3].

68. Pietro del Monte on Giovanni Zabarella, fols. 47v–48, esp. fol. 48: "Quod si P. Scipio et Q. Fabius visis maiorum imaginibus mirum in modum ad virtutem excitatos esse comperimus, si C. Caesar inspecta Alexandri magni statua ad summam rerum accensus est, quo pacto his vivis spirantibusque exemplis Ioannis ingenium ad hoc praeclarum legendi discendique studium excitatum atque inflammatum fuisse credendum est." The allusions are to Sall. *Iug.* 4.5–6 and Suet. *Caes.* 7.

69. Battista Casali on Giovanni Colonna, fols. 30v–32v, esp. fol. 30v: "Bonifacius octavus in totam familiam odio internicino invectus sacris interdixit, anathemate amplissimo notavit, gentem exsecratam appellavit et in decreta pontificia rettulit, Iacobum et Ioannem cardinales et exsilio et sacerdotio multavit. Quos tamen Benedictus XI ad pristinam et dignitatem et auctoritatem restituit. Qui quidem quia plus quam deceret saevit, plus quoque divinitus, ut arbitror, quam par erat supplicii dedit. Nam quem per scelus pontificatum invasit neque sanctius administravit, per scelus quoque a Sciarra Columnensi captus atque in arctissima custodia habitus turpissime cum vita dimisit." For Giovanni's battles with popes Sixtus IV and Alexander VI see F. Petrucci in *DBI*, 27:342–44.

70. Andrea Biglia on Giangaleazzo Visconti (I), pp. 179–80. See also Agostino Camici on Filippo Maria Visconti, fol. 126r–v.

71. Hans Baron identified the ideological character of Bruni's panegyrical writings in his *Crisis*, rev. ed., pp. 191–224, 412–62, and *From Petrarch to Leonardo Bruni*, pp. 151–71. For the continuation of this republican ideology and its application to Cosimo de' Medici see Brown, "Humanist Portrait." Recent scholarship has demonstrated that republican institutions at Florence were manipulated by oligarchic factions before and after Cosimo's return from exile in 1434. See esp. Najemy, *Corporatism and Consensus*, pp. 263–317; Brucker, *The Civic World*; and Rubinstein, *Florence under the Medici*.

72. On Medici funerals see Strocchia, "Burials in Renaissance Florence," pp. 39–46, 268–74, 290–99. She demonstrates, pp. 297–99, that the processional route for Giuliano's funeral in 1516 repeated that followed by Leo X three months earlier. For the political background to these ceremonies see Bullard, *Filippo Strozzi and the Medici*, pp. 9–44.

73. See Brown, "Humanist Portrait," p. 194. Cleofilo praised the Florentines for reviving the use of the title and for awarding it to Cosimo. He advocated that the citizens of Fano do likewise for Antonio Costanzi in 1490. See Cleofilo on A. Costanzi, [fols. 58v–59]. The title *pater patriae* appeared in funeral oratory as early as 1403, when Francesco Zabarella applied it to Arcoano Buzzacarini (p. 143). Gasparino Barzizza called Marciano di Tortona Ligure by the title (fol. 15), and Pietro Donato applied it to Cardinal Francesco Zabarella in 1417 (p. 144b). See also note 78 below.

74. Battista Casali on Giuliano de' Medici, duke of Nemours, fol. 63r–v, esp. fol. 63v: "Itaque quorundam nobilium conspiratione patria eiectus vix annum totum exsulavit cum civium consensu ac patriae humeris reportatus nihil gravius in adversarios consuluit quam ut exsilio solum verterent, tantamque potentiam volentibus civibus est assecutus quanta nulli unquam privato contigit."

75. Marcello Adriani on Giuliano de' Medici, duke of Nemours, fols. 73v–74.

76. Ibid., fol. 74. Cf. also Battista Casali on Giuliano de' Medici, duke of Nemours, fol. 64v.

77. Battista Casali on Giuliano de' Medici, duke of Nemours, fols. 63v–64; Marcello Adriani on Giuliano de' Medici, duke of Nemours, fol. 73v; and Francesco Cattani on Lorenzo de' Medici, duke of Urbino, fols. 362v–63. See also Poggio Bracciolini's remarks in his eulogy for Lorenzo de' Medici (the elder), p. 283; and Gombrich, "The Early Medici as Patrons of Art."

78. Battista Casali on Giuliano de' Medici, duke of Nemours, fol. 64r–v, who stressed that Cosimo successfully defended Florence from the attack of Filippo Maria Visconti; and Marcello Adriani on Giuliano de' Medici, duke of Nemours, fol. 74.

79. Battista Casali on Giuliano de' Medici, duke of Nemours, fols. 64v–65v, esp. fol. 65v: "Nempe simul ea omnia quae quidem divinitus crediderim accidisse ut plus interdum praesidii in pietate, facundia, prudentia quam in armis esse appareret? Quis Codros mihi, quis Decios iactet? Illi moriendo suum patriae sanguinem dumtaxat exhibuerunt, hic paratus etiam mori qui armis occiderat sua se prudentia patriae, patriam sibi sine sanguine incolumem servavit. Ex illo expertus quantum esset in pace boni ad pacem spectare, pacem velle, bellum odisse et tanquam pacis magister motus omnes Italiae suo arbitratu laxare ac reprimere quasi habenas solebat quocum Italiae pax atque tranquillitas simul viguit, simul etiam occidit."

80. Ibid., fols. 65v–66: "Conquisitis enim undique excellenti singularique doctrina viris hisque exceptis hospitio, amicitia, stipendiis, mirum quam brevi Florentia quasi quoddam bonarum artium facultatumque omnium emporium asylumque fuerit. Nam non tam Graeciam viris eruditissimis quam libris et vetustate et fide probatissimis exhausit, ut Florentia non magis Etrusca atque Romana quam Attica perhiberetur quo vel ipsas quoque Athenas migrasse diceres." Casali developed this same theme with reference to the papal library in a discourse delivered in Rome, 1508. See O'Malley, "The Vatican Library and the Schools of Athens."

81. Lorenzo Grana on Clement VII, pp. 262–63; and Marcello Adriani on Giuliano de' Medici, duke of Nemours, fol. 76r–v.

82. Andrea Alamanno on Giovanni di Cosimo de' Medici, fol. 86v; and Marcello Adriani on Giuliano de' Medici, duke of Nemours, fol. 73r–v.

83. Aurelio Bienato on Lorenzo de' Medici, [fol. 5]; Battista Casali on Giuliano de' Medici, duke of Nemours, fol. 66; and Lorenzo Grana on Clement VII, pp. 262–63. For patronage of building see Marcello Adriani on Giuliano de' Medici, duke of Nemours, fol. 73v; Aurelio Bienato on Lorenzo de' Medici, [fol. 5]; and Battista Casali on Giuliano de' Medici, duke of Nemours, fol. 66.

84. Marcello Adriani on Giuliano de' Medici, duke of Nemours, fol. 73r–v; and Brown, "Humanist Portrait," pp. 204–13. For a different assessment of Medici rule from the early Cinquecento see Najemy, "Machiavelli and the Medici."

85. Raffaele Brandolini on Lorenzo Cibò, fol. 83r–v. The reference to Sulla's being greeted by an "ass" seems to be an allusion to Plut. *Sul.* 27.2. Cf. also Ludovico Odassi on Guid'Ubaldo I, pp. 403–4; Marco Vigerio on Sixtus IV, fol. 401v; and Giasone del Maino on Girolamo Torti, [fol. 3r–v]. Maino mentioned incidents from the lives of Midas, Plato, Alexander, and Saint Ambrose. Orators also called attention to omens related to an individual's death. See, e.g., Pietro Barozzi on Giovanni Barozzi, p. 121.

86. Giannantonio Campano on Pius II, [fol. 99]; and on Alessandro Oliva, [fol. 116v]. Campano also relates, [fol. 118r–v] that Oliva foresaw the time of his death prior to any illness, the place where his funeral would be held, and the fact that Campano himself would deliver the eulogy. For other omens related to one's vocation see anonymous on Leonardo Bruni, pp. 149–50; Guglielmo Pagello on Bartolomeo Colleoni, [fols. 4–5]; and Francesco Maturanzio on Leonardo Mansueti, fols. 24v–25v.

87. See, e.g., anonymous, "Oratio in laudem Thadei Quirino [sic]," fol. 145v: "Etenim cum intelligeret cetera caduca et infirma et quasi fortunae ludibria, virtutem autem unam esse quae altissimis sit defixa radicibus quae nulla unquam vi labefactari aut dimoveri loco possit, ad egregia humanitatis

studia et liberales artes animum applicuit." For the place of the *studia humanitatis* in Renaissance thought see Kristeller, "Humanism and Scholasticism."

88. See, e.g., Ermolao Barbaro on Niccolò Marcello, p. 100; Andrea Biglia on a Stefano, fol. 128; Poggio Bracciolini on Francesco Zabarella, p. 252; and Giannantonio Campano on Giovanni della Ratta, [fols. 114v–15]. Giovanni Battista Flavi noted that Cajetan's mother introduced her son to the study of Aquinas [fol. 2v]. Poggio Bracciolini noted, in a contrary sense, that Niccolò Niccoli rejected his father's wish that he become a merchant, preferring the more honest commerce of letters (p. 270).

89. See, e.g., Giannantonio Campano on Pius II, [fol. 99r–v]; Francesco Maturanzio on Leonardo Mansueti, fols. 130v–31; Niccolò Palmeri on Domenico Capranica, fol. 15; and idem on Prospero Colonna, fol. 120v. Cf. Kristeller, "Humanism and Scholasticism," p. 87, and "Philosophy and Rhetoric: The Renaissance," p. 250.

90. Guarino on Margherita Gonzaga, fol. 108v; and Garin, *L'educazione in Europa*, pp. 147–53.

91. Niccolò Capranica on Bessarion, p. 406; and Giovanni Tortelli? on Ludovico Trevisan, fol. 178v. For the study of poetry as part of grammatical instruction in antiquity see O'Malley, "Grammar and Rhetoric in Erasmus."

92. See, e.g., Aurelio Brandolini on Lorenzo Giustini, fol. 220v; Giannantonio Campano on Battista Sforza, [fol. 120]; Battista Casali on Gabriello Gabrielli, fols. 300v–301; Leonardo Giustiniani on Carlo Zeno, p. 142; Elio Lampridio Cerva on Mattia Corvino, fol. 75; Pietro del Monte on Giovanni Zabarella, fol. 47; Ludovico Odassi on Ippolita Maria Sforza, p. 48; idem on Guid'Ubaldo I, pp. 407–8, 414–20; and Sabellico on Benedetto Rugio, fol. 499A.

93. See, e.g., Battista Casali on Gabriello Gabrielli, fol. 301v; Giovanni Cattanei on Francesco Gonzaga, [fols. 16v–17]; Antonio Maggi on Marco Corner (the younger), [fols. 4v–5]; Giannozzo Manetti on Leonardo Bruni, p. c; Francesco Maturanzio on Leonardo Mansueti, fol. 131; idem on Francesco da Porto, fol. 78r–v; Antonio Pacini on Lorenzo de' Medici (the elder), fol. 13; and Niccolò Perotti on Pietro Riario, fol. 152v.

94. For the expression *studia humanitatis* see anonymous, "Oratio in laudem Thadei Quirino [*sic*]," fol. 145; Andrea Alamanno on Giovanni di Cosimo de' Medici, fol. 87; Francesco Barbaro on Giovanni Corradini, fols. 63v–64; Gasparino Barzizza on Marciano di Tortona Ligure, fols. 15v–16; Giacomo Boldù on Tommaso Donato, [fol. 5r–v]; Poggio Bracciolini on Niccolò Niccoli, p. 271; idem on Giuliano Cesarini, p. 727; Pietro Donato on Francesco Zabarella, p. 146b; Guarino on Giannicola Salerno, col. 484; Francesco Maturanzio on Girolamo Pagliello, fol. 116r–v; and Antonio Pacini on Lorenzo de' Medici (the elder), fol. 13. The expression *litterae humanitatis* occurs in the anonymous oration on Bernardo Eroli, [fol. 3v].

95. Kristeller, "Humanism and Scholasticism," p. 98.
96. Andrea Giuliano on Manuel Chrysoloras, pp. 27–28, 31–32. See the detailed discussion of Giuliano's oration at the beginning of chapter 6.
97. Pietro del Monte on Giovanni Zabarella, fol. 47, referring to Cic. *Sen.* 3.9. Del Monte has transferred Cicero's remarks from a context of old age to that of life in general. For Pietro's studies and importance for Renaissance preaching see O'Malley, *Praise and Blame*, pp. 81–83.
98. Guarino on Giannicola Salerno, col. 484.
99. Guarino on Margherita Gonzaga, fol. 108v. For further praise of Vittorino's pedagogy see the anonymous oration on Giberto da Correggio, fol. 26v; and Ludovico Odassi on Federigo da Montefeltro, fol. 3.
100. Ludovico Carbone on Guarino, p. 92.
101. Ibid., p. 94: "Pudendum erat quam parumper litterarum sciebant nostri homines ante Guarini adventum. Nemo erat, non dicam qui oratoriam facultatem nosceret, qui rhetoricam profiteretur, qui graviter et ornate diceret et in publico aliquo conventu verba facere auderet, sed qui veram grammaticae rationem cognosceret, qui vocabulorum proprietatem vimque intelligeret, qui poetas interpretari posset. Iacebat Priscianus, ignorabatur Servius, incognita erant opera Ciceronis, miraculi loco habebatur si quis Crispum Sallustium, si quis C. Caesarem, si quis T. Livium nominaret, si quis ad veterum scriptorum intelligentiam aspiraret. Quadragesimus fere annus cives nostros in ludo puerili occupatos inveniebat in iisdem elementis semper laborantes, semper convolutos, usque adeo bonarum litterarum ruina facta erat."
102. Ibid., p. 95. Carbone continued by mentioning Guarino's lectures on authors like Cicero, Virgil, and Juvenal.
103. Ibid., pp. 95, 98–99. Carbone cited the example of Phoenix, who was assigned to teach Achilles how to speak and act well. The story is recorded initially in Homer *Il.* 9.443 and cited by Cicero *De or.* 3.15.57.
104. See B. Guarini's "De ordine docendi et studendi," ed. Garin, pp. 434–71. Garin discusses its contents in *L'educazione in Europa*, pp. 141–47.
105. Antonio Pacini on Lorenzo de' Medici (the elder), fol. 13: "Quamquam iam aetate provectus studiis humanitatis se contulit. Ex quibus tantum sibi vendicavit ut inter doctos homines disciplinam benevivendi ac benedicendi ignorare non videretur." Pacini went on to admit that Cosimo's brother attained only modest proficiency in oratory. Giannozzo Manetti, p. c. The epitaph on Bruni's tomb in Santa Croce reads: "Historia luget, eloquentia muta est, ferturque Musas tum Graecas tum Latinas lacrimas tenere non potuisse."
106. Francesco Maturanzio on Francesco da Porto, fol. 78r–v. On Maturanzio's career see Zappacosta, *Francesco Maturanzio*. For the creative character of

Vergerio's curriculum see Robey, "Humanism and Education," pp. 43–44, 47; and my "Oratory of Vergerio," p. 6.

107. Sabellico on Benedetto Rugio, p. 499A; and Leonardo Giustiniani on Carlo Zeno, p. 142. See also Ludovico Carbone on Ludovico Casella, fol. 200; Kristeller, "Music and Learning"; and Eörsi, "Lo studiolo di Lionello d'Este," pp. 38–40.

108. Ludovico Carbone on Ludovico di San Bonifacio, fol. 105r–v. Carbone notes that Ludovico drew an illustration in his copy of Plautus. See further Kristeller, "The Modern System of the Arts," pp. 181–83; and Westfall, "Painting and the Liberal Arts."

109. Andrea Navagero on Leonardo Loredan, p. 32.

110. See, e.g., Antonio Maggi on Marco Corner (the younger), [fol. 5]: "Rhetori deinde, cum multum in grammaticis profecisset, traditur ut orandi facultatem doceretur quae natura, arte, et exercitatione consumitur, ut sciret in iudiciis suadere et dissuadere, praeterita laudare vel vituperare, et de futuris deliberare." On the traditional character of this triad see Kennedy, *Classical Rhetoric*, p. 32.

111. Andrea Alamanno on Giovanni di Cosimo de' Medici, fol. 87; and Battista Casali on Aloysius of Aragon, fol. 43. I have been unable to find this saying in the works of Demades.

112. Poggio Bracciolini on Niccolò Niccoli, p. 271: "Contulit se in eius [i.e., Marsili's] familiaritatem ut una cum studiis doctrinae, vitae quoque et morum institutionem perciperet. Hoc quidem mature et sapienter inprimis egit. Nam quibus honesta vivendi ratio proposita est aliquem sibi integrum et probatum virum eligere debent ad cuius imitationem et similitudinem informentur."

113. See, e.g., Poggio Bracciolini on Leonardo Bruni, p. cxix; and Giannozzo Manetti on Leonardo Bruni, p. xciii: "At vero ubi aliquandiu ipsum publice legentem audivit, tanto ac tam magno suavissimae linguae suae amore capiebatur ut iuris civilis studia praetermittere atque in eius disciplinam se totum tradere concupisceret." Manetti's source was Bruni himself, *Commentarius*, pp. 431–32.

114. Niccolò Capranica on Bessarion, p. 406; Andrea Alamanno on Giovanni di Cosimo de' Medici, fol. 87; Giovanni Cattanei on Francesco Gonzaga, [fol. 16v]; and Guarino on Margherita Gonzaga, fol. 108v: "Ipse vero praeceptor Victorinus Feltrensis est tum vita et moribus integerrimus, tum eruditione et omni litterarum genere Graece ac Latine probatissimus, ita ut non minus exemplo quam disciplina ad perdiscendum et ad recte vivendum hortaretur et expediret." Orators regularly commended their subjects for traveling to study with outstanding teachers. See Gasparino Barzizza on Marciano di Tortona Ligure, fol. 15v; Ludovico Carbone on Guarino, p. 92

(referring to Cic. *Tusc.* 4.19.44); Battista Casali on Francesco Remolino, fols. 17v–18; Ludovico da Imola on Pietro Ferrici, [fol. 1v]; Giasone del Maino on Girolamo Torti, [fols. 4v–5v]; Pietro Marsi on Pomponio Leto, [fol. 2r–v]; Francesco Maturanzio on Leonardo Mansueti, fols. 131–32; and Camillo Porcari on Marco Vigerio, fol. 73.

115. Poggio Bracciolini on Francesco Zabarella, pp. 252, 256–57, referring to Cic. *Mur.* 9.19, *Leg.* 1.6.18, *Clu.* 53.146; Antonio Solerio on Pietro Canonici, [fol. 4], referring to Cic. *Off.* 1.7.22, *Fin.* 2.14.45; and Gasparino Barzizza on Marciano di Tortona Ligure, fols. 15v–16.

116. Poggio Bracciolini on Francesco Zabarella, pp. 252–53, 256–57; Pietro Barozzi on Antonio Roselli, pp. 173–74; and Paolo Bigolini on Battista Casali, fol. 3: "Huic tanto ac tam divino ingenio non defuit Lucas Casalius iuris civilis ac pontificii scientia clarissimus, cuius hortatu ac impulsu legibus strenue admodum operam impendit. Videbat enim iuris civilis cognitionem ei vel maxime necessariam esse qui mox tantus in dicendo futurus esset, ut ea ipsi nota essent quae si quis nesciat ad earum rerum scientiam quas Latini scriptores litteris persecuti sunt non facile penetrare potest." Cicero discussed the orator's obligation to know law in *De or.* 1.36.165–46.203. His characterization of Scaevola and Crassus in *Brut.* 39.145 is cited or paraphrased by the following orators: Pietro Barozzi on Antonio Roselli, pp. 173–74; Agostino Dati on Tommaso Docci, fol. xcviii(v); Pietro Donato on Francesco Zabarella, p. 146b; Giovanni Battista Ramusio on Francesco Fasolo, pp. 389–90; Sebastiano Sapia on Giasone del Maino, [fol. 4v]; and Timoteo da Modena on Ludovico da Ferrara, [fol. 2]. Cf. also the anonymous oration on Bernardo Eroli, [fol. 3v]; Cristoforo Marcello on Pietro Barozzi, [fol. 4]; and Armachide Soardi on Pier Francesco Brembati, fol. 164. Coluccio Salutati and Pier Paolo Vergerio complained at the beginning of the Renaissance that eloquence had been excluded from courts of law in their day. See Salutati's *Epistolario*, ed. Novati, 1:341; and Vergerio's *De ingenuis moribus*, ed. Gnesotto, p. 124.

117. For doctors see Ludovico Carbone on Giovanni Ercole, fol. 169r–v; Tommaso Inghirami on Ludovico Podocataro, p. 302; Cristoforo Sassi on Luca Alberto Podiani, [fol. 3r–v]. For theologians see Poggio Bracciolini on Francesco Zabarella, pp. 256–57; idem on Giuliano Cesarini, p. 727; Pietro Donato on Francesco Zabarella, p. 146b; Lorenzo Grana on Giles of Viterbo, pp. 299–301; and Thaddeus of Lyon on Claude de Seyssel, p. 14.

118. Francesco Maturanzio on Leonardo Mansueti, fol. 26r–v. The translation from Cicero's *Pro Archia* is by N. H. Watts, Loeb Library (London: Heinemann; New York: G. P. Putnam's Sons, 1923), p. 9. Robey, "Humanism and Education" and "Vittorino da Feltre," emphasizes that Vergerio's treatise permitted a student to choose those disciplines related to his temperament.

119. See, e.g., Battista de' Giudici on Cristoforo della Rovere, [fol. 1v]: "Et

quoniam et a natura et a parentibus et a praeceptoribus fuerat ad virtutes institutus, didicerit litteras, non generis nobilitatem, non corporis speciem, non marsupium sequi sed sudoris esse comites et laboris, ieiuniorum socias, non saturitatis, continentiae, non luxuriae."

120. See, e.g., the comments of Lorenzo Grana in his oration for Celso Mellini, fol. 138v: "More sapientium Celsus qui ante omnia rerum finem considerant principio scopum sibi eloquentiae ad quam postremo accessurus erat praefixit intelligensque vanam esse omnem dicendi artem et inanem quandam garrulitatem nullis fulgentem hominibus, nulla sententiarum varietate distinctam ni plurima rerum disciplinarumque cognitione niteretur." On the potential dangers of oratory see North, "*Inutilis sibi, perniciosus patriae.*" On perceptions of that danger by Italian humanists see Gray, "Renaissance Humanism."

121. Ludovico Odassi on Guid'Ubaldo I, pp. 415–17; Giordano Orsini on Giovanni Pontano, fols. 18v–19. Odassi observed that it was inappropriate for a ruler like Guid'Ubaldo to cultivate judicial oratory since he himself had to adjudicate many cases. See further Guarino on Giannicola Salerno, cols. 484–85, who adduced Salerno's extemporaneous speech before the Veronese senate and a speech before the pope as proof of his eloquence. Praise for learned eloquence included preaching as well. See, e.g., Pietro Ranzano on Francesco da Toledo, [fol. 2r–v]; and Raffaele Brandolini on Mariano da Genazzano, p. 235.

122. Guarino on Margherita Gonzaga, fol. 108v; anonymous on Leonardo Bruni, pp. 151–52; and Kristeller, "Humanism and Scholasticism," p. 97.

123. Guarino on Margherita Gonzaga, fol. 108v: "divina haec studia velut igniculos ad virtutem accendendam"; and Giovanni Tortelli? on Ludovico Trevisan, fol. 178v: "Magno siquidem semper hominibus adiumento in ea adulescenti aetate hae disciplinae fuerunt ad excitandos ad virtutem animos quas studia humanitatis appellant." See also anonymous, "Oratio in laudem Thadei Quirino [sic]," fol. 145v; Poggio Bracciolini on Niccolò Niccoli, p. 271; and Francesco Maturanzio on Girolamo Pagliello, fols. 116–17. Francesco Cattani, in his eulogy for Lorenzo de' Medici, duke of Urbino, fols. 363–66v, stressed that one's education should be oriented toward the health of the soul and developed his idea in a Platonic framework.

124. Aristotle *Rhet.* 2.12.3; and Cicero *Off.* 1.34.122, *Sen.* 11.36. See the anonymous oration on Ioannes Germanicus, fol. 114; Raffaele Brandolini on Lorenzo Cibò, fols. 82v–83; idem on Mariano da Genazzano, p. 232; Francesco Cardulo on Ardicino II della Porta, [fols. 1v–2]; Andrea Giuliano on Manuel Chrysoloras, p. 27; and Tommaso Inghirami on Pietro Menzi, pp. 198–99. King, *Venetian Humanism,* pp. 31–32, relates the battle against passion to moral ideals of Christianity. Further remedies for lust were sometimes adduced. The anonymous eulogist of Antonio Gonzaga, fol. 156v,

noted that Antonio's parents arranged an early marriage for their son to keep him on the straight and narrow. Cf. also Giovanni Battista Flavi on Cajetan, [fols. 2v–3].

125. Bonifazio Bembo, *In Ludovici Mariae Sfortiae laudes oratio*, [fol. lv]: "Quantum litteris sapientibusque mortales debeant vel hac una re intelligi potest quod omnes bene beateque vivendi rationes litteris a sapientibus traditae continentur."

126. Battista Casali on Niccolò Bufalini, fol. 274r–v; and Antonio Solerio on Pietro Canonici, [fol. 4], referring to Cic. *Off.* 1.7.22, *Fin.* 2.14.45.

127. See esp. Pietro del Monte on Giovanni Zabarella, fol. 47: "ea maxime studia, eas disciplinas delegit in illisque assidue versatus est quae ad bene beateque vivendum plurimum conducere possunt. Quid enim prodest foris doctum ac litteratum videri, intus autem vitiis aestuare? Quid iuvat in coetu hominum alios ad virtutem erudire, se autem libidinibus ac voluptatibus esse subiectum? quae laus illi danda est qui cum tumentibus buccis gloriabundus multa de virtute, de moribus, de rebus bonis ac malis disseruerit et rectum aliis iter ostenderit, se ipse velut amens ac perditus per devia quaeque vagetur atque discurrat? Quanquam igitur Ioannes noster omne litterarum genus degustaverit, ea tamen sibi magis peculiaria esse voluit quibus homines ne dum doctiores sed meliores efficiuntur."

128. See, e.g., Andrea Biglia on Giacomo da Bologna, fol. 127; Matteo Palmieri on Carlo Marsuppini, fol. 69; and esp. George of Trebizond on Fantino Michiel, p. 448: "Cuius tota pueritia, adolescentia, iuventus iis studiis enituit quibus tanquam fundamentis nixus maximas res maximeque necessarias et huic urbi, hoc est libertati, utilissimas gesserit."

129. Cristoforo Landino on Donato Acciaiuoli, fol. 11v, referring to Cic. *De or.* 2.84.342–43; and Poggio Bracciolini on Leonardo Bruni, p. cxix, who refers to the "Tragicus," Aristotle, and the Stoics for support. See further anonymous on the brother of Bartolomeo, fol. 125v; Poggio Bracciolini on Giuliano Cesarini, p. 727; Raffaele Brandolini on Domenico della Rovere, [fol. 6]; Giannantonio Campano on Nello Baglioni, [fol. 105]; Girolamo Crivelli on Bianca Maria Visconti, cols. 426–27; Agostino Dati on Bartolo Bandini, fol. xcviiii(v); Lorenzo Grana on Giles of Viterbo, p. 297; Guarino on Giannicola Salerno, col. 482; Tommaso Inghirami on Galeotto Franciotti, pp. 59–60; Ludovico da Imola on Pietro Ferrici, [fol. 1v]; Giovanni Marini on Antonio Suriani, [fols. 2v–3]; Pietro Marsi on Pomponio Leto, [fols. 1v–2]; Andrea Navagero on Bartolomeo d'Alviano, pp. 4–5; Niccolò da Modrussa on Pietro Riario, [fol. 1v]; Antonio Pacini on Lorenzo de' Medici (the elder), fols. 13v–14; Sabellico on Benedetto Rugio, col. 498B; and Hardison, *The Enduring Monument*, pp. 30–32. Leonardo Bruni, Ludovico Carbone, and Pietro del Monte all contrasted the goods adduced by the Greeks in their symposia with the true goods that stem from virtue. See Bruni on Otto Cavalcanti,

p. 144; Ludovico Carbone on Guarino, p. 102; and Pietro del Monte on Paolo da Lion, fols. 37–38.

CHAPTER FOUR

The quotation in the chapter title is based upon Matthew 25:40.

1. Inghirami on Pietro Menzi, pp. 226–27, refers to his studies under Pietro. For Inghirami's career see Rugiadi, *Tommaso Fedra Inghirami*; O'Malley, *Praise and Blame*, pp. 114–16; and Rosa, "Ciceroniano o cristiano?"
2. Burchard, *Liber notarum*, p. 329.
3. Ibid., p. 457.
4. Inghirami on Pietro Menzi, pp. 215–16. Inghirami traced the rules for panegyric at Athens to Cecrops, legendary founder of the citadel.
5. Ibid., pp. 221–25.
6. Ibid., pp. 227–32. Marius was driven suddenly from Rome in 88 B.C.
7. Ibid., pp. 234–35. Inghirami noted that persons in classical times fixed on the drunkenness of Cimon and Cato, Scipio's sleepiness, the pederasty of Socrates, Pompey's scratching his head with a single finger, and Cicero's boasting about his consulship. Others gossiped of Jerome's familiarity with women, and some had the audacity to suggest that Nicholas V had a weakness for wine. Cf. also Niccolò Palmeri on Domenico Capranica, fol. 18v.
8. Inghirami on Pietro Menzi, pp. 235–37.
9. Ibid., p. 238: "Habuit tamen sibi hoc vitii fateor, non nego nec dissimulo, nihil blandiri, nihil demulcere, nihil noverat assentari, nemo erat simulandi imperitior; iisdem semper vixit moribus, eodem habitu, consuetudine, ac sermone perseveravit, nimia illi loquendi libertas oberat. Non enim illud didicerat: circa puteum non saltandum."
10. This saying of Ortega y Gassett is used in judicious fashion by Brown in his *The Cult of the Saints*, pp. 93–105. For the use of invective in discourses at Rome see O'Malley, *Praise and Blame*, pp. 211–25; and idem, "Historical Thought and the Reform Crisis."
11. Fubini, "Un'orazione di Poggio Bracciolini"; and idem, "Il 'teatro del mondo.'" He supplies a text in the latter study, pp. 93–132.
12. Fubini, "Il 'teatro del mondo,'" pp. 103, 108, 114, and 124–25, esp. p. 114: "Quid isti nostri tam boni vitae magistri nonne personati dici possunt? Cum enim venere in locum excelsum verba facturi, ab aliqua egregia sententia incipiunt, deinde aliorum dictis intexunt orationes suas, multorum advocant exquisitam sapientiam, aut cohortando ad virtutem aut vitia obiur-

gando. . . . Nos vero ulterius querimus: descende ex loco excelso quem ascenderas, depone personam; te ipsum enim scrutari, domesticam vitam videre, mores tuos disquirere cupio. Aveo scire an ea congruant cum praeceptis tuis; aegri quidem nos sumus, medicum quaerimus, non eloquentem sed sanantem."

13. Ibid., p. 108: "Prospicere boni viri vitam, mores intueri, considerare vivendi normam, permagnum est imitandae virtutis incitamentum."

14. Poggio Bracciolini delivered his oration at Constance; Donato spoke in Padua. Vergerio's letter is found in his *Epistolario*, ed. Smith, pp. 362–78. The works at times appeared together in humanist miscellanies of the Quattrocento. The orations by Poggio and Donato are preserved in Udine, Bibl. Arcivescovile, MS 70 (see *Iter*, 2:202, and Bertalot, "Eine Sammlung paduaner Reden"). All three tributes are preserved in Siena, Bibl. Comunale degli Intronati, MS H VI 26, fols. 71–84v (see *Iter*, 2:165). Henry Flemmyng preached a thematic sermon for Zabarella at Constance. Sabbadini, "Lettere e orazioni di Barzizza," p. 827, contends that MS 1139 of the Bibl. Angelica in Rome contains a eulogy for Zabarella by Barzizza on fols. 125–26v (incipit: *Etiamsi ego taceam viri clarissimi*). I question Sabbadini's identification of the author and subject. The speech is for a member of a prestigious Bolognese family whose brother Bartolomeo had recently been named to an important ecclesiastical office (Raimondi? Bolognini?). The oration is found in the codex immediately before two funeral orations, also attributed by Sabbadini to Barzizza, but recently assigned to Andrea Biglia. See Schnaubelt, "Andrea Biglia," p. 220. For Zabarella's rapport with humanists see Zonta, *Zabarella*, pp. 20–22.

15. Poggio Bracciolini on Francesco Zabarella, pp. 252–53; Pietro Donato on Francesco Zabarella, p. 144b (where Donato adverts to the grief of those who pursue the "studia aut humanitatis aut civilitatis") and pp. 145b–46b; and Vergerio, *Epistolario*, pp. 366–68 (who stresses his friend's proficiency in "naturalis philosophia et oratoria facultas").

16. Poggio Bracciolini on F. Zabarella, pp. 252–53, esp. p. 253: "Concurrebant ad eum undique ex toto fere terrarum orbe qui recte sapere volebant, quia non solum notitia legum, quod ipsum erat satis, sed quod est egregius vitae exemplo intuebantur. Natus enim ad decus et honestatem vir sanctissimus, inprimis habuit praecipuam curam virtutis colendae, nec minorem vitae bene agendae rationem habuit quam comparandae doctrinae." See further Donato on F. Zabarella, p. 146a–b (who notes that Zabarella combined philosophy and eloquence); Vergerio, *Epistolario*, pp. 368–69 (who emphasizes that Zabarella instructed his students no less in good morals than in law); and Flemmyng on Zabarella, pp. 550–51 (who speaks of a conjunction of *doctrina* and *fama*).

17. P. Donato on F. Zabarella, p. 144b.

18. Ibid., p. 147a–b. See also Vergerio, *Epistolario*, pp. 373–74; and H. Flemmyng on F. Zabarella, p. 549, who labels Francesco a "pater pauperum."

19. Poggio Bracciolini on F. Zabarella, p. 254; P. Donato on F. Zabarella, p. 147b; and Vergerio, *Epistolario*, pp. 369–70. Vergerio asserts, p. 365, that Zabarella would have been named a cardinal even earlier if Boniface IX had not valued money more than virtue.

20. Poggio Bracciolini on F. Zabarella, p. 254: "Non in fastu, non in pompa et ostentatione decorem dignitatis sitam ducebat, sed placabilitate animi et mansuetudine. Itaque is unus erat maxime ad quem docti homines et Musarum amici sine fastidioso stomacho possent adire."

21. See esp. Poggio Bracciolini on F. Zabarella, p. 255; and Vergerio, *Epistolario*, pp. 374–78.

22. Poggio Bracciolini on F. Zabarella, p. 259 ("copia dicendi"); and P. Donato on F. Zabarella, p. 145a ("tanta vis verborum et sententiarum").

23. Poggio Bracciolini on F. Zabarella, pp. 255, 259–60; P. Donato on F. Zabarella, p. 145a; and H. Flemmyng on F. Zabarella, p. 550.

24. Poggio Bracciolini on F. Zabarella, pp. 255–56; P. Donato on F. Zabarella, p. 148a; Vergerio, *Epistolario*, p. 378; and H. Flemmyng on F. Zabarella, pp. 550–51.

25. See, e.g., Tierney, *Foundations of the Conciliar Theory*, pp. 220–37; Morrissey, "Zabarella"; and idem, "Sigismund, Zabarella, and the Council." Pastor commented negatively on Zabarella's conciliarism in his *History of the Popes*, 1:186–87.

26. Giordano Orsini on Calixtus III, fols. 57v–58. See further Raffaele Brandolini on Domenico della Rovere, [fol. 6]; Francesco Cardulo on Ardicino II della Porta, [fol. 2v]; and Niccolò Palmeri on Nicholas V, fol. 8r–v.

27. Giordano Orsini on Calixtus III, fol. 58. See also Francesco da Vellate on Jean de Broniac, fol. 2v: "Accedit praeterea ad huius famae et gloriae immortalitatem hoc ipsum potissime. Nam cum plurimi aut maiorum suorum potentia, aut divitiarum affluentia, aut aliarum rerum externarum ornamento ut per singulos dies videmus ad honores et dignitates eleventur, ipse autem sui prudentia, virtute, et sapientia ad hunc amplissimum statum in quo paucis ante diebus vidimus perductus est."

28. Battista Casali on Robert Vitrè, fol. 13. See further Poggio Bracciolini on Niccolò Albergati, p. 265; Giannantonio Campano on Alessandro Oliva, [fol. 117r–v]; and Francesco Cardulo on Ardicino II della Porta, [fol. 2v].

29. Ludovico da Imola on Pietro Ferrici, [fol. 2v]: "O dignissimam promotionem ubi sola promoti virtus promoventis animum excitavit, ubi nulla simoniae suspicio fuit, ubi nulla favoris humani sollicitudo intercessit." See further Battista Casali on Robert Vitrè, fol. 13; and Francesco Maturanzio on Giovanni Chiericati, fol. 85v.

30. See, e.g., Pietro del Monte on Calixtus III, fol. 47v; Giovanni Cattanei

on Francesco Gonzaga, [fol. 21]; Cristoforo Marcello on Pietro Barozzi, [fol. 5r–v]; Francesco Maturanzio on Giovanni Chiericati, fol. 85v; and Marco Vigerio on Sixtus IV, fol. 401r–v.

31. Conradus Vegerius on Adrian VI, [fol. 5].

32. Poggio Bracciolini on Niccolò Albergati, p. 264: "O virtutem raram et quam rariores homines secuntur! Recensete alios, et eorum vitam inspicite qui simili praediti sunt dignitate. Quem mihi dabitis qui eiusmodi gradum non appetat, quaerat, enixe procuret, caelum terramque defatiget ut illum consequatur?" See also Cristoforo Marcello on Pietro Barozzi, [fol. 5r–v].

33. Girolamo Gioia on Benedetto Rugio, [fol. 2r–v]. Francesco Cardulo, in his discourse on Ardicino II della Porta, [fol. 3r–v], adduced practically the same list of exemplars (Basil, Gregory of Nazianzus, Celestine V, and Peter Damian). Gioia apparently purloined these examples from Cardulo, for he then added Ardicino as a contemporary example of detachment. Marco Vigerio praised Iacopo da Sarzuela for resigning his position as prior general of the Franciscans, purportedly because of pangs of conscience for the way in which he acquired the post. See Marco Vigerio on Sixtus IV, fol. 400v; and Pastor, *History of the Popes*, 4:206.

34. Gaspare Sighicelli on Niccolò Albergati, fol. 197v: "Non hunc episcopalis dignitas aut cardinalatus officium quod prius habuit quam voluit tametsi hac aetate id raro contingat ab humilitate religionis nulla morum sanctitate separavit." For Albergati's election see Töth, *Nicolò Albergati*, 1:99–152; and E. Pasztor in *DBI*, 1:619–21.

35. On *virtus* as priority see, e.g., Andrea Biglia on a Stefano, fol. 127v; Poggio Bracciolini on Niccolò Albergati, p. 265; Raffaele Brandolini on Lorenzo Cibò, fol. 86; Battista Casali on Robert Vitrè, fol. 13; Leonello Chiericati on Innocent VIII, cols. 1770C–71E; Giovanni Antonio Sangiorgi on Ferry de Clugny, [fol. 5]; Conradus Vegerius on Adrian VI, [fol. 4r–v]; and Marco Vigerio on Sixtus IV, fols. 399v–400, 401r–v. For the added importance of humanist learning see Giannantonio Campano on Alessandro Oliva, [fol. 117r–v]; Giovanni Marini on Antonio Suriani, [fol. 6]; Francesco Maturanzio on Giovanni Chiericati, fol. 85v; and Iacopo Sadoleto on Oliviero Carafa, pp. 323–25.

36. Lorenzo Grana on Giles of Viterbo, pp. 306–9. In 1431 Pietro del Monte criticized Pope Eugene IV for naming his nephew Francesco Condulmer and Angelotto Fosco cardinals. For Pietro, the choices epitomized anti-intellectual currents within the Church. See Sottili, *Studenti tedeschi*, pp. 28, 77–79.

37. Giordano Orsini on Calixtus III, fol. 58r–v.

38. Raffaele Brandolini on Guillaume Pérès, p. 208: "Postremo, cum se iam spectata huius integritas atque peritia magis cottidie dilataret, a Sixto quarto pontifice maximo optimo litterarum ac virtutum remuneratore, praestantissimo huic muneri praefectus est"; and Giannantonio Campano on Alessandro Oliva, [fol. 117]: "Electus est deinde generalis in conventu Piceno, sed ita

electus ut palam clamaret ne se eligerent interminareturque electoribus persecuturum omnes quando singulorum vitia moresque calleret." See also Tommaso Inghirami on Ludovico Podocataro, pp. 306–7.

39. Ibid., pp. 309–12.

40. Leonello Chiericati on Innocent VIII, cols. 1772E–73B. The oration was published three times in the fifteenth century (*GW* 6623–25). In general, see my "Ideal Renaissance Pope," pp. 33–43; O'Malley, *Praise and Blame*, pp. 220–22; and Prodi, *Il sovrano pontefice*, pp. 13–126.

41. Chiericati's sources are Cic. *Leg.* 3.13.30; Plato *Rep.* 3.413–14; and Leo the Great *Epist.* 12.4 (*PL*, 54:649n., where the passage is given as an alternate reading). The biblical narrative concerning Abimelech is found in Judges 9.

42. For Zabarella see Poggio Bracciolini on F. Zabarella, pp. 255–56; Pietro Donato on F. Zabarella, p. 148a; Vergerio, *Epistolario*, ed. Smith, p. 378; and H. Flemmyng on F. Zabarella, pp. 550–51. For Bessarion see Niccolò Capranica on Bessarion, pp. 408–9. Vespasiano da Bisticci narrated the story but mistakenly placed the election after the death of Pius II; see his *Le Vite*, ed. Greco, 1:171. See also Giovanni Battista Flavi on Cajetan, [fol. 11]; and Lorenzo Grana on Giles of Viterbo, p. 314.

43. Angelo Gabrielli on Battista Zeno, p. 228. The story of Prospero Colonna's misfortune is narrated by F. Petrucci in *DBI*, 27:416–18.

44. See, e.g., Poggio Bracciolini on Niccolò Albergati, p. 265; Raffaele Brandolini on Lorenzo Cibò, fol. 85v; Leonello Chiericati on Innocent VIII, col. 1771D–E; Giovanni Battista Flavi on Cajetan, [fol. 5v]; Tommaso Inghirami on Ludovico Podocataro, pp. 320–21; Cristoforo Marcello on Pietro Barozzi, [fol. 4v]; and Francesco Maturanzio on Leonardo Mansueti, fol. 134.

45. Poggio Bracciolini on Niccolò Albergati, p. 263.

46. Giacomo da Alessandria on Fantino Valaresso, pp. ix–x, esp. p. ix: "Quis eo solertior aut vigilantior fuit supra gregem sibi commissum, ut merito pastoris nomen posset sibi ascribere, sicut hic pacis amator, religionis cultor, fidei lumen, Graecorum Latinorumque sanctae unionis protector? Qui fuit metrum et mensura praesidentium in Petri cathedra sedentium? Quotiens hic pastor deificus ovile sibi commissum ad se paterna affectione traxerit, quantum dilexerit, quantum pro eo laboraverit?" The passage on the "good shepherd" is found in John 10. Fantino's authorship of the brief catechism and its reforming purpose are discussed by Peri in "Tre lettere," 1:57–61. For the notion of *diakonia* in the New Testament see Hermann W. Beyer in the *Theological Dictionary of the New Testament*, ed. Gerhard Kittel and trans. Geoffrey W. Bromiley (Michigan: Eerdmans, 1964), 2:81–93; and Küng, *The Church*, pp. 388–93. See also Gabriele Bucci on Francesco de' Bernecci (*Il Memoriale Quadripartitum*, pp. 193–95); Niccolò Palmeri on Domenico Capranica, fols. 30–30'; and Conradus Vegerius on Adrian VI, [fol. 6].

47. Niccolò Palmeri on Nicholas V, fols. 11–12, esp. fols. 11v–12: "En cor-

pus hoc miserabile quod nimia reverentia seu persaepe adulatione pestifera adorabatur in terris contractis nervis carne consumpta adhuc vivens fetidum et ante ipsum obitum cineris prae se ferens similitudinem! Ubi nunc oscula pedum flexis genibus? Ubi interdum illud simulatum et adulatorium nomen 'beatissime pater'? Ubi stans illa turba virorum? quodnam mihi praemium ex his honoribus et terrena et fragili gloria mecum refero miser praeterquam pompam omnium et totius mundi sarcinam?" The *ubi sunt* topic was a purple passage in late medieval preaching. See, e.g., Blench, *Preaching in England*, pp. 135–36, 228–29. See further the anonymous oration on Baldassare Cossa, fol. 54; and O'Malley, *Praise and Blame*, pp. 220–23.

48. Antonio Maggi, in his eulogy for Marco Corner (the younger), [fol. 5], saw the office of cardinal prefigured in the account of Adam's creation in Genesis, for God shaped Adam from a fistful of dirt grabbed from the earth's *cardines*. Giovanni Gatti based his case for divine institution on texts like Luke 22:28–30, 1 Samuel 2:8, and Deuteronomy 17:8–9 in his eulogy for Latino Orsini, fols. 86v–87v. Cf. also Lorenzo Grana on Giles of Viterbo, p. 298. The actual origins of the office seem to be related to the liturgy. See Stephan Kuttner, "*Cardinalis*"; and Andrieu, "L'origine du titre de Cardinal."

49. See Angelo Gabrielli on Battista Zeno, p. 229; Antonio da Montecatini on Niccolò Forteguerri, fol. 141; Iacopo Sadoleto on Oliviero Carafa, p. 325; and esp. Tommaso Inghirami on Julius II, pp. 91–92: "Exquire vota in senatu: libertatem ecclesiasticam tutatum esse, pontificibus maximis, etiam patruo ipsi suo, si quid non rectae fidei iudicaret, acriter obstitisse agnosces."

50. Battista Casali on Domenico Grimani, fol. 74: "Ipsi novistis, patres amplissimi, an non modo ceteris in rebus sed conscribendis etiam in hunc ordinem patribus eundem se semper invictumque praebuerit. Non principum gratiam, non regum auctoritatem, sed suam dumtaxat incorruptam solidamque conscientiam secutus ne temere assentiretur qui interdum etiam pontificibus non dubitavit tanquam Paulus Petro constantissime reluctari." Paul himself described his disagreement with Peter in the second chapter of his letter to the Galatians.

51. See Alessandro Guarini on Ippolito I d'Este, [fol. 4], where he commends the cardinal for refusing to sell his vote in the conclave that elected Julius II (1503) despite overtures that he do so. See further my "Ideal Renaissance Pope," pp. 53–54.

52. Raffaele Brandolini on Domenico della Rovere, [fol. 7]: "Et cum magistratus virum non efficiat sed ostendat illumque excelso et illustri loco in plurium collegarum ac civium plurimorum conspectu qui egregiam aliquam fuerit dignitatem adeptus constituat, fuisse hunc tam excellenti beneficio quam dignissimum verissime patefacit."

53. Niccolò Capranica on Bessarion, p. 412. Cf. also Lorenzo Grana on Giles of Viterbo, pp. 321–22.

54. Tommaso Inghirami on Ludovico Podocataro, pp. 317–18; and Giannantonio Campano on Pius II, [fol. 103]. Orators often supplied lists of a subject's writings including those not directly related to the humanities. Such lists provided empirical proof of a person's learning. See, e.g., Cristoforo Barzizza on Paolo Veneto, pp. 202–3; Niccolò Capranica on Bessarion, p. 410; Giovanni Battista Flavi on Cajetan, [fols. 4v–6]; Niccolò Palmeri on Domenico Capranica, fol. 28r–v; and Marco Vigerio on Sixtus IV, fols. 400v–401.

55. Niccolò Capranica on Bessarion, pp. 406–9, 411. All of the following orations refer to successful embassies by ecclesiastics: Girolamo Aliotti on Bartolomeo Zabarella, p. 314; Michael Apostolis on Bessarion, cols. cxxxiii–cxxxvi; Poggio Bracciolini on Niccolò Albergati, pp. 264–68; idem on Giuliano Cesarini, pp. 727–29, 732; Francesco Cardulo on Ardicino II della Porta, [fol. 2v]; Battista Casali on Jean de Bilhères Lagraulas, fols. 310v–12; Giovanni Cattanei on Francesco Gonzaga, [fols. 21v–22v]; Giovanni Battista Egnazio on Pietro da Bibbiena, fols. 12v–14; Giovanni Battista Flavi on Cajetan, [fols. 8v–9v]; Antonio Gabrielli on Battista Zeno, pp. 229–30; Gerardo da Lucca on Silvestro de' Gigli, fol. 13; Lorenzo Grana on Giles of Viterbo, pp. 304–6, 312–13; Tommaso Inghirami on Julius II, pp. 84–91; Antonio Maggi on Marco Corner (the younger), [fols. 5v–9]; Montorio Mascarelli on Giovan Francesco Capodilista, fol. 73v; Niccolò da Modrussa on Pietro Riario, [fol. 4]; Niccolò Palmeri on Domenico Capranica, fols. 20–21v; Pietro Ranzano on Francesco da Toledo, [fols. 2v–4]; Giovanni Tortelli? on Ludovico Trevisan, fol. 181; and Conradus Vegerius on Adrian VI, [fols. 4, 5r–v].

56. Giannantonio Campano on Pius II, [fol. 99v]; and Niccolò Capranica on Bessarion, p. 408: "Eo cum venisset, Nicaenus pro incredibili sapientia atque animi magnitudine brevi non modo pacatam urbem et quietam reddidit, sed civilem effecit et in litterarum et bonarum artium studia mirifice auxit tanto omnium amore et observantia." Pietro Barozzi, in a eulogy for Antonio Roselli, pp. 177–78, censured the barbarity of the Germans, who refused to be conciliated with Italy and desired to conquer the peninsula.

57. Timoteo da Modena on Ludovico da Ferrara, [fols. 2v, 3v–4]; and Raffaele Brandolini on Mariano da Genazzano, p. 235. See also Lorenzo Grana on Giles of Viterbo, pp. 299, 301–3; Pietro Ranzano on Francesco da Toledo, [fol. 2r–v]; and esp. Giannantonio Campano on Alessandro Oliva, [fol. 117]: "Italia tota praedicavit, semper maximo concursu hominum qui eius altissima rerum scientia delectati, vitae inprimis exemplo movebantur." For praise of the eloquence of ecclesiastics see, e.g., Raffaele Brandolini on Guillaume Pérès, pp. 214–15; Giannantonio Campano on Pius II, [fol. 103r–v]; Guarniero Castiglioni on Branda Castiglioni, fol. 4v; Giovanni Cattanei on Francesco Gonzaga, [fol. 19]; Agostino Dati on Giannantonio Campano, fol. ci; and Jean Jouffroy on Nicholas V, fols. 33v–34.

58. For an evaluation of the preaching of Ludovico da Ferrara see O'Malley, *Praise and Blame*, pp. 105–8. Mariano's preaching and his friendship with the humanists are discussed in ibid., pp. 57n. 52, 120–21; and Greco, "La *docta pietas*," pp. 210–22. Mariano's vernacular panegyric for Saint Jerome mixed elements of a thematic sermon with those more typical of a classicizing epideictic oration. Other orators had abandoned the thematic sermon in the same context much earlier. See my "Vergerio and the Cult of Jerome."

59. Angelo dalla Pergola on Niccolò Capranica, fols. 73v–74; Niccolò Capranica on Bessarion, p. 411; and Eusebio Priuli on Pietro Dolfin, [fol. 8v]. On Nicholas' justifiable anger see Jean Jouffroy on Nicholas V, fols. 31v–32v; and Onofri, "*Sicut fremitus leonis*," pp. 12–20.

60. See, e.g., Alberto da Castelfranco on Urbano Bolzanio, [fol. 9v]; Francesco Maturanzio on Leonardo Mansueti, fol. 134r–v; and Giannantonio Campano on Pius II, [fol. 103].

61. Antonio Maggi on Marco Corner (the younger), [fol. 10]. Renaissance orators often structured their praise of virtues according to the classical canon of prudence, justice, fortitude, and temperance. For further treatment of justice see, e.g., Raffaele Brandolini on Guillaume Pérès, pp. 209–13; Battista Casali on Francesco Remolino, fol. 49r–v; Giovanni Marini on Antonio Suriani, [fol. 5]; and Niccolò da Modrussa on Pietro Riario, [fols. 4v–5].

62. Raffaele Brandolini on Lorenzo Cibò, fols. 88–89. On temperance and continence see, e.g., idem on Guillaume Pérès, pp. 213–14; Giovanni Marini on Antonio Suriani, [fol. 5v]; and Niccolò Palmeri on Domenico Capranica, fol. 23r–v.

63. See Battista Casali on Aloysius of Aragon, fols. 44v–45; Giovanni Battista Egnazio on Marco Corner (the younger), fol. 7r–v; and Antonio Maggi on Marco Corner (the younger), [fol. 12].

64. Battista Casali on Aloysius of Aragon, fol. 45. He uses hunting, fols. 45–46, as a metaphor for the Christian life, with Christ as the heavenly prey. Aloysius' role as director of the hunt is mentioned by G. De Caro in *DBI*, 3:698–701.

65. Poggio Bracciolini on Giuliano Cesarini, pp. 729–31; Girolamo Aliotti on Bartolomeo Zabarella, pp. 313–14; and Camporeale, "Lorenzo Valla *Repastinatio*," pp. 266–67.

66. Borgognone d'Asti on Pietro Emigli, fol. 19v; Cristoforo Barzizza on Paolo Veneto, p. 203; and Niccolò Palmeri on Domenico Capranica, fol. 19v.

67. Cristoforo Barzizza on Paolo Veneto, p. 203; and Lorenzo Grana on Giles of Viterbo, pp. 309–10. Cf. also Giacomo da Alessandria on Fantino Valaresso, p. x.

68. Iacopo Zeno on Giuliano Cesarini, fol. 3r–v, esp. fol. 3r: "Quos cum armis et viribus ab impietate desistere non posse animadverteret, ecclesiastica concertatione vincendos constituens coacta Basileae synodo ut a prin-

cipe praestitutum erat assiduis et miris artibus monendo, disceptando, docendo, suadendo, demulcendo tandem in erroris illos agnitionem et detestationem adduxit." The last three of Cesarini's means—*docendo, suadendo, demulcendo*—are Cicero's "duties of the orator" (see *De or.* 2.27.115, *Or.* 21.69). Cf. also Battista Casali on Francesco Remolino, fol. 19v: "non armis, non gladio, non impotentia, sed oratione, lenitate, mansuetudine coercuit."

69. Lecler, *Toleration and the Reformation*. For Cesarini's career see A. A. Strnad and K. Walsh in *DBI*, 24:188–95.

70. Pietro Barozzi on Giovanni Barozzi, pp. 107–16. On Pietro's life and the specific circumstances that motivated this oration or letter to Paul II see Gios, *L'attività pastorale*, pp. 65–68; and Gasparini, "Sull'episcopato padovano di Barozzi," pp. 87–88.

71. Tommaso Inghirami on Julius II, pp. 95–103. Other popes of the Renaissance were praised for bringing order to the papal state. See, e.g., Giannantonio Campano on Pius II, [fols. 99, 101v–2]; Leonello Chiericati on Innocent VIII, cols. 1771F–72A; Lorenzo Grana on Clement VII, pp. 270–71; and Marco Vigerio on Sixtus IV, fol. 402.

72. Tommaso Inghirami on Julius II, pp. 95–96. Roman orators like Cicero frequently capitalized on the emotional appeal of references to place. See Vasaly, "The Spirit of Place."

73. See Tommaso Inghirami on Julius II, pp. 99–103; and my "Ideal Renaissance Pope," p. 48. The use of the term "golden age" was frequent in sermons and orations delivered at the Renaissance papal court. See O'Malley, *Praise and Blame*, pp. 171, 184, 188–89.

74. Ramage, "Velleius Paterculus 2.126.2–3." For imperial propaganda during the reign of Julius see, e.g., Horrigan, "Imperial and Urban Ideology"; and Stinger, *The Renaissance in Rome*, pp. 235–91.

75. Gaspare Sighicelli on Niccolò Albergati, fols. 198v–200. Cf. also Poggio Bracciolini on Niccolò Albergati, p. 264.

76. Marcello Adriani on Giuliano de' Medici, duke of Nemours, fol. 76 (with reference to Leo X): "qui tam duris rebus tantoque hoc bellorum furore sapientissimis consiliis et divina bonitate ad optatam omnibus tranquillitatem, favente Deo, restituere omnia aliquando velit et possit."

77. See, e.g., Giannantonio Campano on Pius II, [fol. 102]; Lorenzo Grana on Clement VII, pp. 277–78; Niccolò Palmeri on Nicholas V, fol. 9; and Marco Vigerio on Sixtus IV, fol. 402r–v. The anonymous eulogist of Bernardo Eroli, [fol. 4v], praised the cardinal for protecting the Church's unity and peace, which were Christ's heredity.

78. See note 55 above.

79. See Niccolò Palmeri on Domenico Capranica, fols. 22–23; Giordano Orsini on Calixtus III, fols. 56–57; my "Ideal Renaissance Pope," pp. 45–46, 52–53; and O'Malley, *Praise and Blame*, pp. 190–91, 232–35.

80. See Jean Jouffroy on Nicholas V, fol. 34r–v; Niccolò Palmeri on Nicholas V, fol. 10; and Ludovico Carbone on Guarino, p. 100: "Nam si largior vitae mora sanctissimo illi patri data esset, revocabantur antiqua studia, reviviscebant bonae litterae, restituebatur in pristinam dignitatem eloquentia, surgebant moenia Romana."

81. Jean Jouffroy on Nicholas V, fols. 30v, 33r–v. See also Niccolò Palmeri on Nicholas V, fol. 10. Nicholas' program for the city of Rome is described by Westfall, *In This Most Perfect Paradise*.

82. Panegyrics of Nicholas by Giannozzo Manetti, Poggio Bracciolini, and Michele Canensi fostered a myth during the pope's lifetime. See Wittschier, *Manetti*, pp. 79–84; Vasoli, "Poggio e la polemica," pp. 170–71; and Miglio, "Una vocazione in progresso." The myth was fostered after the pope's death in 1455 by epitaphs, funeral orations, and biographies. See, e.g., Kajanto and Nyberg, *Papal Epigraphy*, pp. 54–61; Onofri, "*Sicut fremitus leonis*"; eadem, "Sacralità, immaginazione e proposte politiche"; Westfall, "Biblical Typology"; and D'Amico, *Renaissance Humanism in Papal Rome*, pp. 120–22.

83. Battista Casali on Gabriello Gabrielli, fol. 301v: "Obstupescent posteri animi magnitudinem, constratos montes, moles in caelum erectas, templa restituta, eiectos tyrannos, sed sunt haec cum multis quoque communia. Cum vero te litteras, bonas artes, virtutem extulisse aut audierint aut legerint, eam demum solam et propriam laudem iudicabunt quae neque temporum neque saeculorum iniuria oblitterabitur." See also Giovanni Cattanei on Francesco Gonzaga, [fol. 20v]. For ecclesiastical patronage see my "Ideal Renaissance Pope," pp. 49–50; D'Amico, *Renaissance Humanism in Papal Rome*, pp. 38–60; Strnad, "Francesco Todeschini Piccolomini"; Lee, *Sixtus IV*; and Schröter, "Der Vatikan als Hügel Apollons und der Musen."

84. See, e.g., Guarniero Castiglioni on Branda Castiglioni, fol. 4r–v (cf. Foffano, "La costruzione di Castiglione Olona," pp. 158–61; and idem, "Rapporti tra Italia e Ungheria," pp. 69–77); Francesco Maturanzio on Leonardo Mansueti, fols. 29v–30; Antonio da Montecatini on Niccolò Forteguerri, fol. 141v; and Niccolò Palmeri on Domenico Capranica, fols. 28v–29v. Gaspare Sighicelli recalled that he had studied at the "Scuola dei poveri di Cristo" established by Niccolò Albergati in Bologna. See Gaspare's eulogy, fol. 199v; and Töth, *Albergati*, 1:188–90.

85. Niccolò Perotti on Pietro Riario, fol. 154v: "Pictores, sculptores, oratores, poetae, liberalium artium praeceptores, mathematici, omnes denique in quibus aliqua virtutis scintilla erat munificentiam eius continue experiebantur. Domum ita viris doctis refertam habebat ut Musarum domicilium videretur." Niccolò Capranica and Battista Casali characterized the homes of Bessarion (p. 411) and Giovanni Colonna (fol. 35v) as "academies." See also Giovanni Gatti on Latino Orsini, fol. 92; Niccolò da Modrussa on Pietro Riario, [fol. 3v]; and Niccolò Palmeri on Domenico Capranica, fols. 25v–26.

86. Niccolò made his disparaging reference to Riario in a letter to Francesco Maturanzio. The passage is quoted by Mercati, "Notizie varie," pp. 227–28. The political activities of Riario's court are discussed by Ferroni, "Appunti sulla politica festiva."

87. O'Malley, *Praise and Blame*, pp. 180–81. Further orations that use the topos but are not cited by O'Malley include Angelo dalla Pergola on Niccolò Capranica, fol. 75; Giannantonio Campano on Pius II, [fol. 102v]; Francesco Cardulo on Ardicino II della Porta, [fol. 3]; Battista Casali on Francesco Soderini, fol. 294; idem on Robert Vitrè, fol. 15; Girolamo Gioia on Benedetto Rugio, [fol. 3v]; Giovanni Antonio Sangiorgi on Ferry de Clugny, [fols. 1v–2]; and Thaddeus of Lyon on Claude de Seyssel, pp. 14–15. The orators who mention Pomponius Atticus (Nep. *Att.* 14.1) and the emperor Hadrian are Francesco Cardulo, [fol. 3], and Girolamo Gioia, [fol. 3v].

88. Niccolò Perotti on Pietro Riario, fols. 154v–55. The plan is discussed in Lee, *Sixtus IV*, pp. 120–22.

89. Battista Casali on Domenico Grimani, fol. 73v: "Libros nemo unquam nec cura nec sumptu maiore conquisivit. Nam cum emendis Pici Mirandulae libris nummi deessent, vasa omnia argentea vendidit maluitque suppellectili abacoque pulcherrimo quam libris tanti viri carere, collegitque hoc modo quindecim amplius milia librorum quorum partem erectae Venetiis ad divi Antonii bibliothecae addixit, partem Marino patriarchae nepoti amantissimo ut doctrinae, sic modestiae ac probitatis heredi reliquit." On Grimani's library see Mercati, *Codici Latini Pico Grimani Pio*, pp. 1–38. For praise of the libraries of ecclesiastics see also Ludovico da Imola on Pietro Ferrici, [fol. 3r–v]; Francesco Maturanzio on Leonardo Mansueti, fols. 30v, 32v; Niccolò Palmeri on Domenico Capranica, fol. 28; the panegyric of Adamo di Montaldo for Arnaud Roger, the patriarch of Alexandria, in BAV, MS Vat. lat. 3567, fol. 14; and, in general, Antonovics, "The Library of Capranica."

90. See O'Malley, *Praise and Blame*, pp. 171–74, who refers to Raffaele Brandolini's funeral oration for Domenico della Rovere, [fol. 8r–v]. Brandolini praised the building and restoration of churches, but he implicitly censured spending on private buildings, which in his words was "self-indulgent rather than fruitful for others." At the request of the citizens of Fermo, the reigning pope (Pius II?) blocked the plans for a palace that Bishop Niccolò Capranica intended to build there. Niccolò did carry out other building projects with the cooperation and approval of the local citizens. See Angelo dalla Pergola on Niccolò Capranica, fols. 71v–72; and M. Miglio in *DBI*, 19:161–62.

91. Orators linked the moral reform of religious orders with the physical rebuilding of their monasteries and convents. See, e.g., Francesco Maturanzio on Leonardo Mansueti, fols. 29v–30; Niccolò Palmeri on Domenico Capranica, fols. 28v–29; and esp. Guarniero Castiglioni on Branda Castiglioni,

fol. 4r–v: "Nonnulla etiam monasteria sancta quae praelatorum abbatum negligentia aut aliqua culpa exciderant suis propriis sumptibus reaedificata et devotione et opera sua ad observationem reducta sunt." Masolino figured prominently among the artists whom Castiglioni employed. See Foffano, "La costruzione di Castiglione Olona," pp. 158–61; and idem, "Rapporti tra Italia e Ungheria," pp. 69–77. Italian orators shared with Saint Basil (Hom. 19, par. 2; *PG*, 31:cols. 508C–509A) a conviction that oratory and the visual arts promoted religious reform. See Maguire, *Art and Eloquence in Byzantium*, p. 5. Bernardino da Siena's use of the "IHS" cryptogram motivated Andrea Biglia to conceptualize the value and purpose of a pictorial image. See Arasse, "Andrea Biglia contre Saint Bernardin de Sienne."

92. Niccolò da Modrussa on Pietro Riario, [fols. 2v–3]; and Marco Vigerio on Sixtus IV, fol. 403. See further my "Ideal Renaissance Pope," p. 50; O'Malley, *Praise and Blame*, pp. 207–25; and Stinger, *The Renaissance in Rome*, pp. 14–82, 254–81, passim.

93. Cic. *Off.* 1.20.68. See Raffaele Brandolini on Domenico della Rovere, [fol. 7v]; Battista Casali on Aloysius of Aragon, fol. 44; and Antonio Maggi on Marco Corner (the younger), [fol. 11r–v]. Battista Casali openly defended Francesco Soderini from charges of avarice, fol. 294v. Soderini must have been wealthy given that he paid a fine of 25,000 scudi as punishment for his involvement in a plot to poison Pope Leo X. Poggio Bracciolini especially hammered away at the avarice and hypocrisy of the clergy and vowed religious. See his orations for Francesco Zabarella, p. 258, for Niccolò Albergati, p. 266, and for Giuliano Cesarini, pp. 728–29; and Vasoli, "Poggio e la polemica," pp. 184–88, 194–203; Oppel, "Poggio, San Bernardino of Siena, and the Dialogue *On Avarice*"; and Goldbrunner, "Poggios Dialog über die Habsucht." The financial pressures that these expectations created for Roman cardinals are discussed by Chambers, "The Housing Problems of Gonzaga."

94. See, e.g., Raffaele Brandolini on Lorenzo Cibò, fols. 86v–87; Giovacchino Castiglioni on a Iacopo, fol. 73; Giovanni Cattanei on Francesco Gonzaga, [fol. 20v]; Leonello Chiericati on Innocent VIII, cols. 1771C–72B; Giacomo da Alessandria on Fantino Valaresso, pp. ix–x; Girolamo Gioia on Benedetto Rugio, [fols. 2v–3]; Sabellico on Benedetto Rugio, col. 499B; and O'Malley, *Praise and Blame*, p. 174. On the biblical injunction to care for widows and orphans see Dibelius, *James: A Commentary*, p. 121. As a papal legate, Alessandro Oliva was explicitly instructed to accept gifts only from the wealthy and only to assist the needy. See Giannantonio Campano on Alessandro Oliva, [fol. 117v]. On the importance of charity see also Gios, *L'attività pastorale*, pp. 360–62; Gasparini, "Sull'episcopato padovano di Barozzi," p. 119; Camporeale, "Lorenzo Valla *Repastinatio*," pp. 266–67; and Vauchez, "Assistance et charité."

95. The anonymous oration on Bernardo Eroli, [fol. 4r–v], based upon John 10:11–14. Poggio Bracciolini on Giuliano Cesarini, pp. 725–26. The debate over the circumstances of Cesarini's death is noted by A. A. Strnad and K. Walsh in *DBI*, 24:188–95. Enea Silvio Piccolomini was the source for the unflattering version because he considered Cesarini a traitor to the conciliarist cause. Cf. also Giovanni Cattanei on Francesco Gonzaga, [fols. 22v–23]; Niccolò Palmeri on Domenico Capranica, fols. 22–23; and Pietro Ranzano on Francesco da Toledo, [fol. 4].

96. See the anonymous oration on Pandolfo II Malatesta, p. xxvi; Giovanni Pontano on Gattamelata, pp. 356–57; Baldassare Rasini on Francesco Sforza, fol. 21v; and esp. Giovanni Cattanei on Barbara Gonzaga, [fols. 6v–7]: "Non recensebo quemadmodum non pauci religiosi ab ea discedentes pectus suum pugnis percutiebant exclamantes 'Vae nobis peccatoribus qui religiosorum nomina gerimus. Pudet nos coram Deo nostro cum sub amictu purpureo et insignito habitu tam religiosum, tam castum, tam integrum prae nobis contemplati sumus spiritum.'"

97. Guarino on Leonello d'Este, fols. 64v–65; Battista Mantovano on Eleanor of Aragon, [fol. 7r–v]; and Battista Guarini on Eleanor of Aragon, [fol. 3v]. For further instances of women praised for reciting the divine office see Giannantonio Campano on Battista Sforza, [fol. 120v]; Guarino on Teodora Zilioli, col. 1242; and Martino Filetico on Gentile Brancaleoni, fol. 3. The inspiration for these descriptions of "ideal feminine piety" may have been Jerome's advice to his female followers. See Rice, *Jerome in the Renaissance*, pp. 96–97.

98. See, e.g., Battista Mantovano on Eleanor of Aragon, [fol. 7]; Giannantonio Campano on Battista Sforza, [fol. 121]; Guarino on Teodora Zilioli, col. 1243; and Battista Guarini on Eleanor of Aragon, [fol. 3v]. Cf. also Giovanni Cattanei on Federigo I Gonzaga, [fol. 27r–v], where Cattanei relates that Federigo withdrew to pray for guidance, an activity that the orator compares to the Roman custom of reading auspices.

99. See, e.g., Battista Mantovano on Eleanor of Aragon, [fol. 7]; Giovanni Cattanei on Barbara Gonzaga, [fol. 7r–v]; idem on Federigo I Gonzaga, [fols. 27v–28]; Guarino on Teodora Zilioli, cols. 1242–43; and Elio Lampridio Cerva on Damianus Gotius, fol. 94. Niccolò da Rimini claimed that Galeotto Roberto Malatesta had to be ordered by his confessors to fulfill his marriage duty (p. 545). In his eulogy for Teodora Zilioli, col. 1244, Guarino related that Teodora took a vow of continence after bearing her husband children. Teodora thus fulfilled two Scriptural imperatives in one lifetime: (1) "Increase and multiply" (Genesis 1:28), and (2) "Deny yourself, take up your cross, and follow me" (Matthew 16:24).

100. Giovanni Garzoni often praised those who assisted the poor, widows, and virgins. See, e.g., his orations on Giorgio Manzoli, fol. xxxiiii(v); on an

Alessandro, fol. xxxvii; and on Giovanni Zambeccari, fol. cv(v). In a eulogy for Cristoforo della Rovere, [fol. 3], Battista de' Giudici emphasized that, while governor of Castel Sant'Angelo, Cristoforo ate only after all the prisoners had been fed. Guglielmo Pagello argued that a fund Bartolomeo Colleoni endowed for dowries had helped rid Bergamo of sexual crimes like rape and incest. See G. Pagello on B. Colleoni, [fol. 14r–v]; and cf. the anonymous oration on Elisabetta Malatesta, p. xxxii. For further examples of generous giving see Battista Mantovano on Eleanor of Aragon, [fol. 7]; Battista Casali on a Stefano, fols. 279v–80; Giovanni Cattanei on Barbara Gonzaga, [fol. 9r–v]; Guarino on Teodora Zilioli, cols. 1248–49; idem on Giannicola Salerno, col. 483; Ludovico Odassi on Federigo da Montefeltro, fols. 11v–12; Giovanni Pontano on Gattamelata, p. 357; and Stefano Sterponi on Alessandro Pucci, fol. 23v.

101. See, e.g., the anonymous oration on Giangaleazzo Visconti, fol. 95r–v; Poggio Bracciolini on Lorenzo de' Medici (the elder), pp. 281–82; Gabriele Bucci on Ludovico I, marchese di Saluzzo (*Il Memoriale Quadripartitum*, pp. 177–78); Ludovico Carbone on Borso d'Este, fol. 93v; Battista Casali on Niccolò Bufalini, fol. 275v; Battista Guarini on Eleanor of Aragon, [fol. 4]; Giovanni Montano on Filippo Maria Visconti, col. 440A–B; and Guglielmo Pagello on Bartolomeo Colleoni (regarding his burial chapel), [fols. 13v–14]. Ludovico Bruno characterized Isabella of Castile as another Saint Helen for her enrichment of the holy places in Jerusalem. He claimed that the queen was able to insure those improvements by bribing the appropriate sultan. See Bruno on Isabella, [fol. 9].

102. Guarino on Leonello d'Este, fol. 65; and Battista Casali on a Stefano, fol. 280v: "quibus dumtaxat natum se ipse adserebat reque ita esse comprobavit ut mentem a religione nunquam alienam gesserit nec a civilibus muneribus unquam abhorruerit usque ad magnorum virorum testimonia eum omnibus meritis absolutum civem fuisse praedicantium." Cf. also Elio Lampridio Cerva on Bartolomeo Resti, fol. 11v; and Giovanni Pontano on Gattamelata, p. 357.

103. Agostino Dati on Bartolo Bandini, fol. c: "Illud affirmare non dubitem, hunc unum cum inprimis contemplationem cum actione coniunxisse." The phrase "a contemplative even in action" was used to describe the ideal Jesuit in the sixteenth century. For the influence of Italian humanism on the order's orientation see O'Malley, "The Jesuits, St. Ignatius, and the Counter Reformation."

104. Poggio Bracciolini on Lorenzo de' Medici (the elder), p. 281: "Unam virtutem, ea est caritas, virtutum omnium parens, quam colebat maxime. Egenorum domicilium erat, ille viduas, ille pupillos, ille virgines suis facultatibus sustentabat."

105. Antonio Solerio on Pietro Canonici, [fol. 5r–v], quoting Cic. *Lig.* 12,

Tusc. 1.14.32, and James 1:27. For allusions to the passage in Matthew's Gospel see, e.g., Pietro Barozzi on Antonio Roselli, p. 179; and Giusto Baldini on Giovanni da Lucca, fol. 106.

106. Raffaele Brandolini on Domenico della Rovere, [fol. 3]: "neque ad hanc quam agimus vitam bene beateque degendam, neque ad illam quam maximopere exoptamus beatitudinem adipiscendam aut certius aut firmius aut verius ac opportunius quippiam virtutibus non dicam inveniri, sed ne cogitari quidem posse perquam facile intelligetis." Repeated reference has been made throughout this chapter to O'Malley's penetrating analysis of the "ideal of the Christian life" found in Roman oratory (*Praise and Blame*, pp. 165–237). I believe that the ideal, which O'Malley derived on the basis of Roman sources, can be shown to have been as diffuse as was humanism in the Italian Renaissance. Criticism of Renaissance prelates became muted in the period after the Council of Trent, when the Church was presented primarily as a "perfect society" and Rome as the "holy city." See McGinness, "Rhetoric and Counter-Reformation Rome."

CHAPTER FIVE

The quotation in the chapter title is based upon Virgil *Aen.* 6.853.

1. Zeno's career is summarized in Lane, *Venice*, pp. 189–96, 227–28.
2. On Giustiniani's life see Oberdorfer, "Di Leonardo Giustiniano"; and Labalme, *Bernardo Giustiniani*, pp. 8–90. I have found sixty-four manuscript copies of the eulogy in volumes 1–3 of Kristeller's *Iter*, a total more than double that of its nearest rival. Bertalot, "Uno zibaldone umanistico," p. 245, lists six editions of the speech published between 1492 and 1798. Orators like the panegyrist of Mattia Lupi (Bartolo Nerucci?) lifted whole sections verbatim from Giustiniani's oration. In a letter of July 1418 (*Epistolario*, ed. Sabbadini, 1:196–98), Guarino praised the contents of the speech and the manner in which Giustiniani delivered it.
3. Leonardo Giustiniani on Carlo Zeno, p. 142. For lacunae in Themistocles' cultural formation see Cic. *Tusc.* 1.2.4 and Quint. 1.10.19. Cicero commented on the unjust character of Themistocles' exile in *Am.* 12.42; *Brut.* 10.41–42; and *Rep.* 1.3.5. Guarino, Giustiniani's professor of rhetoric, had dedicated his translation of Plutarch's *Themistocles* to Carlo Zeno the year before Zeno's death (1417). It became a commonplace in subsequent Renaissance funeral orations to praise the deceased for devoting his leisure to the study of music. See, e.g., Guarino on Leonello d'Este, fol. 65v, where Guarino borrowed and developed his student's idea.
4. Leonardo Giustiniani on Carlo Zeno, p. 145.

5. Ibid., p. 144. Giustiniani compared Zeno to other figures from antiquity. He noted, for example, that Zeno combined the ability to memorize things, for which Lucius Lucullus was renowned, with Hortensius' ability to memorize words (p. 143). The reference is to Cic. *Acad.* 2.1.2. Immediately after this passage, Cicero speaks of the memory of Themistocles, "the greatest man of Greece."

6. Leonardo Giustiniani on Carlo Zeno, p. 142. Guarino, in his eulogy for Giannicola Salerno, col. 482, emphasized the value of travels for a legislator and mentioned Lycurgus and Solon as prototypes from antiquity.

7. Leonardo Giustiniani on Carlo Zeno, p. 143: "Quod cum philosophiam potissimum ac oratorium munus, tum ad bene beateque vivendum, tum ad publicam hominum utilitatem conferre intellexisset, non quantum occupatissimo viro et in cottidiana maximarum rerum varietate versato, sed quantum aut philosopho aut oratori par fuerat in his est artibus assecutus. Quid enim illam sublimem philosophiae cognitionem extollam? Quid illum dicendi usum et rationem?" The passage adducing places as witnesses is modeled upon Cic. *Manil.* 11.30–31.

8. Ibid., pp. 143–45, esp. p. 144: "Non itaque minorem sibi gloriam vendicavit virtute propria quam militum adiumento. Cum enim rebus tota Citeriore Gallia a se clarissime gestis, omnes fere eius aetatis imperatores superasset, sibi tamen ipse cessisse visus est, cum in Cumanas Alpes profectus, cum parva admodum militum manu, ferocissimam et vi ac armis ante indomitam multitudinem, comitate et consilio sibi conciliavit. Quot ibi militum legiones ante trucidatae fuerant? Quot exercitus deleti? Quot duces caesi? Non ferro, non viribus, non acierum conflictu gens ea, tum animorum immanitate, tum difficultate locorum debellari poterat, sed novo quodam et inusitato bellandi genere, id est, auctoritate, humanitate, clementia, affabilitate, comitate, eloquentia. Quibus Carolus invictas urbes et agrestes animos vicit, domuit, atque subegit."

9. See Kohl, "Political Attitudes"; and my "Oratory of Vergerio," pp. 12–24. Gundersheimer, *Ferrara*, pp. 129–31, describes a similar cultural program from the Quattrocento as "courtly humanism." On the general development of political thought in the Italian Renaissance see Skinner, *Foundations of Modern Political Thought*, vol. 1.

10. Petrarch on Giovanni Visconti, p. 337: "tanti potentissimi Cittadini, tante Terre, Tanti Popoli, e tutti viveano in pace e giustizia sotto il nostro Signore"; and p. 339: "Questa parola si conviene con fondamento considerare un buon Signore n'è tolto, tre ne sono rimasi; se questi non fussino assai possenti a consolarne de la perdita del'uno, dubitarei che noi per amore del Signore morto non fussimo ingiuriosi a' Signor vivi." Petrarch apparently had to interrupt his speech when an astrologer signaled that the propitious

moment had arrived to confer power on the three Visconti. See Tiraboschi, *Storia della letteratura italiana*, 5:30.

11. Pier Paolo Vergerio on Francesco il Vecchio da Carrara, col. 196B–D (the crowd of mourners), col. 197C–E (visible proof of great deeds in war and peace), and col. 198A–C (concluding exhortation to Francesco Novello). See further my "Oratory of Vergerio," pp. 12–24.

12. The language of "crisis" consciously recalls Baron's *Crisis of the Early Italian Renaissance*. See also Mattingly, *Renaissance Diplomacy*, pp. 55–95; and Mesquita, "The Place of Despotism." For the propagandistic purpose of much humanist oratory see Gombrich, "Renaissance and Golden Age."

13. I cite from the edition of Bruni's *Laudatio* in Baron, *From Petrarch to Leonardo Bruni*, pp. 232–65. The ecphrasis of the city is found on pp. 235–40; see esp. p. 238: "Sed haec tanta admiratio, hic tantus stupor, tam diu apud homines est quam diu hanc pulcherrimam urbem non aspexerunt neque viderunt eius magnificentiam. Ceterum ubi illam intuiti sunt, omnis talis evanescit abitque admiratio." On the work's date and political significance see Baron, *Crisis*, rev. ed., pp. 47–48, 191–224; idem, *From Petrarch to Leonardo Bruni*, pp. 102–23, 151–71; and Vasoli, "Considerazioni." Burckhardt chose "The State as a Work of Art" as the title for part 1 of his *Civilization*.

14. Bruni, *Laudatio*, pp. 243–48, esp. p. 244: "Atqui si nobilitatem in auctore quaeris, nihil in toto orbe terrarum nobilius populo Romano poteris invenire; si divitias, nihil opulentius; si amplitudinem ac magnificentiam, nihil omnino clarius neque gloriosius; si magnitudinem imperii, nihil intra Oceanum est quod non armis subactum in eius fuerit potestate. Quamobrem ad vos quoque, viri Florentini, dominium orbis terrarum iure quodam hereditario ceu paternarum rerum possessio pertinet. Ex quo etiam illud fit, ut omnia bella quae a populo Florentino geruntur iustissima sint, nec possit hic populus in gerendis bellis iustitia carere, cum omnia bella pro suarum rerum vel defensione vel recuperatione gerat necesse est, quae duo bellorum genera omnes leges omniaque iura permittunt."

15. Ibid., pp. 258–63, esp. p. 262: "Cum enim potentiores, suis opibus confisi, tenues ledere aspernarique viderentur, causas eorum qui minus poterant ipsa res publica suscepit, maiorique poena res illorum personasque munivit. Rationi quippe consentaneum arbitrata est ut disparem condicionem hominum dispar poena sequeretur, et qui magis indigebat ei plus auxilii tribuere suae prudentiae iustitiaeque putavit. Itaque ex diversis ordinibus facta est quaedam aequabilitas, cum maiores sua potentia, minores res publica, utrosque vero metus poenae defendat."

16. Poggio Bracciolini on Lorenzo de' Medici, pp. 282, 284; and Antonio Pacini on Lorenzo de' Medici, fols. 5r–v, 10v–11. Pacini's oration was never recited publicly, probably to the relief of Cosimo de' Medici. In several places

Pacini depicts the Medici as princes. He affirms that Medici homes seemed worthy of a royal lord ("regio domino," fol. 6v), that their lands generated riches like a royal household ("tanquam ex regia domo," fols. 6v–7), that the presence of so many cardinals at Lorenzo's funeral befitted a king or prince ("regi ac illustrissimo cuique principi," fol. 9), that the family kept servants in the manner of nobles ("more nobilium," fol. 10), and that Lorenzo possessed a regal bearing ("Ducis enim et regis aspectum," fol. 10v). Pacini dedicated the work to Cardinal Giuliano Cesarini.

17. Bruni on Nanni Strozzi, p. 3; and Baron, *Crisis*, rev. ed., pp. 412–39.

18. For the dating of the oration see Baron's comments in the first edition of *Crisis*, 2:430–39. He argues that the oration was begun in the summer or autumn of 1427 but completed only in the spring of 1428.

19. Bruni, *Laudatio*, pp. 249–52; and idem on Nanni Strozzi, pp. 3–4, 7, esp. p. 7: "Bellum autem iustius esse nullum potest quam quod aut lacessitus referas, aut pro patria libertateque suscipias. . . . Bellum erat pro patria, pro libertate, pro salute civium susceptum, quod lacessita primo civitas tunc iustissime referebat, periculum ab hoste ingens atque horrendum."

20. Bruni on Nanni Strozzi, pp. 5–7.

21. Skinner, *Foundations of Political Thought*, 1:75–77.

22. Bruni, *Laudatio*, p. 244; idem on Nanni Strozzi, pp. 3–4; and the dedicatory letter of Antonio Pacini to Cardinal Giuliano Cesarini, fol. 1r–v.

23. Baron, *Crisis*, rev. ed., pp. 413–14; and Witt, *Coluccio Salutati and His Public Letters*, pp. 4, 57–68.

24. The funeral obsequies for Giangaleazzo lasted fourteen hours and are described in Corio, *Storia di Milano*, ed. Butti and Ferrario, 2:439–47. Pietro Castelleto preached during those ceremonies. Other orations delivered at funeral commemorations in the year of Giangaleazzo's death are recorded below in the Appendix under "anonymous"; Capogallo, Giovanni; and Lampugnano, Giovanni. The scribe of the Riccardiana codex, which contains the orations of Capogallo and Lampugnano, made the following judgment about them: "qui sermo est incorrectus nec mihi placet nec ipsum intelligo et nescio quid formaliter suum thema voluerit dicere cum reverentia loquendo" (fol. 89v); "est incorrecter scriptus nec mihi placet nec materia nec forma" (fol. 165v). The thematic character of these orations makes them less ideological than those by Gasparino Barzizza and Andrea Biglia. For the circumstances of Decembrio's panegyric see Garin, "La cultura milanese," pp. 581–82.

25. See the anonymous oration on Giangaleazzo Visconti, fols. 94v–96 (which provides the most complete list of churches that the duke patronized); Gasparino Barzizza on Giangaleazzo Visconti, fol. 17; Andrea Biglia on Giangaleazzo (I), pp. 181–83; idem on Giangaleazzo (II), fols. 55v–56; and

Pietro Castelleto on Giangaleazzo, col. 1044B–D. The anonymous orator contrasted a Christian sense of *magnificentia*, which fosters the divine cult, with Aristotle's conception, restricted to secular matters. Barzizza described Giangaleazzo's intention to retire to the Certosa: "Quid autem deinceps acturus esset, si vita ei longior data esset, certissimis monumentis demonstravit. Quibus nemini dubium esse debet quin, rebus regni compositis, totum se divino cultui sacrisque caerimoniis tradidisset."

26. A. Biglia on Giangaleazzo Visconti (I), p. 181.

27. A. Biglia on Giangaleazzo Visconti (I), pp. 179–80; idem on Giangaleazzo (II), fol. 51; and Decembrio, *Panegyricus*, ed. Petraglione, p. 1017. Biglia (I), pp. 179–80, described the Visconti as "timocrats," i.e., those who deserved to be first in love and honor for creating the Milanese state.

28. The quotation from the Book of Wisdom is included in Caterina Visconti's final instructions to her son, which functioned as a compendium of good government for the Visconti; see anonymous on Caterina Visconti, fol. 85. See further Francesco Filelfo on Stefano Federigo Todeschini, fol. 77r–v; Mesquita, "The Place of Despotism," pp. 316–18; and cf. Rubinstein, "Political Ideas in Sienese Art."

29. See, e.g., Pietro Castelleto on Giangaleazzo Visconti, col. 148C–D; and the anonymous oration on Caterina Visconti, fol. 85r–v. The anonymous orator mentions "the Carthusian cardinal of Santa Croce" in that passage. He is referring to Niccolò Albergati. The oration was therefore delivered after 24 May 1426. The speaker also notes, fol. 84, that he had already delivered a sermon on Giangaleazzo not long before.

30. See, e.g., Pietro Castelleto on Giangaleazzo Visconti, col. 1039C; Andrea Biglia on Giangaleazzo (I), p. 179; and idem on Giangaleazzo (II), fols. 50v–53v, esp. fols. 51v–52: "Quibus rebus plane significatum arbitror nullum administrandarum rerum imperium summo illi totius orbis rectori esse gratius quam hunc ducum ordinem, dum sese divinae bonitatis iudicio dignos exhibeant, quando quidem ipse Deus omnium rerum atque imperiorum dominator in suo, hoc est, in electo ab se populo primum duces esse voluit qui subiectam plebem fide ac ratione gubernarerit [*sic*]."

31. See the anonymous oration on Giangaleazzo Visconti, fols. 96, 97, 101v–02; Decembrio, *Panegyricus*, ed. Petraglione, pp. 1022–23; idem on Niccolò Piccinino, p. 1001; and Andrea Biglia on Giangaleazzo Visconti (I), p. 180.

32. On Giangaleazzo's conduct of war see the anonymous oration on Giangaleazzo, fol. 93r–v; Gasparino Barzizza on Giangaleazzo, fols. 16–17; Andrea Biglia on Giangaleazzo (I), pp. 180, 183; idem on Giangaleazzo (II), fols. 53–54v; Pietro Castelleto on Giangaleazzo, cols. 1039B–C, 1040B, 1042B–D, 1045A–D; and Giovanni Lampugnano on Giangaleazzo, fol. 164. For Filippo

Maria see Antonio da Rho on Niccolò Piccinino, fols. 144v–45, 146v–47; and Pier Candido Decembrio on Niccolò Piccinino, pp. 994–95, 1000–1001, 1008–9.

33. See esp. Andrea Biglia on Giangaleazzo (I), p. 183: "Quis autem ingenio aut sermone comprehenderit quibus artibus totius ferme Italiae imperium quaesiverit? nec quicquam a summis Boiorum Alpibus ad Romanum solum praeter exiguum quendam Tusciae agrum supererat, quod non iussa ducis audiret"; Mattingly, *Renaissance Diplomacy*, pp. 72–75; and Mesquita, "The Place of Despotism," pp. 313–14.

34. See Bernardo Giustiniani on Francesco Foscari, fols. 181v–82: "Quod autem ad instituta pertinet gubernandique rationem libet profecto dicere et constanti voce asseverare non Solonis aut Licurgi praeclarissima inventa, non Platonis philosophorum principis stilo descriptam potius quam oculis, oculis visam civitatem"; George of Trebizond on Fantino Michiel, p. 448: "Cuius tota pueritia, adolescentia, iuventus iis studiis enituit, quibus tanquam fundamentis nixus maximas res maximeque necessarias et huic urbi, hoc est, libertati, utilissimas gesserit"; and Leonardo Giustiniani on Giorgio Loredan, p. 14: "Addamus et illud quod universum rei publicae corpus ab eis semper ita curatum et in commune consultum, ut in aliqua diligentius parte tuenda, ne aliquas unquam desertas amiserint. Quae res adeo civiles discordias et populares omnino seditiones avertit, ut huic dumtaxat civitati post hominum memoriam sine factionibus intestinis contentionibus tam immensum, tam diuturnum gerere licuit imperium." On the public spirit of Venetian patricians see also Pietro del Monte on Giovanni Zabarella, fol. 46v; Filippo da Rimini on Francesco Barbaro, fols. 10–11, 12r–v; Finlay, *Politics in Venice*, pp. 27–37; and King, *Venetian Humanism*, pp. 92–205. Sixteenth-century funeral orations also demonstrated that Venetian political thinkers portrayed the republic as a realization of Platonic ideals. See Andrea Navagero on Leonardo Loredan, pp. 34–37; and Libby, "Venetian History and Political Thought after 1509," pp. 9–15. Contarini's treatise was first printed in 1543, though it was probably begun ca. 1523–24 and completed ca. 1532. See Gilbert, "The Date of Contarini's and Giannotti's Books."

35. I refer to the manuscript version of Bernardo's speech and make reference to subsequent orations for the doges Niccolò Marcello, Andrea Vendramin, and Leonardo Loredan to demonstrate the continuity of ideals. I have not seen the funeral oration of Antonio Contarini for Andrea Contarini (d. 1382) in Venice, Museo Correr, MS Cicogna 2755, apparently in Italian. F. Cavazzana Romanelli, *DBI*, 28:103, describes it as the first ever for a doge. A list of the names of eulogists for doges who held office during the period under consideration is in Mosto, *I dogi*, pp. 191–286. For discussion of the ducal funeral and coronation rites see Muir, *Civic Ritual*, pp. 263–89.

36. Bernardo Giustiniani on Francesco Foscari, fols. 183–86. See also Ermo-

Iao Barbaro on Niccolò Marcello, pp. 100–102; Pietro Marcello on Andrea Vendramin, pp. 150–54; Andrea Navagero on Leonardo Loredan, pp. 32–34; and King, *Venetian Humanism*, p. 179.

37. Bernardo Giustiniani on Francesco Foscari, fol. 186.

38. Ibid., fol. 190: "Cum autem Franciscus videret quotnam Ecclesiae dissidia pararentur, statuit hos bellorum motus novo quodam vincendi genere superare. Mittitur ex illius sententia ad Eugenium et Sigismundum Andreas Donatus, Francisci gener. Mandati ea virtus exstitit ut paucis diebus ex longinquo bello pax fieret, qui venerat infestissimus amicissimus in Germania rediret, qui Phippi [sic] partes fovisset adversus Philippum converteret." See further Muir, *Civic Ritual*, pp. 103–34.

39. B. Giustiniani on Francesco Foscari, fols. 186v–88v, 192–93, 196; and Labalme, *Bernardo Giustiniani*, pp. 114–25, who based her analysis on the revised, printed version of the speech. Similar justifications are supplied by Leonardo Giustiniani on Giorgio Loredan, p. 14; and Giovanni Pontano on Gattamelata, pp. 354, 358.

40. Pietro del Monte on Paolo da Lion, fol. 40r–v. For his dedication, Paolo was voted the unusual reward of a patrician wife. Pietro probably intended the example as a spur to patricians to support Venetian policy. Cf. also Leonardo Giustiniani on Giorgio Loredan, pp. 17–19, who describes how Giorgio was killed in an ambush while attempting to protect Venice's liberty on the sea against pirates led by Ambrogio Spinola.

41. Bernardo Giustiniani on Francesco Foscari, fol. 181: "qui maximis suis laboribus (et periculis) imperii nostri fines terra marique propagavit"; and fols. 182v–83: "Non enim praeclarus civis aliquis sed princeps nobilissimus, non una aliqua virtus sed omnium virtutum exemplar, non qui civibus ornamento fuerit, sed qui civitatis huius gloriam apud omnes exteras nationes celeberrimam amplissimamque reddiderit est laudandus, (ut unus sit post hominum memoriam cuius virtutes, gesta, terraque et mari summa cum gloria propagatum imperium amplam atque uberem orationis copiam desideret)." The phrases in parentheses were omitted in the printed version, perhaps in the latter case to soften the imperialist tone.

42. See, e.g., Tomasi, *Ritratto del Condottiero*; Mallett, *Mercenaries*; Griffiths, "Uccello's *Battle*"; Kajanto and Nyberg, *Papal Epigraphy*, pp. 60–61; and Mallett and Hale, *Military Organization*, pp. 186–98. To demonstrate continuities in humanist ideals, I also cite from funeral orations for prominent military leaders, who were active after 1454.

43. George of Trebizond on Fantino Michiel, pp. 450–51, who calls the Parthians "copiae Armeniorum." George apparently alludes to the accounts of the military heroics of Miltiades in Nep. *Milt.* 4.1 and of Lucullus in Plut. *Luc.* 24–32, esp. 28. Giovanni Pontano on Gattamelata, pp. 358–60; and Lauro Quirini on Gattamelata, pp. 351–52.

44. Antonio da Rho on Niccolò Piccinino, fol. 147r–v; and Pier Candido Decembrio on Niccolò Piccinino, pp. 1001–7.

45. See, e.g., Giovanni Pontano on Gattamelata, p. 354; and Andrea Navagero on Bartolomeo d'Alviano, pp. 14–15. Clemency was shown by not conquering the conquerable. Antonio da Rho, fol. 147, claimed that Filippo Maria Visconti overrode Niccolò Piccinino's plan to launch a surprise attack on Florence because his aim was not conquest: "Decreverat tunc mente sua Pizininus Florentiam omni spe, omni praesidio destitutam invadere et in servitutem redigere; et fortasse actum esset, nisi principis illustrissimi nostri natura quam mitis et humana quae inimicos potius conciliatos habere quam funditus delere semper cupiebat obstitisset." Antonio sought to shape future policy by praising the past. For the model of the "clement Caesar" see Agostino Camici on Filippo Maria Visconti, fol. 127r–v; Giovanni Cattanei on Francesco Gonzaga, [fol. 18v]; Francesco Filelfo on Bianca Maria Visconti, fol. 27v; and Andrea Navagero on Bartolomeo d'Alviano, pp. 5–6.

46. Giovanni Battista Egnazio on Niccolò Orsini, [fol. 13v]: "Temperantia autem in quo uno maior? Quid ipse miles quam continens, quam disciplinae militaris observator ut vestigium militis nedum manus pacato obfuerit nulli? neque vero hoc mirum, si is imperator militem facile contineat qui continentiae leges sibi primus imponat." Cf. also Giovanni Pontano on Gattamelata, p. 354; and Celio Calcagnini on Antonio Costabili, p. 276.

47. For the example of ancient generals see Antonio Telesio on Giangiacomo Trivulzi, [fol. 7]. For that of contemporary generals see Giovanni Battista Egnazio on Niccolò Orsini, [fol. 10r–v]; Francesco Maturanzio on Orazio I Baglioni, fol. 54r–v; and idem on Giovanni Chiericati, fol. 88. Eloquent generals were praised by Andrea Navagero on Bartolomeo d'Alviano, pp. 9, 16; and Lauro Quirini on Gattamelata, p. 350.

48. Anonymous on Bartolomeo Padovano, fol. 290v. See also the anonymous oration on Pandolfo II Malatesta, p. xxv; Gabriele Mauro on Benedetto Pesaro, [fols. 2v–3]; Lauro Quirini on Gattamelata, p. 353; and Antonio Telesio on Giangiacomo Trivulzi, [fol. 4r–v]. For a knight's pledge of honor see Leonardo Bruni on Nanni Strozzi, p. 5; and Mallett, *Mercenaries*, pp. 101–6. Cases of eulogies for soldiers killed in ambushes include Aurelio Brandolini on Lorenzo Giustini, fols. 217–19, 223–25v; Leonardo Bruni on Nanni Strozzi, pp. 6–7; and Leonardo Giustiniani on Giorgio Loredan, pp. 17–19. Cf. also Francesco Maturanzio on Orazio I Baglioni, fols. 55v–56v.

49. Sallust *Cat.* 10.3–13.5. Orators who criticized the mercenary system include Leonardo Bruni on Nanni Strozzi, p. 5; and Gabriele Mauro on Benedetto Pesaro, [fol. 4]. For a general's *humanitas*, see, e.g., Giovanni Battista Egnazio on Niccolò Orsini, [fols. 13v–14]; Andrea Navagero on Bartolomeo d'Alviano, p. 13; Giovanni Pontano on Gattamelata, pp. 356–57; and Lauro Quirini on Gattamelata, pp. 352–53.

50. Baron, *Crisis*, rev. ed., pp. 370–96, 430–33; Bayley, *War and Society*; and Oppel, "Peace vs. Liberty."

51. Gasparino Barzizza on Giangaleazzo Visconti, fol. 16r–v, esp. fol. 16v: "Tum etiam illa me res magnopere, patres insignes, movet quod non tam de his principibus orta oratio est qui ceteros dilatatis finibus imperiis excesserunt quam de illis qui virtute animi omnibus praestiterunt. Mea quidem semper sententia fuit unam vel quidem minimam ex omnibus virtutem pluris omnibus regnis atque triumphis quamvis maximis habendam." The remainder of the oration is cast as a proof that Giangaleazzo possessed virtues like modesty and clemency, which Alexander the Great and Julius Caesar lacked. The scruple of Filippo Maria is described by Cognasso, "Istituzioni comunali e signorili," pp. 523–24.

52. B. Giustiniani on Francesco Foscari, fols. 186v, 190, 192r–v, 196, 197–98v, esp. fol. 190: "Eat nunc aliquis et belli gloriam afferat, sapientiam aspernetur, quasi non plus interdum fieri viderimus moderatione prudentiaque quam caedibus aut rapinis. At non sic Lacedaemonii qui, cum ferro acieque vicissent, gallinae sacrificio diis agere gratias, cum vero comitate et suadella, bovis [MS: bonis] quasi maius et, ut ita dicam, divinius quiddam esset, sicuti est, ducere hominem quam cogere et animi ratione quam viribus belligerare. Ne semper autem Spartam aut Athenas defatigemus, ecce, Fuscarus noster in hoc genere laudis perpetuum sese posteritati exemplum offert." The conjunction of Athens and Sparta suggests that Italy in the mid-Quattrocento faced a situation as potentially destructive as Greece during the Peloponnesian War. Finlay, *Politics in Venice*, pp. 116–17, has challenged the interpretation that Foscari was deposed in a vendetta led by the Loredan family and motivated by his conduct of foreign policy; he argues that Foscari was simply incapable or unwilling to fulfill the responsibilities of his office. Cf. also Leonardo Giustiniani on Carlo Zeno, p. 144; George of Trebizond on Fantino Michiel, p. 449; and Bessarion on the emperor Manuel, *PG*, 161:col. 618.

53. Cic. *Brut.* 12.45: "Nec enim in constituentibus rem publicam nec in bella gerentibus nec in impeditis ac regum dominatione devinctis nasci cupiditas dicendi solet. Pacis est comes otique socia et iam bene constitutae civitatis quasi alumna quaedam eloquentia."

54. Andrea Biglia on Battista? Bentivoglio, fol. 26v. For the justification of war by various orators see Antonio da Rho on Niccolò Piccinino, fols. 144v–45; Leonardo Bruni on Nanni Strozzi, p. 7; Agostino Camici on Filippo Maria Visconti, fol. 127; and Giovanni Pontano on Gattamelata, p. 358.

55. Guarino on Leonello d'Este, fol. 65: "Ex quo functus singularis atque beatus collectus est, quod, cum in tota Mars impius saeviret Italia et ferrum ignisque per finitimos sonaret agros, providentissimus marchio a bellicis detrimentis et vastationibus et ab hostili impetu suum incolume tutus est regnum. Clementia quae generi Estensi propria et innata est in Leonello id

efficit ut, cum irrogandis insontes poenis mitis esset, infelicibus misericordiam impertiret. Ad donandam reis vitam saepissime pronus erat, Senecae clarissimi et philosophi et poetae scitum illud amplexatus: sanguine humano abstine quicumque regnas. Meminerat enim reges Dei imitatores ad benefaciendum esse datos; quodque homo ipse hominibus ut membris praeesset, fixum habebat animo saevitiam non homini sed beluarum esse. Idcirco saevitiam nunquam, severitatem nonnunquam, sed clementiam semper in homines exercendam legerat et libens imitabat." See Seneca *Herc.* 745; and cf. Sen. *Clem.* 1.11.2–3; and Virg. *Geor.* 1.511. Guarino expressed the same sentiments in a consolatory letter to Leonello for the death of his father, Niccolò III; see *Epistolario*, ed. Sabbadini, 2:414–16.

56. D. Acciaiuoli on Cosimo de' Medici, p. 261: "Verum, praestantissimi cives, ante omnia in oculis atque animis vestris habere vos decet illius perpetuum studium in libertate servanda, amorem et propensam voluntatem in re publica tuenda atque in ea tranquillitate locanda, quam sapientes viri optimis rerum publicarum gubernatoribus propositam esse voluerunt"; and p. 262: "et posterorum exemplum quod eos excitet alacrioresque reddat ad libertatem patriae tuendam." The phrase "alacrior ad tutandam rem publicam" is cited from Cic. *Rep.* 6.13.13; cf. also *Rep.* 2.29.51. See further Brown, "Humanist Portrait." Acciaiuoli's attitude toward Cosimo had been one of tepid support and even hostility until Cosimo helped to engineer the peace settlement. Afterwards Donato became an active servant in the Medici regime. See Garin, "Acciaiuoli"; and Ganz, "Acciaiuoli and the Medici."

57. Francesco Filelfo on Francesco Sforza, fol. 23: "Quam ipsam [pacem] princeps moderatissimus non solum non recusavit, sed ultro etiam castella omnia, municipia omnia, oppida omnia quae iure belli sibi vendicarat Venetis dono cessit quo nihil deesset omnino ad perpetuae pacis stabilimentum ac robur. Imitatus sane quod scriptum est, 'Pacem meam relinquo vobis, pacem meam do vobis.' Cum enim delectaretur omnem per se pacari Italiam, nihil per sese deesse voluit ad tollendam omnem belli non materiam modo, sed etiam suspitionem. Altius certe animus eius suspiciebat qui mortalia despiceret omnia, immortalis illius vitae gloriam beatitudinemque contemplans, ad quam sola iustitia nos perducit." Bernardo Giustiniani on Francesco Foscari, fols. 196, 198r–v. For Colleoni's contribution see Guglielmo Pagello on Bartolomeo Colleoni, [fols. 7r–v, 9r–v]; Giovanni Michele Alberto Carrara on Bartolomeo Colleoni, pp. 260, 265, 267; and M. E. Mallett in *DBI*, 27:9–19.

58. Montaldo, "De vita Alfonsi oratio," p. 227; and Giannozzo Manetti on Giannozzo Pandolfini, fols. 11v–15v. The role of Nicholas V was praised by Jean Jouffroy, fols. 36v–37; and by Niccolò Palmeri, fols. 8v–10.

59. On a perpetual crusade against the Turk see esp. Donato Acciaiuoli? on Ioannes Hunyadi, fol. 84r–v. Guglielmo Pagello adduced as one proof of

Bartolomeo Colleoni's *pietas* the funds that Colleoni assigned in his will for the purpose of "crushing the inhuman Turk," [fol. 14r–v]. Cf. also O'Malley, *Praise and Blame*, pp. 233–35. For the hunt see, e.g., Montaldo, "De vita Alfonsi oratio," p. 226; Guarino on Leonello d'Este, fol. 65v; and Gundersheimer, *Ferrara*, pp. 127–45.

60. Giovanni Montano on Filippo Maria Visconti, col. 442A–B. See also Agostino Camici on Filippo Maria Visconti, fols. 125v–26; Girolamo Crivelli on Bianca Maria Visconti, cols. 428B–C, 431B–C; Francesco Filelfo on Francesco Sforza, fol. 3r–v; Giovanni Montano on Filippo Maria Visconti, col. 442C; and Bembo, *In Ludovici Mariae Sfortiae laudes oratio*, [fol. 4r–v]. Filelfo, in his oration for Bianca Maria Visconti, fol. 32, accused Pope Calixtus III of inducing Borso d'Este to fight against Milan.

61. Filelfo on Francesco Sforza, fol. 22: " 'Absit,' inquit, 'ut ego in patriam meam tam liberaliter veluti revocatus triumphans ingrediar. Quod si me cupitis pro benignitate vestra maxime honoratum, operam date ut omnia pacata inter vos esse offendam. Cessent civiles omnes discordiae, exstinguantur omnia odiorum incendia, iniuriae omnes mea gratia condonentur. Quod ut etiam ipsi et privatim faciatis et publice, ego primus quicquid est adversus me meosque perpetratum aut iniuste aut pervicaciter non ignosco solum, sed omnes rogo atque oro ut sempiterna id oblivione ex animo deleatis.' "

62. Francesco Filelfo on Francesco Sforza, fols. 4v–5 (regarding the Castello), and fol. 13v (regarding his severity with the soldier). Filelfo also praised Francesco for his clemency in disobeying his father's orders to slaughter rebellious troops under his command (fol. 7r–v), for his compassionate treatment of a wounded enemy general (fols. 8v–9v), and for his continence in resisting the temptation to rape a captured virgin (fol. 20v). See also Baldassare Rasini on Francesco Sforza, fols. 13–17v, esp. fol. 15. Rasini also called attention, fols. 22v–23, to Sforza's clemency in pardoning those who had plotted against him. For further reference to Visconti patronage for religious buildings see Giovanni Montano on Filippo Maria Visconti, col. 440A–B.

63. G. Campano on Nello Baglioni, [fol. 110r–v], esp. [fol. 110r]: "O rem admirabilem et aetate nostra inauditam, summum pontificem privati hominis morte temperare a dolore et lacrimis tenere non posse. Cur ita? Quoniam eum inquit virum solum Perusinam civitatem prudentia et consilio regere solitum, solum praesentia populi saepe furores atque impetus repressisse." The context in which the oration was delivered is discussed by Bernardo, *Campano*, pp. 75–76.

64. Giannantonio Campano on Nello Baglioni, [fols. 105–9v]. Cf. also idem on Giovanni della Ratta, [fol. 115].

65. Francesco Maturanzio on Braccio Baglioni, fols. 16v–18, 20r–v. In general, see the article on Braccio by R. Abbondanza in *DBI*, 5:207–12; Black,

"The Baglioni"; and Blanshei, "Population, Wealth, and Patronage." Maturanzio credited Niccolò Chiericati with repressing crime and settling discords during his administrative tenure in Perugia, fol. 91v. Cf. also the anonymous oration on Uguccione? Contrari, fol. 120; Celio Calcagnini on Alfonso I d'Este, pp. 272–73; Benedetto Colucci on Antonio Partini, pp. 70, 72; and Ludovico Odassi on Federigo da Montefeltro, fol. 14. Andrea Biglia extolled a Bentivoglio (Battista?) for marrying several times and thereby spinning a web of affinities to nurture concord in Bologna, fol. 29r–v.

66. See, e.g., Cristoforo Landino on Donato Acciaiuoli, fol. 13r–v; Alamanno Rinuccini on Matteo Palmieri, p. 83; Lorenzo Rocca on Luigi Dardani, [fol. 4v]; Ermolao Barbaro on Niccolò Marcello, p. 101: "et quascumque provincias adiisset non ante discessit quam, urbe et agro perlustrato universo, purgatissimam malis hominibus redderet. Simultates vero ita undique compressit, ita lites maximas composuit aut diremit, ut capitales antea inimicitias et odia desperatae concordiae ad pacem tranquillitatemque revocaverit"; and Piero Valeriano on Girolamo della Torre, [fol. 2r–v], esp. [fol. 2]: "Accedebat huc concors et rara haec magistratuum unanimitas ac fraterna propemodum caritas quae tranquillitatem civitati pacatissimam praestaret, siquidem Platonis testimonio tales sunt civitates quales earum moderatores."

67. See, e.g., Ermolao Barbaro on Niccolò Marcello, pp. 101–2; Pietro Contarini on Marco Corner, [fols. 5v–6]; Bernardo Giustiniani on Francesco Foscari, fol. 185r–v; Pietro Marcello on Andrea Vendramin, pp. 153–54; Andrea Navagero on Leonardo Loredan, pp. 33–34; Antonio Pacini on Lorenzo de' Medici (the elder), fols. 10v–14; Giovanni Battista Ramusio on Francesco Fasolo, p. 391; Baldassare Rasini on Francesco Sforza, fol. 15; and esp. Poggio Bracciolini on Lorenzo de' Medici (the elder), pp. 283–85, esp. 284: "Etenim prudentia, temperantia, frugalitas, continentia, rerum scientia illis tantum videtur prodesse in quibus consistunt, parum quidem ad alios declinantes. At vero iustitia, liberalitas, humanitas, comitas, munificentia communi rei publicae conservationi ac praesidio accommodantur iuvantque quam plurimos." Alamanno Rinuccini, in the decree he prepared for Cosimo de' Medici's award as "pater patriae," spoke of the republic's two principal concerns as rewards and punishments (*Lettere ed orazioni*, ed. Giustiniani, p. 125). Pietro Barozzi suggested that citizens were equal before the law; see Barozzi on Antonio Roselli, pp. 181–82.

68. Montaldo, "De vita Alfonsi oratio," p. 226. Cf. also Ludovico Carbone on Bartolomeo Pendaglia, fols. 85v–87.

69. Montaldo, "De vita Alfonsi oratio," p. 226.

70. On the Venetian myth of justice and its celebration in public art see Chambers, *The Imperial Age of Venice*, pp. 94–107; and Sinding-Larsen, *Christ in the Council Hall*. For discussion of the procurator's office and social assistance in Venice during the Renaissance see Pullan, *Rich and Poor*, pp. 209–10,

351–54; and Mueller, "The Procurators of San Marco." An anonymous eulogist for Paolo Tron, fol. 101v, emphasized that the office of procurator of San Marco embraced the philosophers' ideals of justice and generosity and the theologians' ideals of compassion and charity.

71. Pietro Marcello on Andrea Vendramin, pp. 155–57. The story of L. Iunius Brutus is told by Livy 2.5.5–9. Cf. also Bernardo Giustiniani on Francesco Foscari, fol. 186r–v; and Ermolao Barbaro on Niccolò Marcello, pp. 102–3.

72. The phrase refers specifically to Borso d'Este's founding of the Certosa. I have borrowed it from Rosenberg, " 'Per il bene di . . . nostra cipta.' " See also Gundersheimer, *Ferrara*; and idem, "Patronage of Ercole."

73. Celio Calcagnini on Alfonso I d'Este, pp. 268–69; Guarino on Leonello d'Este, fols. 64v–65; and Gundersheimer, *Ferrara*, pp. 98–100, 276.

74. Ludovico Carbone on Borso d'Este, fol. 93v. He also, fol. 94r–v, applauded the fact that the senate and people of Ferrara awarded Borso a statue while still alive. See further Rosenberg, " 'Per il bene di . . . nostra cipta,' " pp. 330–31; and Gundersheimer, *Ferrara*, pp. 127–72.

75. Francesco Negro on Ercole I d'Este, fol. 10v: "longaeque prius Ferrariae hemicyclium agrum addit quem vallo fossaque latissima muniens in totius populi commodum et urbis honestamentum praeclarissimis civium aedibus augustissimisque deorum templis exornat ita ut, si quondam Semiramis quae Ninam civitatem, si Ascanius qui Laurentum, si Romulus qui Romam feliciter ampliavit merita sunt divinitate donati, sic Hercules et augustus et divinus merito possit appellari." See further Gundersheimer, *Ferrara*, pp. 184–99; and idem, "Patronage of Ercole," pp. 16–18. These building projects forced orators to treat certain of government's less pleasant necessities. Celio Calcagnini claimed that Ercole Strozzi had been forced against his will to exact taxes and assured his listeners that every ducat collected had gone toward public works like the walls, gates, and bridges of the city. See Calcagnini on Ercole Strozzi, pp. 284–85.

76. Gundersheimer, "Women, Learning, and Power."

77. Battista Guarini on Eleanor of Aragon, [fols. 2–3]; and Battista Mantovano on Eleanor of Aragon, [fols. 4v–5, 6–7].

78. When praising a woman's domestic virtue, humanist eulogists particularly underlined her efforts to assure a liberal education for her children. See, e.g., Elio Lampridio Cerva on Paula Zamagna, fol. 5v; Francesco Maturanzio on Dorotea da Porto, fol. 81v; and esp. Guarino on Teodora Zilioli, col. 1247: "Cum contra morandis pro aetate filiis, ad litterarum studia provehendis, ad bene beateque vivendum instituendis nullis parcatur impensis, argentum liberaliter et libenter effundatur, munera libentissime dimittantur, bonarum artium praeceptores conducantur, scriptitandis et comparandis codicibus largior impendatur opera." Francesco Filelfo ap-

plauded Bianca Maria Visconti for assuring that her son Galeazzo Maria Sforza be wise and eloquent; much of his eulogy for her (fols. 28v–33) consists of a demonstration of the young man's wise eloquence. On the public contributions of women see, e.g., the anonymous oration on Louise of Savoy, fols. 3–4; anonymous on Elisabetta Malatesta, p. xxxi; Battista Mantovano on Eleanor of Aragon, [fols. 4v–5]; Giannantonio Campano on Battista Sforza, [fols. 119–20v]; Pandolfo Collenuccio on Battista Sforza, p. 53; Girolamo Crivelli on Bianca Maria Visconti, cols. 428C–E, 429B–C; Carlo Curro on Isabella? of Portugal, [fol. 4]; Giovanni Mario Filelfo on Margherita Gonzaga, fol. 27r–v; Battista Guarini on Eleanor of Aragon, [fols. 1–2v]; and Niccolò Lucaro on Beatrice Sforza, fol. 132. The anonymous eulogist of Louise of Savoy, fols. 6–8, stressed that Louise ruled France after her son Francis I's capture at Pavia and worked with Margaret, the aunt of the emperor Charles V, to establish peace between the houses of Habsburg and Valois. See further Freeman, "Louise of Savoy"; and Griffiths, "Louise of Savoy."

79. Anonymous on Elisabetta Malatesta, p. xxx: "Quid illum dicendi usum et orationem? Testis es tu, illustrissime princeps, vosque conscripti patres, qui saepe cum in senatu rogati venissetis, suavissimam vocem, gravissimas sententias maxima semper cum admiratione audivistis." Guarino on Margherita Gonzaga, fol. 108v (a passage transcribed by Sabbadini in his edition of Guarino's *Epistolario*, 3:322). Giannantonio Campano on Battista Sforza, [fols. 119v–20v]. See also the anonymous oration on Louise of Savoy, fol. 8v; Martino Filetico on Gentile Brancaleoni, fol. 2; Giacomo da Pesaro? on Costanza Varano, [fols. 82–83]; Ludovico Odassi on Ippolita Maria Sforza, p. 49; and Baldassare Rasini on Francesco Sforza, fol. 7r–v. Giovanni Cattanei and Ludovico Odassi emphasized the power of a woman's example to persuade others to "good and holy living." See Cattanei on Barbara Gonzaga, [fols. 9, 14]; and Odassi on Ippolita Maria Sforza, p. 46.

80. See Bruni, "De studiis et litteris," ed. Garin, p. 154. Giannantonio Campano on Battista Sforza, [fol. 120v]: "Audita est a Pio secundo pontifice maximo tanta cum attentione aut stupore potius ut excusaverit se ille, parem adhibere orationem non posse, et dolere atque angi quod tantum miraculum eloquentiae publicae et freqnenti [sic] collegio non admisisset, facturum id fuisse affirmavit, si vel dimidium sperasset ex femina, nec minore admiratione prosecutus est familiarem eius sermonem, castigatum et modicum, gravitatis simul et prudentiae plenum ut saepe repetierit hanc unam esse quae recte sciret et multum et parum loqui sensisseque nunc dicendi vim in femina quantam nunquam antea percepisset in viro, et inique actum esse cum feminis quibus passim erepta esset occasio dandi litteris operam cum in earum aliqua tantum natura cumulasset ingenii." See also Giovanni Cattanei on Barbara Gonzaga, [fol. 6v]; Jordan, "Feminism and the Humanists"; King, "Book-Lined Cells"; and Kristeller, "Learned Women of Early Modern Italy."

81. See, e.g., Pietro Castelleto on Giangaleazzo Visconti, col. 1041B; Niccolò da Rimini on Galeotto Roberto Malatesta, p. 545; Montaldo, "De vita Alfonsi oratio," p. 225; Gundersheimer, *Ferrara*, pp. 186–91; Weissman, *Ritual Brotherhood*, pp. 99–104; and Küng, *The Church*, pp. 388–93.

82. Gundersheimer, *Ferrara*, pp. 98–100; Pullan, *Rich and Poor*, pp. 197–215; and E. Micheletti on Santi Buglioni in *DBI*, 15:27–28. The majority of scenes on the frieze were completed by 1528, though the work was not finished until 1585. The second scene, which depicts "housing the stranger," shows Christ disguised as a pilgrim who points out the *spedalingo* of the hospital, Leonardo Buonafede, washing the feet of John the Baptist. See Marquand, *Benedetto and Santi Buglioni*, pp. 168–69.

83. Ludovico Strassoldo on Francesco Corner, fol. 92r–v, esp. fol. 92r: "Qui tum dissuadentibus cognatis ac propinquis propter variam instabilemque rerum humanarum fortunam sanctissimum illud omnique memoria dignum respondebat, 'Iniquum esse et ab humanitate semotum tum cum maxime opus esset amicis auxilio deesse atque tam sanctum amici officium tum desertum habere cum maxime confirmandum foret.'" Pietro Contarini on Marco Corner, [fols. 4, 5, 7v]; Carlo Cappello on Giorgio Corner, pp. 184–86. The decision to annex Cyprus was made by the Venetian senate. Giorgio managed to overcome his sister's opposition through a combination of bribes and threats. The senate frequently interfered in Giorgio's affairs, for his fabulous wealth meant power. See G. Gullino in *DBI*, 29:212–16.

84. See, e.g., Tommaso Acerbo on Giovanni Britannico, [fol. 86r–v]: "Is sane timor ingenuus Britanici cordi erat calcar adhibitum ad liberalitatem atque beneficentiam, quae iure sancta a nobis appellari debet. Ea enim large magnificeque usus est non tantum in splendida hominum nobilium principumque hospitalitate, at, quod est longe sanctius longeque praestantius in egenorum susceptione et illis divinis actionibus, quas Sacrae Scripturae misericordiae opera vocitant assiduus fuit"; and [fol. 87v]: "O singularem viri probitatem atque misericordiam! Vicit in eius pectore erga Deum et proximum pietas avaritiae insatiabilem famem." He uses the familiar biblical categories of the "orphans and widows," [fol. 87], to define the proper objects for a knight's care in peacetime. On magnificence see, e.g., Poggio Bracciolini on Lorenzo de' Medici (the elder), pp. 283, 285; Antonio Pacini on Lorenzo de' Medici (the elder), fols. 3v–6, 11v–12v; and Fraser-Jenkins, "Cosimo de' Medici's Patronage."

85. On Girolamo's career see Pastor, *History of the Popes*, 4:300–85, 413–30; 5:271–72.

86. Pietro Marsi on Girolamo Riario, [fol. 2r–v]: "Testis est et illa civitas quae proh dolor non sua culpa sed quorundam factiosorum vesania et immanitate sui principis ossa non meruit. Pontifice vita defuncto, ad suos cum thori genialis consorte ac filiis eo animo se recepit, ut non minus subditorum

quam propriae utilitati consuleret, a bello, quantum per tempora licuisset, penitus alienus ut pacis commodo securi fruerentur. Quos prudentiae suae regendos et gubernandos Pontifex commiserat. Non enim ad bellicos tumultus, non ad classica furibundum incedentia Martem, sed ad pacem pro qua certandum est et concordiam nati sumus." Pedro Flores's praise of peace in a sermon before the election of a successor to Pope Julius II, Girolamo's cousin, is a similar example of implicit criticism of the deceased's policies (*Oratio*, [fol. 7r–v]).

87. Pietro Marsi on Girolamo Riario, [fol. 4r–v]: "Meus ille cruor non aliam vindictam exposcit quam vindicare potuisse. Magnanimum principem decere scias rebus acri iudicio discussis scelerum punire auctores, multitudinem vero quae instar freti parvo huc et illuc momento impellitur clementi animo conservare, ac in omni fortuna humanitatis habere rationem quae in homine ferum animum penitus detestatur. Qui omnibus certe formidolosus est is in suam cladem irritat omnis atque accendit; prudentia lateri tuo quorundam defendat insidias. Clementia vero populum conciliet, liberalitas illum tibi perinde ac patri devinctum reddat generosi spiritus Iulium Caesarem imitare cuius clementia communi praeconio celebratur. Parcere subiectis et debellare superbos olim prima fuit laus Romanorum principum." See Virg. *Aen*. 6.853.

88. Pietro Marsi on Girolamo Riario, [fols. 4v–5]: "Itala gens, quae inprimis humanitate ceteris antecellit tot tantisque nationibus censetur, quae Italo nomini ac famae prospicientes interdum graves tollerant dominos ne infami appellatione notentur. . . . Heia igitur omnis quos honoris causa appello Forocornelienses, Forolivienses, et Foropompilienses Romana progenies in medium consulite ac ut coepistis bona fide sequimini et non minus honori quam usui prospicientes."

89. Francesco Vigilio on Francesco II Gonzaga, fols. 127v–29. Cf. Jacomuzzi, "Un modello."

90. Francesco Vigilio on Francesco II Gonzaga, fols. 133–34, where he treats all of these actions under the rubric of *caritas*. See also Celio Calcagnini on Alfonso I d'Este, p. 269: "Ad securitatem vero et perennem suorum defensionem urbem nostram foveis, aggeribus, alioque item apparatu muniit et prope inexpugnabilem fecit. Cum igitur multo maxima Italiae pars bello, caedibus, vastitate conflagraverit, nos et Dei optimi maximi ope et sapientissimi principis consilio extra omnem fortunae aleam in alta pace viximus."

91. George of Trebizond on Fantino Michiel, p. 453: "Nam ut nullum unquam ille magistratum concupivit nisi quem ex dignitate atque utilitate rei publicae gerere poterat, ita in omnibus semper primus electus cunctisque suffragiis renunciatus est; et, quod admirandum Venetis, qui haec omnia sciunt, ceteris, siqui nesciunt, incredibile videbitur, iis semper se abdicabat magistratibus qui utilitatis multum, laboris parum afferebant. Censebat enim sincerus Fantini animus pecunias aliis, sibi gloriam expetendam, quod non

in honoribus solum, verum etiam in ceteris diligenter observabat." Battista Guarini (fols. 11v–14) and Ludovico Carbone (fols. 200–201) emphasized the integrity of Ludovico Casella, who refused all bribes and only accepted a larger home at the insistence of Borso d'Este. They placed Casella in the tradition of Greeks like Xenocrates (cf. Cicero *Tusc.* 5.32.91) and Romans like Curius and Fabius (cf. Cicero *Sen.* 4.10, 16.55–56). See also Pietro Barozzi on Antonio Roselli, pp. 181–82; Poggio Bracciolini on Lorenzo de' Medici (the elder), p. 282; Celio Calcagnini on Antonio Costabili, p. 278; Pietro Contarini on Marco Corner, [fols. 5v–6, 8v–9]; Francesco da Grado on Giovanni Almerici, fol. 124r–v; Pietro del Monte on Paolo da Lion, fol. 40r–v; Giovanni Battista Ramusio on Francesco Fasolo, p. 391; Lorenzo Rocca on Luigi Dardani, [fol. 4r–v]; and Ludovico Strassoldo on Francesco Corner, fol. 92v.

92. See esp. Giannantonio Campano on Giovanni della Ratta, [fol. 115].

93. Gilbert, "The Humanist Concept of the Prince and *The Prince* of Machiavelli."

94. Trans. John W. Basore, *Seneca, Moral Essays*, Loeb Library (London: W. Heinemann; New York: G. P. Putnam's Sons, 1928), 1:399. In general, see *Der kleine Pauly: Lexikon der Antike*, ed. K. Ziegler, W. Sontheimer, and H. Gartner, 5 vols. (Munich: A. Druckenmüller, 1964–75), 4:cols. 547–48; and Brown, "Humanist Portrait." Cf. also Orlando, "L'ideologia negli *Apologi* di Collenuccio."

95. Francesco Zabarella on Arcoano Buzzacarini, p. 143; Antonio Pacini on Lorenzo de' Medici (the elder), fols. 3v–5; Donato Acciaiuoli on Cosimo de' Medici, pp. 261–62; and Brown, "Humanist Portrait," pp. 190–91. See also the tribute to Cosimo composed by Rinuccini, *Lettere ed orazioni*, pp. 125–26; and Gundersheimer, *Ferrara*, pp. 67–69, who describes the application of the title to Niccolò III d'Este by the time of his death in 1441.

96. Giannantonio Campano on Nello Baglioni, esp. [fol. 110v]; Francesco Maturanzio on Braccio Baglioni, fols. 17–18, 20; anonymous on Lazzaro Becci, fol. 224; and Celio Calcagnini on Alfonso I d'Este, pp. 268–69. Cf. also Francesco Negro on Ercole I d'Este, [fol. 11v].

97. Leonardo Giustiniani on Carlo Zeno, p. 143, where examples of ancient patronage are drawn from Plutarch *Lys.* 18.4, *Cat. min.* 10.2, *Luc.* 10.3, 42.1–4.

98. Battista Guarini on Ludovico Casella, fol. 15r–v: "Nonne cum doctrinae portus et sanctitatis exemplar Guarinus parens meus occidisset, quem ille in omni sermone patrem appellare consueverat mirabilem humanitatem gratitudini immensae coniunctam exhibuit? Nam cum in funus prodiisset quod ab eo propter magistratus occupationes raro fiebat secumque reputaret non modo se ab illius fontibus doctrinam hausisse sed illum fuisse qui et de domo Estensi bene meritus esset et civitatem hanc omnesque Italorum ac barbarorum provincias et litterarum studiis et probis moribus adornasset,

cupiens optimi discipuli officio fungi speransque se gloriosissimo Duci Borsio rem gratissimam facturum cadaveri humeros subiicere non recusavit reliquosque qui aderant amplissimos viros ad idem faciendum exemplo suo incitavit. O mansuetudinem inauditam! O humanitatem omnium praeconiis celebrandam!"

99. Guarino on Leonello d'Este, fol. 65r–v; and Gundersheimer, *Ferrara*, pp. 92–126. Ludovico Odassi on Federigo da Montefeltro, fol. 11v; and Clough, "Federigo da Montefeltro's Patronage of the Arts." Aurelio Bienato on Lorenzo de' Medici, [fols. 5–6]; and Chastel, *Art et humanisme à Florence*. Bienato delivered his oration at Naples. Lorenzo had ordered that his funeral in Florence be as simple as possible; see Poliziano's letter to Iacobus Antiquarius, *Opera omnia*, ed. Maïer, 1:47. For princely patronage see also Francesco Negro on Ercole I d'Este, [fol. 10r–v], who applauded Ercole for reintroducing comedy and music at Ferrara; and Bessarion on Manuel II Palaeologus (*PG*, 161:col. 619), who emphasized the emperor's contribution to a rebirth of Greek letters.

100. Celio Calcagnini on Beatrice of Aragon, pp. 257–58, esp. p. 258: "bonisque artibus regna instituere, efferatos animos emollire, bene educatis ingeniis favere, litteratos undecumque accersere eosque omni munificentia honestare. Quo factum est ut in Pannonias omne ferme Latium ea tempestate migrarit atque in media barbarie Athenae excitarentur."

101. The first funeral was held in 1406 for Coluccio Salutati, but the eulogy, by Ser Viviano di Neri, has not survived. See Witt, *Hercules at the Crossroads*, pp. 414–15; and Strocchia, "Burials in Renaissance Florence," pp. 29–32. Giannozzo Manetti, Poggio Bracciolini, and an anonymous orator wrote eulogies for Leonardo Bruni after his death in 1444. Fubini, in a brief introduction to Poggio's oration, *Opera*, 2:657, argues that it was composed shortly after Bruni's death in March 1444. He bases his argument on an undated letter of Poggio to Giovanni Cirignani da Lucca that mentions the oration and is normally included among the letters from 1444. I would propose a date after 1453 for the published redaction of the speech, on the basis of a passage in the oration that indicates that Poggio is continuing the *History of Florence* begun by Bruni and Marsuppini (p. cxxiv; Poggio Bracciolini, *Opera*, 2:670). Poggio began work on the *History* in 1453 when, he became chancellor of Florence; see Wilcox, *Florentine Humanist Historiography*, p. 207. Matteo Palmieri commemorated Carlo Marsuppini in 1453, and Alamanno Rinuccini celebrated Palmieri in 1475. In general, see Martines, *The Social World*, pp. 239–45.

102. Manetti on Leonardo Bruni, pp. xcvii–ic.

103. Ibid., pp. xcv–xcvi. Manetti has adapted the story from Bruni, *Commentarius*, pp. 445–46.

104. Alamanno Rinuccini on Matteo Palmieri, p. 83. Cristoforo Landino on

Donato Acciaiuoli, fols. 12v–13v, esp. 13v: "Erat vera religio, semper paci, semper concordiae favebat."

105. See Cristoforo Landino on Donato Acciaiuoli, fol. 14r–v, for the ecphrasis of Giuliano's murder and, fols. 17v–18, for Florence's tribute to Acciaiuoli. See further Garin, "Acciaiuoli," pp. 272–79; and Ganz, "Acciaiuoli and the Medici," pp. 66–69.

106. Alamanno Rinuccini on Matteo Palmieri, p. 83.

107. Poggio Bracciolini on Leonardo Bruni, p. cxxi: "Quia autem duo genera sunt hominum qui procul a laude militari vitam honestam secuntur, alterum eorum qui animum suum applicant ad rem publicam gubernandam inque ea administranda labores pro communi utilitate suscipiunt, alterum eorum qui otio dediti litterarum quiescunt procul a turbine populari, utrumque Leonardus noster est summa cum laude complexus." Matteo Palmieri on Carlo Marsuppini, fol. 69r–v: "Erat enim naturali ingenio et industria uberrime praeditus et bonarum omnium artium studiis disciplinisque ornatus quibus naturae et doctrinae laudibus peregregie floruit cum universali civitatis fructu ac rei publicae dignitate. Omnem enim doctrinam divinarum et humanarum artium uno quodam societatis vinculo continebat. Erat summa clementia et humanitate probatissimus, virtute et moribus gravis, studiis accuratissimus, ingenio acri et copiosa vehementique ubertate peracutus, doctrina praestans omnibus et in omni liberalium artium scientia iudicio et praeceptione plene cumulateque perfectus adeo ut nullus ei deesset orationis ornatus neque rerum scientia divinitus praestita."

108. See the letters of Poggio and Vergerio in praise of Salutati, *Epistolario*, ed. Novati, 4:471–73, 479; Giannozzo Manetti on Leonardo Bruni, pp. xcvii, cxiv; Poggio Bracciolini on Leonardo Bruni, pp. cxviii, cxix (referring to Manuel Chrysoloras), cxxiv (referring to Carlo Marsuppini); Matteo Palmieri on Carlo Marsuppini, fol. 69v; and Seigel, *Rhetoric and Philosophy*.

109. Cristoforo Landino on Donato Acciaiuoli, fols. 15v–17. Alamanno Rinuccini on Matteo Palmieri, pp. 80–81: "Cum enim duplex felicitatis genus a philosophis propositum duplicem vivendi rationem nobis ostendat, et earum una in communibus vitae civilis actionibus versetur, altera procul ab omni actione remota, altissimarum rerum adipiscendae cognitioni dumtaxat intenta sit, prudentissimus vir, medium quendam inter utramque viam modum secutus, magnam statim ab initio futurae virtutis concitavit exspectationem quam subsecuta mox vita longe superavit." See further Garin, "Acciaiuoli," pp. 234–69; Giustiniani, *Rinuccini*, p. 228; and Kristeller, "The Humanist Movement," pp. 29–30.

110. Poggio Bracciolini on Leonardo Bruni, pp. cxxv–cxxvi: "Inprimis autem virtutem colant et habeant vitae ducem, sine qua et litterae contemnendae sunt et doctrina omnis videtur esse repudianda. Nam quibus pluris est scientia quam virtutis indagatio, ii viri evadunt callidi et perniciosi et tum rei

publicae, tum ceteris inutiles. Longe enim errant illi a quorum mentibus abest virtus, suorum actuum atque operum moderatrix, doctrinamque ad salutem hominum comparatam ad perniciem gentium convertunt. Re enim honesta abutuntur ad scelus et perfidiam et tanquam virginem castam videntur prostituere in nefarios usus. Itaque omnes qui viri magni et ceteris praestantiores esse volunt nomenque suum reddere clarum litterarum studiis et doctrinae exercitia virtutum adiungant, eaque ad rei publicae et ad singulorum utilitatem conferant. Praestat enim indoctum civem esse quam malum, minusque malus civis rudis quam doctus qui rem publicam perturbat et nocet civitati."

111. Matteo Palmieri on Carlo Marsuppini, fol. 69r–v, esp. fol. 69: "Cuius immortalitate maxime dignum ingenium et summum sicut omni genere doctrinarum, ita exemplis ac praeceptis culmen nuper est acerbissima et lugubri morte peremptum. Quod quidem est omnibus maxime condolendum, sed praecipue animo et cogitatione cernentibus quod hic omni genere laudum egregius ac praestantissimus nostrae aetatis vir quod rarissimum est in terris et apud mortales arduum atque difficile simul coniunxerat." Cristoforo Landino on Donato Acciaiuoli, fols. 15v–17, esp. fol. 16: "Neque didicit solum, verum etiam de sese praestitit ut non modo doctrina sed vita quoque et moribus quod eius scientiae esse proprium philosophum cognosceretur."

CHAPTER SIX

The quotation in the chapter title is based upon Cicero *Rep.* 1.17.28.

1. See Guarino, *Epistolario*, ed. Sabbadini, 1:102, 114; Sabbadini, *Guarino*, pp. 28–29; and my "Oratory of Vergerio," p. 22n. 2.

2. A. Giuliano on Manuel Chrysoloras, pp. 25–26. On Giuliano's life see Troilo, *Giuliano*.

3. See the pertinent comments by G. Cracco in *DBI*, 5:104.

4. A. Giuliano on Manuel Chrysoloras, p. 26: "auctoritas huius nobilissimi viri clarissimique philosophi."

5. Ibid., pp. 26–27, alluding to Cic. *Sen.* 23.84, *Rep.* 6.13.13. Chrysoloras accompanied John XXIII to the Council and was considered to be a worthy candidate for the papacy. See Cammelli, *Crisolora*, pp. 161–69.

6. A. Giuliano on Manuel Chrysoloras, pp. 27–30, alluding to Val. Max. 4.1.15 ext. 1–2; Cic. *Sen.* 12.39–41, *Off.* 1.7.22, *Fin.* 2.14.45, *Am.* 5.17–19.

7. A. Giuliano on Manuel Chrysoloras, pp. 31–35, alluding to Cic. *Sen.* 14.49, 15.51, 16.56–57, *Am.* 6.21.

8. A. Giuliano on Manuel Chrysoloras, p. 34.

9. Cic. *Sen.* 11.36, 12.39, 18.62. Andrea Giuliano on Manuel Chrysoloras, pp. 27–28. Cammelli, *Crisolora*, pp. 25–26.

10. Andrea Giuliano on Manuel Chrysoloras, pp. 31–32.

11. Ibid., p. 33: "Quam plura Platonis et Plutarchi monumenta, Demosthenis reliquorumque virorum illustrium libri, nostrorum excellentissimorum hominum atque Graecorum gesta apud nos velut antea latuissent, nisi tantum Manuelis beneficium nostris hominibus Graecarum litterarum scientiam studiumque suasisset." See, in general, Kristeller, "Italian Humanism and Byzantium," pp. 145–49.

12. Andrea Giuliano on Manuel Chrysoloras, pp. 27–28: "qui teneris adhuc annis se sic ad philosophiam liberaliumque scientiarum studia contulit ut adolescens inter philosophos et doctrina et vita numeraretur?" Ibid., pp. 29–30: "Unum tamen Guarinum nostrum dicam, qui cum Graecarum litterarum in quibus nunc peritissimus est, Manuelem sibi praeceptorem delegisset, ab eo non modo doctrina et moribus ornatus fuit, sed multis aliis perpetuis ac maximis beneficiis saepenumero adiutus." Ibid., pp. 32–33, esp. p. 32: "Quas paulo post civitates tum Graecis disciplinis, tum optimis artibus summisque virtutibus ita ornavit ac instituit ut et peritos et bonos viros permultos efficeret." On Manuel's teaching methods see Cammelli, *Crisolora*, pp. 81–98.

13. Guarino's letter to Poggio is lost. We have only Poggio's response from Florence in June 1455. See Guarino, *Epistolario*, ed. Sabbadini, 2:636–37, 3:459–61, 470; Poggio Bracciolini, *Opera*, ed. Fubini, 3:178–80; and Fubini, "Il 'teatro del mondo,'" p. 20.

14. Poggio Bracciolini, *Opera*, ed. Fubini, 3:180: "Nam et patria complectanda erat de cuius laudibus infinita paene enarrari possunt et doctrina singularis et eius viri eximia in omni genere virtus, tum mores probatissimi, tum castissima vita. Utilitas praetereaquam Latinis litteris attulit, quae ante suum adventum mutae, mancae, debiles videbantur. Excitata sunt eius opera ingenia ad Graecarum litterarum studia, quae magnum doctrinae lumen nostro saeculo attulerunt. Tum ad eloquentiam commoti sunt permulti in qua pristinum fere dicendi ornatum recuperatum videmus."

15. Baron, *Crisis*, rev. ed., pp. 191–224; idem, *From Petrarch to Leonardo Bruni*, pp. 151–71; Vasoli, "Considerazioni"; and O'Malley, *Praise and Blame*, pp. 77–78.

16. Leonardo Bruni, "Prologus in Basilii Epistolam," ed. Baron. See in general Witt, *Hercules at the Crossroads*, pp. 395–413.

17. Leonardo Bruni, "Prologus in Phaedonem Platonis," ed. Baron, p. 4: "Quod etsi temporum supputatio non patitur, tamen ex hoc intelligi potest— id quod ego nunc ostendere volo—: me scilicet eum philosophum ad te mittere, qui a vera religione, cui tu divino nutu praefectus es, nequaquam

abhorret, sed tantam habet convenientiam, ut fundamenta sententiarum suarum ex nostris libris putetur sumpsisse." For Cicero's use of *convenientia* see, e.g., *Fin.* 3.6.21.

18. I am unaware of evidence that would establish that Bruni's panegyric of Florence was delivered publicly. Nineteen manuscripts listed in the first three volumes of Kristeller's *Iter* contain Bruni's oration on Otto Cavalcanti. It was also published in the fifteenth century with Bruni's translation of Aristotle, *Oeconomica Liber I* ([Cologne: Arnold ter Hoernen, ca. 1475]); GW 2434. Ludovico Carbone used sections of the speech for inspiration in his oration for Guarino.

19. Leonardo Bruni on Otto Cavalcanti, p. 144. Cf. Griffiths, "Leonardo Bruni and the University of Rome."

20. Bruni, *Commentarius*, p. 428; anonymous on Leonardo Bruni, p. 150; and Giannozzo Manetti on Leonardo Bruni, p. xcii.

21. See in general Weisinger, "Renaissance Accounts of the Revival of Learning"; and Ferguson, *The Renaissance in Historical Thought*, pp. 1–28.

22. Bruni, *Commentarius*, pp. 431–32: "Itaque in adventu Chrysolorae anceps equidem factus sum, cum et studium iuris deserere flagitiosum ducerem et tantam occasionem litterarum Graecarum ediscendarum praetermittere scelus quodammodo arbitrarer, saepiusque ipse ad me iuvenili motu inquiebam: 'Tu cum tibi liceat Homerum et Platonem et Demosthenem ceterosque poetas et philosophos et oratores, de quibus tanta ac tam mirabilia circumferuntur, intueri atque una colloqui, ac eorum mirabili disciplina imbui, te ipsum deseres atque destitues? Tu occasionem hanc divinitus tibi oblatam praetermittes? Septingentis iam annis nemo per Italiam Graecas litteras tenuit; et tamen doctrinas omnes ab illis esse confitemur. Quanta igitur vel ad cognitionem utilitas vel ad famam accessio vel ad voluptatem cumulatio tibi ex linguae huius cognitione proveniet? Iuris quidem civilis doctores passim complurimi sunt; nec te deficiet unquam discendi facultas. Hic autem unus solusque litterarum Graecarum doctor, si e conspectu se auferet, a quo postmodum ediscas nemo reperietur.' His tandem rationibus expugnatus, Chrysolorae me tradidi, tanto discendi ardore, ut quae per diem vigilans percepissem, ea noctu quoque dormiens agitarem." Giannozzo Manetti on Leonardo Bruni, pp. xciii–xciv, esp. p. xciii: "At vero ubi aliquandiu ipsum [Chrysoloram] publice legentem audivit, tanto ac tam magno suavissimae linguae suae amore capiebatur ut iuris civilis studia praetermittere atque in eius disciplinam se totum tradere concupisceret." Poggio Bracciolini on Leonardo Bruni, p. cxix: "Ibi quadriennio iuri civili operam dedit. Quo in studio cum plurimum profecisset, . . . supervenit Manuel Chrysoloras ex urbe Constantinopoli Graecorum omnium sapientia et eloquentia tum facile princeps, qui studia Graecarum litterarum quae iam diu in Italia oblita et sepulta erant apud nos primus excitavit. Et cum plures ad eius doctrinam conflue-

rent haberenturque coetus praestantiores, Leonardus illorum gloria commotus, cum in eo studio magnam laudem propositam videret, posthabita iuris civilis cura adhaesit Manueli, brevique effecit ut omnes coauditores tum bonitate ingenii, tum studio diligenti facile superaret." See further Wittschier, *Manetti*, pp. 74–78; and Garin, "Ritratto di Leonardo Bruni Aretino."

23. Poggio Bracciolini on Niccolò Niccoli, p. 272. Ludovico Carbone on Guarino, pp. 92–93.

24. Poggio Bracciolini on Niccolò Niccoli, p. 272: "Quae quantum utilitatis nostris hominibus attulerint, tum ad eloquentiam, tum ad plurimarum rerum scientiam quis ignorat? Videntur prisca illa tempora quibus eloquentia cum sapientia coniuncta vigebat esse hoc saeculo renovata." Poggio Bracciolini on Leonardo Bruni, p. cxix. On the ideal union of wisdom and eloquence see Kristeller, "The Humanist Movement," p. 29; idem, "Philosophy and Rhetoric: The Renaissance," p. 243; Gray, "Renaissance Humanism"; and Seigel, *Rhetoric and Philosophy*.

25. Anonymous on Leonardo Bruni, p. 153: "Hic est enim vir ille qui praecepta excolendi mores quos bene meritos probaverit honestissima civitas in Latinam linguam reduxit. Hic exoletam iam antiquam Florentinae civitatis memoriam ac paene deletam ex cohibentibus undique tenebris in lucem revocavit. Hic eruditionem Graecarum litterarum per septingentos iam annos in Italiam non notam primus relevavit. Latinarum quoque litterarum elegantiam et copiam iam pridem perditam adeo diligenter ornateque conquisivit ut post octingentos annos illam primus resumpserit tantaque eloquentia tractavit ut illis antiquis quos legentes admirari solemus nulla ex parte inferior esse videatur."

26. Giannozzo Manetti on Leonardo Bruni, pp. cii–civ; and Poggio Bracciolini on Leonardo Bruni, p. cxxii. Poggio further contends, p. cxxiii, that Bruni's history of Florence was his finest piece of scholarship. See further Baron, *From Petrarch to Leonardo Bruni*, pp. 123–27; Marsh, *The Quattrocento Dialogue*, pp. 24–37; and Quint, "Humanism and Modernity."

27. Leonardo Bruni on Nanni Strozzi, p. 4. Poggio Bracciolini on Leonardo Bruni, pp. cxxii–cxxiii, who states that Bruni translated Basil of Caesarea, Plutarch, Xenophon, Plato, Aristotle, Polybius, and Procopius. For the importance of Greek learning see also Alberto da Castelfranco on Urbano Bolzanio, [fols. 6v–7]; and Battista Casali on Gabriello Gabrielli, fols. 300v–301.

28. Anonymous on Leonardo Bruni, p. 151: "Ac inde maiora iam ausus, Platonis sex, Aristotelis vero viginti libros qui ad mores et rectam vivendi viam scribuntur, diligenter et ornate Latine dictavit." On Bruni's translations see Bertalot, "Zur Bibliographie"; Soudek, "Bruni's Annotated Latin Version of the *Economics*"; and idem, "Leonardo Bruni and His Public." Battista de' Giudici defended the scholastic translation of Aristotle's *Ethics* and criticized Bruni's version. See Grabmann, "Eine ungedruckte Verteidigungsschrift."

29. See the anonymous oration on Bruni, p. 151; Giannozzo Manetti on Bruni, p. ci; and Poggio Bracciolini on Bruni, p. cxxiii. Scholars have yet to compare in a systematic way the medieval Latin translations and their Renaissance counterparts. See Kristeller, "Italian Humanism and Byzantium," pp. 147–49.

30. Giannozzo Manetti on Leonardo Bruni, p. ci. For further praise of translations see Pietro Barozzi on Antonio Roselli, p. 167; and Ludovico Carbone on Guarino, pp. 99–100. On the tradition of an "eloquent Aristotle," see Seigel, *Rhetoric and Philosophy*, pp. 99–136. Italian panegyrists also celebrated Thomas Aquinas for his eloquence. See O'Malley, "Some Panegyrics of Aquinas," pp. 184–86.

31. Anonymous on Leonardo Bruni, p. 152: "Qui omnes inscribuntur libri LXXIIII quorum aliqui ad morem et rectam bene vivendi rationem spectant, plerique ad memoriam rerum antiquarum quarum exemplo maximo emolumento suis civibus esse possit, reliqui partim bene dicendi copiam, partim vero cum familiare ac domesticum, tum commune atque usitatum scribendi genus prosecuntur adeo ut nulla penitus sit neque sufficientia bene dicendi, neque recte intelligendi prudentia quae in eo non sit plene cumulateque perfecta." Baron, *Humanistic and Political Literature*, pp. 149–50, argues that the eulogist worked from a list of Bruni's writings compiled by a member of Bruni's circle (Manetti?) shortly before his death.

32. Giovanni Quirini on Benedetto Brugnoli, [fol. 4v]: "Quid recenseam quantum in historicis quoque exponendis valuerit? Quorum cognitio non solum iocunda, verum etiam utilissima est. Liberalibus enim ingeniis et his qui publicis in rebus hominumque communitate versaturi sunt, historiarum notitia convenientior est ac moralis philosophiae studium. . . . In horum quidem altero praecepta invenire possumus quid sequi quidve fugere conveniens nobis sit, in altero exempla"; and my "Oratory of Vergerio," p. 6.

33. Poggio Bracciolini on Francesco Zabarella, p. 253: "Cum vero ad virilem aetatem pervenisset, existimans non solum sibi se natum esse, sed procreatum quoque ad utilitatem ceterorum palam coepit docere, non tam questus gratia, quem semper ille contempsit ac pro nihilo habuit quam officii et communis utilitatis quo laborum suorum fructus ad multos perveniret." See further Cic. *Off.* 1.7.22., *Fin.* 2.14.45; and Ludovico Carbone on Guarino, p. 93. Cf. Cristoforo Landino on Donato Acciaiuoli, fol. 15v; and Alamanno Rinuccini on Matteo Palmieri, p. 80.

34. Cabrino Cabrini on Gasparino Barzizza, fol. 247v. I have been unable to find the citations from Cassiodorus and Justinian's *Institutes*.

35. Ludovico Carbone on Guarino, pp. 98–99: "Nec enim solum recta litteratura sed boni etiam mores a Guarino discebantur, ut veterum oratorum consuetudinem revocaret qui non minus erant vivendi praeceptores quam dicendi auctores." Carbone is referring to Homer *Il.* 9.443, a passage cited by

Cic. *De or.* 3.15.57. See also Paolo Bigolini on Battista Casali, fols. 3v–4; Poggio Bracciolini on Niccolò Niccoli, p. 274; Gian Giacomo Crotti on Niccolò Lucaro, [fol. 2r–v]; Cristoforo Landino on Donato Acciaiuoli, fol. 16; and Matteo Palmieri on Carlo Marsuppini, fol. 69. In his eulogy for Bruni, p. cxx, Poggio claimed that he obtained a secretarial post for Bruni at the papal court by praising the elegance of his speaking and his virtue ("laudando Leonardum et orationis elegantiam virtutemque prae ceteris extollendo").

36. Agostino Dati on Bartolo Bandini, fol. xcviiii(v): "Eloquentia tanquam humanae conciliationis princeps magno semper in honore est habita, si tamen cum sapientia fuerit et moderatione coniuncta." Ludovico Carbone on Guarino, p. 100: "Eloquentiam ad hominum salutem a natura concessam in nullius exitum, in nullius perniciem convertebat." See also Lorenzo Grana on Celso Mellini, fol. 141r–v; Guarino on Leonello d'Este, fol. 65; and Tommaso Inghirami on Ludovico Podocataro, pp. 306–7. On Cicero's concept of the ideal orator see Michel, *Rhétorique et philosophie chez Cicéron*; and Gilleland, "Cicero's Ideal Orator."

37. Matteo Palmieri on Carlo Marsuppini, fol. 69: "Erat enim naturali ingenio et industria uberrime praeditus et bonarum omnium artium studiis disciplinisque ornatus; quibus naturae et doctrinae laudibus peregregie floruit cum universali civitatis fructu ac rei publicae dignitate. Omnem enim doctrinam divinarum et humanarum artium uno quodam societatis vinculo continebat." Cf. Cic. *Arch.* 1.2, 7.15, *Fin.* 5.23.65, *Brut.* 12.45. Tacitus, in his *Dial.* 40.3–4, criticized Cicero's position. See North, "*Inutilis sibi, perniciosus patriae,*" pp. 261–67.

38. Poggio Bracciolini on Francesco Zabarella, p. 256: "Audistis enim persaepe illum verba facientem, etiam ex tempore, quae magna est in oratore difficultas. Audistis non orationem, sed quasi fluvium quendam redundantem, tum verborum copia, tum gravitate sententiarum." Cicero used the phrase "flumen gravissimorum optimorumque verborum" in *De or.* 2.45.188 and "flumen orationis aureum" in *Acad.* 4.38.119, with reference to Aristotle. See also Giannantonio Campano on Pius II, [fol. 99]; Gian Giacomo Crotti on Niccolò Lucaro, [fol. 5r–v]; Jean Jouffroy on Nicholas V, fols. 33v–34; and Niccolò Perotti on Severo Perotti, fol. 50.

39. Gian Giacomo Crotti on Niccolò Lucaro, [fol. 4r–v]. Giasone del Maino on Girolamo Torti, [fol. 6v]: "Pronuntiatio eius in initio remissior, sed in clausularum extremo elevatior altius acutiusque desinebat. Longas periodos uno spiritu tanquam torrente contorquebat. Nonnunquam altius provocante materia sic incalescebat ut intonare, fulgurare, et quasdam quasi igneas verborum coruscationes faucibus emittere videretur." For the orations by Campano, Giustiniani, and Manetti see Bernardo, *Campano*, pp. 61–62; Mosto, *I dogi*, p. 208; and Tiraboschi, *Storia*, 6:part 1:40.

40. See my "Oratory of Vergerio," pp. 7–9; Ward, "Renaissance Commen-

tators on Ciceronian Rhetoric," pp. 164, 169–71; Fumaroli, "Rhetoric, Politics, and Society," pp. 257–59; and Trinkaus, "The Question of Truth," pp. 209–12.

41. Giannantonio Campano on Pius II, [fol. 103r–v]: "oratio illa divina non permovisset qua caedes nostrorum, qua hostium barbaries inter orandum spectari et cerni videbatur." Campano repeated elements of a topos from antiquity when he described potential ravages by the Turk. See Paul, "*Urbs Capta.*"

42. Celio Calcagnini on Ercole Strozzi, pp. 282–83: "Quantus erat in omni orationis genere, seu vorsam seu prorsam conderet! Quanta naturae indulgentia omnis generis carmen effingebat, seu mordax iambicum seu grande heroicum seu dulce elegum tentaret!" Cf. Giovanni Garzoni on Andromaco Milani, p. 124; idem on Battista Manzoli, fol. 23; and Giannozzo Manetti on Leonardo Bruni, p. cii. On the tradition of *orator et poeta*, see Macr. *Sat.* 5.1.1; Kristeller, "Humanism and Scholasticism," pp. 97–98; idem, "Philosophy and Rhetoric: The Renaissance," pp. 242–43, 251; Hardison, *The Enduring Monument*; and idem, "The Orator and the Poet."

43. Petrarch acquired the codex of Pliny at Mantua in 1350. It is now conserved in Paris, Bibl. Nationale, MS Lat. 6802 (Maurizio Bettini supplied this reference). Contemporary scholars have begun to differentiate between an oratorical and a poetic or grammatical humanism. See, e.g., Witt, "*Ars dictaminis*"; O'Malley, "Egidio da Viterbo"; and idem, "Grammar and Rhetoric in Erasmus."

44. Witt, *Hercules at the Crossroads*, pp. 414–15. Trapp, "The Poet Laureate," has suggested that the coronation of Petrarch's teacher, Convenevole da Prato, in 1336 may have been funerary. In his coronation oration Petrarch cited Ovid's conviction (*Pont.* 4.2.35–36) that virtue increased with praise. The Latin text of the oration has recently been reedited; see Godi, "La Collatio laureationis." An English translation is in Wilkins, *Studies in Petrarch*, pp. 300–313. Orators also commemorated that their subjects received a laurel crown during their lifetimes. See, e.g., Cleofilo on Antonio Costanzi, [fol. 53v]; and Pietro Marsi on Pomponio Leto, [fol. 3v].

45. Giannozzo Manetti on Leonardo Bruni, pp. cv–cxiv; and Wittschier, *Manetti*, pp. 70–78. Manetti quotes Cic. *De or.* 1.16.70, 3.7.27. For the tomb see Schulz, *Bernardo Rossellino*, pp. 32–51 (a reference given me by Eve Borsook).

46. Poggio Bracciolini on Niccolò Niccoli, p. 270.

47. Ibid., p. 271: "Ad eam [virtutem] capescendam sentiebat maxime esse accommodata studia litterarum, quae sola verum virtutis iter demonstrare et vitia compescere existimantur. Cum autem variae essent discendi facultates quibus homines pro animi affectione applicare ingenium solent, humanitatis studia sibi delegit velut ea quibus boni viri effici maxime consueverunt et minime rerum cupidi. Haec enim sola ad virtutem videntur spectare, quippe

cum in eis honestum ipsum et agitatio quaedam mentis ac melioris vitae cultus quaeratur." Poggio also lists, pp. 273–74, the disciplines that Niccoli mastered: Greek and Latin letters, history, cosmography, Latin literature, sacred letters, the meaning of words, and eloquence.

48. Ibid., pp. 272–76, esp. pp. 272–73: "O vere doctorum omnium parens et studiorum domicilium, quantum tibi Latina eloquentia, quantum docti homines, quantum studiosi litterarum nomini tuo debent! Tu inprimis viam ad humanitatis studia ostendisti; tu iter ad veram eloquentiam demonstrasti; tu Graecas litteras ad Italiam reduxisti; tu consilio, tu libris, tu opera, tu cohortationibus semper omnibus recta sentientibus affuisti; tu diligentissimus rerum perpensor, tu gravis eloquentiae censor, tu peracutus doctorum existimator magno adiumento omnibus exstitisti. Tu denique tum corripiendo, tum laudando effecisti ut ad aliquam dignitatem facultas eloquentiae perveniret." The force of the passage is heightened by Poggio's use of anaphora and apostrophe.

49. Giovanni da Vecchiano on Gian Pietro d'Avenza, esp. p. 152: "Hic noster vates benignitate et magnitudine sua feros homines mitigabat duriorem barbarum ad caritatem flectens, ad humanitatem convertens"; and Bartolo Nerucci? on Mattia Lupi. See further Giannantonio Modesti on Luca a Ripa, fol. 30r–v; Percival, "Grammar and Rhetoric"; Grafton and Jardine, "Humanism and the School of Guarino"; and Fioravanti, "La cultura in Valdelsa."

50. Cleofilo on Antonio Costanzi, [fols. 52–53v].

51. Gian Giacomo Crotti on Niccolò Lucaro, [fol. 4v]; Ludovico Carbone on Guarino, pp. 93–94, 97–98; and Bartolomeo Pagello, "Oratio habita in senatu," fol. 55v.

52. Ludovico Carbone on Guarino, pp. 95–96; Elio Lampridio Cerva on Ioannes Gotius, fols. 126v–27; Gian Giacomo Crotti on Niccolò Lucaro, [fol. 4v]; and esp. Pietro Marsi on Pomponio Leto, [fol. 1r–v]: "Hic Romanam linguam barbara inquinatione pollutam, cum nescio quid Geticum blateraret et Vandalum, penitus expurgavit et longo postliminio revocatam prisca iterum dignitate ac iure Latii benignissime honestavit"; and [fol. 2v]: "Alter quasi aetate nostra clarissimus et vivendi et dicendi magister Isocrates."

53. Isocrates, *To Demonicus* 48–49, *To Nicocles* 38, *Nicocles* 1–2, 61, *Antidosis* 274–82 (regarding ethos); *To Demonicus* 5–8, 45–47, *Nicocles* 47 (regarding virtue); *To Demonicus* 3–4, *Antidosis* 284–85, *Panathenaicus* 87, *To Nicocles* 11–12 (regarding character and education). Isocrates labeled his panegyric of Evagoras (8–11) the first such work in prose. See further Kristeller, "Philosophy and Rhetoric: Classical Antiquity," p. 218; Jaeger, *Paideia*, 3:46–155; and Rosa, *La fede nella "paideia,"* pp. 19–83.

54. See Pier Paolo Vergerio on Francesco il Vecchio da Carrara, col. 197D–E, and my "Oratory of Vergerio," p. 17; Guarino on Leonello d'Este, fol. 65r–

v; Battista Casali on Francesco Remolino, fol. 18r–v; Mercati, "Pescennio Francesco Negro," pp. 54–57; and Lee, "The *Studium Urbis.*"

55. Gian Giacomo Crotti on Niccolò Lucaro, [fol. 4v]. Crotti adverted to the voyage of the queen of Sheba to visit Solomon for his wisdom (1 Kings 10, 2 Chronicles 9), Plato's journey to study with Archytas of Tarentum (see, e.g., Cic. *Rep.* 1.10.16), and Cicero's journey to Rhodes to see Apollonius Molo (*Brut.* 91.316). The following orators praised educators who traveled in order to learn: Poggio Bracciolini on Leonardo Bruni, p. cxix; Ludovico Carbone on Guarino, p. 92; Pietro Marsi on Pomponio Leto, [fol. 3r–v]; and Pietro del Monte on Paolo da Lion, fol. 38v.

56. Pietro Marsi on Pomponio Leto, [fol. 3]; and Tiraboschi, *Storia della letteratura italiana*, 6:part 2:13–14.

57. Poggio Bracciolini on Niccolò Niccoli, p. 276: "Templum quoddam virtutis et decoris existimabatur domus illa et tanquam habitaculum honestatis in qua accendebantur omnes ad virtutem et bonarum artium disciplinas." Battista Casali on Domenico Grimani, fol. 73: "Ingenti cogendarum statuarum, nomismatum, et quoruncumque veterum monumentorum studio flagrabat quod, his spectandis, non minus tacito quodam stimulo animi ad virtutem quam legendis historiis excitentur." See also Perry, "Grimani's Legacy of Ancient Art." Ludovico Carbone filled his study in Ferrara with paintings and statues. See Frati, "Carbone," pp. 57–58.

58. Gian Giacomo Crotti on Niccolò Lucaro, [fol. 5v]: "Domus Lucarica perfectae virtutis officina exstitit, qua virtutum incitamenta, monitus salutares, fructusque liberalium artium emergebant. Sermo eius iugiter circa litteras, innocentiam, probitatem, sapientiam, mores, religionem versabatur. Inter cenandum et prandendum memoriam priscorum cuiuscumque generis sapientium usurpabat, et quod quisque laudis et gloriae vel scribendo vel dicendo nactus esset diserto colloquio ostendebatur. Sublata mensa, paulisper cum aliquo ex contubernalibus doctiore aut fabulabatur aut disserebat." Cicero, *Brut.* 8.32, used the phrase "officina dicendi," which Ludovico Carbone applied to the home of Guarino, p. 95. Paduan humanists habitually repaired to the countryside to discuss classical texts. When a "bestius homo" denounced that practice, Ermolao Barbaro enlisted Pietro del Monte to compose an invective on their behalf. See Sottili, *Studenti tedeschi*, pp. 12–14. See further Montaldo, "De vita Alfonsi oratio," p. 226, who describes that learned discussions at the Neapolitan court were followed by performances of jesters; and the discussion of "godly feasts" sponsored by Renaissance cardinals and bishops in chapter 4 above.

59. Poggio Bracciolini on Niccolò Niccoli, p. 276; and Filippo da Rimini on Francesco Barbaro, fols. 11v–12. See also Tommaso Inghirami on Pietro Menzi, pp. 199–201; and Poggio Bracciolini on Leonardo Bruni, pp. cxvi–cxvii, where he bemoans the passing of Salutati, Roberto Rossi, Niccoli, and

Bruni, all of whom had helped to found a "revived Academy." On the Roman academies of Pomponio Leto see Pietro Marsi on Leto, [fols. 2v, 3v, 4v]; and D'Amico, *Renaissance Humanism in Papal Rome*, pp. 89–112.

60. See, e.g., Giannantonio Campano on Pius II, [fol. 103r–v]; Niccolò Capranica on Bessarion, p. 410; and Kristeller, "Philosophy and Rhetoric: The Renaissance," pp. 247–52.

61. Alberto da Castelfranco on Urbano Bolzanio, [fols. 5v–6]; and Bustico, *Bolzanio e Valeriano*. Cleofilo on Antonio Costanzi, [fols. 53v–54], esp. [fol. 54]: "Quid, inquam, alii sentirent perquirebat Antonius, non indoctus, non rerum ignarus, non ut ab aliis sciret quod ipse nesciret, sed ut ponderatis omnium sententiis quae esset optima iudicaret." On the commentary see Kristeller, "Humanism and Scholasticism," pp. 96–97; idem, "The Scholar and His Public," pp. 6–10; and *Der Kommentar in der Renaissance*, ed. Buck and Herding.

62. Alamanno Rinuccini on Matteo Palmieri, pp. 82–83; Giustiniani, *Rinuccini*, pp. 226–27; and Elio Lampridio Cerva on Ioannes Gotius, fols. 127–28. Cf. also Pomponio Leto on Leonardo Grifi, fol. 88v.

63. Manetti, "Vita Senecae," ed. Moreschini, pp. 869–70: "Ceterum nos hanc veterem et antiquam ac sane futilem controversiam multiplicibus causis et variis auctoritatibus hinc inde munitam esse animadvertentes, ambiguam et non solutam relinquere quam ancipitibus et incertis rationibus solvere maluimus, ac demum satis esse duximus frivola haec et inutilia grammaticis perquirenda dimittere, quam tempus, cuiuscumque suppellectilis pretiosissimum, in parvarum et minimarum rerum investigatione frustra conterere. . . . Sed si forte quadam paulo graviori vel publica vel privata cura tenerentur, profecto ab huiusmodi tam parvarum et tam minimarum ac tam denique frivolarum rerum cogitationibus longe abhorrerent." Gasparino Barzizza described the short texts he compiled for rhetorical instruction in a letter published by Mazzuconi, "Dell'epistolario di Gasparino Barzizza," pp. 183–84, 198–99.

64. Poggio Bracciolini on Niccolò Niccoli, pp. 271–72: "Etenim eos qui libros suos occultarent neque cum ceteris participarent, cum essent editi ad communem viventium utilitatem, quodammodo abhorrebat, affirmans huiusmodi homines teneri crimine expilatae hereditatis"; and *Two Renaissance Book Hunters: The Letters of Poggius Bracciolini to Nicolaus de Niccolis*. Jean Jouffroy on Nicholas V, fol. 34r–v; and Niccolò Palmeri on Nicholas V, fol. 10. See also Alberto da Castelfranco on Urbano Bolzanio, [fol. 6r–v]; Giusto Baldini on Giovanni da Lucca, fol. 105v; and Battista Casali on Domenico Grimani, fol. 73v.

65. Poggio Bracciolini on Niccolò Niccoli, pp. 276–77, esp. p. 276: "Sed excellentissima eius virtus atque optimum omnium facinus nequaquam est silentio praetereundum. Cum vivens omnibus profuisset, cum semper publi-

cae consuluisset commoditati, curavit ut etiam post exactam sanctissime vitam, laborum suorum fructus ad posteros emanaret. Id egit vir egregius doctorum virorum amantissimus, quod nullum multis antea saeculis fecisse, neque memoria hominum constat, neque ullae litterae prodiderunt. Rem sane statuit temporum omnium ac saeculorum laudibus celebrandam. Ex libris, quos homo nequaquam opulentus et rerum persaepe inops supra octingentos codices summo labore et diligentia comparaverat, decrevit testamento fieri per amicos publicam bibliothecam ad utilitatem hominum sempiternam." Alberto da Castelfranco on Urbano Bolzanio, [fol. 9]. See also Niccolò Capranica on Bessarion, p. 411; Battista Casali on Domenico Grimani, fol. 73; Francesco Maturanzio on Leonardo Mansueti, fol. 134v; Ludovico Odassi on Federigo da Montefeltro, p. 400; and Davies, "The Senator and the Schoolmaster," pp. 6–21.

66. See, e.g., the following, which deal with the libraries of funeral orators: Sambin, "La biblioteca di Donato"; Manfré, "La biblioteca dell'umanista Giovanni Garzoni"; and Diller, "The Library of Francesco and Ermolao Barbaro."

67. Perreiah, "Paul of Venice"; Sambin, "Su Giacomo della Torre"; Vescovini, "Medicina e filosofia"; Rose, *The Italian Renaissance of Mathematics*, pp. 46–50; and Kristeller, "Philosophy and Medicine."

68. Cristoforo Barzizza on Paolo Veneto, pp. 202–3; Pietro Partenio on Antonio Fracanziani, [fol. 13]; and Gilbert, "The Early Italian Humanists and Disputation."

69. See, e.g., Agostino Dati on Pietro Rossi, fol. xcviiii; Gian Luigi Faccino on Sigismondo d'Este, fol. 172; Giovanni Garzoni on Antonio Penzo, fols. 168v–70; and esp. Tommaso Inghirami on Ludovico Podocataro, p. 300: "quam rem perspiciens Varinus invidi esse putans tantum ingenium primis rudimentis diutius detinere, suasit adolescenti iam facto ut cum bonarum artium affatim hausisset, philosophiae animum adiiceret, quae sola hominem expoliret, extremam manum imponeret, ac virtutis et bene vivendi in se disciplinam contineret." For Socrates see Niccolò Lucaro on Battista Piasi, fol. 133v; and Giovanni Quirini on Benedetto Brugnoli, [fols. 4v–5]. For the tendency to harmonize systems of thought see Kristeller on Cattani in *DBI*, 22:507–9; Garin, "Acciaiuoli," pp. 236–41; and Branca, "Ermolao Barbaro," pp. 225–29. See also Perreiah, "Humanist Critiques."

70. Sebastiano Sapia on Giasone del Maino, [fols. 4v–5], esp. [fol. 4v]: "Mirum profecto iureconsultum consummatissimum tamen in mansuetioribus Musis versatum, quo plane refutanda est eorum opinio qui non bene cum legibus humaniores litteras convenire contendunt, asserentes Musas adeo ad delectationem pellicere, ut postmodum legibus vacare difficillimum sit." Paolo Bigolini on Battista Casali, fol. 3: "Videbat enim iuris civilis cognitionem ei vel maxime necessariam esse qui mox tantus in dicendo futurus

esset, ut ea ipsi nota essent quae si quis nesciat ad earum rerum scientiam quas Latini scriptores litteris persecuti sunt non facile penetrare potest." Cf. also Andrea Biglia? on Vestio? Fiori, fol. 129; and Francesco Zabarella on Giovanni Ludovico Lambertazzi, fol. 10r–v.

71. Pietro Barozzi on Antonio Roselli, pp. 172–73; and Maffei, *Gli inizi dell'umanesimo giuridico*.

72. Giasone del Maino on Girolamo Torti, [fols. 6–8v]; and Sebastiano Sapia on Giasone del Maino, [fol. 5r–v]. See further the anonymous oration on Bernardo Eroli, [fol. 3v]. Orators used Cicero's statement about the abundance of disciples produced by Isocrates (*De or.* 2.22.94) to characterize the number of lawyers issuing from Renaissance universities. See, e.g., Pietro Donato on Francesco Zabarella, p. 146a; Giasone del Maino on Girolamo Torti, [fol. 7v]; and Antonio Solerio on Pietro Canonici, [fols. 4v–5].

73. Sebastiano Sapia on Giasone del Maino, [fols. 3v–4]: "Inspicite, quaeso, inspicite omnes stili elegantiam, nitorem, argutias, fecunditatem. Quis eo clarius inextricabiles nodos explicavit? Quis elimatius confusas doctorum sententias et inter se discordes ad veram semitam reduxit? Quis copiosius quidpiam exornavit? Quis absolutius obscura enodavit? Quis denique elegantius atque ordinatius omnia concinnavit?" Giasone del Maino on Girolamo Torti, [fols. 4v, 7v], esp. [fol. 4v]: "Iuri itaque Caesareo ascriptus legales libros insatiabili discendi cupiditate revolvens, in ipsis studiorum exordiis non contentus litterali sensu quem adolescentuli iuniores observant, interiorem et abditum nucleum eruebat, legum causas acutius inquirebat et fundamentalem iuris rationem in ipsis usque radicibus accurate perscrutabatur." See also Pietro Donato on Francesco Zabarella, p. 146a.

74. Agostino Dati on Mariano Sozzini, fol. xcviii: "Exstant multa et praeclara huius viri monumenta, scripta compluria, ingentia volumina, libri rerum maximarum cognitione referti. Earum praesertim quae ad rectam vivendi viam, ad humanorum actuum directionem spectant, ad pellendam iniuriam, ad colendam iustitiam, ad virtutes exercendas, ad vitia exsecranda." The most recent study of Sozzini (Nardi, *Sozzini*, pp. 100–13) argues that he followed traditional logical schemes and methods and was little affected by humanism.

75. Antonio Solerio on Pietro Canonici, [fol. 5v]: "Pacis et concordiae tam verus erat amator quod quae proficiscebantur a legibus et a iuris civilis rigore semper ad facilitatem aequitatemque referens, non constituere litium actiones malebat quam controversias tollere." Canonici's body was carried in a solemn funeral procession through Bologna seated on a chair in the act of lecturing. See Fantuzzi, *Notizie*, 3:81–82.

76. Pietro Barozzi on Antonio Roselli, pp. 175–78. For honest lawyers in the tradition of Plutarch's Aristides see, e.g., anonymous on a Bernardino, fol. 226r–v; Pietro Barozzi on Antonio Roselli, pp. 164–65, 179–80; Andrea

Biglia on a Giacomo, fol. 166; idem on a Niccolò, fol. 172r–v; Poggio Bracciolini on Francesco Zabarella, p. 258; and Giovanni Garzoni on Vincenzo Paleotti, fols. 107v–08.

77. Antonio Solerio on Pietro Canonici, [fol. 4]: "Nam is animadvertens hominem aliorum hominum utilitate natum esse legibus operam dedit, quibus non solum sibi, sed et patriae et parentibus et amicis plurimum conferre posset." The reference is again to Cic. *Off.* 1.7.22, *Fin.* 2.14.45. Poggio Bracciolini on Francesco Zabarella, pp. 256–57, referring to Cic. *Mur.* 9.19, *Leg.* 1.6.18, *Clu.* 53.146. Poggio had rediscovered the text of the *Pro Murena* in 1415.

78. McClure, "Healing Eloquence." Cf. also Siraisi, *Arts and Sciences at Padua*, pp. 55–58, who argues that the development of the medical school at Padua in the first half of the fourteenth century helped the cause of rhetoric and classical studies in general.

79. Gasparino Barzizza on Iacopo da Forlì, pp. 24–25; Francesco Barbaro on Giovanni Corradini, fol. 64r–v; and Cristoforo Sassi on Luca Alberto Podiani, [fol. 4].

80. See, e.g., Gasparino Barzizza on Iacopo da Forlì, pp. 24–25; Agostino Dati on Bartolo Bandini, fol. c; and Francesco Pucci on Silvestro Galeota, fol. 8.

81. Piero Valeriano on Girolamo della Torre, [fol. 5v]; and Pietro Partenio on Girolamo della Torre, [fol. 10]. Gasparino Barzizza on Iacopo da Forlì, pp. 23, 25–26; and Ludovico Carbone on Giovanni Ercole, fol. 169v. See also Francesco Barbaro on Giovanni Corradini, fol. 64r–v; and Giovanni Garzoni on Girolamo Ranuzzi, p. 121.

82. Agostino Dati on Bartolo Bandini, fol. c. See further Gasparino Barzizza on Iacopo da Forlì, p. 24; Ludovico Carbone on Giovanni Ercole, fol. 169v; Pietro Partenio on Girolamo della Torre, [fol. 10]; Francesco Pucci on Silvestro Galeota, fol. 8; and Piero Valeriano on Girolamo della Torre, [fol. 6].

83. Agostino Dati on Bartolo Bandini, fol. c; Elio Lampridio Cerva on Andrea da Modena, fols. 131–33v; Giovanni Tortelli? on Ludovico Trevisan, fol. 179v; and McClure, "Healing Eloquence."

84. Francesco Barbaro on Giovanni Corradini, fols. 64–65; and Ludovico Carbone on Giovanni Ercole, fols. 169v–70. Gabriele Bucci compared Matteo Punzoni to the good Samaritan (Luke 10:30–37) for providing necessary medical care for the destitute (see *Il Memoriale Quadripartitum*, p. 189).

85. Agostino Dati on Niccolò Ricoveri, fol. xcvii(r–v); and Pietro Partenio on Antonio Fracanziani, [fol. 13v]. See also Elio Lampridio Cerva on Andrea da Modena, fol. 130v. The program of the facade of the Ospedale del Ceppo in Pistoia is discussed in chapter 5 above.

86. Niccolò Capranica on Bessarion, p. 407: "Plus tamen apud eum valuit

fidei veritas quam suorum et patriae amor. Finita enim disputatione, eloquentia, sapientia, atque auctoritate sua imperatoris et reliquorum animos dimissis erroribus ad Latinorum opinionem et verum ritum profitendum permovet atque inducit"; Michael Apostolis on Bessarion, cols. cxxxiii–cxxxvi; and Gill, "The Sincerity of Bessarion." Giacomo da Alessandria on Fantino Valaresso, pp. ix–x.

87. Raffaele Brandolini on Mariano da Genazzano, pp. 235–36; and Gutiérrez, "Testi e note." For further praise of Augustinian reform preaching see Giannantonio Campano on Alessandro Oliva, [fol. 117]; and Lorenzo Grana on Giles of Viterbo, pp. 301–3. For Dominican preaching and the theological contribution made by the order see Giacomo Boldù on Tommaso Donato, [fol. 5v]; Francesco Maturanzio on Leonardo Mansueti, fols. 131–32, 134r–v; Pietro Ranzano on Francesco da Toledo, [fol. 2r–v]; Timoteo da Modena on Ludovico da Ferrara, [fols. 2v–3]; and Gargan, *Lo studio teologico e la biblioteca dei Domenicani*. For the Franciscan contribution and the order's relationship to humanism see Camillo Porcari on Marco Vigerio, fols. 71v–74v; Marco Vigerio on Sixtus IV, fol. 399v; Lee, *Sixtus IV*; and Porzi, *Umanesimo e francescanesimo*. On Sixtus' role in settling the controversy over the blood of Christ in favor of his Franciscans see Marco Vigerio on Sixtus IV, fols. 400v–401; and Lee, pp. 19–20.

88. G. B. Flavi on Cajetan, [fols. 5–10v], esp. [fol. 7v]: "Exspectabam id dicerent potius, cur illum nefandissimum hominem in secretum colloquium accersitum non statim necari iussisset, et si ministri defuissent ipse suismet manibus confecisset, aut saltem, si id non posset, occulto aliquo veneno administrato e medio sustulisset. Pium esse impium hominem qua velis et possis ratione interficere. Quibus quid tandem respondeam non habeo nisi dignos esse qui ad talia ministeria perpetranda mittantur. Ille didicit ex Paulo apostolo non esse facienda mala ut eveniant bona [Romans 3:8]. Utinam omnes divinum Xysti nostri iudicium secuti fuissent, non ita esset profecto res ista Martini exulcerata. Adversus quem nunquam suae lucubrationis gladium distringere voluit ne (ut ipse dicebat) dum unum hominem insectaretur, imperiti vulgi rerum novarum cupidi studia excitaret." He goes on to berate Catholic polemicists for making Luther more famous by their controversial works. Flavi's work may be a biography cast in the form of an oration. See Kalkoff, "Flavio."

89. The phrase "sacred philology" is Kristeller's, in "Paganism and Christianity," p. 72. See also Garofalo, "Gli umanisti e la Bibbia"; Fois, *Il pensiero cristiano di Valla*, pp. 251–60, 383–440; Trinkaus, *In Our Image and Likeness*, 2:563–614; Camporeale, *Lorenzo Valla*, pp. 277–403; idem, "Da Lorenzo Valla a Tommaso Moro"; idem, "Lorenzo Valla: *Encomion S. Thomae*"; idem, "Umanesimo e teologia"; and Bentley, *Humanists and Holy Writ*. Italian humanists

placed their philological criticism of Scripture under the patronage of Jerome. See my "Vergerio and the Cult of Jerome"; and Rice, *Jerome in the Renaissance*, pp. 84–136.

90. Conradus Vegerius on Adrian VI, [fol. 3v]; and Bentley, "New Testament Scholarship at Louvain." Thaddeus of Lyon on Claude de Seyssel, p. 14: "Ea sunt inprimis excellens viri doctrina ac multiiuga eruditio tam Caesareo quam pontificio in iure, praecipue in sacra pagina cui uni ita semper erat addictus ut prae illa ceteras flacci faceret disciplinas, nec mirum. Ipsa est nempe domina, aliae ancillulae ac pedisequae. Hanc sibi asciverat, hanc a iuventute exquisierat formae illius amator factus. Theologiam dico non qualis moderna quaedam conspicitur languens circa contentiones et pugnas verborum, sed antiqua illa Hieronimiana, Augustiniana, Ambrosiana, mystica recondita"; and O'Malley, "Erasmus and Luther."

91. Giovanni Battista Flavi on Cajetan, [fols. 2v, 4v, 6]. Kristeller, "Thomism and Italian Thought"; Wicks, "Thomism between Renaissance and Reformation: Cajetan"; O'Malley, "Some Panegyrics of Aquinas"; idem, *Praise and Blame*, pp. 127–29, 147–49; and idem, "The Feast of Thomas Aquinas."

92. Lorenzo Grana on Giles of Viterbo, pp. 309–10: "Nam dum perpetuos dies et noctes legem Domini meditatur [Psalms 1:2], secreta quaedam atque abdita Hebraeorum volumina quae ab illius gentis magistris celari audierat omni studio ac diligentia conquisivit, tantumque illius cura indefessa ac liberalitas valuit (nullis etenim laboribus, nullis sumptibus parcens ad tercentos aliquando aureos nummos vel exigui legendi ac describendi voluminis causa erogavit), ut enuntiata innumera de quibus durae illa cervicis natio nobiscum contendere audebat suorummet testimonio Christianae fidei veritatem approbare aeterno Aegidii in rem publicam beneficio convinceretur." See further O'Malley, *Giles of Viterbo*; and the papers in *Egidio da Viterbo, O.S.A. e il suo tempo*.

93. Agostino Dati on Pietro Rossi, fol. xcviiii(r v); and Fioravanti, "Pietro de' Rossi."

94. Bartolomeo Zamberti on Giorgio Valla, pp. 305–7.

95. Cristoforo Marcello on Pietro Barozzi, [fols. 3v–4]. For Calcagnini, see Hybertson, "Celio Calcagnini"; Blumenberg, "Der archimedische Punkt des Celio Calcagnini"; and V. Marchetti, A. De Ferrari, and C. Mutini in *DBI*, 16:492–98.

CHAPTER SEVEN

1. Giustiniani, "*Homo, Humanus* and the Meanings of 'Humanism.'"
2. Trans. Clinton Walker Keyes, Loeb Library (1928; reprinted London: W. Heinemann, 1961), p. 495.
3. Bernardo Navagero, "In funere Andreae Gritii laudatio," fol. 41v: "Is cum ab ipsis philosophorum libris in scholis didicisset praeclarum hoc et divinum animal hominem ad res gerendas esse procreatum et virtutum ipsarum igniculos animis nostris natura ingenitos, non facile apparere nisi assiduo honestarum actionum usu quasi excitati collucerent ad maiora se quaedam et his fortasse potiora natum esse intellexit." Cf. Cic. *Fin.* 5.7.18, *Leg.* 1.12.33, *Tusc.* 3.1.2. Because Gritti died on 28 December 1538, this eulogy is not included in the appendix; a full reference appears in the bibliography. Tiraboschi, *Storia della letteratura italiana*, 7:part 3:406–7, reports that Gritti had Navagero recite the oration for him before he died and that the doge wept during certain passages.
4. Ludovico Carbone on Giovanni Ercole, fol. 170r-v: "Proficiscar autem non solum ad eos viros quos in philosophia cognovi eruditos qui mecum familiarissime ac coniunctissime vixerunt, verum etiam ad Platonem, Aristotelem, Marcum Tullium Ciceronem, disciplinarum sidera fulgentissima qui de bene ac beate vivendi ratione, de immortalitate animorum praeclarissima et disertissima scripta reliquerunt."
5. Stefano Sterponi on Alessandro Pucci, fol. 23v: "Mira in illo lenitas erat cum summa gravitate coniuncta, mira comitas, summa urbanitas, tanta morum facilitas tamque affabilis animus, ut saepe accusaretur a multis quod nimium perhumane foveret omnes rusticos, agrarios, artifices, aratores et vilissimos quosque homines, quodque se nimis facilem adeuntibus se praeberet, nec intelligebant hunc imitari humani generis redemptorem dicentem, 'Sinite parvulos ad me venire; talium est enim regnum caelorum' [Matt. 19:14], et illud, 'Discite a me quia mitis sum et humilis corde' [Matt. 11:29], 'Beati enim pauperes spiritu' [Matt. 5:3], superbiae inflantis. Nihil enim tam sanctum, tam amabile, tam probatum apud Deum et homines quam in omne genus hominum uti mansuetudine atque clementia et in omnes prae se ferre humanitatem unde nostrae excellentiae nomen accepimus."

APPENDIX

A SHORT-TITLE FINDING LIST OF FUNERAL ORATIONS FROM THE ITALIAN RENAISSANCE, CA. 1374–1534

This list contains the results of a systematic search for funeral eulogies undertaken during the writing of this book. It makes no claim to be exhaustive. I have included works cast in the form of an oration but never actually delivered in public, and a few eulogies from places outside Italy proper, e.g., Dubrovnik and Cyprus. The place and date of an oration's delivery are given whenever I have been able to determine that information. Question marks are used to indicate uncertain data. When a question mark precedes a title, it means that authorship cannot be established with certainty. Titles marked by an asterisk (*) signify that I have not seen the oration and have included it on the basis of information in the catalogues. Where appropriate, the entry ends with a short-title reference by which the oration is cited in the notes.

ACCIAIUOLI, DONATO (1428–78)
1.? "Oratio funebris acta in funere . . . Ioannis Vaivodae." Florence, Bibl. Nazionale, MS Magl. IX 123, fols. 83–86; *Iter*, 1:137. Place unknown, 1456. Donato Acciaiuoli? on Ioannes Hunyadi.
2. ". . . oratio habita quando Cosmus Medices . . . factus fuit PATER PATRIAE." In Angelo Fabroni, *Magni Cosmi Medicei vita*, 2 vols. (Pisa: A. Landi, 1789), 2:260–62. Florence, 1465. Donato Acciaiuoli on Cosimo de' Medici.

ACERBO, TOMMASO, O.P.
"Oratio funera [sic] in quemcunque equitem auratum . . . ." In Gregorio Britannico, *Sermones funebres et nuptiales* (Milan: L. Pachel, 14 March 1496), [fols. 83v–89v]; *GW* 5549. Brescia, date unknown. Tommaso Acerbo on Giovanni Britannico.

ADRIANI, MARCELLO VIRGILIO (1464–1521)
1. "Oratio . . . habita in funere . . . Iuliani de Medicis . . . ducis Ne-

mursiae." Florence, Bibl. Riccardiana, MS 811, fols. 71–78; *Iter*, 1:204. Florence, 1516. Marcello Adriani on Giuliano de' Medici, duke of Nemours.

2.? "Orazione funerale in morte di . . . [Cosimo] de' Pazzi arcivescovo di Firenze." Modena, Bibl. Estense, MS Gamma I 1, 48 (Campori app. 1614), [fols. 1–3 (fragm.)]. The text is in Latin. Florence, 1513. Marcello Adriani? on Cosimo de' Pazzi.

ALAMANNO, ANDREA (1421–after 1473)
"Oratio in funere Ioannis Medicis Cosmi filii . . . ." Florence, Bibl. Laurenziana, MS Plut. 54.10, fols. 86–89. Florence, 1463. Andrea Alamanno on Giovanni di Cosimo de' Medici.

ALATUS, PETRUS SIMON (DA ASCOLI)
* *Oratio pro morte Montaninae uxoris Hieronymi Petruccii Senensis* (Siena: [Heinrich von Haarlem and Heinrich von Köln], 1498); GW 513. Siena?, date unknown.

ALBERTI, LEON BATTISTA (1404–72)
"Canis." In *Opera*, ed. Girolamo Massaini ([Florence: Bartolomeo de' Libri, ca. 1501]), [fols. 39–45v]; GW 571. Republished in Grayson, "Il *Canis* di Leon Battista Alberti." Leon Battista Alberti on his dog.

ALBERTO DA CASTELFRANCO
Oratio habita in funere Urbani Bellunensis . . . (Venice: Bernardinus de Vitalibus, 1524). Venice, 1524. Alberto da Castelfranco on Urbano Bolzanio.

ALBERTO, GIOVANNI MICHELE, DA CARRARA. *See* CARRARA, GIOVANNI

ALIOTTI, GIROLAMO, O.S.B. (1412–80)
"In funere . . . Bartholomaei Zabarellae archiepiscopi Florentini oratio." In *Epistolae et opuscula*, ed. G. M. Scarmalius, 2 vols. (Arezzo: M. Bellottus, 1769), 2:311–16. Florence, 1445. Girolamo Aliotti on Bartolomeo Zabarella.

ALTAFLORES (ALBIFLORIUS) PAMPHILUS, IOANNES HERCULES
* ". . . oratio funebris pro . . . Ioanne Francisco ex nobilibus . . . Spilimbergi." Udine, Bibl. Capitolare, MS Bini 21.3; *Iter*, 2:574. Place and date unknown.

ANGELO DALLA PERGOLA (ANGELUS PERGULENSIS)
"Oratio in funere . . . Nicolai episcopi ac principis Firmani . . . ." Naples, Bibl. Nazionale, MS IX F 49, fols. 71–76; *Iter*, 1:429. Fermo?, 1473. Angelo dalla Pergola on Niccolò Capranica.

Appendix: List of Funeral Orations 251

ANONYMOUS

* 1. "Oratio habita in morte domini Vincentii de Albertis de Mevania." Paris, Bibl. Nationale, MS Lat. 8642, fols. 29–30v; *Iter*, 3:226. Bevagna?, date unknown.
2. ["Oratio in morte Andreae (Amalphitanensis?)"]. BAV, MS Vat. lat. 2906, fols. 86–87; *Iter*, 2:356. Place and date unknown. Anonymous on Andrea (d'Amalfi?).
* 3. "Mediolani pro funere magistri Angeli de Vicemalis." West Berlin, Staatsbibliothek, MS Lat. fol. 613, fol. 106; *Iter*, 3:483–84. Milan, date unknown.
4. "Sermo pro domino Archimbaldo de Fuxo . . . ." Florence, Bibl. Laurenziana, MS Conventi soppressi 449, fols. 48–50v (fragm.); *Iter*, 1:73. Rome?, date unknown. Anonymous on Archimbaldus de Fuxo.
5. "Sermo in morte domini Raynerii de Forlivio." Florence, Bibl. Riccardiana, MS 784, fols. 154v–55; *Iter*, 1:201–2. Padua, 1358? Anonymous on Raniero Arsendi.
6. "Oratio in funere Lazzari Beccii." Florence, Bibl. Nazionale, MS Conventi soppressi J VII 5, fols. 223–24; *Iter*, 1:163. San Gimignano?, date unknown. Anonymous on Lazzaro Becci.
7. "Oratio funebris [pro Bernardino]." Florence, Bibl. Nazionale, MS Conventi soppressi J VII 5, fols. 225v–26v; *Iter*, 1:163. Place and date unknown. Anonymous on a Bernardino.
8. "Oratio funebris habita in morte . . . Brachii de Fortebrachiis de Montone . . . ." Rome, Bibl. Corsiniana, MS 33 E 27 (Nic. Rossi 229), fols. 140–44v; *Iter*, 2:115. Perugia, 1424. Anonymous on Braccio Fortebracci da Montone.
9. "Laudatio Leonardi historici et oratoris." In Santini, "Leonardo Bruni Aretino," pp. 149–55. Florence, 1444. Anonymous on Leonardo Bruni.
10. "In funere Ioannis Antonii Burgii pii sacerdotis . . . ." Modena, Bibl. Estense, MS Gamma G 1, 12 (Campori 55), fols. 68–71v; *Iter*, 1:390. Ferrara?, date unknown. Anonymous on Giovanni Antonio Borghi.
11. "Sermo in exsequiis [Thomasii Caciae]." Milan, Bibl. Naz. Braidense, MS A E XII 10, fol. 136r–v; *Iter*, 1:357. Milan?, date unknown. Anonymous on Tommaso Caccia.
12. "In funere . . . Baptistae Capitanei . . . oratio." Milan, Bibl. Ambrosiana, MS & 179 sup., fols. 74–79v; *Iter*, 1:317. Novara, 1509. Anonymous on Battista Capitani.
13. ["Oratio in funere Contrarii Ferrariensis"]. BAV, MS Vat. lat. 8761, fols. 119–22; *Iter*, 2:345. Ferrara, 1448? Anonymous on Uguccione? Contrari.

14. "Sermo factus in exsequiis . . . Balthasaris Cossae cardinalis Florentini . . . ." Milan, Bibl. Ambrosiana, MS P 259 sup., fols. 53–56; *Iter,* 1:307. Florence, 1420. Anonymous on Baldassare Cossa.
15. *Oratio in funere Bernardi Heruli Cardinalis Spoletani* ([Rome: Stephan Plannck, 1481–87]); Hain 12021. Rome?, 1479. Anonymous on Bernardo Eroli.
16. "Oratio funebris [pro imperatore Giberto]." Bergamo, Bibl. Civica, MS Delta IV 40 (MA 273), fols. 26–27v; *Iter,* 1:10. Parma?, ca. 1455. Anonymous on Giberto da Correggio.
17. "Oratio in funere Georgii rectoris." Milan, Bibl. Ambrosiana, MS C 145 inf., fols. 276v–79; *Iter,* 1:320. Place and date unknown. Anonymous on a Giorgio.
18. "Sermo ad funera unius lapsi [Antonii Gongiagi]." Palermo, Bibl. Comunale, MS 4 Qq A 8 n. XI, [fols. 155v–58v]; *Iter,* 2:26. Place and date unknown. Anonymous on Antonio Gonzaga.
19. ["Oratio funebris pro Ioanne Germanico"]. BAV, MS Vat. lat. 8750, fols. 113–15; *Iter,* 2:385–86. Perugia, 1488. Anonymous on Ioannes Germanicus.
*20. "Sermo in exsequiis cuiusdam dominae Isabelinae de Capella de Clavaxio." West Berlin, Staatsbibliothek, MS Lat. fol. 613, fol. 127; *Iter,* 3:483–84. Place and date unknown.
21. ["Oratio funebris pro Ludovica Engoliomense"]. BAV, MS Barb. lat. 1880, fols. 1–9v; *Iter,* 2:448. Rome, 1531. Anonymous on Louise of Savoy.
22. "Funebris oratio [pro Malatesta]." BAV, MS Vat. lat. 8750, fols. 88v–90; *Iter,* 2:385–86. Place and date unknown. Anonymous on a Malatesta.
23. "Oratio in officio . . . Helisabeth consortis . . . Malatestae de Pensauro . . . ." In Olivieri degli Abbati, *Orazioni in morte,* pp. xxviii–xxxiv. Pesaro, 1405. Anonymous on Elisabetta Malatesta.
24. "Oratio habita in funere . . . Galeotti Roberti de Malatestis . . . ." BAV, MS Ottob. lat. 2854, fols. 43v–50; *Iter,* 2:437. Rimini, 1432. Anonymous on Galeotto Roberto Malatesta.
25. "Oratio in laudem . . . Pandulphi Malatestae de Pensauro." In Olivieri degli Abbati, *Orazioni in morte,* pp. xxiv–xxvii. Pesaro, 1373? Anonymous on Pandolfo II Malatesta.
26. ["Bernardini Marimenii Eulogium"]. Naples, Bibl. Gov. dei Gerolamini, MS M.C.F. 2, 12 (cart. 163), fols. 42–43 (fragm.); *Iter,* 1:397, 2:546. Sorrento?, date unknown. Anonymous on Bernardino Marimeni.
27. "Sermo mortui [Bartholomaei Patavini]." BAV, MS Palat. lat. 327, fols.

289v–91v; *Iter*, 2:390. Place and date unknown. Anonymous on Bartolomeo Padovano.

*28. "Oratio in funere Nicolai Pandulfini . . . ." Munich, Staatsbibliothek, MS Clm 766, pp. 223ff.; *Iter*, 3:616. Rome?, 1518.

*29. "Oratio habita in morte domini Gasparis Petrutii de Mevania." Paris, Bibl. Nationale, MS Lat. 8642, fols. 27–28v; *Iter*, 3:226. Bevagna?, date unknown.

30. "In funere eiusdem cardinalis Zabarellae." Rome, Bibl. Angelica, MS 1139, fols. 125–26v. Listed among the works of Gasparino Barzizza by Remigio Sabbadini, *Archivio storico lombardo* 13 (1886): 828–29, who identified the subject as Francesco Zabarella. I believe from the oration's content that it is not by Barzizza and that the subject is the brother of an important ecclesiastic named Bartolomeo (Raimondi? Bolognini?). Bologna, date unknown. Anonymous on the brother of Bartolomeo.

*31. "In funere archiepiscopi [Ioannis de Rupescissa]." Casale Monferrato, Seminario Vescovile, MS 1 b 20, fols. 69ff.; *Iter*, 1:40. Basel?, 1437.

32. "Oratio funebris [pro patre Stephano]." Florence, Bibl. Nazionale, MS Conventi soppressi J VII 5, fols. 207–9; *Iter*, 1:163. Ascoli-Piceno?, date unknown. Anonymous on a Stefano, O.F.M.

33. ["Oratio funebris pro Stephano de Burgo"]. Florence, Bibl. Laurenziana, MS Conventi soppressi 449, fols. 46–47v; *Iter*, 1:73. Rome, 1424. Anonymous on Stefano da Borgo, O. Serv.

*34. "Pro Paulo T. funebris oratio." Trent, Bibl. Comunale, MS 4964; *Iter*, 2:191. Place unknown, 1524.

35. "Oratio funebris pro . . . senatore Veneto . . . Paulo Throno . . . procuratore Sancti Marci . . . ." BAV, MS Capponiani 3, fols. 95v–107v. Venice, 1460. Anonymous on Paolo Tron.

36. "Oratio funebris anniversaria in laudem Catherinae de Vicecomitibus ducissae Mediolani." Venice, Bibl. Naz. Marciana, MS 3788 (Marc. lat. X 254), fols. 84–85v; *Iter*, 2:233. Milan, after 24 May 1426. Anonymous on Caterina Visconti.

37. "Oratio habita in laudem . . . Ioannis Galeazi Vicecomitis ducisque Mediolani." BAV, MS Ottob. lat. 1834, fols. 90v–103v; *Iter*, 2:433. Milan?, 1402? Anonymous on Giangaleazzo Visconti.

38. "Funebris oratio optimae matronae defunctae." Milan, Bibl. Ambrosiana, MS C 145 inf., fols. 274v–76; *Iter*, 1:320. Place and date unknown.

39. "In exsequiis oratio." Milan, Bibl. Naz. Braidense, MS A E XII 10, fol. 134r–v; *Iter*, 1:357. Subject is a woman. Place and date unknown.

The same codex (fols. 135v–36v) contains three further orations, perhaps on the same subject.

ANTONIO DA RHO, O.F.M. (ca. 1398–ca. 1450)
"Oratio . . . de laudibus . . . Nicholai Pizinini." Milan, Bibl. Ambrosiana, MS B 124 sup., fols. 143–48v; *Iter*, 1:328. Milan, 1444. Antonio da Rho on Niccolò Piccinino.

APOSTOLIS, MICHAEL (ca. 1422–ca. 1480)
"Epitaphios . . . epi tō theiotatō Bēssariōni . . . ." In *PG*, 161:cols. cxxvii–cxl (with Latin translation). Crete, 1472. Michael Apostolis on Bessarion.

ARRIGONI, GIACOMO, O.P. (ca. 1368–1435)
1. "Sermo in exsequiis Landulphi Maramaldi . . . cardinalis Barensis." Vienna, Nationalbibliothek, MS Lat. 4292, fols. 117v–21v; Kaeppeli, *Scriptores*, 2:300–301. Constance, 1415. Giacomo Arrigoni on Landolfo Maramaldi.
2. "Oratio . . . in exsequiis Ferdinandi Aragonum regis . . . ." Florence, Bibl. Riccardiana, MS 784, fols. 248–50v; *Iter*, 1:201–2. Constance, 1416. Giacomo Arrigoni on Ferdinand I of Aragon.

ASTENSIS, BERGOGNONUS. See BORGOGNONE D'ASTI

BADOER, BONAVENTURA (DA PERAGA), O.E.S.A. (1332–85)
"Sermo habitus in exsequiis . . . Francisci Petrarcae . . . ." In Bucci, *Il Memoriale Quadripartitum*, pp. 162–71. Arquà, 1374. Bonaventura Badoer on Petrarch.

BALDINI, GIUSTO
". . . in Ioannis Lucensis . . . funere oratio." BAV, MS Regin. lat. 1370, fols. 105–8v; *Iter*, 2:598. Bruges, 1472. Giusto Baldini on Giovanni da Lucca.

BAPTISTA DE IUDICIBUS, O.P. See GIUDICI, BATTISTA DE', O.P.

BAPTISTA MANTUANUS, O. CARM. See BATTISTA MANTOVANO, O. CARM.

BARBARO, ERMOLAO (1453–93)
"In funere Nicolai Marcelli Venetiarum principis … . oratio." In *Epistolae, orationes et carmina*, ed. Vittore Branca (Florence: Bibliopolis, 1943), 2:99–103. Venice, 1474. Ermolao Barbaro on Niccolò Marcello.

BARBARO, FRANCESCO (ca. 1390–1454)
"Pro insigni viro Ianino Coradino sua epitaphios logos, id est, funebris oratio." BAV, MS Palat. lat. 1364, fols. 61v–65v. Printed in *Diatriba praeliminaris ad Francisci Barbari epistolas*, ed. Ang. Maria Quirini

(Brescia: I. Rizzardus, 1741), pp. clvi–clxi. Venice, 1416. Francesco Barbaro on Giovanni Corradini.

BAROZZI, PIETRO (ca. 1444–1507)
1. ". . . in morte Ioannis patrui patriarchae Venetiarum . . . oratio." In *Orazioni, elogi e vite*, ed. Molin, 1:103–27. Padua?, 1466. Pietro Barozzi on Giovanni Barozzi.
2. ". . . in funere Antonii Roicelli . . . oratio." In Valier, *De cautione adhibenda in edendis libris*, pp. 163–82. Padua, 1466–71. Pietro Barozzi on Antonio Roselli.

BARTOLOMEO (BISHOP OF VALVA AND SULMONA)
"In morte . . . Petri de Celano . . . ." Naples, Bibl. Nazionale, MS VIII A A 6, fols. 137–42; *Iter*, 1:424. Place and date unknown. Bartolomeo (Vinci?) on Pietro Celani.

BARZIZZA, CRISTOFORO (d. 1445)
"Pro funere Pauli religiosi viri . . . ." In Felice Momigliano, "Paolo Veneto e le correnti del pensiero religioso e filosofico nel suo tempo," *Atti della Accademia di Udine*, ser. 3, 13 (1906–7): 197–204. Padua, 1429. Cristoforo Barzizza on Paolo Veneto.

BARZIZZA, GASPARINO (ca. 1360–1431)
[*See also* ANONYMOUS, no. 30; and BIGLIA, ANDREA]
1. "Oratio in funere Iacobi de Turre Foroliviensis . . . ." In *Opera*, ed. Furietti, 1:23–26. Padua, 1414. Gasparino Barzizza on Iacopo da Forlì.
2. "Funebris oratio in mortem cuiusdam doctoris edita." Rome, Bibl. Angelica, MS 1139, fols. 15–16. Milan?, date unknown. Gasparino Barzizza on Marciano di Tortona Ligure.
3. "Oratio in laudem Ioannis Galeazi . . . habita in eius anniversario obitus die." Ibid., fols. 16–17v. Pavia, date unknown. Gasparino Barzizza on Giangaleazzo Visconti.

BARZIZZA, GUINIFORTE (1406–63)
1. ". . . oratio ad Ioannem Iacobum Palaeologum Montisferrati marchionem in morte eius filiae Medeae reginae Cypri." In *Opera*, ed. Furietti, 2:33–39. Place unknown, 1441. Guiniforte Barzizza on Medea Palaeologa.
2. ". . . in proxima notata legatione ab ipso habenda funebris oratio." Ibid., 2:45–56. Place unknown, 1451. Guiniforte Barzizza on Amadeus VIII of Savoy.

BATTISTA MANTOVANO, O. CARM. (1448–1516)
1. "Oratio funebris . . . [pro Ludovico Caciolupo]." In Benedicto Maria

Zimmerman, O. Carm., "B. Baptistae Mantuani opera soluta oratione scripta hucusque inedita," *Analecta ordinis Carmelitarum Discalceatorum* 7 (1932): 174–75. Bologna?, 1476. Battista Mantovano on Ludovico Caccialupi.

2. *Oratio habita in exsequiis . . . Leonorae ducissae Ferrariae . . .* ([Cremona: Carlo Darleri, after 22 October 1493]); GW 3274. Mantua, 1493. Battista Mantovano on Eleanor of Aragon.

3. *. . . in funere Ferrandi regis oratio* (Brescia: Bernardino Misinta, 8 December 1496); GW 3275. Mantua, 1496. Battista Mantovano on Ferrante II of Naples.

BECICHEMO, MARINO (ca. 1468–1526)

* ". . . funebris laudatio . . . de meritis Ioannis Petri Stellae magni Venetiarum cancelarii habuit." In *Orationes duae . . .* (Venice: Sumptibus Comini Querensis, 1524). Venice, 1523.

BEMBO, BERNARDO (1433–1519)

". . . in funere Bertholdi marchionis Estensis . . . oratio." BAV, MS Vat. lat. 13709, fols. 272–307v; *Iter*, 2:388. Venice, 1464. Bernardo Bembo on Bertoldo d'Este.

BENIGNO SALVIATI, GIORGIO, O.F.M. (d. 1520)

Oratio funebris pro Iunio Georgio habita ([Florence?: s.t., after 17 February 1500?]); GW 3844. Dubrovnik, 1499. Giorgio Benigno Salviati on Iunius Georgius.

BERGOGNONUS ASTENSIS. *See* BORGOGNONE D'ASTI

BIANCHI, APOLLONIO (DA PIACENZA), O.F.M. (15th cent.)

1. ". . . funebris oratio incipit." Venice, Bibl. del Museo Civico Correr, MS Cicogna 797 (1048), fols. 47–48v; *Iter*, 2:283. Borgo Vercelli?, date unknown. Apollonio Bianchi on Caterina Centori.

2. ". . . funebris oratio incipit feliciter." Ibid., fols. 48v–50v. Place and date unknown. This and the following oration may simply be models. Apollonio Bianchi on anonymous (I).

3. ". . . funebris oratio." Ibid., fols. 50v–51v. Place and date unknown. Apollonio Bianchi on anonymous (II).

BIENATO, AURELIO (d. 1496)

Oratio in funere Laurentii de Medicis Neapoli habita ([Milan: Filippo Mantegazza, 1492, after 8 April]); GW 4346. Naples, 1492. Aurelio Bienato on Lorenzo de' Medici.

BIGLIA, ANDREA, O.E.S.A. (ca. 1394–1435)

Critical editions of nos. 1 and 2 are in Schnaubelt, "Andrea Biglia," pp. 368–447. Nos. 8–10 were attributed to Gasparino Barzizza by Sabbadini, "Lettere e orazioni di Barzizza," pp. 828–29.

1. "In exsequiis Ioannis Galeatii Vicecomitis . . . laudatio funerea." In Lidia Alberti, "Una orazione inedita dell'umanista Andrea Bigli," *Athenaeum* 3 (1915): 178–85. Milan, date unknown. Andrea Biglia on Giangaleazzo Visconti (I).
2. ". . . secunda collaudatio anniversaria Ioannis Galeazi Vicecomitis . . . ." Milan, Bibl. Ambrosiana, MS F 55 sup., fols. 50–57; *Iter*, 1:298. Milan, date unknown. Andrea Biglia on Giangaleazzo Visconti (II).
3. "Oratio edita . . . [in funere Bentivoli]." Venice, Bibl. Naz. Marciana, MS 4351 (Marc. lat. XI 3), fols. 25–30; *Iter*, 2:238. Bologna, 1425. Andrea Biglia on Battista? Bentivoglio.
4. ["Oratio funebris Iacobi"]. BAV, MS Palat. lat. 607, fols. 165v–66v (160v–61v); *Iter*, 2:396. Bologna?, 1423–28. Andrea Biglia on a Giacomo.
5. "Collaudatio funerea Ioannis Gislerii militis Bononiensis . . . ." Ibid., fols. 168v–69 (163v–64). Bologna, 1423–28. Andrea Biglia on Giovanni Ghislieri.
6. ["Oratio funebris in laudem Laurentii Bononiensis"]. Ibid., fols. 169v–70 (164v–65). Bologna?, 1423–28. Andrea Biglia on Lorenzo da Bologna.
7. ["Oratio funebris in laudem Nicolai iurisconsulti"]. Ibid., fols. 171v–72v (166v–67v). Bologna?, 1423–28. Andrea Biglia on a Niccolò.
8. ["Oratio funebris in laudem Iacobi Bononiensis doctoris iuris"]. Rome, Bibl. Angelica, MS 1139, fols. 126v–27v. Bologna?, 1423–28. Andrea Biglia on Giacomo da Bologna.
9. ["Oratio funebris in laudem Stephani"]. Ibid., fols. 127v–28v. Bologna, 1423–28. Andrea Biglia on a Stefano.
10.? ["Oratio funebris in laudem Vestii? Florii"]. Ibid., fols. 128v–29v. Bologna?, 1423–28? Andrea Biglia? on Vestio? Fiori.

BIGOLINI, PAOLO (DA TREVISO)
"De vita et moribus Ioannis Baptistae Casalii oratio . . . ." Milan, Bibl. Ambrosiana, MS G 33 inf., part 1, fols. 1–6; *Iter*, 1:324. Rome, 1525. Paolo Bigolini on Battista Casali.

BOLDÙ, GIACOMO (ca. 1475–1545)
. . . *oratio funebris pro Thoma Donato* . . . (Venice: I. Tacuinus, 1504). Venice, 1504. Giacomo Boldù on Tommaso Donato.

BONAVENTURA DA PERAGA, O.E.S.A. *See* BADOER, BONAVENTURA, O.E.S.A.

BONISOLI, OGNIBENE (DA LONIGO) (ca. 1412–74)
"Oratio funebris pro clarissima domina Elizabetha de Nogarolis . . . ." In *Isotae Nogarolae Veronensis opera quae supersunt omnia accedunt Angelae et Zeneverae Nogarolae epistolae et carmina*, ed. Eugenius Abel (Vienna: apud Gerold et socios, 1886), 2:407–17. Vicenza, date unknown. Ognibene Bonisoli on Elisabetta Nogarola.

BORGOGNONE D'ASTI
"Oratio funebris pro Petro de Miliis." Florence, Bibl. Nazionale, MS Rossi-Cassigoli 372, part 1, fols. 18–20v; *Iter*, 1:165–66 (without the author's name). Ascoli-Piceno?, 1426. Borgognone d'Asti on Pietro Emigli.

BRACCIOLINI, POGGIO (1380–1459)
1. "Oratio funebris in obitu Leonardi Arretini." In *Leonardi Bruni Arretini epistolarum libri VIII*, ed. Mehus, pp. cxv–cxxvi. Rome, 1444 (final redaction apparently completed at Florence and not before 1453). Poggio Bracciolini on Leonardo Bruni.
2. "In funere domini Francisci cardinalis Florentini habita." In *Opera*, ed. Fubini, 1:252–61. Constance, 1417. Poggio Bracciolini on Francesco Zabarella.
3. "Oratio in funere cardinalis Sanctae Crucis." Ibid., 1:261–69. Siena, 1443. Poggio Bracciolini on Niccolò Albergati.
4. "Oratio in funere Nicolai Nicoli civis Florentini." Ibid., 1:270–77. Written at Bologna and sent to Florence, 1437. Poggio Bracciolini on Niccolò Niccoli.
5. "Oratio in funere Laurentii de Medicis." Ibid., 1:278–86. Florence, 1440. Poggio Bracciolini on Lorenzo de' Medici (the elder).
6. "Oratio in funere . . . cardinalis . . . Iuliani de Caesarinis Romani." Ibid., 2:719–35. Rome, 1445. Poggio Bracciolini on Giuliano Cesarini.

BRANDOLINI, AURELIO (1440–97)
". . . pro Laurentio Iustino . . . oratio in funere habita." Rome, Bibl. Angelica, MS 1503, fols. 216–27. Rome?, after 1482. Aurelio Brandolini on Lorenzo Giustini.

BRANDOLINI, RAFFAELE (ca. 1465–1515)
1. ". . . oratio parentalis de obitu magistri Mariani Zenazanensis . . . ." In Greco, "La *docta pietas*," pp. 230–38. Rome, 1499. Raffaele Brandolini on Mariano da Genazzano.
2. "Oratio parentalis de obitu Guillermi Perrerii . . . ." In Ch. Samaran, "Un français à Rome au XVe siècle: Guillaume Pérès condomois auditeur de rote (1420?-1500)," *Annuaire-Bulletin de la Société de l'histoire*

de France 68 (1931): 199–218. Rome, 1500. Raffaele Brandolini on Guillaume Pérès.
3. *Oratio de obitu Dominici Ruvere* (Rome: E. Silber, 1501). Rome, 1501. Raffaele Brandolini on Domenico della Rovere.
4. ". . . parentalis oratio in obitu Laurentii Cibae . . . ." BAV, MS Barb. lat. 1868, fols. 81–91v; *Iter*, 2:461. Rome, 1504. Raffaele Brandolini on Lorenzo Cibò.

BRITANNICO, GIOVANNI (d. after 26 November 1518)
"Oratio . . . in obitu magni. magistratus Brixiani Nicolai Duodo [*sic*] habita Brixiae." In Britannico, *Sermones funebres et nuptiales*, [fols. 93v–96v]. Brescia, 1491. Giovanni Britannico on Niccolò Duodo.

BRITANNICO, GREGORIO
These orations may simply be models for instruction. *Sermones funebres et nuptiales* contains eight further orations by Gregorio, [fols. 109–19v], that all appear to be generic.
1. "Oratio pro aliquo doctore sive aliquo philosopho defuncto [Antonio Britannico] . . . ." In his *Sermones funebres et nuptiales*, [fols. 89v–93v]. Brescia?, date unknown. Gregorio Britannico on Antonio Britannico (I).
2. "Oratio funebris communis pro quocunque comite . . . ." Ibid., [fols. 103–4v]. Brescia, date unknown. Gregorio Britannico on Andrea Britannico.
3. "Oratio funebris communis . . . ." Ibid., [fols. 104v–5]. Brescia?, date unknown. Gregorio Britannico on a Britannico.
4. "Oratio funebris pro muliere communis . . . ." Ibid., [fols. 105–7v]. Brescia?, date unknown. Gregorio Britannico on Antonia Cinili.
5. "Sermo funebris pro biothanato communis . . . ." Ibid., [fols. 107v–9]. Gregorio Britannico on Giovanni Britannico.
6. "Oratio funebris communis . . . ." Ibid., [fols. 119v–20v]. Brescia, date unknown. Gregorio Britannico on Antonio Britannico (II).

BRUNI, LEONARDO (ca. 1370–1444)
1. "Laudatio in funere Othonis." In Santini, "Leonardo Bruni Aretino," pp. 142–45. Viterbo, 1405. Leonardo Bruni on Otto Cavalcanti.
2. "Oratio in funere Ioannis Strozzae." In E. Baluze, . . . *Miscellanea novo ordine digesta et aucta*, ed. G. D. Mansi (Lucca: V. Junctinius, 1761–64), 4:2–7. Florence, 1428. Leonardo Bruni on Nanni Strozzi.

BRUNO, LUDOVICO (1434–1508)
De obitu Helisabeth Hispaniarum . . . reginae oratio (Rome: J. Besicken?, 1505). Rome, 1505. Ludovico Bruno on Isabella of Castile.

BUCCI, GABRIELE, O.E.S.A. (ca. 1430–ca. 1497)
Il Memoriale Quadripartitum, ed. Curlo, 4:174–310, contains seventy-four funeral orations by Bucci. Page numbers for this edition are given in the notes when one of his orations is cited.

CABRINI, CABRINO
1. "Sermonculum [in morte Gasparini de Barzizis]." Stresa, Centro di Studi Rosminiani, MS 22, fols. 246v–48; Iter, 2:171–72. Milan?, 1430. Cabrino Cabrini on Gasparino Barzizza.
2. "Sermonculum [post exsequias filiae Ioannis Moresini]." Ibid., fol. 248. Milan, 1430. Cabrino Cabrini on a Moresini.

CAIETANUS, DANIEL. See GAETANI, DANIELE

CALCAGNINI, CELIO (1479–1541)
1. ". . . in funere Beatricis Pannoniarum reginae oratio." In Orationes funebres (Hanau, 1613), pp. 256–59. Ferrara, 1508. Celio Calcagnini on Beatrice of Aragon.
2. ". . . in funere Hippolyti cardinalis Estensis oratio." Ibid., pp. 259–65. Ferrara, 1520. Celio Calcagnini on Ippolito I d'Este.
3. ". . . in funere Alphonsi primi . . . oratio." Ibid., pp. 266–73. Ferrara, 1534. Celio Calcagnini on Alfonso I d'Este.
4. ". . . in funere Antonii Constabilis oratio." Ibid., pp. 273–79. Ferrara, 1527. Celio Calcagnini on Antonio Costabili.
5. ". . . in funere Herculis Strozzae oratio." Ibid., pp. 280–85. Ferrara, 1508. Celio Calcagnini on Ercole Strozzi.

CALDIERA, GIOVANNI (ca. 1400–by 1474)
* "Oratio in funere Orsati Justiniani Sancti Marci Procuratoris ad senatum populumque habita . . . ." London, British Library, MS Add. 15406, fols. 91–97v; King, Venetian Humanism, pp. 345, 457. Venice, date unknown.

CAMICI, AGOSTINO, O.E.S.A.
["Oratio in funere Philippi Mariae Vicecomitis"]. BAV, MS Capponiani 3, fols. 125–28v. The Vatican printed catalogue gives Francesco Sforza as the oration's subject. Cremona, 1447? Agostino Camici on Filippo Maria Visconti.

CAMPANO, GIANNANTONIO (1429–77)
1. "In exsequiis divi Pii II . . . oratio." In Opera omnia (Rome, 1495; reprinted Farnsborough, England: Gregg International, 1969), [fols. 99–104]. Siena, 1465. Giannantonio Campano on Pius II.
2. "In funere magnifici Nelli de Balionibus oratio." Ibid., [fols. 104–14]. Perugia, 1457. Giannantonio Campano on Nello Baglioni.

3. "In funere parentis domini archiepiscopi Beneventani . . . oratio." Ibid., [fols. 114v–16]. Perugia, 1456. Giannantonio Campano on Giovanni della Ratta.
4. "In funere cardinalis Sanctae Susannae Saxoferratensis oratio." Ibid., [fols. 116–19]. Rome, 1463. Giannantonio Campano on Alessandro Oliva.
5. "In funere Urbinatis ducissae oratio." Ibid., [fols. 119–22v]. Urbino, 1472. Giannantonio Campano on Battista Sforza.

CAPOGALLO, GIOVANNI
["Sermo in morte Ioannis Galeazi"]. Florence, Bibl. Riccardiana, MS 784, fols. 85v–89v; *Iter*, 1:201–2. Milan?, 1402. Giovanni Capogallo on Giangaleazzo Visconti.

CAPPELLO, CARLO (1492–1546)
". . . in funere Georgii Cornelii . . . oratio." In *Orazioni, elogi e vite*, ed. Molin, 1:198–212. Venice, 1527. Carlo Cappello on Giorgio Corner.

CAPRANICA, NICCOLÒ (d. 1473)
". . . oratio in funere Bessarionis." In Mohler, *Kardinal Bessarion*, 3:404–14. Rome, 1472. Niccolò Capranica on Bessarion.

CARBONE, LUDOVICO (1436–82)
1. "Oratio habita in funere . . . Guarini Veronensis." In *Reden und Briefe*, ed. Müllner, pp. 89–107. Ferrara, 1460. Ludovico Carbone on Guarino.
2. ". . . oratio Bononiae habita in funere . . . Iacobi Linensis." BAV, MS Ottob. lat. 1153, fols. 13v–15v; *Iter*, 2:427. Bologna, date unknown. Ludovico Carbone on Giacomo Dal Lino.
3. "Oratio in funere Ioannis Herculis Veronensis." Ibid., fols. 168v–73. Ferrara, date unknown. Ludovico Carbone on Giovanni Ercole.
4. ". . . oratio in funere Ioannis Amanserii Galli." Ibid., fols. 176–77. Ferrara, date unknown. Ludovico Carbone on Jean Amanseur.
5. "Oratio habita in funere clarissimi equitis Bartholomaei Pendaliae." Venice, Bibl. Naz. Marciana, MS 4451 (Marc. lat. XII 137), fols. 78v–89v; *Iter*, 2:258. Place and date unknown. Ludovico Carbone on Bartolomeo Pendaglia.
6. ["Oratio in funere Ludovici de Sancto Bonifacio"]. Ibid., fols. 102v–7 (repeated on fols. 152–55v). Place and date unknown. Ludovico Carbone on Ludovico di San Bonifacio.
7. ". . . oratio in funere . . . ducis Borsii Ferrariensis habita . . . ." Venice, Bibl. Naz. Marciana, MS 4679 (Marc. lat. XIV 229), fols. 91–97v; *Iter*, 2:248. Ferrara, 1471. Ludovico Carbone on Borso d'Este.

8. ". . . oratio acta in funere . . . referendarii Lodovici Casellae . . . ." Modena, Bibl. Estense, MS Alpha O 6, 15 (Est. lat. 174), fols. 196–203; *Iter*, 1:378–79. Ferrara, 1469. Ludovico Carbone on Ludovico Casella.

* 9. ". . . oratio habita in funere . . . Bertholdi Estensis." Coburg, Landesbibliothek, MS S IV 2, 41, fols. 252–62v; *Iter*, 3:510–11. Este, 1463–64. Ludovico Carbone on Bertoldo d'Este.

CARDULO, FRANCESCO (DA NARNI)
Oratio in exsequiis Ardicini II. de Porta cardinalis Aleriensis habita ([Rome: Andreas Freitag, after 4 March 1493]); GW 6134. Rome, 1493. Francesco Cardulo on Ardicino II della Porta.

CARRARA, GIOVANNI MICHELE ALBERTO (1438–90)
"Oratio extemporalis habita in funere Bartholomaei Coleonis . . . ," ed. Petrus de Comitibus. In Pietro Spino, *Istoria della vita e fatti dell'eccellentissimo capitano di guerra Bartolomeo Colleoni* (Bergamo: G. Santini, 1732), pp. 259–72. Bergamo, 1476. Giovanni Michele Alberto Carrara on Bartolomeo Colleoni.

CASA, ANGELO, O.F.M.
1. ["Oratio in funere Gregorii Carmagnolae theologi"]. Treviso, Bibl. Comunale, MS 38, fols. 1–3v; *Iter*, 2:196. Place and date unknown. Angelo Casa on Gregorio Carmagnola.
2. ["Oratio in funere Ioannis Antonii Patelae"]. Ibid., fols. 4–8v. Padua, date unknown. Angelo Casa on Giannantonio Patela.
3. ["Oratio in funere Iacobini Borgii theologi"]. Ibid., fols. 9–14v. Padua, date unknown. Angelo Casa on Giacobino Borgia.

CASALI, ANTONIO
* 1. "Funeralis Fratris Antonii in funere . . . Iacobi Alvarottis." West Berlin, Staatsbibliothek, MS Lat. fol. 486, fol. 100r–v; *Iter*, 3:482. Padua?, date unknown.
* 2. ". . . [oratio] habita Paduae in funere magistri Bartholomaei d. An." Ibid., fol. 101r–v. Padua, date unknown.

CASALI, BATTISTA (1473–1525)
1. "Oratio funebris pro Dominico [Capranica] . . . ." Milan, Bibl. Ambrosiana, MS G 33 inf., part 1, fols. 263v–64v; *Iter*, 1:324. Rome?, date unknown. Battista Casali on Domenico Capranica (the younger).
2. "Funebris oratio pro Nicolao Tifernate." Ibid., part 1, fols. 273–78v. Rome, 1506? Battista Casali on Niccolò Bufalini.

Appendix: List of Funeral Orations 263

3. "Oratio funebris pro Stephano." Ibid., part 1, fols. 278v–82. Rome, date unknown. Battista Casali on a Stefano.
4. "Oratio funebris pro Laurentio." Ibid., part 1, fols. 282v–86. Place and date unknown. Battista Casali on a Lorenzo.
5. "Oratio funebris pro Francisco Antonio." Ibid., part 1, fols. 287v–88. Place and date unknown. Battista Casali on a Francesco Antonio.
6. "Oratio funebris pro Petro Borgia." Ibid., part 1, fols. 288–90. Rome, date unknown. Battista Casali on Pietro Borgia.
7. "Oratio pro Soderino." Ibid., part 1, fols. 291–95. Rome, 1524. Battista Casali on Francesco Soderini.
8. "Oratio in funere Gabrielis cardinalis Sancti Praxedis." Ibid., part 1, fols. 297v–303. Rome, 1511. Battista Casali on Gabriello Gabrielli.
9. "Oratio in funere cardinalis Sancti Dionysii." Ibid., part 1, fols. 309–15. Rome, 1499. Battista Casali on Jean de Bilhères Lagraulas.
10. "In funere cardinalis Columnae." Ibid., part 2, fols. 29–37. Rome, 1508. Battista Casali on Giovanni Colonna.
11. ". . . in funere Francisci Luxemburgi oratio." Ibid., part 2, fols. 37v–45. Rome, date unknown. Battista Casali on Francis of Luxemburg.
12. "In funere Iuliani Medices." Ibid., part 2, fols. 62v–68v. Rome, 1516. Battista Casali on Giuliano de' Medici, duke of Nemours.
13. "In funere cardinalis Grimani." Ibid., part 2, fols. 69–75. Rome, 1523. Battista Casali on Domenico Grimani.
14. "In funere Roberti cardinalis Nanetensis." BAV, MS Vat. lat. 8106, fols. 11–16; Iter, 2:344. Rome, 1513. Battista Casali on Robert Vitrè.
15. "Pro cardinale Surentino." Ibid., fols. 16v–20v, 49r–v. Rome, 1518. Battista Casali on Francesco Remolino.
16. "Pro cardinale Aloysio Aragonio." Ibid., fols. 40–46. Rome, 1519. Battista Casali on Aloysius of Aragon.

CASCIOTTI, BARTOLOMEO (d. ca. 1478)
"Oratio funebris . . . [pro Nicolao Saturnino]." Milan, Bibl. Naz. Braidense, MS A D XIV 27, fols. 61v–62; Iter, 1:356. The work is a letter cast in the form of a speech. Ferrara, 1441. Bartolomeo Casciotti on Niccolò Saturnino.

CASTANEA (CRISTOFORO DI S. EUFEMIA)
"Sermo funeralis . . . ." Florence, Bibl. Laurenziana, MS Ashb. 270, fols. 169v–70v; Iter, 1:82–83. Place and date unknown. Castanea on a Maria?

CASTELLETO, PIETRO, O.E.S.A.
"Sermo . . . in exsequiis . . . domini Ioannis Galeazi." RIS, 16:cols. 1038C–50D. Milan, 1402. Pietro Castelleto on Giangaleazzo Visconti.

CASTIGLIONI, GIOVACCHINO, O.P. (d. ca. 1472)
Excerpts from twenty-four orations are in Verani, "Notizie del P. M. Giovacchino Castiglioni." The manuscripts at Chieri and Asti that contained the discourses were destroyed during the Second World War.
1. "Oratio lugubris super funus Margaritae uxoris . . . Ioannis Simonetae . . . ." Milan, Bibl. Ambrosiana, MS E 124 sup., fols. 92–93v; *Iter*, 1:298. Milan, date unknown. Giovacchino Castiglioni on Margherita Simonetta.
2. ". . . in funere . . . marchionis Rolandi Palavicini oratio." Parma, Archivio di Stato, MS 90 bis, fols. 1–4v; *Iter*, 2:552. Milan?, 1457. Giovacchino Castiglioni on Rolando Pallavicini.
3. ". . . in funere dominae Poloniae . . . Antonii et Bartholomaei de Canobio matris oratio . . . ." Ibid., fols. 4v–7. Milan, date unknown. Giovacchino Castiglioni on Polonia Ligurni.
4. ". . . in funere . . . Merchionis de Vizano senatoris Romani." Paris, Bibl. Nationale, MS Lat. 7843, fols. 66v–70; *Iter*, 3:221–22. Rome, 1447? Giovacchino Castiglioni on Merchione da Vizzano.
5. ". . . in funere . . . Doroteae Castilioneae oratio." Ibid., fols. 70–72. Pavia, date unknown. Giovacchino Castiglioni on Dorotea Castiglioni.
6. ". . . in funere domini Iacobi praepositi Sancti Felicis oratio." Ibid., fols. 72–74. Venice, date unknown. Giovacchino Castiglioni on a Giacomo.

CASTIGLIONI, GUARNIERO (d. 1460)
"Oratio . . . habita in funeralibus . . . cardinalis Brandae Castilionei." Milan, Bibl. Ambrosiana, MS B 124 sup., fols. 1–5; *Iter*, 1:328. Milan?, 1443. Guarniero Castiglioni on Branda Castiglioni.

CASTRIFRANCANUS, ALBERTUS. See ALBERTO DA CASTELFRANCO

CATTANEI, GIOVANNI LUCIDO (ca. 1462–1505)
1. ". . . oratio in funere illustrissimae Barbarae marchionissae Mantuae . . . ." In *Orationes variae* ([Parma: Angelo Ugoletti, after 1 August 1493?]), [fols. 3–14]; *GW* 6219. Mantua, 1482. Giovanni Cattanei on Barbara Gonzaga.
2. ". . . oratio funebris pro . . . Francisco Gonzaga . . . ." Ibid., [fols. 14v–25v]. Mantua, 1483. Giovanni Cattanei on Francesco Gonzaga.
3. ". . . Frederici Gonzagae . . . epicedion . . . ." Ibid., [fols. 25v–35v]. Mantua, 1484. Giovanni Cattanei on Federigo I Gonzaga.

CATTANI, FRANCESCO (DA DIACCETO) (1466–1522)
". . . oratio in funere Laurentii Medicis Urbini principis." Florence,

Bibl. Nazionale, MS Naz. II IV 34, fols. 362–67; *Iter*, 1:114. Florence, 1519. Francesco Cattani on Lorenzo de' Medici, duke of Urbino.

CERETA, LAURA (1469–99)
"Divae Laurae in Asinarium funus oratio." In Albert Rabil, Jr., *Laura Cereta: Quattrocento Humanist*, Medieval and Renaissance Texts and Studies 3 (Binghamton, N.Y.: Center for Medieval and Early Renaissance Studies, 1981), pp. 118–34. Laura Cereta on an ass.

CERVA, ELIO "LAMPRIDIO" (ca. 1462–1520)
1. ". . . laudatio funebris in obitum Georgii Crucii . . . ." BAV, MS Vat. lat. 2939, fols. 1–4v; *Iter*, 2:357. Dubrovnik, 1513. Elio Lampridio Cerva on Georgius Crucius.
2. "Laudatio . . . in . . . matronam Paulam uxorem Marini Zamani." Ibid., fols. 5–6v. Dubrovnik, date unknown. Elio Lampridio Cerva on Paula Zamagna.
3. "Oratio in funere Bartholomaeus [sic] Restius [sic]." Ibid., fols. 7–12v. Dubrovnik, date unknown. Elio Lampridio Cerva on Bartolomeo Resti.
4. "Oratio in funere Nicolai Morelli Florentini." Ibid., fols. 18–23. Dubrovnik, date unknown. Elio Lampridio Cerva on Niccolò Morelli.
5. "Oratio funebris in regem Mathiam." Ibid., fols. 66v–81. Dubrovnik, 1490. Elio Lampridio Cerva on Mattia Corvino.
6. ". . . in obitum Nicolai Gocei oratio." Ibid., fols. 84–86v. Dubrovnik, 1502. Elio Lampridio Cerva on Nicolaus Gotius.
7. "Oratio in funere Orsati Gotii." Ibid., fols. 87–90. Dubrovnik, 1514. Elio Lampridio Cerva on Orsatus Gotius.
8. "Oratio in funere Pauli Basillii." Ibid., fols. 90–92v. Place and date unknown. Elio Lampridio Cerva on Paolo Basilli.
9. "Oratio in funere Damiani Gocii." Ibid., fols. 92v–95v. Dubrovnik, 1515. Elio Lampridio Cerva on Damianus Gotius.
10. "Oratio in funere Bartholomaei Gocii." Ibid., fols. 102v–7. Dubrovnik, date unknown. Elio Lampridio Cerva on Bartholomaeus Gotius.
11. "Oratio funebris in Marinum Gradaeum." Ibid., fols. 107v–13. Dubrovnik, 1493. Elio Lampridio Cerva on Marinus Gradaeus.
12. "Oratio funebris in Martullum Zamanum . . . ." Ibid., fols. 113v–19. Dubrovnik, date unknown. Elio Lampridio Cerva on Martullus Zamagna.
13. "Oratio in funere Ioannis Gotii." Ibid., fols. 119–29v. Dubrovnik, 1502. Elio Lampridio Cerva on Ioannes Gotius.
14. "Oratio in funere Andreae Mutinensis medici." Ibid., fols. 129v–34v.

Dubrovnik, date unknown. Elio Lampridio Cerva on Andrea da Modena.

15. "... in Iunium Sorgium avunculum suum funebris oratio." Ibid., fols. 138v–49. Dubrovnik, date unknown. Elio Lampridio Cerva on Iunius Sorgius.

*16. "Oratio ... in funere Michaelis Zamagnii Stephani filii." Dubrovnik, Bibl. Male Braće, MS 1247. Dubrovnik, date unknown.

CHIERICATI, LEONELLO (1443–1506)

1. "Oratio in funere Innocentii Papae VIII." In *Thesaurus Novus Anecdotorum*, ed. E. Martène and U. Durand (Paris, 1717; reprinted Farnsborough, England: Gregg International, 1968–69), 2:cols. 1768–73. Rome, 1492. Leonello Chiericati on Innocent VIII.

* 2. "Sermo ... in funere Philippi cardinalis Bononiensis habita." Munich, Staatsbibliothek, MS Clm 24837, fols. 25ff. Rome, 1476.

CHRISTOPHORUS DE MEDIOLANO, O.P. *See* CRISTOFORO DA MILANO, O.P.

CIPELLI, GIOVANNI BATTISTA. *See* EGNAZIO, GIOVANNI BATTISTA

CIRIACO D'ANCONA (KYRIACUS ANCONITANUS) (1391–1452)
"Epitaphios logos." Milan, Bibl. Ambrosiana, MS R 93 sup., fols. 24–25; *Iter*, 1:341. Ancona, date unknown. Ciriaco d'Ancona on anonymous.

CLEOFILO, FRANCESCO OTTAVIO (1447–90)
"... oratio ad senatum Fanensem [pro morte Antonii Constantii]." In A. Constantius, [*Opera*], [fols. 52–59]. Fano, 1490. Francesco Cleofilo on Antonio Costanzi.

COCCIO, MARC ANTONIO. *See* SABELLICO

COLLENUCCIO, PANDOLFO (1444–1504)
"... oratio in funere Baptistae Sfortiae habita Pisauri." In Adolfo Cinquini, *Il codice Vaticano-Urbinate latino 1193: documenti ed appunti per la storia letteraria d'Italia nel Quattrocento*, 3 fascicles (Aosta: G. Allasia, 1905–9), 1:51–56. Pesaro, 1472. Pandolfo Collenuccio on Battista Sforza.

COLUCCI, BENEDETTO (ca. 1438–ca. 1506)
"... funebris oratio in mortem Antonii Partini." In L. Manicardi, "Di una *oratio funebris* inedita di Benedetto Colucci," *Bullettino storico pistoiese* 15 (1913): 67–74 (fragm.). Florence, 1455–56. Benedetto Colucci on Antonio Partini.

Appendix: List of Funeral Orations

COMINO, BARTOLOMEO (1468–1544)
* *Oratio pro funere Ioannis Dedi veneti scribae maximi* (Venice: Greg. de Gregoriis, 1511); King, *Venetian Humanism*, p. 458. Venice, date unknown.

CONTARINI, ANTONIO
* "Orazione funebre per il doge Andrea Contarini, 1382." Venice, Bibl. del Museo Civico Correr, MS Cicogna 2755. Venice, 1382.

CONTARINI, PIETRO (ca. 1446–1495)
Oratio in funere Marci Cornelii habita (Venice: Filippo di Pietro, 7 October 1479); GW 7442. Venice, 1479. Pietro Contarini on Marco Corner.

CORNELIUS PARISIENSIS
"Oratio in funere Petri de Lonato." BAV, MS Vat. lat. 4380, fols. 67–69; *Iter*, 2:326. Place and date unknown. Cornelius Parisiensis on Petrus de Lonato.

COSTANZI, ANTONIO (1435–90)
1. "Oratio funebris . . . per eundem Antonium . . . ." In [*Opera*], [fols. 44v–45]. Iesi, ca. 1458. Antonio Costanzi on anonymous.
2. "Oratio in funere Antonii Perutii . . . ." Ibid., [fol. 45r–v]. Fano, date unknown. Antonio Costanzi on Antonio Peruzzi.

CRISTOFORO DA MILANO, O.P.
* *Sermones ad funera*. Taggia, Conv. Domenicano, MS Arch. 2, pp. 305–30; Kaeppeli, *Scriptores*, 1:266.

CRIVELLI, GIROLAMO
"Oratio parentalis in laudem Blancae Mariae Sfortiae Vicecomitis." *RIS*, 25:cols. 425–32. Milan?, 1468. Girolamo Crivelli on Bianca Maria Visconti.

CROTTI, GIAN GIACOMO
Oratio . . . qua deflet Nicolaum Lucarum oratorem . . . (Pavia?: Iacobus de Burgofranco, 1518). Pavia, 1517? Gian Giacomo Crotti on Niccolò Lucaro.

CURRO, CARLO
1. *Oratio in funere reginae Lusitaniae habita . . .* (Messina: Wilhelm Schomberger, 20 December 1498); GW 7859. Messina, 1497? Carlo Curro on Isabella? of Portugal.
2. *Oratio in cenotaphio Ioannis principis Aragonensis* ([Messina: Johann Schade, ca. 1498]); GW 7858. Messina?, 1498? Carlo Curro on Juan of Aragon.

DATI, AGOSTINO (ca. 1420–78)
1. ". . . oratio I in funere Loysii Comparii . . . ." In *Opera* (Siena: S. Nicolai Nardi, 1503), fols. xcvi(v)–xcvii. Siena?, date unknown. Agostino Dati on Luigi Compari.
2. ". . . funebris oratio altera habita . . . pro Nicolao Recupero . . . ." Ibid., fol. xcvii(r–v). Siena, 1476. Agostino Dati on Niccolò Ricoveri.
3. ". . . funebris oratio III habita . . . in funere Mariani Sozini civis Senensis . . . ." Ibid., fols. xcvii(v)–xcviii. Siena, 1467. Agostino Dati on Mariano Sozzini.
4. ". . . funebris oratio IIII quam habuit in laudem Thomae Doccii iurisconsulti . . . ." Ibid., fols. xcviii–xcviiii. Siena, 1461. Agostino Dati on Tommaso Docci.
5. ". . . funebris oratio V quam ipse habuit in funere . . . Petri Russii Senensis . . . ." Ibid., fol. xcviiii(r–v). Siena, 1459. Agostino Dati on Pietro Rossi.
6. ". . . oratio VI de vita et obitu . . . Bartholi Turei Senensis . . . ." Ibid., fols. xcviiii(v)–c(v). Siena, 1477. Agostino Dati on Bartolo Bandini.
7. ". . . funebris oratio VII de morte et laudibus . . . Francisci Aringherii." Ibid., fols. c(v)–ci. Siena, date unknown. Agostino Dati on Francesco Aringhieri.
8. ". . . de laudibus . . . Campani Episcopi . . . ." Ibid., fol. ci (fragm.). Siena, 1477. Agostino Dati on Giannantonio Campano.

DATI, LEONARDO, O.P. (ca. 1365–1425)
"Sermo pro exsequiis Frederici Frezzi episcopi Fulginatis." Vienna, Nationalbibliothek, MS Lat. 4300, fols. 212–14v; Kaeppeli, *Scriptores*, 3:73–77. Constance, 1416. Leonardo Dati on Federigo Frezzi.

DECEMBRIO, PIER CANDIDO (1392–1477)
"Oratio in funere Nicolai Picinini, sive vita eiusdem bellicosissimi ducis." *RIS*, n.s. 20, no. 1:991–1009. Milan, 1444. Pier Candido Decembrio on Niccolò Piccinino.

DEL MAINO, GIASONE. *See* MAINO, GIASONE DEL

DIACCETO, FRANCESCO DA. *See* CATTANI, FRANCESCO

DOMINICUS DE FURNO
"Oratio in funere reverendi magistri Gabrielis Nasii . . . ." In Bucci, *Il Memoriale Quadripartitum*, ed. Curlo, pp. 310–12. Place and date unknown. Dominicus de Furno on Gabriele Nasi.

DONATO, PIETRO (ca. 1380–1447)
"Oratio in exsequiis domini Francisci Zabarellae." In *Thesaurus anec-*

dotorum novissimus, ed. B. Pez (Augsburg: Veit, 1721–29), Codex Diplomatico-Historico-Epistolaris, 5:part 3:144a–48b, where the oration is attributed to Gasparino Barzizza. Padua, 1417. Pietro Donato on Francesco Zabarella.

EGNAZIO, GIOVANNI BATTISTA (CIPELLI, GIOV. BATT.) (1473–1553)
1. ". . . *oratio in Laurentii Hispaniarum regis . . . legati clarissimi funere habita* (Venice: I. Leucius, 1506). Venice, 1501. Giovanni Battista Egnazio on Lorenzo Suarez de la Vega.
* 2. [Funeral oration for Benedetto Brugnoli] (Venice: ex Academia Aldi Romani, 1502). Venice, 1502.
3. ". . . *funebris oratio pro Aloysio Dardano archigrammateo* (Venice: B. Imperator, 1554). Venice, 1506. Giovanni Battista Egnazio on Luigi Dardani.
4. ". . . *oratio habita in funere . . . Nicolai Ursini Nolae Petilianique principis* (Venice: G. de Gregoriis, 1509). Venice, 1509. Giovanni Battista Egnazio on Niccolò Orsini.
5. ". . . pro Petro Bibienio oratore pontificio habita oratio . . . ." Venice, Bibl. Naz. Marciana, MS 4736 (Marc. lat. XIV 230), fols. 8–15; *Iter*, 2:268. Venice, 1514. Giovanni Battista Egnazio on Pietro da Bibbiena.
6. "Oratio funebris pro . . . cardinali Cornelio . . . ." BAV, MS Vat. lat. 7179, fols. 1–8; *Iter*, 2:383. Venice, 1525. Giovanni Battista Egnazio on Marco Corner (the younger).

FACCINO, GIAN LUIGI
"Funesta in . . . Sigismundi Estensis morte . . . oratio." BAV, MS Vat. lat. 8761, fols. 165–74v; *Iter*, 2:345. Place unknown, 1524? Gian Luigi Faccino on Sigismondo d'Este.

FAUSTO, VETTORE (1480–1551)
"In funere Francisci Rubrii . . . oratoris regii . . . oratio." In *Orationes clarorum hominum* (Cologne, 1560), pp. 469–84. Venice, 1521. Vettore Fausto on Francesco Rosso.

FILELFO, FRANCESCO (1398–1481)
1. ". . . oratio in funere domini Baldesaris [sic] Castellioni." Milan, Bibl. Ambrosiana, MS N 165 sup., fols. 63v–65v; *Iter*, 1:302. Milan, 1444? Francesco Filelfo on Baldassare Castiglioni.
2. "Oratio parentalis de divi Francisci Sphortiae . . . felicitate." In *Orationes Francisci Philelfi cum quibusdam aliis eiusdem operibus ad oratoriam summopere conducentibus* (Paris: Nic. de Pratis, 1515), fols. 3–25v. Milan, 1467. Francesco Filelfo on Francesco Sforza.
3. ". . . oratio habita in funere . . . Blancae Mariae Mediolanensium

ducissae." Ibid., fols. 25v–34. Milan, 1468. Francesco Filelfo on Bianca Maria Visconti.

4. "Oratio funebris pro . . . Philippo Borrhomaeo comite Haronae." Ibid., fols. 74–76. Milan, 1464. Francesco Filelfo on Filippo Borromeo.

5. "Oratio funebris pro . . . senatore Stephano Frederico Thedoschino." Ibid., fols. 76–78v. Milan, 1440. Francesco Filelfo on Stefano Federigo Todeschini.

FILELFO, GIOVANNI MARIO (1426–80)
"Epitaphion de obitu . . . Margharitae Gonzagae marchionessae Mantuae . . . ." Naples, Bibl. Nazionale, MS IX F 49, fols. 25–32; *Iter*, 1:429. Mantua, 1479. Giovanni Mario Filelfo on Margherita Gonzaga.

FILETICO, MARTINO (d. ca. 1490)
"Fune[b]ris oratio . . . pro obitu . . . Gentilis Montisferetri . . . comitissae." Padua, Bibl. del Seminario, MS 84, fols. 1–4v; *Iter*, 2:11. Urbino?, 1457. Martino Filetico on Gentile Brancaleoni.

FILIPPO DA LUCCA, O.F.M.
"Praedicatio funebris in obitu . . . Iacobae quondam dominae Lucani principis habita . . . ." Rome, Bibl. Casanatense, MS 1861, fols. 114–15v; *Iter*, 2:103. Lucca?, 1400? Filippo da Lucca on Iacoba (Guinigi?).

FILIPPO DA RIMINI (ca. 1407–97)
"Oratio in funus illustris Francisci Barbari." Venice, Bibl. Naz. Marciana, MS 4717 (Marc. lat. XIV 250), fols. 10–14; *Iter*, 2:249. Venice, 1454. Filippo da Rimini on Francesco Barbaro.

FLAVI, GIOVANNI BATTISTA (1482–1544)
Oratio et carmen de vita . . . Thomae de Vio Caietani . . . (Rome: A. B. Asulanus, 1535), bound into BAV, MS Vat. lat. 4912, fols. 387–402; *Iter*, 2:330. Rome, 1534. Giovanni Battista Flavi on Cajetan.

FLEMMYNG, HENRY
1. "Oratio . . . in exsequiis Francisci Zabarellae, cardinalis Florentini . . . ." In *Magnum oecumenicum Constantiense concilium*, ed. H. von der Hardt, 6 vols. (Frankfurt and Leipzig: C. Genschius, 1696–1700), 1:part 2:546–52. Constance, 1417. Henry Flemmyng on Francesco Zabarella.
* 2. [Funeral oration for Robert Halam, bishop of Salisbury]. Vienna, Nationalbibliothek, MS Lat. 4710, fols. 285ff. Constance, 1417.

FLORENTINUS, FRANCISCUS, O.F.M. *See* PADOVANO, FRANCESCO, O.F.M.

FRANCESCO DA GRADO
"Oratio . . . funebris . . . edita in funere . . . Ioannis de Almericis de Pensauro . . . ." Padua, Bibl. Universitaria, MS provv. 197, fols. 123–25v; *Iter*, 2:19. Mantua?, 1451. Francesco da Grado on Giovanni Almerici.

FRANCESCO DA TOLEDO
Oratio in funere illustris domini Leonardi de Robore . . . ([Rome: Eucharius Silber, 1483–90]); Copinger 2575, Reichling, 1:146. Rome?, 1475. Francesco da Toledo on Leonardo della Rovere.

FRANCESCO DA VELLATE
"Oratio . . . edita in funere . . . cardinalis Ostiensis summi pontificis vicecancellarii." BAV, MS Vat. lat. 8919, fols. 1–6v; *Iter*, 2:346. Rome, 1426. Francesco da Vellate on Jean de Broniac.

GABRIELLI, ANGELO
". . . in funere . . . cardinalis Baptistae Zeni . . . ." In Valier, *De cautione adhibenda in edendis libris*, pp. 226–32. Venice, 1501. Angelo Gabrielli on Battista Zeno.

GAETANI, DANIELE (1460–1528)
* 1. "In obitu . . . dominae Helisabetae Savorganae [sic] matris . . . Nicolai . . . Epicedion." San Daniele del Friuli, Bibl. Civ. Guarneriana, MS 183. Udine, date unknown.
* 2. "Funerarium . . . ductoris Iacobi Savorgnan . . . ." Udine, Bibl. Capitolare, MS Bini 21.1; *Iter*, 2:574. Udine?, 1499.

GARZONI, GIOVANNI (1419–1505)
1. "Oratio funebris . . . in funere Peregrini Zambeccari." In Giovanni Fantuzzi, *Notizie degli scrittori bolognesi*, 9 vols. (Bologna, 1781–94; reprinted Bologna: Arnaldo Forni, 1965), 9:115–19. Bologna, date unknown. Giovanni Garzoni on Peregrino Zambeccari.
2. "In funere magistri Nestoris Morandi." Ibid., 9:119–20. Bologna, 1503. Giovanni Garzoni on Nestore Morandi.
3. "In funere Hieronymi Ranuzzi." Ibid., 9:120–23. Bologna, 1496. Giovanni Garzoni on Girolamo Ranuzzi.
4. "Oratio funebris pro Andromaco Milano." Ibid., 9:123–24. Bologna, 1496? Giovanni Garzoni on Andromaco Milani.
5. "Oratio funebris in laudem Virgilii Malvetii." Ibid., 9:124–28. Bologna, 1481. Giovanni Garzoni on Virgilio Malvezzi.
6. "In laudem merchatorum [pro Antonio] . . . ." Bologna, Bibl. Universitaria, MS Lat. 1896, part 1, fols. 34v–36; *Iter*, 1:24. Bologna?,

date unknown. Giovanni Garzoni on an Antonio (I).
7. "Oratio funebris in qua tota ars consistit [pro Antonio]." Ibid., part 1, fols. 42v–44v. Bologna?, date unknown. Giovanni Garzoni on Antonio (II).
8. "Oratio funebris pro domino Vincentio Palliotto." Ibid., part 1, fols. 107–8v. Bologna, 1498. Giovanni Garzoni on Vincenzo Paleotti.
9. "Oratio funebris pro quodam magistro et theologiae professore." Ibid., part 1, fols. 114v–15v. Bologna, date unknown. Giovanni Garzoni on Giacomo Gandulfi.
10. "Oratio funebris [pro Georgio Manzolo]." Bologna, Bibl. Universitaria, MS Lat. 1622, part 1, fols. xxxiiii–xxxv. Bologna, date unknown. Giovanni Garzoni on Giorgio Manzoli.
11. "Oratio funebris [pro Alexandro]." Ibid., part 1, fols. xxxv–xxxviii(v). Bologna?, date unknown. Giovanni Garzoni on an Alessandro.
12. ["Oratio funebris pro Antonio"]. Ibid., part 1, fols. lxxii(v)–lxxiii(v). Bologna?, date unknown. Giovanni Garzoni on Antonio (III).
13. "In funere Ioannis Zambecharii." Ibid., part 1, fol. cv(r–v). Bologna?, date unknown. Giovanni Garzoni on Giovanni Zambeccari.
14. ". . . oratio funebris in laudem mulieris . . . ." Ibid., part 1, fols. 160v–63. Bologna?, date unknown. Giovanni Garzoni on Cassandra Lambertazzi (I).
15. "Oratio funebris [pro Ludovico] . . . ." Ibid., part 1, fols. 163v–64v. Bologna?, date unknown. Giovanni Garzoni on a Ludovico.
16. "Oratio funebris [pro Antonio] . . . ." Ibid., part 1, fols. 164v–67. Bologna?, date unknown. Giovanni Garzoni on an Antonio (IV).
17. ". . . oratio funebris [pro Antonio]." Ibid., part 1, fols. 167–69v. Bologna?, date unknown. Giovanni Garzoni on an Antonio (V).
18. "Haec oratio habenda erat in funere prioris Sancti Salvatoris sed beneficio episcopi liberatus est." Ibid., part 1, fols. 193–94v. Bologna?, date unknown. Giovanni Garzoni on Niccolò Ludovisi?
19. "Laudatio funebris pro Matthia Pannoniae rege . . . ." Ibid., part 1, fols. 359v–62v. Bologna?, 1490. Giovanni Garzoni on Mattia Corvino.
20. "Oratio funebris pro muliere." Ibid., part 1, fols. 390–93. Bologna?, date unknown. Giovanni Garzoni on Francesca Lambertazzi.
21. "Oratio funebris pro viro." Ibid., part 1, fols. 393–94. Bologna?, date unknown. Giovanni Garzoni on Francesco Basso?
22. "Oratio funebris in laudanda mercatura [pro Antonio]." Ibid., part 1, fols. 396–98 (revised version of no. 6 above). Bologna?, date unknown. Giovanni Garzoni on Antonio (Ia).
23. ["Oratio funebris? pro Antonio Penso"]. Bologna, Bibl. Universitaria, MS Lat. 741, fols. 167v–74v. Bologna?, date unknown. Giovanni Garzoni on Antonio Penzo.

24. "Oratio funebris pro Andrea Bentivolo." Bologna, Bibl. Universitaria, MS Lat. 742, fols. 8–9v. Bologna, 1491. Giovanni Garzoni on Andrea Bentivoglio.
25. "Oratio funebris [pro Antonio]." Ibid., fols. 28v–30. Bologna?, date unknown. Giovanni Garzoni on an Antonio (VI).
26. ["Oratio funebris pro quodam provinciali"]. Ibid., fols. 30–31. Bologna?, date unknown. Giovanni Garzoni on anonymous (provincial).
27. "Oratio funebris [pro Cassandra]." Ibid., fols. 31–33. Bologna, date unknown. Giovanni Garzoni on Cassandra Lambertazzi (II).
28. "Oratio funebris in laudem Antonii Linensis . . . ." Bologna, Bibl. Universitaria, MS Lat. 746, fols. 18–21v. Bologna?, 1472? Giovanni Garzoni on Antonio Dal Lino.
29. "Oratio funebris in laudem Baptistae Mancoli . . . ." Ibid., fols. 21v–27. Bologna?, 1473? Giovanni Garzoni on Battista Manzoli.

GASPAR DE SANCTO IOANNE, O.P. *See* SIGHICELLI, GASPARE, O.P.

GATTI, GIOVANNI, O.P. (d. 1484)
". . . oratio quam habuit in funere Latini cardinalis Ursini . . . ." BAV, MS Vat. lat. 2918, fols. 76–97; *Iter*, 2:256, Kaeppeli, *Scriptores*, 2:441. Rome, 1477. Giovanni Gatti on Latino Orsini.

GERARDO DA LUCCA
". . . oratio . . . in funere . . . Silvestri episcopi Anglici Lucensis civis de Giglis . . . ." Lucca, Bibl. Governativa, MS 762, fols. 11v–15v; *Iter*, 1:258. Lucca, 1521. Gerardo da Lucca on Silvestro de' Gigli.

GIACOMO DA ALESSANDRIA, O.F.M.
"Oratio in funere . . . Fantini Valaressi . . . archiepiscopi Cretensis . . . ." In Bernard Schultze's edition of Fantinus Vallaressus, *Libellus de ordine generalium conciliorum et unione Florentina*, Concilium Florentinum: Documenta et scriptores ser. B, 2:part 2 (Rome: Pontificium Institutum Orientalium Studiorum, 1944), pp. viii–xi. Crete, 1443. Giacomo da Alessandria on Fantino Valaresso.

GIACOMO DA PESARO
1. ". . . oratio funebris . . . in morte Caroli [Malatestae] . . . ." In Olivieri degli Abbati, *Orazioni in morte*, pp. xxxiv–xxxix. Pesaro, 1438. Giacomo da Pesaro on Carlo Malatesta.
2.? "Oratio funebris pro quacunque Imperatrice, Regina, Ducissa, Marchionissa in Constantiam directa Pisaurensium dominam." In Gregorio Britannico, *Sermones funebres et nuptiales*, [fols. 80v–83v]. Pesaro, 1447. Giacomo da Pesaro? on Costanza Varano Sforza.

GIOIA, GIROLAMO
Oratio in Rucii abbatis funere Venetiis habita ([Venice: Bernardino Benagli, ca. 1495]); Reichling 196 (1:44). Venice, 1495? Girolamo Gioia on Benedetto Rugio.

GIOVANNI DA VECCHIANO (DI PISA)
". . . in solemni Ioannis Petri poetae clarissimique orationis [sic] laureatione feliciter incipit." In Mariarosa Cortesi, "Alla scuola di Gian Pietro d'Avenza in Lucca," *Quellen und Forschungen aus italienischen Archiven und Bibliotheken* 61 (1981): 109–67, esp. 148–53. Lucca, 1457. Giovanni da Vecchiano on Gian Pietro d'Avenza.

GIUDICI, BATTISTA DE', O.P. (d. 1484)
1. *Oratio in funere Christophori Rovere Cardinalis* ([Rome: Georg Lauer, after 9 February 1478]); Hain 9467. Rome, 1478. Battista de' Giudici on Cristoforo della Rovere.
2. ". . . in funere . . . Roberti Malatestae Ariminensis funebris oratio." Rimini, Bibl. Civ. Gambalunga, MS SC–157 (4 B I 43), fols. 2–11; *Iter*, 2:89. Rome, 1482. Battista de' Giudici on Roberto Malatesta.

GIULIANO, ANDREA (ca. 1384–1452)
"Pro Manuele Chrysolora funebris oratio." In Boerner, *De doctis hominibus Graecis liber*, pp. 16–35. Venice, 1415. Andrea Giuliano on Manuel Chrysoloras.

GIUSTINIANI, BERNARDO (1408–89)
". . . oratio funebris de laudibus Francisci Fuscari ducis Venetiarum." BAV, MS Chig. I VI 215, fols. 180v–98v; *Iter*, 2:484. A revised version is in *Orazioni, elogi e vite*, ed. Molin, 1:21–59. Venice, 1457. Bernardo Giustiniani on Francesco Foscari.

GIUSTINIANI, LEONARDO (ca. 1389–1446)
1. "Funebris oratio praestantissimi viri Leonardi Iustiniani pro Carlo Zeno." *RIS*, n.s. 19, no. 6:141–46. Venice, 1418. Leonardo Giustiniani on Carlo Zeno.
2. "AD C. V. Georgium Lauredanum funebris oratio . . . ." In *Orazioni, elogi e vite*, ed. Molin, 1:12–20. For the attribution to Giustiniani rather than Guarino, see Guarino's *Epistolario*, ed. Sabbadini, 3:132–33. Venice, 1421. Leonardo Giustiniani on Giorgio Loredan.

GRADENSIS, FRANCISCUS. See FRANCESCO DA GRADO

GRANA, LORENZO (d. 1539)
1. "Oratio in funere Clementis VII." In *Anecdota litteraria*, ed. Ama-

duzzi and Bianconi, 4:255–84. Rome, 1534. Lorenzo Grana on Clement VII.
2. "Oratio in funere Aegidii Canisii cardinalis Viterbiensis." Ibid., 4:285–322. Rome, 1532. Lorenzo Grana on Giles of Viterbo.
3. "In funere Celsi Mellini . . . lacrimae." BAV, MS Vat. lat. 11761, fols. 134v–43v; *Iter*, 2:386. Rome, 1519. Lorenzo Grana on Celso Mellini.

GUARINI, ALESSANDRO (1486–1556)

. . . *funebris oratio in . . . Hippolytum Estensem* . . . ([s.l.: s.t., after 20 September 1520]). Ferrara, 1520. Alessandro Guarini on Ippolito I d'Este.

GUARINI, BATTISTA (ca. 1435–1503)
1. *Funebris oratio in reginam Eleanoram Aragoniam* . . . ([Ferrara: André Belfort, after 12 October 1493]); Hain 8132. Ferrara?, 1493. Battista Guarini on Eleanor of Aragon.
2. ". . . in clarissimum et amplissimum virum Ludovicum Casellium . . . funebris oratio." Modena, Bibl. Estense, MS Alpha J 9, 43 (Est. lat. 1269), fols. 1–21v (followed by Italian translation that is incomplete at beginning); *Iter*, 1:384. Parma, 1469? Battista Guarini on Ludovico Casella.

GUARINI, GUARINO (1370–1460)
1. ". . . funebris oratio." Bergamo, Bibl. Civica, MS Delta IV 40 (MA 273), fols. 21v–22; *Iter*, 1:10. Verona, date unknown. Guarino on anonymous.
2. "Oratio funebris in morte . . . Ioannis Nicolae Salerni . . . Veronensis." In Mittarelli, *Bibliotheca codicum manuscriptorum*, cols. 481–88. Verona, 1426. Guarino on Giannicola Salerno.
3. "Oratio in funere Theodorae matris . . . Iacobi Zilioli." Ibid., cols. 1241–51. Ferrara, 1429–30. Guarino on Teodora Zilioli.
4. "Oratio [pro Ovizone de Polenta]." Milan, Bibl. Ambrosiana, MS N 339 sup., fols. 33v–34v; *Iter*, 1:336. Ravenna, 1431. Guarino on Obizzo da Polenta.
5. ". . . ad illustrem dominum Leonellum pro uxoris Margaritae morte funebris oratio." Padua, Bibl. del Seminario, MS 692, fols. 107v–10. Rovigo, 1439. Guarino on Margherita Gonzaga.
6. "[In] funere Leonelli Estensis clarissimi marchionis . . . oratio . . . ." BAV, MS Ottob. lat. 1834, fols. 63v–67; *Iter*, 2:433. Ferrara, 1450. Guarino on Leonello d'Este.

HYVANUS, ANTONIUS. *See* IVANI, ANTONIO

IACOBUS DE ALEXANDRIA, O.F.M. *See* GIACOMO DA ALESSANDRIA, O.F.M.

IACOBUS ARRIGONI, O.P. See ARRIGONI, GIACOMO, O.P.

IACOBUS BONONIENSIS. See IACOPO DA BOLOGNA

IACOBUS PISAURUS. See GIACOMO DA PESARO

IACOPO DA BOLOGNA
"Oratio . . . habita in funere atque exsequiis pro quodam suo monaco." Florence, Bibl. Nazionale, MS Magl. VIII 1390, fols. 127–28; *Iter*, 1:133. Ferrara?, date unknown. Iacopo da Bologna on a Fabiano.

INGHIRAMI, TOMMASO "FEDRA" (ca. 1470–1516)
1. "Pro Iulio II. pontifice maximo funebris oratio." In *Orationes duae*, ed. P. L. Galletti (Rome: G. Salomonus, 1777), pp. 77–105. Rome, 1513. Tommaso Inghirami on Julius II.
2. "Galeotti cardinalis Sancti Petri ad Vincula . . . laudatio." Ibid., pp. 57–76. Rome, 1507. Tommaso Inghirami on Galeotto Franciotti.
3. "Laudatio in obitu Ludovici Podocathari Cypri . . . cardinalis." In *Anecdota litteraria*, ed. Amaduzzi and Bianconi, 1:289–333. Rome, 1504. Tommaso Inghirami on Ludovico Podocataro.
4. "In laudem Petri de Vicentia . . . oratio funebris." Ibid., 3:191–244. Rome, 1505. Tommaso Inghirami on Pietro Menzi.

IOANNES CAPOGALLO. See CAPOGALLO, GIOVANNI

IOANNES GATTI DE MESSANA, O.P. See GATTI, GIOVANNI, O.P.

IOANNES DE LAMPUGNANO. See LAMPUGNANO, GIOVANNI

IVANI, ANTONIO (ca. 1430–82)
* ". . . oratio funebris per eundem adolescentulum Clementis Benefacii filium in funere Antoni Tranchedi[ni]." Sarzana, Bibl. Comunale, MS XXVI F 175, fol. 94r–v; *Iter*, 2:145. Sarzana?, date unknown.

JOUFFROY, JEAN (d. 1473)
1. "Oratio . . . habita Romae in funeralibus Nicolai papae quinti." BAV, MS Vat. lat. 3675, fols. 30–37; *Iter*, 2:322. Published in Onofri, "*Sicut fremitus leonis*," pp. 21–28. Rome, 1455. Jean Jouffroy on Nicholas V.
* 2. ". . . oratio funebris pro Alberto rege Romanorum . . . Florentiae in generali concilio habita." Fulda, Landesbibliothek, MS C 10, fols. 51–55; *Iter*, 3:537–38. Florence, 1439.

KYRIACUS ANCONITANUS. See CIRIACO D'ANCONA

LAMBERTAZZI, GIOVANNI LUDOVICO (d. 1401)
"Sermo in morte magni domini Francisci senioris de Carraria." *RIS*,

n.s. 17, no. 1:443–46n. Padua, 1393. Giovanni Ludovico Lambertazzi on Francesco il Vecchio da Carrara.

LAMPRIDIUS CERVINUS, AELIUS. *See* CERVA, ELIO "LAMPRIDIO"

LAMPUGNANO, GIOVANNI
"Sermo in morte et exsequiis ducis Mediolani." Florence, Bibl. Riccardiana, MS 784, fols. 161–65v; *Iter*, 1:201–2. Milan, 1402. Giovanni Lampugnano on Giangaleazzo Visconti.

LANDINO, CRISTOFORO (1425–98)
1. "In funere Donati Acciaroli oratio . . . ." BAV, MS Vat. lat. 13679, fols. 11–18; *Iter*, 2:387. Italian translation in *Delle orazioni*, ed. F. Sansovino, 1:286–94. Florence, 1478. Cristoforo Landino on Donato Acciaiuoli.
2. ". . . in funere Iordani Ursini oratio." Ed. Manfred Lentzen, in *Studien zur Dante-Exegese Cristoforo Landinos (mit einem Anhang bisher unveröffentlichter Briefe und Reden)*, Studi italiani 12 (Cologne and Vienna: Böhlau, 1971), pp. 271–76. Florence, 1483. Cristoforo Landino on Giordano Orsini.

LANDULPHUS
"In morte regis Andreae." BAV, MS Vat. lat. 4376, fols. 26v–30; *Iter*, 2:326. Naples?, 1345? Magister Landulphus on King Andrew (of Anjou?).

LEONARDI, NICCOLÒ (ca. 1370–after 1452)
"Oratio habita in funere . . . Magistri Andreae phisici Venetiarum." Venice, Bibl. Naz. Marciana, MS 4002 (Marc. lat. XIV 12), fols. 119v–20v; *Iter*, 2:246. Venice?, date unknown. Niccolò Leonardi on an Andrea.

LETO, POMPONIO (1428–98)
". . . oratio dicta in funere Leonardi Griphi . . . ." BAV, MS Vat. lat. 6850, fols. 86–90; *Iter*, 2:382. Rome, 1485. Pomponio Leto on Leonardo Grifi.

LOLLIO, ANTONIO (DA SAN GIMIGNANO)
1. *Oratio habita in funere . . . Philiberti . . . cardinalis Matisconensis . . .* ([Rome: Stephan Plannck, not before 30 September 1484]); Hain 10178. Rome, 1484. Antonio Lollio on Philibert Hugonet.
2. "Oratio in funere . . . Laudomiae de Picholominis . . . ." In Mittarelli, *Bibliotheca codicum manuscriptorum*, cols. 686–90. Siena, date unknown. Antonio Lollio on Laudomia Piccolomini.

LOSCHI, FRANCESCO (1412–1462/63)
* "Oratio pro Francisco de Portis." Munich, Universitätsbibliothek, MS 2/607, fols. 77v–79v; *Iter*, 3:648. Place and date unknown.

LUCARO, NICCOLÒ
1. "Deploratio illustrissimae Beatricis . . . ." In Gregorio Britannico, *Sermones funebres necnon nuptiales*, fols. 131v–33. Cremona, 1496. Niccolò Lucaro on Beatrice Sforza.
2. "Baptistae Piasii astronomi . . . funebris laudatio . . . ." Ibid., fols. 133–34v. Cremona, 1492. Niccolò Lucaro on Battista Piasi.

LUDOVICO DA IMOLA, O.F.M.
Oratio in funere Petri Ferrici cardinalis ([Rome: Georg Lauer, not before 1479]); Hain 9160. Rome, 1478. Ludovico da Imola on Pietro Ferrici.

LUDOVICUS DE PIRANO, O.F.M. See STRASSOLDO, LUDOVICO, O.F.M.

LUGDUNENSIS, THADDEUS, O.E.S.A. See THADDEUS OF LYON, O.E.S.A.

MAGGI, ANTONIO
. . . *pro* . . . *cardinale Cornelio funebris oratio* (Venice: I. Tacuinus de Tridino, 1525). Verona?, 1524. Antonio Maggi on Marco Corner (the younger).

MAGNO, MARCANTONIO (ca. 1480–1549)
Oratio in funere regis Catholici (Naples: S. Mayr, 1516). Naples, 1516. Marcantonio Magno on Ferdinand of Aragon.

MAINO, GIASONE DEL (1435–1519)
Oratio in funere Hieronymi Torti habita ([Pavia: Francesco Girardengo, after 11 August 1484]); Hain 10973. Pavia, 1484. Giasone del Maino on Girolamo Torti.

MAIUS, ANTONIUS. See MAGGI, ANTONIO

MANETTI, GIANNOZZO (1396–1459)
1. "Oratio funebris in solemni Leonardi (Arretini) historici, oratoris, ac poetae laureatione." In Bruni, *Epistolarum libri VIII*, ed. Mehus, pp. lxxxix–cxiv. Florence, 1444. Giannozzo Manetti on Leonardo Bruni.
2. ". . . funebris oratio in funere . . . Iannotii Pandolfini equitis Florentini." Florence, Bibl. Riccardiana, MS 3903, fols. 1–20v; *Iter*, 1:183. Written at Naples and sent to Florence, 1456. Giannozzo Manetti on Giannozzo Pandolfini.

MARCELLO, CRISTOFORO (d. 1527)
. . . *in reverendissimi episcopi Petri Barrocii funus* . . . ([s.l.: s.t., after 10

January 1507]). Padua, 1507. Cristoforo Marcello on Pietro Barozzi.

MARCELLO, PIETRO (ca. 1454–after 7 June 1502)
* 1. ". . . in obitu Iacobi Marcelli oratio." Venice, Conte Alessandro Marcello del Maino, MS ser. A I, Busta 4; *Iter,* 2:578. Venice?, 1484?
2. ". . . oratio in funere Andreae Vendrameni Venetiarum principis." In *Orazioni, elogi e vite,* ed. Molin, 1:141–60. Venice, 1478. Pietro Marcello on Andrea Vendramin.

MARCO DA VERONA, O.E.S.A.
1. "Oratio in funere Aegidii Hispani cardinalis." In *Oratio in funere Aegidii Hispani cardinalis, cum aliis eiusdem orationibus* ([Bologna: Iustinianus de Ruberia, ca. 1500]), [fols. 1–2v]; Reichling 1567 (5:46). Bologna, 1497. Marco da Verona on Gil Albornoz.
2. "Oratio habita Papiae in funere Dominici Costae." Ibid., [fol. 7r–v]. Pavia, 1487. Marco da Verona on Domenico Costa.
3. "Oratio . . . infunere [sic] habita Bartholomaeae Squarzaficae." Ibid., [fol. 8r–v]. Alessandrina, 1488. Marco da Verona on Bartolomea Squarciafici.

MARINI, GIOVANNI
Pro Antonio Suriano Venetiarum patriarcha funebris oratio (Venice: Greg. de Gregoriis, 1508). Venice, 1508. Giovanni Marini on Antonio Suriani.

MARSI, PIETRO
1. *Oratio dicta in funere Hieronymi Forocorneliensis et Foroliviensis comitis* ([Bologna: Platone de' Benedetti, after 14 April 1488]); Hain 10793. Place unknown, 1488. Pietro Marsi on Girolamo Riario.
2. *Oratio habita Romae in obitu Pomponii Laeti* ([Rome: Eucharius Silber, after 2 May 1497]); Hain 10792. Rome, 1497. Pietro Marsi on Pomponio Leto.

MASCARELLI, MONTORIO
"Oratio . . . acta in funere . . . Ioannis Francisci de Capitibus Listae . . . ." Venice, Bibl. Naz. Marciana, MS 4296 (Marc. lat. XIV 264), fols. 71–74; *Iter,* 2:250. Padua, 1447–59. Montorio Mascarelli on Giovan Francesco Capodilista.

MATURANZIO, FRANCESCO (1443–1518)
1. *Oratio in funere Grifonis Balionii* ([Perugia: printer of Robertus Anglicus, *BMC,* 6:789 = Pietro da Colonia, Giovanni di Corrado, and Federico Eber, after 1 May 1477]); Hain 10896. Perugia, 1477. Francesco Maturanzio on Grifo Baglioni.

2. "... oratio habita in funere Braccii Balioni...." BAV, MS Vat. lat. 5358, fols. 13–21v; *Iter*, 2:375. Perugia, 1479. Francesco Maturanzio on Braccio Baglioni.
3. "... oratio Perusiae in funere imaginario Fratris Leonardi Mansueti ...." Ibid., fols. 22–33. Perugia, 1480. Francesco Maturanzio on Leonardo Mansueti.
4. "... funebris laudatio habita Romae in funere Laurentii Zani Veneti patriarchae Antiocheni...." Ibid., fols. 45–52v. Rome, 1484. Francesco Maturanzio on Lorenzo Zane.
5. "... funebris oratio habita Perusiae in funere Horatii Balioni ad Beneventum defuncti et in patriam reportati." Ibid., fols. 52v–57v. Perugia, 1486. Francesco Maturanzio on Orazio I Baglioni.
6. "... funebris oratio habita in funere... Francisci Portensis Vicentini...." Ibid., fols. 76v–81. Vicenza, date unknown. Francesco Maturanzio on Francesco da Porto.
7. ["Oratio in funere Dorotheae uxoris Ioannis Portensis"]. Ibid., fols. 81v–83v. Vicenza, date unknown. Francesco Maturanzio on Dorotea da Porto.
8. "... funebris laudatio habita... in funere... Ioannis Clerigati ...." Ibid., fols. 83v–88v. Vicenza, 1495. Francesco Maturanzio on Giovanni Chiericati.
9. "... funebris oratio habita... in funere... Nicolai Clarigati [sic] ...." Ibid., fols. 88v–92v. Vicenza, 1492. Francesco Maturanzio on Niccolò Chiericati.
10. "Funebris oratio... in funere... Antonii[?] Aquensis." Ibid., fols. 113v–14v. Vicenza, date unknown. Francesco Maturanzio on Tommaso d'Acqui.
11. "... funebris laudatio in funere... Isotheae Portensis Vicentinae." Ibid., fols. 114v–15v. Vicenza, date unknown. Francesco Maturanzio on Isotta da Porto.
12. "Funebris oratio habita... in funere... Hieronymi Paelli...." Ibid., fols. 115v–18. Vicenza, date unknown. Francesco Maturanzio on Girolamo Pagliello.
*13. "In funere Pauli Portensis habita Vicentiae." Perugia, Bibl. Com. Augusta, MS F 73 (399); *Iter*, 2:56. Vicenza, date unknown.
*14. "In funere patris Andreae Castaldi ordinis servorum." Perugia?, codex formerly in San Domenico and apparently now lost. See Vermiglioli, *Memorie*, pp. 97–102.

MAURO, GABRIELE

... *oratio in funere Benedicti Pisauri classis Venetae imperatoris* ...

(Venice: Bernardinus de Vitalibus, 1503). Venice, 1503? Gabriele Mauro on Benedetto Pesaro.

MODESTI, GIANNANTONIO (1479–1523)
"Oratio funebris Ferrariae habita pro Luca a Ripa." Rimini, Bibl. Civ. Gambalunga, MS SC-415 (4 D II 38), fols. 29–31v; *Iter*, 2:89. Ferrara, date unknown. Giannantonio Modesti on Luca a Ripa.

MONACI, LORENZO DE' (ca. 1351–1428)
"Sermo . . . in celebritate exsequiarum . . . Vitalis Lando." BAV, MS Vat. lat. 5223, fols. 66–67v; *Iter*, 2:372–73. Venice, 1407. Lorenzo de' Monaci on Vitale Lando.

MONTANO, GIOVANNI
"Ad . . . principem Blancam Mariam illustrissimi genitoris eius funebris oratio." *RIS*, 25:cols. 435–42. Milan?, after 1447. Giovanni Montano on Filippo Maria Visconti.

MONTANO, ROBERTO
? * "Oratio lugubris in funere . . . Opizonis de Polenta . . . ." Venice, Bibl. del Museo Civico Correr, MS Correr 225. Information supplied by Professor Kristeller. Ravenna, 1441?

MONTE, PIETRO DEL (ca. 1400–1457)
1. "Oratio . . . in funere . . . Pauli de Leone equitis Patavini." BAV, MS Vat. lat. 2694, fols. 36v–42; *Iter*, 2:350. Padua, 1431. Pietro del Monte on Paolo da Lion.
2. "Oratio . . . pro funere . . . Ioannis Zabarellae." Ibid., fols. 46–49. Padua, 1433. Pietro del Monte on Giovanni Zabarella.
3. ". . . oratio in funere Calisti tercii . . . ." BAV, MS Vat. lat. 4872, fols. 39–51v; *Iter*, 2:369. Rome, 1456. Pietro del Monte on Calixtus III.

MONTECATINI, ANTONIO DA
"Oratio habita . . . in funere . . . cardinalis Theanensis . . . ." Florence, Bibl. Nazionale, MS Magl. VII 1095, fols. 140–42v; *Iter*, 1:130–31. Pistoia, 1473. Antonio da Montecatini on Niccolò Forteguerri.

MORANDI, FILIPPO. *See* FILIPPO DA RIMINI

NAVAGERO, ANDREA (1483–1529)
1. "Oratio habita in funere Bartholomaei Liviani." In *Opera omnia*, ed. I. Antonius and C. Vulpius (Venice: Remondiniana, 1754), pp. 3–23. Venice, 1515. Andrea Navagero on Bartolomeo d'Alviano.
2. "Oratio habita in funere Leonardi Lauretani Venetiarum principis."

Ibid., pp. 24–53. Venice, 1521. Andrea Navagero on Leonardo Loredan.

NEGRO, PESCENNIO FRANCESCO (1452–after 9 November 1523)
1. "... in Agnesinae Bondinae ... Petri Rocabonellae genetricis ... interitum ... pullata oratio." In Pietro Verrua, "Cinque orazioni dette dall'umanista Francesco Negri nello studio di Padova," *Archivio veneto-tridentino*, ser. 4, 1 (1922): 204–9. Padua, 1487–90. Francesco Negro on Agnesina Bondina Roccabonella.
2. "... in Ioannis Iacobi Putei ... luctuosum obitum ... pullata funebris oratio." Ibid., pp. 213–17. Padua, 1487–90. Francesco Negro on Gianiacopo Dal Pozzo.
3. *Pullata Nigri contio in Domini Herculis inferias* (Ferrara: s.t., after 1 February 1505). Ferrara, 1505. Francesco Negro on Ercole I d'Este.

NERUCCI, BARTOLO (d. after 1473)
? "Oratio habita in funere praestantissimi et reverendi viri Mathiae Lupii per M. B." in Guido Traversari, "Di Mattia Lupi (1380–1468) e de' suoi *Annales Geminianenses*," *Miscellanea storica della Valdelsa* 12 (1904): 123–25. San Gimignano, 1468. Bartolo Nerucci? on Mattia Lupi.

NICCOLÒ DA MODRUSSA
Oratio in funere ... Petri cardinalis Sancti Sixti ... ([Rome: Stephan Plannck, 1481–87]); Hain 11771. Rome, 1474. Niccolò da Modrussa on Pietro Riario.

NICCOLÒ DA RIMINI, O.F.M.
"Sermo de vita et morte ... Galeocti Ruberti de Malatestis ...." In Constantinus Bartolucci, O.F.M., "Legenda B. Galeoti Roberti de Malatestis tertii ordinis S. Francisci (1411–1432)," *Archivum Franciscanum historicum* 8 (1915): 539–57. Rimini, 1432–33. Niccolò da Rimini on Galeotto Roberto Malatesta.

NICOLAUS DE LEONARDIS. See LEONARDI, NICCOLÒ

ODASSI, LUDOVICO (1455–1509)
1. "Oratio habita in funere ... Federici Urbinatium ducis." BAV, MS Urb. lat. 1233, fols. 1–14; Stornajolo, *Codices Urbinates latini*, 3:229–30. Urbino, 1482. Ludovico Odassi on Federigo da Montefeltro.
2. "... oratio habita in funere Hippolytae Aragoniae Calabriae ducissae." In *Studi e ricerche di letteratura umanistica*, ed. A. Altamura (Naples: S. Viti, 1956), pp. 46–52. Urbino, 1488. Ludovico Odassi on Ippolita Maria Sforza.

3. "In funere Guidi Ubaldi Feretrii Urbini ducis . . . ." In *Orationes clarorum hominum* (Cologne, 1560), pp. 393–445. Urbino, 1508. Ludovico Odassi on Guid'Ubaldo I.

OLIVA, ALESSANDRO (d. 1463)

"Oratio funeralis in morte domini Ugolini Farnetae de Michaelis . . . ." Modena, Bibl. Estense, MS Gamma G 7, 18 (Campori 1365), fols. 35–38v; *Iter*, 1:389. Perugia, date unknown. Alessandro Oliva on Ugolino de' Micheli.

OLIVIERO

"Oratio fune[b]ris in . . . Helisabeth de Aragonia . . . ." Naples, Bibl. Nazionale, MS XII E 7, fols. 257–64v; *Iter*, 1:430. Taranto?, 1505? Oliviero on Isabella of Castile.

ORSINI, GIORDANO

1. "Oratio facta in funere Ioannis Pontani . . . ." Florence, Bibl. Laurenziana, MS Ashb. 271, fols. 17v–21; *Iter*, 1:83. Padua, 1446. Giordano Orsini on Giovanni Pontano.
2. ["Oratio . . . ad sacrum cardinalium collegium edita pro successore Calisti papae III eligendo . . ."]. BAV, MS Vat. lat. 4872, fols. 54–59v; *Iter*, 2:369. Rome, 1456. Giordano Orsini on Calixtus III.

PACINI, ANTONIO

"Oratio in funere Laurentii de Medicis senioris." Florence, Bibl. Riccardiana, MS 928, fols. 2–14v; *Iter*, 1:210–11. Florence, 1440. Antonio Pacini on Lorenzo de' Medici (the elder).

PADOVANO, FRANCESCO (DA FIRENZE), O.F.M.

1. ". . . pro . . . Leonardo Sabellio apostolicae camerae prothonotario funebris oratio." Florence, Bibl. Nazionale, MS Landau Finaly 152, fols. 85v–87; *Iter*, 1:171. Rome, date unknown. Francesco Padovano on Leonardo Savelli.
2. ". . . pro . . . Petro Naldi rotae pontificalis auditore funebris oratio incipit." Ibid., fols. 87–88v. Rome, date unknown. Francesco Padovano on Pietro Naldi.
3. ". . . pro devotissima matrona Marina Foscarina funebris oratio." Trieste, Bibl. Civica, MS Sez. Petrar. I 4, pp. 333–37; *Iter*, 2:199. Place and date unknown. Francesco Padovano on Marina Foscarina.

PAGELLO, GUGLIELMO

Laudatio in funere Bartholomaei Coleonii Venetorum imperatoris (Vicenza: [Iohannes de Reno], 28 January 1476); Hain 12265. Bergamo, 1476. Guglielmo Pagello on Bartolomeo Colleoni.

PALMERI, NICCOLÒ, O.E.S.A. (d. 1467)
1. "Oratio funebris . . . in funere Nicolai papae quinti." BAV, MS Vat. lat. 5815, fols. 3–12v; *Iter*, 2:376–77. Rome, 1455. Niccolò Palmeri on Nicholas V.
2. "Oratio funebris . . . cardinalis Firmani . . . ." Ibid., fols. 13–32v. Rome, 1458. Niccolò Palmeri on Domenico Capranica.
3. ["Oratio in funere cardinalis Prosperi Columnensis"]. Ibid., fols. 119–26. Rome, 1463. Niccolò Palmeri on Prospero Colonna.

PALMIERI, MATTEO (1406–75)
"Dicta in coronatione Caroli Aretini poetae cancellarii Florentini . . . ." Florence, Bibl. Riccardiana, MS 660, fols. 69–70; *Iter*, 1:195. Florence, 1453. Matteo Palmieri on Carlo Marsuppini.

PAMPHILUS, IOANNES HERCULES ALTAFLORES. *See* ALTAFLORES PAMPHILUS, IOANNES

PANNIZZATI, NICCOLÒ MARIO (d. 1529)
1.? "Oratio in funere domini Herculis Aestensis." Modena, Bibl. Estense, MS Alpha O 6, 15 (Est. lat. 174), fols. 216–19; *Iter*, 1:378–79. Ferrara?, 1505? Niccolò Pannizzati? on Ercole I d'Este.
2.? ". . . oratio funebris pro . . . Hippolyte . . . cardinale Ferrariensi." Ibid., fols. 220–24. Ferrara?, 1520? Niccolò Pannizzati? on Ippolito I d'Este.
* 3. *Oratio in funere Herculis Cantelmi Sorani Ducis* (Ferrara: Gio. Mazzochi?, 1509). Ferrara, 1509.

PARTENIO, PIETRO
1. "Laudatio . . . in Hieronymi Turriani medici . . . funere Patavii publice habita." In *Orationes* (Venice: s.t., after 1507), [fols. 8v–10]; Reichling 1020 (3:66–67). Padua, 1506. Pietro Partenio on Girolamo della Torre.
2. ". . . laudatio in Antonii Fracantiani philosophi . . . funere publice habita." Ibid., [fols. 11–14]. Padua, 1506. Pietro Partenio on Antonio Fracanziani.

PERGULENSIS, ANGELUS. *See* ANGELO DALLA PERGOLA

PERLEONE, PIETRO (ca. 1400–before 22 April 1463)
* "Oratio in funere Iani Campofregosi, D. Senensium." BAV, MS Vat. lat. 5336, fols. 35–43v; *Iter*, 2:374, King, *Venetian Humanism*, p. 467. Siena?, date unknown.

PEROTTI, NICCOLÒ (1429–80)
1. ". . . monodia in obitu Severi Perotti fratris . . . ." BAV, MS Vat. lat.

6835, fols. 45v–51v; *Iter*, 2:381–82. Rome?, ca. 1466. Niccolò Perotti on Severo Perotti.

2. ". . . oratio habita in funere Peri [*sic*] cardinalis Divi Sixti . . . ." BAV, MS Vat. lat. 8750, fols. 152–61v; *Iter*, 2:385–86. Rome, 1474. Niccolò Perotti on Pietro Riario.

PETRARCA, FRANCESCO (1304–74)
"Arringa facta Mediolani . . . de morte domini archiepiscopi Mediolanensis . . . ." In *Scritti inediti*, ed. Hortis, pp. 335–40. Milan, 1354. Petrarch on Giovanni Visconti.

PETRUS DE CASTELLETO, O.E.S.A. See CASTELLETO, PIETRO, O.E.S.A.

PETRUS DE MONTE. See MONTE, PIETRO DEL

PETRUS DE TRAVERSINIS, O. CARM. See TRAVERSINI, PIETRO, O. CARM.

PHILETICUS, MARTINUS. See FILETICO, MARTINO

PHILIPPUS DE LUCA, O.F.M. See FILIPPO DA LUCCA, O.F.M.

PHILOMUSUS. See SUPERCHI, GIAN FRANCESCO

PHILOPONUS. See STERPONI, STEFANO

PISAURUS, IACOBUS. See GIACOMO DA PESARO

POGGIO BRACCIOLINI. See BRACCIOLINI, POGGIO

PONTANO, GIOVANNI (d. 1446)
"Acta in funere magistri Gatemelatae in civitate Patavina." In Eroli, *Erasmo Gattamelata*, pp. 354–61. Padua, 1443. Giovanni Pontano on Gattamelata.

PONTICO VIRUNIO, LUDOVICO (ca. 1460–1520)
. . . *oratio in funere Elisabeth Vicedominae Trimeris* (Reggio: P. Virunius, after 2 April 1517). Place unknown, 1517. Ludovico Pontico Virunio on Elisabetta Visdomini.

PORCARI, CAMILLO (d. 1521)
"Oratio funebris pro cardinalis [*sic*] Senogalliensis [*sic*]." BAV, MS Vat. lat. 8106, fols. 70–76v; *Iter*, 2:344. Rome, 1516. Camillo Porcari on Marco Vigerio.

POZZO, FRANCESCO DAL (called "PUTEOLANO")
"Oratio funebris pro . . . Sfortia Maria Vicecomite duce . . . ." Cremona, Bibl. Governativa, MS Civico BB 2.5.2 (second bundle beginning with a letter of Francesco Filelfo a Ludovico Maria Sforza),

[fols. 6–7 (fragm.)]; *Iter*, 1:52. Place unknown, 1479. Francesco Dal Pozzo on Sforza Maria Sforza.

PRIULI, EUSEBIO, O. CAMALD. (d. ca. 1531)
... *pro* ... *Petro Delphino eiusdem ordinis generali* ... *funebris oratio* ([s.l.: s.t., s.a.]). Venice?, 1525. Eusebio Priuli on Pietro Dolfin.

PUCCI, FRANCESCO (1463–1512)
1. "Oratio habita in funere Francisci Minutoli . . . ." Naples, Bibl. Nazionale, MS V F 2, fols. 1–4v; *Iter*, 1:418. Naples, before 1491. Francesco Pucci on Francesco Minutolo.
2. "Oratio . . . habita in funere Silvestri Galeoti regis archiatri." Ibid., fols. 5–11. Naples, 1488? Francesco Pucci on Silvestro Galeota.
3. "Oratio . . . dicta Neapoli in aede divi Dominici . . . [in funere Regis Mathiae]." In *Nuovi documenti*, ed. De Marinis and Perosa, pp. 251–58. Naples, 1490. Francesco Pucci on Mattia Corvino.

PUTEOLANUS, FRANCISCUS. *See* POZZO, FRANCESCO DAL

QUIRINI, GIOVANNI (DI NICCOLÒ)
... *oratio in eximii viri Benedicti Brugnoli laudem* (Venice: s.t., 1502). Venice, 1502. Giovanni Quirini on Benedetto Brugnoli.

QUIRINI, LAURO (ca. 1420–81)
"In funere . . . imperatoris Cattamelatae de Narnia oratio." In Eroli, *Erasmo Gattamelata*, pp. 348–53. Padua?, 1443. Lauro Quirini on Gattamelata.

RAMUSIO, GIOVANNI BATTISTA (1485–1557)
"In funere Francisci Faseoli magni Venetiarum cancellarii . . . oratio." In *Orationes clarorum hominum* (Cologne, 1560), pp. 386–93. Venice, 1516. Giovanni Battista Ramusio on Francesco Fasolo.

RANSANUS, PETRUS, O.P. *See* RANZANO, PIETRO, O.P.

RANZANO, PIETRO, O.P. (ca. 1427/28–92)
Oratio in funere Francisci Toletani Cauriensis episcopi ([Rome: Iohann Bulle, after 15 March 1479]); Hain 13692. Rome, 1479. Pietro Ranzano on Francesco da Toledo.

RASINI, BALDASSARE (d. 1468)
1. "Oratio funerea in commemorationem doctorum atque scholasticorum hac qui achademia vita excesserunt . . . ." London, British Library, MS Arundel 138, fols. 354–55v. Pavia, date unknown. Baldassare Rasini on professors and students (I).
2. "Oratio . . . in funerabilibus [*sic*] electorum et scolarium . . . ." BAV,

MS Palat. lat. 1592, fols. 93v–96v; *Iter*, 2:397–98. Pavia, 1447? Baldassare Rasini on professors and students (II).
3. ". . . oratio de . . . Francisci Sfortiae ligurum ducis laudibus . . . ." BAV, MS Ottob. lat. 1834, fols. 1–26v; *Iter*, 2:433. Pavia, 1467. Baldassare Rasini on Francesco Sforza.

RAUDENSIS, ANTONIUS, O.F.M. *See* ANTONIO DA RHO, O.F.M.

RINUCCINI, ALAMANNO (1426–99)
"In funere Matthaei Palmerii oratio . . . ." In *Lettere ed orazioni*, ed. Giustiniani, pp. 78–85. Florence, 1475. Alamanno Rinuccini on Matteo Palmieri.

ROCCA, LORENZO
. . . *oratio pro funere Aloysii Dardanii Veneti scribae maximi* (Venice: P. F. de Consortibus, 1511). Venice?, 1511? Lorenzo Rocca on Luigi Dardani.

RUFFO, MATTEO
"Oratio . . . habita paene ex tempore in funere . . . archiepiscopi Dyrachiensis in urbe Verona suffraganei." Padua, Bibl. del Seminario, MS 116, fols. 1–4v; *Iter*, 2:11–12. Verona, 1487. Matteo Ruffo on Marco Cattanei.

SABELLICO (COCCIO, MARC ANTONIO) (1436–1506)
1. "Oratio dicta Venetiis in funere Zacchariae Barbari . . . ." In *Opera omnia* (Basel: I. Hervagius, 1560), 4:cols. 494B–97A. Venice, ca. 1492. Sabellico on Zaccaria Barbaro.
2. "Oratio dicta Venetiis in funere Benedicti Rugii regii oratoris . . . ." Ibid., 4:cols. 497B–501A. Venice, date unknown. Sabellico on Benedetto Rugio.

SADOLETO, IACOPO (1477–1547)
1. "Oratio . . . in funere Oliverii Carafae cardinalis Neapolitani . . . ." In Antonio Altamura, "Il Cardinale Oliviero Carafa in un'orazione inedita del Sadoleto," *Rassegna storica napolitana*, n.s. 1 (1940): 320–28. Rome, 1511. Iacopo Sadoleto on Oliviero Carafa.
2. "De obitu . . . Cardinalis Federici Fregosi homilia." In *Opera omnia*, 4 vols. (Verona, 1737–38; reprinted Ridgewood, N.J.: Gregg, 1964), 3:14–29. Rome, 1541. Iacopo Sadoleto on Federigo Fregoso.

SANGIORGI, GIOVANNI ANTONIO (d. 1509)
Oratio funebris . . . in exsequiis . . . cardinalis Tornacensis ([Rome: Stephan Plannck, after 16 October 1483]); Hain 7597. Rome?, 1483. Giovanni Antonio Sangiorgi on Ferry de Clugny.

SAPIA, SEBASTIANO (1462–1523)
. . . *oratio in funere iureconsultorum principis Iasonis Maini* . . . (Pavia: Iacobus de Burgo Franco, 1520). Pavia?, 1519. Sebastiano Sapia on Giasone del Maino.

SASSI, CRISTOFORO (1499–1574)
* 1. [Funeral oration for Francesco Maturanzio]. Perugia, 1518.
2. ". . . oratio in funere Lucae Alberti Podiani Perusini medici praestantissimi." BAV, MS Vat. lat. 5891, fols. 1–6; *Iter*, 2:336. Perugia, 1552. Cristoforo Sassi on Luca Alberto Podiani.

SCEVOLA, NICCOLÒ (d. 1555)
1. ". . . in funere Alfonsi Cardonii." Florence, Bibl. Nazionale, MS Conventi soppressi J VII 5, fols. 187–88v; *Iter*, 1:163. Spoleto?, date unknown. Niccolò Scevola on Alfonso Cardoni.
2. "In funere Clarelii? Lupi Spoletini oratio . . . ." Ibid., fols. 189–93v. Spoleto?, date unknown. Niccolò Scevola on Chiarello? Lupi.
3. ". . . in funere Sebastiani Rachiani?." Ibid., fols. 194–96v. Spoleto?, date unknown. Niccolò Scevola on Sebastiano Racchiani?.

SCLARICI DAL GAMBARO, TOMMASO (1455–1507)
"Oratio funebris quam in adverso Galli fato Boazanus habuit ad Cocos . . . ." In *Oratio funebris sed faceta; Epistola asini ad asinos; Due dialogi* (Bologna: B. Hectoris, 1510), [fols. 2–12v].

SCYLLACIUS, NICOLAUS
* 1. "Oratio in funere Franchinae Bechariae et Hieronymi filii." In *Opuscula* ([Pavia: Giovanni Andrea Bosco, Michele e Bernardino Garaldi], 9 March 1496); Hain 14572. Pavia?, date unknown.
* 2. "Oratio in funere Iohannis Attenduli." Ibid. Pavia?, date unknown.

SERATTI, GIOVANNI PEREGRINO
". . . funebris oratio ex tempore." Florence, Bibl. Riccardiana, MS 771, fol. 55r–v; *Iter*, 1:200–201. Place and date unknown. Giovanni Peregrino Seratti on Giovanni da Roma.

SIBILLA, BARTOLOMEO (DA MONOPOLI), O.P. (d. before 31 October 1493)
1. "Oratio . . . in lucubractionibus exsequiarum . . . Francisci de Baucio et aliis." Florence, Bibl. Nazionale, MS Conventi soppressi J VII 5, fols. 211–17v; *Iter*, 1:163. Place unknown, 1483. Bartolomeo Sibilla on Franciscus de Baucio and companions.
2. "Oratio . . . in exsequiis . . . ducissae Calabriae . . . ." Ibid., fols. 218–22v. Monopoli?, 1488? Bartolomeo Sibilla on Ippolita Maria Sforza.

Appendix: List of Funeral Orations 289

SIGHICELLI, GASPARE, O.P. (d. 1457)
"In funere Nicolai Albergati bononiensis . . . ." Milan, Bibl. Ambrosiana, MS L 69 sup., fols. 196–201; *Iter*, 1:333–34. Bologna, 1443. Gaspare Sighicelli on Niccolò Albergati.

SOARDI, ARMACHIDE
". . . in laudibus Petri Francisci Brembati eiusdem ordinis ac civitatis viri funebris oratio." Padua, Bibl. Capitolare, MS B 62, fols. 163–68; *Iter*, 2:6. Padua?, 1465. Armachide Soardi on Pier Francesco Brembati.

SOLERIO, ANTONIO (DA CARPI)
. . . *in funere Petri Canonici . . . oratio* (Bologna: Caligula de Bazaleriis, 1502), [fols. 3v–6v]. Bologna, 1502. Antonio Solerio on Pietro Canonici.

SPAGN[U]OLI, BATTISTA, O. CARM. *See* BATTISTA MANTOVANO, O. CARM.

STELLA, GIROLAMO, O. CARM.
* "In funere archiepiscopi Mediolanensis, videlicet . . . Bartholomaei." Casale Monferrato, Seminario Vescovile, MS 1 b 20, fols. 63vff.; *Iter*, 1:40. Basel, 1433.

STERPONI, STEFANO (DA PESCIA, called PHILOPONUS)
1. ". . . oratio funebris in parentalia Laurentii Medicis Urbini ducis . . . ." Florence, Bibl. Riccardiana, MS 911, fols. 12–19v; *Iter*, 1:208–9. Florence, 1519. Stefano Sterponi on Lorenzo de' Medici, duke of Urbino.
2. ". . . oratio funebris in parentalia Alexandri Puccii equitis aurati . . . ." Ibid., fols. 20–26. Florence, date unknown. Stefano Sterponi on Alessandro Pucci.

STRASSOLDO, LUDOVICO, O.F.M. (d. 1446)
1. "Oratio funerea . . . pro . . . Francisco Cornario . . . ." Siena, Bibl. Comunale degli Intronati, MS H VI 26, fols. 91–93v; *Iter*, 2:165. Padua?, 1420. Ludovico Strassoldo on Francesco Corner.
* 2. "Oratio habita in funere clarissimi viri Bartholomaei Cermisono [sic]." Leningrad, Archive of the Institute of History of the Academy of Sciences (LOII), MS 1/614, fols. 55–58. Padua, 1429.

SUARDUS, ARMACHIDES. *See* SOARDI, ARMACHIDE

SUPERCHI, GIOVANNI FRANCESCO, called PHILOMUSUS
". . . oratio in funere . . . equitis Nicolai Savorgnani." Milan, Bibl. Trivulziana, MS 783, fols. 6–12v; *Iter*, 1:363. Cividale del Friuli?, date unknown. Giovanni Francesco Superchi on Niccolò Savorgnan.

TELESIO, ANTONIO (DA COSENZA) (1482–1534)
. . . *oratio quam habuit in funere illustrissimi Ioannis Iacobi Trivultii*
(Milan: Aug. de Vicomercato, 1519). Milan?, 1518. Antonio Telesio
on Gian Giacomo Trivulzi.

THADDEUS OF LYON, O.E.S.A.
"Oratio funebris habita in funere . . . Claudii Seyssellii archiepiscopi
Taurinensis . . . ." Turin, Archivio di Stato (Sezione 1), MS Bibl.
Antica H II 25, pp. 11–18; *Iter*, 2:176. Turin, 1520. Thaddeus of Lyon
on Claude de Seyssel.

TICIONUS, LUDOVICUS. *See* TIZZONE, LUDOVICO

TIMOTEO DA MODENA, O.P. (TIMOTHEUS DE TOTIS DE MUTINA)
"Oratio de funere . . . Ludovici de Ferraria totius ordinis praedicato-
rum procuratoris dignissimi." In *Oratio in funere Ludovici de Ferraria.
Sermones duo coram Alexandro VI* ([Rome: Eucharius Silber, after 4
May 1497]); Hain 15584. Rome?, 1496. Timoteo da Modena on Ludo-
vico da Ferrara.

TIZZONE, LUDOVICO
"Oratio edita . . . in funerali pompa . . . comitissae Maxini sed non
habita." Turin, Bibl. Nazionale, MS J III 13, fols. 364–65; *Iter*, 2:181–
82. Place and date unknown. Ludovico Tizzone on Countess Maxine.

TORTELLI, GIOVANNI (1400–1466)
? ["Oratio in funere Ludovici Scarampi cardinalis Aquileiensis"]. BAV,
MS Barb. lat. 1952, fols. 178–82v; *Iter*, 2:448. Rome, 1465. Giovanni
Tortelli? on Ludovico Trevisan.

TRAVERSINI, PIETRO, O. CARM.
". . . sermo in funere . . . Petri Spagnoli vulgari sermone recitatus."
Mantua, Bibl. Comunale, MS F II 6, fols. 439–44 (in Latin); *Iter*,
1:274. Place and date unknown. Pietro Traversini on Pietro Spagnoli.

TREBIZOND (TRAPEZUNTIUS), GEORGE OF (1395–1486)
"Oratio funebris in Fantinum Michaelem." In *Collectanea Trapezuntiana*, ed. Monfasani, pp. 445–58. Venice, 1434. George of Trebizond
on Fantino Michiel.

TUDERTINUS, ANTONIUS PACINUS. *See* PACINI, ANTONIO

UBALDINO
"Pro Cardinali Puccio." BAV, MS Vat. lat. 8106, fols. 23–30v (repeated
on fols. 32–39); *Iter*, 2:344. Rome, 1531. Ubaldino on Lorenzo Pucci.

UBERTI, FRANCESCO (ca. 1440–1518)
* "Oratio in funere Malatestae Novelli." Rimini, Bibl. Civ. Gambalunga, MS 4 H IV 2, fols. 2ff.; *Iter*, 2:89. The manuscript is apparently now MS SC-1251 (information supplied by Professor Kristeller). Cesena, 1465.

URSINUS, IORDANUS. See ORSINI, GIORDANO

VALERIANO, PIERO (or PIERIO or GIANPIETRO) (1477–1558)
. . . *oratio in funere Hieronymi Turriani Veronensis* (Padua: Lazarus Soardus, 1506). Padua, 1506. Piero Valeriano on Girolamo della Torre.

VARINI, GIAN FRANCESCO
1. "In funere Hieronymi Cassinarii oratio." BAV, MS Vat. lat. 2850, fols. 51v–53v; *Iter*, 2:354. Place and date unknown. Gian Francesco Varini on Girolamo Cassinari (I).
2. "Pro eodem domi eiusdem." Ibid., fols. 53v–54. Place and date unknown. Gian Francesco Varini on Girolamo Cassinari (II).
3. "Pro Bartholomaeo Cassinario oratio." Ibid., fols. 54–55. Place unknown, 1495? Gian Francesco Varini on Bartolomeo Cassinari (I).
4. "Pro eodem domi eiusdem." Ibid., fol. 55. Place unknown, 1495? Gian Francesco Varini on Bartolomeo Cassinari (II).
5. "Pro eodem in exsequiis quae septimo die fiunt." Ibid., fols. 55–56. Place unknown, 1495? Gian Francesco Varini on Bartolomeo Cassinari (III).
6. "In funere Catharinae Scarpae oratio." Ibid., fol. 56r–v. Place and date unknown. Gian Francesco Varini on Caterina Scarpa.
7. "Pro Hieronymo Gripho oratio." Ibid., fol. 120. Place and date unknown. Gian Francesco Varini on Girolamo Grifi.
8. "In funere Ioannis Baptistae Cassandrae Perusini oratio." Ibid., fols. 155–56. Place unknown, 1497. Gian Francesco Varini on Gian Battista Cassandra.

VEGERIUS, CONRADUS
. . . *funebris oratio in mortem . . . Hadriani VI . . . habita Romae* (Rome: s.t., 1523). Rome, 1523. Conradus Vegerius on Adrian VI.

VERGERIO, PIER PAOLO (ca. 1368–1444)
"Oratio in funere Francisci senioris de Carraria Patavii principis." *RIS*, 16:cols. 194B–98C. Padua, 1393. Pier Paolo Vergerio on Francesco il Vecchio da Carrara.

VIGERIO, MARCO, O.F.M. (1446–1516)
"Oratio habita . . . in funere . . . Sixti papae quarti . . . ." BAV, MS

Urb. lat. 1023, fols. 397–403v; Stornajolo, *Codices Urbinates latini*, 3:12–16. Savona, 1484. Marco Vigerio on Sixtus IV.

VIGILIO, FRANCESCO

"Oratio . . . habita in funere . . . domini Francisci Gonzagae marchionis Mantuae." Mantua, Archivio di Stato, MS Archivio Gonzaga 85 (B XXXIII 10), fols. 126–34v; *Iter*, 1:269. Mantua, 1519. Francesco Vigilio on Francesco II Gonzaga.

ZABARELLA, FRANCESCO (1360–1417)

1. "Oratio in obitu . . . domini Francisci eius genitoris obnixe plorans." *RIS*, 16:cols. 243A–48A. Padua, 1393. Francesco Zabarella on Francesco il Vecchio da Carrara.
2. "Consolatio de morte filii." In Zonta, *Zabarella*, pp. 139–41. Padua, 1398. Francesco Zabarella on Niccolò da Carrara.
3. "In funere . . . Arcoani Buzzacharini oratio." Ibid., pp. 142–44. Padua, 1403. Francesco Zabarella on Arcoano Buzzacarini.
4. "In exsequiis et funere . . . Ioannis Ludovici de Lambertatiis . . . oratio." Naples, Bibl. Nazionale, MS V E 40, fol. 10r–v; *Iter*, 1:401. Padua, 1401. Francesco Zabarella on Giovanni Ludovico Lambertazzi.
* 5. "Pro domino Andrea de Vicecomitibus generali humiliatorum in conventu . . . ." Vienna, Nationalbibliothek, MS Lat. 5513, fols. 99v–100v; *Iter*, 3:64–66. Place unknown, 1410.
* 6. "Pro funebri honore domini Anthonii quondam cardinalis Aquilegensis oratio." Ibid., fols. 105–7. Rome?, 1412.
* 7. "In memoria defuncti [Bartholomaei Paradisii]." Ibid., fols. 152–53. Place and date unknown.
* 8. "In morte [Omneboni] rectoris." Ibid., fols. 158v–59. Place and date unknown.
* 9. "In funere strenui militis Patari de Buzacharinis." Ibid., fols. 190v–91v. Padua?, date unknown.
*10. "Pro filio domini Medii Comitis defuncto . . . in exsequiis." Ibid., fols. 198v–99. Padua?, 1391.

ZAMBERTI, BARTOLOMEO (ca. 1473–after July 1539)

". . . in funere Georgii Vallae Placentini . . . oratio." In Rose, "Bartolomeo Zamberti's Funeral Oration," pp. 303–7. Venice, 1500. Bartolomeo Zamberti on Giorgio Valla.

ZENO, IACOPO (1418–81)

"Oratio in funere cardinalis Iuliani Caesarini." Cortona, Bibl. Comunale, MS 162 (243), fols. 1–6; Mazzatinti, 18:70. Rome, 1445. Iacopo Zeno on Giuliano Cesarini.

Acta Concilii Constanciensis. Edited by Heinrich Finke et al. 4 vols. Münster i. W.: Regensbergsche Buchhandlung, 1896–1928.
Adalbert of Prague. *Leben und Schriften des Prager Magisters Adalbert Rankonis de Ericinio*. Edited by Jaroslav Kadlec. Beiträge zur Geschichte der Philosophie und Theologie des Mittelalters, Neue Folge 4. Münster i. W.: Aschendorff, 1971.
Adamo di Montaldo. *See* Montaldo, Adamo di.
Alberti, Leon Battista. *Il cane*. Translated by Piero di Marco Parenti. Ancona: Aurelli G. E. Comp., 1847.
Andrieu, Michel. "L'origine du titre de Cardinal dans l'Eglise romaine." In *Miscellanea Giovanni Mercati*, vol. 5, pp. 113–44. Studi e testi 125. Vatican City: BAV, 1946.
Anecdota litteraria. Edited by G. C. Amaduzzi and G. L. Bianconi. 4 vols. Rome: A. Fulgonius, 1773–83.
Anonymous. "Oratio in laudem Thadei Quirino [sic]." BAV, MS Chigi. I VI 215, fols. 144v–46.
Antonovics, A. V. "The Library of Cardinal Domenico Capranica." In *Cultural Aspects of the Italian Renaissance: Essays in Honour of Paul Oskar Kristeller*, edited by Cecil H. Clough, pp. 141–59. Manchester: Manchester University Press; New York: A. F. Zambelli, 1976.
Approaches to the Second Sophistic: Papers Presented at the 105th Annual Meeting of the American Philological Association. Edited by G. W. Bowersock. University Park, Pa.: American Philological Association, 1974.
Arasse, Daniel. "Andrea Biglia contre Saint Bernardin de Sienne: l'humanisme et la fonction de l'image religieuse." In *Acta conventus neo-latini Turonensis*, edited by Jean-Claude Margolin, 2 vols., 1:417–37. Paris: J. Vrin, 1980.
Arbesmann, Rudolph, O.S.A. *Der Augustinereremitenorden und der Beginn der humanistischen Bewegung*. Cassiciacum 19. Würzburg: Augustinus, 1965.
Arendt, Paul. *Die Predigten des Konstanzer Konzils: ein Beitrag zur Predigt- und Kirchengeschichte des ausgehenden Mittelalters*. Freiburg: Herder, 1933.
Aurelius Romanus. "Ex Menandro Rhetore in secundo divisionis demonstrativi generis capite de oratione funebri caput XIIII." Perugia, Bibl. Comunale Augusta, MS Fondo Vecchio C 61, fols. 121v–23v.

Austin, R. G. "Quintilian on Painting and Statuary." *Classical Quarterly* 38 (1944): 17–26.
Barker, John W. *Manuel II Palaeologus (1391–1425): A Study in Late Byzantine Statesmanship.* New Brunswick: Rutgers University Press, 1969.
Baron, Hans. "Cicero and the Roman Civic Spirit in the Middle Ages and the Early Renaissance." *Bulletin of the John Rylands Library* 22 (1938): 72–97.
———. *The Crisis of the Early Italian Renaissance.* 1st ed. 2 vols. Princeton: Princeton University Press, 1955. Rev. ed. Princeton: Princeton University Press, 1966.
———. *From Petrarch to Leonardo Bruni: Studies in Humanistic and Political Literature.* Chicago: University of Chicago Press, 1968.
———. *Humanistic and Political Literature in Florence and Venice at the Beginning of the Quattrocento: Studies in Criticism and Chronology.* Cambridge: Harvard University Press, 1955.
Barzizza, Gasparino, and Guiniforte Barzizza. *Gasparini Barzizii et Guinifortis filii opera.* Edited by G. A. Furietti. Rome: I. Salvonius, 1723.
Baxandall, Michael. *Giotto and the Orators: Humanist Observers of Painting in Italy and the Discovery of Pictorial Composition, 1350–1450.* Oxford: Clarendon Press, 1971.
———. "Guarino, Pisanello and Manuel Chrysoloras." *Journal of the Warburg and Courtauld Institutes* 28 (1965): 183–204.
Bayley, C. C. *War and Society in Renaissance Florence: The "De Militia" of Leonardo Bruni.* Toronto: University of Toronto Press, 1961.
Beale, Walter. "Rhetorical Performative Discourse: A New Theory of Epideictic." *Philosophy and Rhetoric* 11 (1978): 221–46.
Bembo, Bonifazio. *In Ludovici Mariae Sfortiae (cognomine Mauri) laudes oratio.* [Milan: Leonhard Pachel, after 28 November 1490]; GW 3809.
Bentley, Jerry H. *Humanists and Holy Writ: New Testament Scholarship in the Renaissance.* Princeton: Princeton University Press, 1983.
———. "New Testament Scholarship at Louvain in the Early Sixteenth Century." *Studies in Medieval and Renaissance History,* n.s. 2 (1979): 51–79.
Bernardo, Flavio di. *Un vescovo umanista alla Corte Pontificia: Giannantonio Campano (1429–1477).* Miscellanea Historiae Pontificiae 39. Rome: Gregorian University Press, 1975.
Berrigan, Joseph R. "Benzo d'Alessandria and the Cities of Northern Italy." *Studies in Medieval and Renaissance History* 4 (1967): 125–92.
Bertalot, Ludwig. "Eine Sammlung paduaner Reden des XV. Jahrhunderts." In *Studien zum italienischen und deutschen Humanismus,* edited by Paul Oskar Kristeller, 2 vols., 2:209–35. Raccolta di studi e testi 129–30. Rome: Storia e letteratura, 1975.
———. "Uno zibaldone umanistico latino del Quattrocento a Parma." In *Studien zum italienischen und deutschen Humanismus,* edited by Paul Oskar

Kristeller, 2 vols., 2:241–64. Raccolta di studi e testi 129–30. Rome: Storia e letteratura, 1975.

———. "Zur Bibliographie der Übersetzungen des Leonardus Brunus Aretinus." *Quellen und Forschungen aus italienischen Archiven und Bibliotheken* 27 (1937): 178–95.

Bettini, Maurizio. *Antropologia e cultura romana: parentela, tempo, immagini dell'anima*. Rome: La Nuova Italia Scientifica, 1986.

Beyer, Hermann W. "Diakonia." In *Theological Dictionary of the New Testament*, edited by Gerhard Kittel and translated by Geoffrey W. Bromiley, 2: 81–93. Grand Rapids, Mich.: Eerdmans, 1964.

Bitzer, Lloyd. "The Rhetorical Situation." *Philosophy and Rhetoric* 1 (1968): 1–14.

Black, C. F. "The Baglioni as Tyrants of Perugia, 1488–1540." *English Historical Review* 85 (1970): 245–81.

Blanshei, Sarah. "Population, Wealth, and Patronage in Medieval and Renaissance Perugia." *Journal of Interdisciplinary History* 9 (1978–79): 597–619.

Blench, J. W. *Preaching in England in the Late Fifteenth and Sixteenth Centuries: A Study of English Sermons 1450–c. 1600*. New York: Barnes & Noble, 1964.

Blumenberg, Hans. "Der archimedische Punkt des Celio Calcagnini." In *Studia Humanitatis Ernesto Grassi zum 70. Geburtstag*, edited by E. Hora and E. Kessler, pp. 103–12. Munich: W. Fink, 1973.

Boerner, Chr. Frid. *De doctis hominibus Graecis litterarum Graecarum in Italia instauratoribus liber*. Leipzig: I. F. Gleditschius, 1750.

Bombe, Walter. "Der Palast des Braccio Baglioni in Perugia und Domenico Veneziano." *Repertorium für Kunstwissenschaft* 32 (1909): 295–301.

Bonisoli, Ognibene. Untitled panegyric for Pietro Foscari. BAV, MS Regin. lat. 1555, fols. 48–58.

Bowersock, G. W. *Greek Sophists in the Roman Empire*. Oxford: Clarendon Press, 1969.

Bracciolini, Poggio. *Opera omnia*. Edited by Riccardo Fubini. 4 vols. Turin: Bottega d'Erasmo, 1964–66.

———. "Oratio ad patres reverendissimos." Edited by Riccardo Fubini. In "Il 'teatro del mondo' nelle prospettive morali e storico-politiche di Poggio Bracciolini." In *Poggio Bracciolini 1380–1980 (nel VI centenario della nascita)*, pp. 93–132. Istituto Nazionale di Studi sul Rinascimento, Studi e Testi 8. Florence: Sansoni, 1982.

———. *Two Renaissance Book Hunters: The Letters of Poggius Bracciolini to Nicolaus de Niccolis*. Translated by Phyllis Gordan. Records of Civilization: Sources and Studies 91. New York: Columbia University Press, 1974.

Branca, Vittore. "Ermolao Barbaro and Late Quattrocento Venetian Humanism." In *Renaissance Venice*, edited by J. R. Hale, pp. 218–43. London: Faber & Faber, 1973.

Britannico, Gregorio. *Sermones funebres et nuptiales.* Milan: L. Pachel, 14 March 1496; *GW* 5549.

———. *Sermones funebres necnon nuptiales.* Venice: per Victorem .q. Petri a Rabanis et socios, 1533.

Brown, Alison M. "The Humanist Portrait of Cosimo de' Medici, Pater Patriae." *Journal of the Warburg and Courtauld Institutes* 24 (1961): 186–221.

Brown, Peter. *The Cult of the Saints.* Chicago: University of Chicago Press, 1981.

Brucker, Gene. *The Civic World of Early Renaissance Florence.* Princeton: Princeton University Press, 1977.

Bruni, Leonardo. "De studiis et litteris." In *Il pensiero pedagogico dell'umanesimo*, edited by Eugenio Garin, pp. 147–71. I classici della pedagogia italiana 2. Florence: Giuntine and Sansoni, 1958.

———. "Laudatio Florentinae urbis." Edited by Hans Baron. In *From Petrarch to Leonardo Bruni: Studies in Humanistic and Political Literature*, pp. 232–63. Chicago and London: University of Chicago Press, 1968. English translation by Benjamin Kohl in *The Earthly Republic: Italian Humanists on Government and Society*, edited by Benjamin Kohl and Ronald Witt, pp. 135–75. Philadelphia: University of Pennsylvania Press, 1978.

———. *Leonardi Bruni Arretini Epistolarum libri VIII.* Edited by L. Mehus. Florence: Paperinius, 1741.

———. "Prologus in Basilii Epistolam. . . ." In *Humanistisch-philosophische Schriften*, edited by Hans Baron, pp. 99–100. Berlin and Leipzig: B. G. Teubner, 1928.

———. "Prologus in Phaedonem Platonis." In *Humanistisch-philosophische Schriften*, edited by Hans Baron, pp. 3–4. Berlin and Leipzig: B. G. Teubner, 1928.

———. *Rerum suo tempore gestarum Commentarius.* In *RIS*, n.s. 19, no. 3 (fasc. 4–5): 403–69.

Bucci, Gabriele, O.E.S.A. *Il Memoriale Quadripartitum di Fra Gabriele Bucci da Carmagnola.* Edited by Faustino Curlo. Biblioteca della Società Storica Subalpina 63. Pinerolo: G. Brugnolo, 1911.

Buchheit, Vinzenz. *Untersuchungen zur Theorie des Genos Epideiktikon von Gorgias bis Aristoteles.* Munich: M. Hueber, 1960.

Büchner, Karl. *Somnium Scipionis: Quellen, Gestalt, Sinn.* Hermes Einzelschriften Heft 36. Wiesbaden: F. Steiner, 1976.

Bullard, Melissa. *Filippo Strozzi and the Medici: Favor and Finance in Sixteenth-Century Florence and Rome.* Cambridge and New York: Cambridge University Press, 1980.

Burchard, Johann. *Liber Notarum.* Edited by Enrico Celani. In *RIS*, n.s. 32, nos. 1–2.

Burckhardt, Jacob. *The Civilization of the Renaissance in Italy*. Translated by S. G. C. Middlemore. Oxford and London: Phaidon, 1945.
Burgess, Theodore. "Epideictic Literature." *University of Chicago Studies in Classical Philology* 3 (1902): 89–261.
Bustico, Guido. *Due umanisti veneti: Urbano Bolzanio e Pierio Valeriano*. Florence: A. Vallecchi, 1932. Reprinted from *Civiltà moderna* 4 (1932): 6–24.
Cammelli, Giuseppe. *I dotti bizantini e le origini dell'umanesimo*, vol. 1, *Manuele Crisolora*. Florence: Vallecchi, 1941.
Camporeale, Salvatore. "Da Lorenzo Valla a Tommaso Moro: lo statuto umanistico della teologia." *Memorie Domenicane*, n.s. 4 (1973): 9–102.
———. "Lorenzo Valla *Repastinatio, Liber Primus*: retorica e linguaggio." In *Renaissance Studies in Honor of Craig Hugh Smyth*, 2 vols., 1:261–79. Florence: Giunti Barbèra, 1985.
———. "Lorenzo Valla tra Medioevo e Rinascimento: *Encomion S. Thomae* (1457)." *Memorie Domenicane*, n.s. 7 (1976): 11–194.
———. *Lorenzo Valla: umanesimo e teologia*. Florence: Istituto nazionale di studi sul Rinascimento, 1972.
———. "Umanesimo e teologia tra '400 e '500." *Memorie Domenicane*, n.s. 8–9 (1977–78): 411–36.
Chambers, D. S. "The Housing Problems of Cardinal Francesco Gonzaga." *Journal of the Warburg and Courtauld Institutes* 39 (1976): 21–58.
———. *The Imperial Age of Venice 1380–1580*. London and New York: Harcourt Brace Jovanovich, 1970.
Charland, Th.-M. *Artes praedicandi: contribution à l'histoire de la rhétorique au Moyen Age*. Publications de l'Institut d'Etudes Médiévales d'Ottawa 7. Paris: J. Vrin, 1936.
Chastel, André. *Art et humanisme à Florence au temps de Laurent le Magnifique: études sur la Renaissance et l'humanisme Platonicien*. Paris: Les presses universitaires, 1961.
Chiappini, Luciano. *Gli Estensi*. Milan: Dall'Oglio, 1967.
Cipriani, Giovanni. *Il mito etrusco nel Rinascimento fiorentino*. Biblioteca di storia toscana moderna e contemporanea, Studi e documenti 22. Florence: L. Olschki, 1980.
Clough, Cecil H. "Federigo da Montefeltro's Patronage of the Arts, 1468–1482." *Journal of the Warburg and Courtauld Institutes* 36 (1973): 129–44.
Cognasso, Francesco. "Istituzioni comunali e signorili di Milano sotto i Visconti." In *Storia di Milano*, vol. 6, *Il ducato visconteo e la repubblica ambrosiana 1392–1450*, pp. 449–544. Milan: Fondazione Treccani degli Alfieri, 1955.
Constantius, Antonius, and Iacobus Constantius. [*Opera*]. Fano: H. Soncinus, 1502.

Corio, Bernardino. *Storia di Milano*. Edited by Angelo Butti and Luigi Ferrario. 3 vols. Milan: F. Colombo, 1856.
Cousin, Jean. *Etudes sur Quintilien*. 2 vols. Paris: Boivin, 1936.
Curtius, Ernst Robert. *European Literature and the Latin Middle Ages*. Translated by W. Trask. 1953. Reprinted New York: Harper & Row, 1963.
D'Amico, John. *Renaissance Humanism in Papal Rome: Humanists and Churchmen on the Eve of the Reformation*. The Johns Hopkins University Studies in Historical and Political Science, ser. 101, no. 1. Baltimore: The Johns Hopkins University Press, 1983.
Dati, Leonardo. *Epistolae XXXIII*. Edited by L. Mehus. Florence: Io. Paulus Giovannelli, 1743.
Davies, M. C. "The Senator and the Schoolmaster: Friends of Leonardo Bruni Aretino in a New Letter." *Humanistica Lovaniensia* 33 (1984): 1–21.
Davis, Charles. "An Early Florentine Political Theorist: Fra Remigio de' Girolami." *Proceedings of the American Philosophical Society* 104 (1960): 662–76.
Decembrio, Pier Candido. "De laudibus Mediolanensium urbis panegyricus." Edited by Giuseppe Petraglione. In *RIS*, n.s. 20, no. 1:1011–25.
Delle orazioni volgarmente scritte da diversi uomini illustri. Edited by Francesco Sansovino. 2 vols. Lyon: G. and V. Lanais, 1741.
DeNeef, A. Leigh. "Epideictic Rhetoric and the Renaissance Lyric." *Journal of Medieval and Renaissance Studies* 3 (1973): 203–31.
Dibelius, Martin. *James: A Commentary on the Epistle of James*. Revised by Heinrich Greeven and translated by Michael Williams. Philadelphia: Fortress, 1976.
Diedo, Francesco. "Laudatio in Bartholomaeum Paierinum." Venice, Bibl. Naz. Marciana, MS 4499 (Marc. lat. XIV 236), fols. 64v–76.
Diller, Aubrey. "The Library of Francesco and Ermolao Barbaro." *Italia medioevale e umanistica* 6 (1963): 253–62.
Downey, G. "Ekphrasis." In *Reallexikon für Antike und Christentum*, 4:921–44. Stuttgart: Hiersemann, 1950–.
Drury, Marcel. "*Laudatio funebris* et rhétorique." *Revue de philologie de littérature et d'histoire anciennes*, ser. 3, 16 (1942): 105–14.
The Earthly Republic: Italian Humanists on Government and Society. Edited by Benjamin Kohl and Ronald Witt. Philadelphia: University of Pennsylvania Press, 1978.
Egidio da Viterbo, O.S.A. e il suo tempo. Rome: ed. Analecta Augustiniana, 1983.
Eörsi, Anna K. "Lo studiolo di Lionello d'Este e il programma di Guarino da Verona." *Acta historiae artium Academiae Scientiarum Hungaricae* 21 (1975): 15–52.

Eroli, Giovanni. *Erasmo Gattamelata da Narni, suoi monumenti e sua famiglia*. Rome: Salviucci, 1876.

Fantuzzi, Giovanni. *Notizie degli scrittori bolognesi*. 9 vols. 1781–94. Reprinted Bologna: Arnaldo Forni, 1965.

Fasoli, Gina. "La coscienza civica nelle *laudes civitatum*." In *Scritti di storia medievale*, edited by F. Bocchi, A. Carile, and A. I. Pini, pp. 293–318. Bologna: La Fotocromo Emiliana, 1974.

———. "Nascita di un mito." In *Scritti di storia medievale*, edited by F. Bocchi, A. Carile, and A. I. Pini, pp. 445–72. Bologna: La Fotocromo Emiliana, 1974.

Fehl, Philipp. *The Classical Monument: Reflections on the Connection between Morality and Art in Greek and Roman Sculpture*. New York: New York University Press, 1972.

Ferguson, Wallace. *The Renaissance in Historical Thought: Five Centuries of Interpretation*. Boston: Houghton Mifflin, 1948.

Ferroni, Giulio. "Appunti sulla politica festiva di Pietro Riario." In *Umanesimo a Roma nel Quattrocento*, edited by Paolo Brezzi and Maristella de Panizza Lorch, pp. 47–65. Rome: Istituto di Studi Romani; New York: Barnard College, 1984.

Finlay, Robert. *Politics in Renaissance Venice*. New Brunswick: Rutgers University Press, 1980.

Fioravanti, Gianfranco. "La cultura in Valdelsa al tempo di Callimaco." In *Callimaco esperiente poeta e politico del '400*, edited by Gian Carlo Garfagnini, pp. 217–45. Florence: L. Olschki, 1987.

———. "Pietro de' Rossi: Bibbia ed Aristotele nella Siena del '400." *Rinascimento* 20 (1980): 87–159.

Flores, Pedro. *Oratio . . . de summo pontifice eligendo Julii II Pontificis maximi successore*. Rome: s.t., 1513.

Foffano, Tino. "La costruzione di Castiglione Olona in un opuscolo inedito di Francesco Pizolpasso." *Italia medioevale e umanistica* 3 (1960): 153–87.

———. "Rapporti tra Italia e Ungheria in occasione delle legazioni del cardinale Branda Castiglioni (1350–1443)." In *Venezia e Ungheria nel Rinascimento*, edited by Vittore Branca, pp. 67–78. Civiltà veneziana: Studi 28. Florence: L. Olschki, 1973.

Fois, Mario. *Il pensiero cristiano di Lorenzo Valla nel quadro storico-culturale del suo ambiente*. Analecta Gregoriana 174. Rome: Gregorian University Press, 1969.

Franceschi, Dora. "L'*Oculus pastoralis* e la sua fortuna." *Atti dell'Accademia delle Scienze di Torino* 99, no. 2 (1964–65): 205–61.

Fraser-Jenkins, A. D. "Cosimo de' Medici's Patronage of Architecture and the Theory of Magnificence." *Journal of the Warburg and Courtauld Institutes* 33 (1970): 162–70.

Frati, Lodovico. "Di Lodovico Carbone e delle sue opere." *Atti e memorie della deputazione ferrarese di storia patria* 20, no. 1 (1910): 53–80.

Freeman, John F. "Louise of Savoy: A Case of Maternal Opportunism." *Sixteenth Century Journal* 3, no. 2 (1972): 77–98.

Fubini, Riccardo. "Un'orazione di Poggio Bracciolini sui vizi del clero scritta al tempo del Concilio di Costanza." *Giornale storico della letteratura italiana* 142 (1965): 24–33.

———. "Osservazioni sugli *Historiarum florentini populi libri XII* di Leonardo Bruni." In *Studi di storia medievale e moderna per Ernesto Sestan*, 2 vols., 1:403–48. Florence: L. Olschki, 1980.

———. "Il 'teatro del mondo' nelle prospettive morali e storico-politiche di Poggio Bracciolini." In *Poggio Bracciolini 1380–1980 (nel VI centenario della nascita)*, pp. 1–135. Istituto nazionale di studi sul Rinascimento, Studi e testi 8. Florence: Sansoni, 1982.

Fumaroli, Marc. "Rhetoric, Politics, and Society: From Italian Ciceronianism to French Classicism." In *Renaissance Eloquence: Studies in the Theory and Practice of Renaissance Rhetoric*, edited by James J. Murphy, pp. 253–73. Berkeley, Los Angeles, and London: University of California Press, 1983.

Gaeta, Franco. "Alcune considerazioni sul mito di Venezia." *Bibliothèque d'humanisme et Renaissance* 23 (1961): 58–75.

———. "Sull'idea di Roma nell'umanesimo e nel Rinascimento (appunti e spunti per una ricerca)." *Studi romani* 25 (1977): 169–86.

Galletti, Alfredo. *L'eloquenza (dalle origini al XVI secolo)*. Storia dei generi letterari italiani. Milan: F. Vallardi, 1904–38.

Ganz, Margery. "Donato Acciaiuoli and the Medici: A Strategy for Survival in '400 Florence." *Rinascimento*, n.s. 22 (1982): 33–73.

Gargan, Luciano. *Lo studio teologico e la biblioteca dei Domenicani a Padova nel Tre e Quattrocento*. Padua: Antenore, 1971.

Garin, Eugenio. "La cultura milanese nella prima metà del XV secolo." In *Storia di Milano*, vol. 6, *Il ducato visconteo e la repubblica ambrosiana 1392–1450*, pp. 545–608. Milan: Fondazione Treccani degli Alfieri, 1955.

———. "Donato Acciaiuoli, cittadino fiorentino." In *Medioevo e Rinascimento*, pp. 211–87. Bari: Laterza, 1961.

———. *L'educazione in Europa 1400–1600: problemi e programmi*. Bari: Laterza, 1957.

———. "Ritratto di Leonardo Bruni Aretino." *Atti e memorie della Accademia Petrarca di lettere, arti e scienze*, n.s. 40 (1970–72): 1–17.

Garofalo, Salvatore. "Gli umanisti italiani del secolo XV e la Bibbia." In *La Bibbia e il Concilio di Trento*, pp. 338–75. Scripta Pontifici Instituti Biblici 96. Rome: Pontifical Biblical Institute, 1947.

Gasparini, Giuseppina De Sandre. "Uno studio sull'episcopato padovano di Pietro Barozzi (1487–1507) e altri contributi sui vescovi veneti nel Quattrocento: problemi e linee di ricerca." *Rivista di storia della Chiesa in Italia* 34 (1980): 81–122.

Geanakoplos, Deno. *Greek Scholars in Venice*. Cambridge: Harvard University Press, 1962.

———. *Interaction of the "Sibling" Byzantine and Western Cultures in the Middle Ages and Italian Renaissance (330–1600)*. New Haven and London: Yale University Press, 1976.

Giannetto, Nella. *Bernardo Bembo: umanista e politico veneziano*. Civiltà veneziana: Saggi 34. Florence: L. Olschki, 1985.

Giesey, Ralph. *The Royal Funeral Ceremony in Renaissance France*. Geneva: Droz, 1960.

Gilbert, Felix. "The Date of the Composition of Contarini's and Giannotti's Books on Venice." *Studies in the Renaissance* 14 (1967): 172–84.

———. "The Humanist Concept of the Prince and *The Prince* of Machiavelli." *Journal of Modern History* 11 (1939): 449–83. Reprinted in *History: Choice and Commitment*, pp. 91–114. Cambridge: Harvard University Press, 1977.

———. *Machiavelli and Guicciardini: Politics and History in Sixteenth-Century Florence*. Princeton: Princeton University Press, 1965.

———. "The Renaissance Interest in History." In *Art, Science, and History in the Renaissance*, edited by Charles S. Singleton, pp. 373–87. Baltimore: The Johns Hopkins University Press, 1967.

Gill, Joseph. "The Sincerity of Bessarion the Unionist." *Journal of Theological Studies*, n.s. 26 (1975): 377–92.

Gilleland, Brady B. "The Development of Cicero's Ideal Orator." In *Classical, Mediaeval, and Renaissance Studies in Honor of Berthold Louis Ullman*, edited by Charles Henderson, Jr., 2 vols., 1:91–98. Rome: Storia e letteratura, 1964.

Gios, Pierantonio. *L'attività pastorale del vescovo Pietro Barozzi a Padova (1487–1507)*. Fonti e ricerche di storia ecclesiastica padovana 8. Padua: Istituto per la storia ecclesiastica padovana, 1977.

Girolami, Remigio de'. *Sermones de mortuis*. Florence, Bibl. Nazionale, MS Conventi soppressi G 4, 936, fols. 376–404v.

Giustiniani, Vito R. *Alamanno Rinuccini 1426–1499: Materialen und Forschungen zur Geschichte des florentinischen Humanismus*. Cologne and Graz: Böhlau, 1965.

———. "*Homo, Humanus,* and the Meanings of 'Humanism.'" *Journal of the History of Ideas* 46 (1985): 167–95.

———. "Sulle traduzioni latine delle 'Vite' di Plutarco nel Quattrocento." *Rinascimento*, n.s. 1 (1961): 3–62.

Godi, Carlo. "La *Collatio laureationis* del Petrarca." *Italia medioevale e umanistica* 13 (1970): 1–27.

———. "L'orazione del Petrarca per Giovanni il Buono." *Italia medioevale e umanistica* 8 (1965): 45–83.
Goldbrunner, Hermann. "Poggios Dialog über die Habsucht: Bemerkungen zu einer neuen Untersuchung." *Quellen und Forschungen aus italienischen Archiven und Bibliotheken* 59 (1979): 436–52.
Gombrich, E. H. "The Debate on Primitivism in Ancient Rhetoric." *Journal of the Warburg and Courtauld Institutes* 29 (1966): 24–38.
———. "The Early Medici as Patrons of Art: A Survey of Primary Sources." In *Italian Renaissance Studies*, edited by E. F. Jacob, pp. 279–311. London: Faber & Faber, 1960.
———. "Renaissance and Golden Age." *Journal of the Warburg and Courtauld Institutes* 24 (1961): 306–9.
Grabmann, Martin. "Eine ungedruckte Verteidigungsschrift der scholastischen Übersetzung der Nikomachischen Ethik gegenüber dem Humanisten Lionardo Bruni." In *Mittelalterliches Geistesleben*, 3 vols., 1:440–48. Munich: M. Hueber, 1926–56.
Grafton, A. T., and Jardine, L. "Humanism and the School of Guarino: A Problem of Evaluation." *Past and Present*, no. 96 (August 1982): 51–80.
Gray, Hanna. "Renaissance Humanism: The Pursuit of Eloquence." *Journal of the History of Ideas* 24 (1963): 497–514.
Grayson, Cecil. "Il *Canis* di Leon Battista Alberti." In *Miscellanea di studi in onore di Vittore Branca*, part 3, *Umanesimo e Rinascimento a Firenze e Venezia*, 2 vols., 1:193–204. Biblioteca dell'*Archivum Romanicum* 180. Florence: L. Olschki, 1983.
Greco, Aulo. "La *docta pietas* degli umanisti e un documento della Biblioteca Angelica." *Accademie e biblioteche d'Italia* 47 (1979): 210–38.
Gregg, Robert C. *Consolation Philosophy: Greek and Christian Paideia in Basil and the Two Gregories*. Cambridge, Mass.: Philadelphia Patristic Foundation, 1975.
Griffiths, Gordon. "Leonardo Bruni and the Restoration of the University of Rome (1406)." *Renaissance Quarterly* 26 (1973): 1–10.
———. "Louise of Savoy and the Reform of the Church." *Sixteenth Century Journal* 10, no. 3 (1979): 29–36.
———. "The Political Significance of Uccello's *Battle of San Romano*." *Journal of the Warburg and Courtauld Institutes* 41 (1978): 313–16.
Guarini, Battista. "De ordine docendi et studendi." In *Il pensiero pedagogico dell'umanesimo*, edited by Eugenio Garin, pp. 434–71. Florence: Giuntine and Sansoni, 1958.
Guarini, Guarino, da Verona. *Epistolario*. Edited by Remigio Sabbadini. 3 vols. Miscellanea di storia veneta, 8, 11, 14. Venice: C. Ferrari, 1915–19.
Güldner, F. "Jakob Questemberg, ein deutscher Humanist in Rom." *Zeitschrift des Harz-Vereins für Geschichte und Altertumskunde* 38 (1905): 213–76.

Gundersheimer, Werner L. *Ferrara: The Style of a Renaissance Despotism.* Princeton: Princeton University Press, 1973.
―――. "The Patronage of Ercole I d'Este." *Journal of Medieval and Renaissance Studies* 6 (1976): 1–18.
―――. "Women, Learning, and Power: Eleanora of Aragon and the Court of Ferrara." In *Beyond Their Sex: Learned Women of the European Past*, edited by Patricia Labalme, pp. 43–65. New York and London: New York University Press, 1984.
Gutiérrez, David. "Testi e note su Mariano da Genazzano (†1498)." *Analecta Augustiniana* 32 (1969): 117–204.
Hammer, William. "The Concept of the New or Second Rome in the Middle Ages." *Speculum* 19 (1944): 50–62.
Hardison, O. B., Jr. *The Enduring Monument: A Study of the Idea of Praise in Renaissance Literary Theory and Practice.* Chapel Hill: University of North Carolina Press, 1962.
―――. "The Orator and the Poet: The Dilemma of Humanist Literature." *Journal of Medieval and Renaissance Studies* 1 (1971): 33–44.
Hertter, Fritz. *Die Podestàliteratur Italiens im 12. und 13. Jahrhundert.* Berlin and Leipzig: B. G. Teubner, 1910.
Horrigan, J. Brian. "Imperial and Urban Ideology in a Renaissance Inscription." *Comitatus* 9 (1978): 73–86.
Hunger, Herbert. *Die hochsprachliche profane Literatur der Byzantiner*, vol. 1, *Philosophie, Rhetorik, Epistolographie, Geschichtsschreibung, Geographie.* Handbuch der Altertumswissenschaft, 12, no. 5, part 1. Munich: Beck, 1978.
Hybertson, Larry. "Celio Calcagnini: A Pre-Copernican Renaissance Astronomer." *Rinascimento*, n.s. 6 (1966): 295–304.
Hyde, J. K. "Medieval Descriptions of Cities." *Bulletin of the John Rylands Library* 48 (1965–66): 308–40.
―――. *Padua in the Age of Dante.* New York: Barnes & Noble, 1966.
Ilardi, Vincent. " 'Italianità' among Some Italian Intellectuals in the Early Sixteenth Century." *Traditio* 12 (1956): 339–67.
Ioannes Viterbiensis. *De regimine civitatum.* Edited by Gaetano Salvemini. In *Bibliotheca Iuridica Medii Aevi: Scripta Anecdota glossatorum*, 3:217–80. Bologna: Successores Monti, 1901.
Jacomuzzi, Stefano. "Un modello del principe rinascimentale: Francesco II Gonzaga nella *Chronica di Mantua* dell'Equicola." In *Miscellanea in onore di Vittore Branca*, part 3, *Umanesimo e Rinascimento a Firenze e Venezia*, 2 vols., 2:701–15. Biblioteca dell'*Archivum Romanicum* 180. Florence: L. Olschki, 1983.
Jaeger, Werner. *Paideia: The Ideals of Greek Culture.* Translated by Gilbert Highet. 3 vols. Oxford: Oxford University Press, 1939–44.
Janson, H. W. "The Equestrian Monument from Cangrande della Scala to

Peter the Great." In *16 Studies*, pp. 157–88. New York: Abrams, 1974.
Jenkins, Romilly. "The Hellenistic Origins of Byzantine Literature." *Dumbarton Oaks Papers* 17 (1963): 37–52.
Jordan, Constance. "Feminism and the Humanists: The Case of Sir Thomas Elyot's *Defence of Good Women*." *Renaissance Quarterly* 36 (1983): 181–201.
Kaeppeli, Thomas. *Scriptores Ordinis Praedicatorum Medii Aevi*. 3 vols. Rome: Typis Polyglottis Vaticanis, 1970–.
Kajanto, Iiro. "*Pontifex Maximus* as the Title of the Pope." *Arctos: Acta Philologica Fennica* 15 (1981): 37–52.
⸻, and Nyberg, Ulla. *Papal Epigraphy in Renaissance Rome*. Helsinki: Academia scientiarum fennica, 1982.
Kalkoff, Paul. "G. B. Flavio als Biograph Kajetans und sein Bericht über Luthers Verhör in Augsburg." *Zeitschrift für Kirchengeschichte* 33, no. 2 (1912): 240–67.
Kennedy, George. *The Art of Persuasion in Greece*. London: Routledge & Kegan Paul, 1963.
⸻. *The Art of Rhetoric in the Roman World 300 B.C.–A.D. 300*. Princeton: Princeton University Press, 1972.
⸻. *Classical Rhetoric and Its Christian and Secular Tradition from Ancient to Modern Times*. Chapel Hill: University of North Carolina Press, 1980.
⸻. *Greek Rhetoric under Christian Emperors*. Princeton: Princeton University Press, 1983.
⸻. *New Testament Interpretation through Rhetorical Criticism*. Chapel Hill: University of North Carolina Press, 1984.
Kessler, Eckhard. *Petrarca und die Geschichte: Geschichtsschreibung, Rhetorik, Philosophie im Übergang vom Mittelalter zur Neuzeit* (Munich: W. Fink, 1978).
⸻. "Petrarch's Contribution to Renaissance Historiography." *Res Publica Litterarum: Studies in the Classical Tradition* 1 (1978): 129–49.
⸻. *Das Problem des frühen Humanismus: seine philosophische Bedeutung bei Coluccio Salutati*. Humanistische Bibliothek, Reihe 1, Abhandlungen 1. Munich: W. Fink, 1968.
Kierdorf, Wilhelm. *Laudatio Funebris: Interpretationen und Untersuchungen zur Entwicklung der römischen Leichenrede*. Beiträge zur klassischen Philologie, Heft 106. Meisenheim am Glan: A. Hain, 1980.
King, Margaret L. "Book-Lined Cells: Women and Humanism in the Early Italian Renaissance." In *Beyond Their Sex: Learned Women of the European Past*, edited by Patricia Labalme, pp. 66–90. New York and London: New York University Press, 1984.
⸻. *Venetian Humanism in an Age of Patrician Dominance*. Princeton: Princeton University Press, 1986.
Kohl, Benjamin. "Political Attitudes of North Italian Humanists in the Late Trecento." *Studies in Medieval Culture* 4 (1974): 418–27.

Der Kommentar in der Renaissance. Edited by August Buck and Otto Herding. Boppard: Boldt, 1975.

Kristeller, Paul Oskar. "Francesco Bandini and His Consolatory Dialogue upon the Death of Simone Gondi." In *Studies in Renaissance Thought and Letters*, pp. 411–35. Rome: Storia e letteratura, 1956.

———. "Humanism and Scholasticism in the Italian Renaissance." In *Renaissance Thought and Its Sources*, edited by Michael Mooney, pp. 85–105. New York: Columbia University Press, 1979.

———. "The Humanist Movement." In *Renaissance Thought and Its Sources*, edited by Michael Mooney, pp. 21–32. New York: Columbia University Press, 1979.

———. "Italian Humanism and Byzantium." In *Renaissance Thought and Its Sources*, edited by Michael Mooney, pp. 137–50. New York: Columbia University Press, 1979.

———. "Learned Women of Early Modern Italy: Humanists and University Scholars." In *Beyond Their Sex: Learned Women of the European Past*, edited by Patricia Labalme, pp. 91–116. New York and London: New York University Press, 1984.

———. "The Modern System of the Arts." In *Renaissance Thought*, vol. 2, *Papers on Humanism and the Arts*, pp. 163–227. New York: Harper, 1965.

———. "Music and Learning in the Early Italian Renaissance." In *Renaissance Thought*, vol. 2, *Papers on Humanism and the Arts*, pp. 142–62. New York: Harper, 1965.

———. "Paganism and Christianity." In *Renaissance Thought and Its Sources*, edited by Michael Mooney, pp. 66–81. New York: Columbia University Press, 1979.

———. "Philosophy and Medicine in Medieval and Renaissance Italy." In *Organism, Medicine, and Metaphysics: Essays in Honor of Hans Jonas*, edited by Stuart F. Spicker, pp. 29–40. Dordrecht: D. Reidel, 1978.

———. "Philosophy and Rhetoric: Classical Antiquity." In *Renaissance Thought and Its Sources*, edited by Michael Mooney, pp. 217–28. New York: Columbia University Press, 1979.

———. "Philosophy and Rhetoric: The Middle Ages." In *Renaissance Thought and Its Sources*, edited by Michael Mooney, pp. 228–42. New York: Columbia University Press, 1979.

———. "Philosophy and Rhetoric: The Renaissance." In *Renaissance Thought and Its Sources*, edited by Michael Mooney, pp. 242–59. New York: Columbia University Press, 1979.

———. "The Scholar and His Public in the Late Middle Ages and the Renaissance." In *Medieval Aspects of Renaissance Learning*, edited and translated by Edward Mahoney, pp. 1–25. Duke Monographs in Medieval and Renaissance Studies 1. Durham: Duke University Press, 1974.

———. "Thomism and the Italian Thought of the Renaissance." In *Medieval Aspects of Renaissance Learning*, edited and translated by Edward P. Mahoney, pp. 27–91. Duke Monographs in Medieval and Renaissance Studies 1. Durham: Duke University Press, 1974.

Küng, Hans. *The Church*. Translated by Ray and Rosaleen Ockendeen. New York: Sheed & Ward, 1967.

Kustas, George L. "The Function and Evolution of Byzantine Rhetoric." *Viator* 1 (1970): 55–73.

———. *Studies in Byzantine Rhetoric*. Analecta Vlatadon 17. Thessalonica: Patriarchal Institute, 1973.

Kuttner, Stephan. "*Cardinalis*: The History of a Canonical Concept." *Traditio* 3 (1945): 129–214.

Labalme, Patricia. *Bernardo Giustiniani: A Venetian of the Quattrocento*. Uomini e dottrine 13. Rome: Storia e letteratura, 1969.

Lane, Frederic C. *Venice: A Maritime Republic*. Baltimore and London: The Johns Hopkins University Press, 1973.

Lausberg, Heinrich. *Handbuch der literarischen Rhetorik*. 2 vols. Munich: M. Hueber, 1960.

Lecler, Joseph. *Toleration and the Reformation*. Translated by T. L. Westow. 2 vols. New York: Association Press, 1960.

Lee, Egmont. "Humanists and the *Studium Urbis*, 1473–1484." In *Umanesimo a Roma nel Quattrocento*, edited by Paolo Brezzi and Maristella de Panizza Lorch, pp. 127–46. Rome: Istituto di studi romani; New York: Barnard College, 1984.

———. *Sixtus IV and Men of Letters*. Temi e testi 26. Rome: Storia e letteratura, 1978.

Leichenpredigten als Quelle historischer Wissenschaften. Edited by Rudolf Lenz. Cologne and Vienna: Böhlau, 1975.

Libby, Lester, Jr. "Venetian History and Political Thought after 1509." *Studies in the Renaissance* 20 (1973): 7–45.

Lombardi, Giuseppe. "Aspetti della produzione e circolazione del libro a Roma nel XV secolo." In *Umanesimo a Roma nel Quattrocento*, edited by Paolo Brezzi and Maristella de Panizza Lorch, pp. 67–80. Rome: Istituto di studi romani; New York: Barnard College, 1984.

Loschi, Antonio. *Inquisitio super XI orationes Ciceronis*. Paris: I. Parvus, 1536.

McClure, George. "Healing Eloquence: Petrarch, Salutati, and the Physicians." *Journal of Medieval and Renaissance Studies* 15 (1985): 317–46.

———. "The Renaissance Vision of Solace and Tranquillity: Consolation and Therapeutic Wisdom in Italian Humanist Thought." 2 vols. Ph.D. dissertation, University of Michigan, 1981.

MacCormack, Sabine. *Art and Ceremony in Late Antiquity*. The Transformation of the Classical Heritage 1. Berkeley, Los Angeles, and London: University of California Press, 1981.

―――. "Latin Prose Panegyrics: Tradition and Discontinuity in the Later Roman Empire." *Revue des études Augustiniennes* 22 (1976): 29–77.

McGinness, Frederick John. "Rhetoric and Counter-Reformation Rome: Sacred Oratory and the Construction of the Catholic World View, 1563–1621." Ph.D. dissertation, University of California, Berkeley, 1982.

McManamon, John. "The Ideal Renaissance Pope: Funeral Oratory from the Papal Court." *Archivum Historiae Pontificiae* 14 (1976): 9–70.

―――. "Innovation in Early Humanist Rhetoric: The Oratory of Pier Paolo Vergerio (the Elder)." *Rinascimento*, n.s. 22 (1982): 3–32.

―――. "Pier Paolo Vergerio (the Elder) and the Beginnings of the Humanist Cult of Jerome." *Catholic Historical Review* 71 (1985): 353–71.

Maffei, Domenico. *Gli inizi dell'umanesimo giuridico*. Milan: Giuffrè, 1956.

Maguinness, W. S. "Some Methods of the Latin Panegyrists." *Hermathena* 47 (1932): 42–61.

Maguire, Henry. *Art and Eloquence in Byzantium*. Princeton: Princeton University Press, 1981.

Mallett, Michael E. *Mercenaries and Their Masters: Warfare in Renaissance Italy*. London: Bodley Head, 1974.

―――. "Venice and Its Condottieri, 1404–54." In *Renaissance Venice*, edited by J. R. Hale, pp. 121–45. London: Faber & Faber, 1973.

―――, and J. R. Hale. *The Military Organization of a Renaissance State: Venice c. 1400 to 1617*. Cambridge, New York, and Melbourne: Cambridge University Press, 1984.

Manetti, Giannozzo. "Praefatio in laudatione non funebri sed potius triumphali . . . Agnetis Numantinae ad Nunnium Gusmanum . . . ." BAV, MS Palat. lat. 1606, fols. 1–4.

―――. "Vita Senecae." Edited by Claudio Moreschini. In *Annali della Scuola Normale Superiore di Pisa: Classe di lettere e filosofia*, ser. 3, 6 (1976): 847–75.

Manfré, Guglielmo. "La biblioteca dell'umanista bolognese Giovanni Garzoni (1419–1505)." *Accademie e biblioteche d'Italia* 27 (1959): 249–78, 28 (1960): 17–72.

Marquand, Allan. *Benedetto and Santi Buglioni*. Princeton Monographs in Art and Archaeology 9. Princeton: Princeton University Press, 1921.

Marsh, David. *The Quattrocento Dialogue: Classical Tradition and Humanist Innovation*. Harvard Studies in Comparative Literature 35. Cambridge: Harvard University Press, 1980.

Martines, Lauro. *The Social World of the Florentine Humanists 1390–1460*. Princeton: Princeton University Press, 1963.

Mattingly, Garrett. *Renaissance Diplomacy*. London: Jonathan Cape, 1955.

Mattioli, Emilio. *Luciano e l'umanesimo*. Naples: Istituto italiano per gli studi storici, 1980.
Mazzocco, Angelo. "Decline and Rebirth in Bruni and Biondo." In *Umanesimo a Roma nel Quattrocento*, edited by Paolo Brezzi and Maristella de Panizza Lorch, pp. 249–66. Rome: Istituto di studi romani; New York: Barnard College, 1984.
Mazzuconi, Daniela. "Per una sistemazione dell'epistolario di Gasparino Barzizza." *Italia medioevale e umanistica* 20 (1977): 183–241.
Medieval Eloquence: Studies in the Theory and Practice of Medieval Rhetoric. Edited by James J. Murphy. Berkeley, Los Angeles, and London: University of California Press, 1978.
Mercati, Giovanni. *Codici Latini Pico Grimani Pio. . . .* Studi e testi 75. Vatican City: BAV, 1938.
———. "Notizie varie sopra Niccolò Modrussiense." In *Opere minori*, vol. 4, *1917–1936*, pp. 205–67. Studi e testi 79. Vatican City: BAV, 1937.
———. *Per la cronologia della vita e degli scritti di Niccolò Perotti arcivescovo di Siponto*. Studi e testi 44. Vatican City: BAV, 1925.
———. "Pescennio Francesco Negro Veneto protonotario apostolico." In *Ultimi contributi alla storia degli umanisti (fascicolo II)*, pp. 24–109. Studi e testi 91. Vatican City: BAV, 1939.
———. "Questenbergiana." In *Opere minori*, vol. 4, *1917–1936*, pp. 437–59. Studi e testi 79. Vatican City: BAV, 1937.
Mesquita, D. M. Bueno de. "The Place of Despotism in Italian Politics." In *Europe in the Late Middle Ages*, edited by J. R. Hale, J. R. L. Highfield, and B. Smalley, pp. 301–31. London: Faber & Faber; Evanston: Northwestern University Press, 1965.
Michel, Alain. *Rhétorique et philosophie chez Cicéron*. Paris: Les presses universitaires, 1960.
Michel, Paul-Henri. *Un idéal humain au XVe siècle: la pensée de L. B. Alberti (1404–1472)*. Paris: Société d'éditions "Les Belles Lettres," 1930.
Miglio, Massimo. "Una vocazione in progresso: Michele Canensi, biografo papale." *Studi medievali*, ser. 3, 12 (1971): 463–524.
Mittarelli, G. B. *Bibliotheca codicum manuscriptorum monasterii S. Michaelis Venetiarum prope Murianum . . . .* Venice: Fentiana, 1779.
Mohler, Ludwig. *Kardinal Bessarion als Theologe, Humanist und Staatsmann*. 3 vols. 1923–42; reprinted Paderborn: F. Schöningh, 1967.
Mollat, G. "L'oeuvre oratoire de Clement VI." *Archives d'histoire doctrinale et littéraire du Moyen Age* 3 (1928): 239–74.
Monfasani, John. "Bessarion Latinus." *Rinascimento*, n.s. 21 (1981): 165–209.
———. "The Byzantine Rhetorical Tradition and the Renaissance." In *Renaissance Eloquence: Studies in the Theory and Practice of Renaissance Rhetoric*,

edited by James J. Murphy, pp. 174–87. Berkeley, Los Angeles, and London: University of California Press, 1983.

―――. *George of Trebizond: A Biography and a Study of His Rhetoric and Logic.* Columbia Studies in the Classical Tradition 1. Leiden: Brill, 1976.

Montaldo, Adamo di. " . . . ad Calistum tertium . . . de clara vita divi Regis Alfonsi oratio." In Tammaro De Marinis, *La biblioteca napoletana dei re d'Aragona*, 4 vols., 1:225–27. Milan: U. Hoepli, 1947–52.

Morrissey, Thomas. "Emperor-Elect Sigismund, Cardinal Zabarella, and the Council of Constance." *Catholic Historical Review* 69 (1983): 353–70.

―――. "Franciscus Zabarella (1360–1417): Papacy, Community, and Limitations Upon Authority." In *Reform and Authority in the Medieval and Reformation Church*, edited by Guy Lytle, pp. 37–54. Washington, D.C.: Catholic University Press, 1981.

Mosto, Andrea da. *I dogi di Venezia nella vita pubblica e privata.* Milan: Aldo Martello, 1966.

Mueller, Reinhold C. "The Procurators of San Marco in the Thirteenth and Fourteenth Centuries: A Study of the Office as a Financial and Trust Institution." *Studi veneziani* 13 (1971): 105–220.

Muir, Edward. *Civic Ritual in Renaissance Venice.* Princeton: Princeton University Press, 1981.

Murphy, James J. *Medieval Rhetoric: A Select Bibliography.* Toronto: University of Toronto Press, 1971.

―――. *Rhetoric in the Middle Ages: A History of Rhetorical Theory from Saint Augustine to the Renaissance.* Berkeley, Los Angeles, and London: University of California Press, 1974.

Najemy, John. *Corporatism and Consensus in Florentine Electoral Politics, 1280–1400.* Chapel Hill: University of North Carolina Press, 1982.

―――. "Machiavelli and the Medici: The Lessons of Florentine History." *Renaissance Quarterly* 35 (1982): 551–76.

Nardi, Paolo. *Mariano Sozzini giureconsulto senese del Quattrocento.* Quaderni di *Studi senesi* 32. Milan: Giuffrè, 1974.

Navagero, Bernardo. " . . . in funere Andreae Gritii principis Veneti laudatio." BAV, MS Ottob. lat. 489, fols. 40–48.

North, Helen. "*Inutilis sibi, perniciosus patriae*: A Platonic Argument against Sophistic Rhetoric." *Illinois Classical Studies* 6 (1981): 242–71.

Nuovi documenti per la storia del Rinascimento. Edited by Tammaro De Marinis and Alessandro Perosa. Florence: L. Olschki, 1970.

Oberdorfer, Aldo. "Di Leonardo Giustiniano umanista." *Giornale storico della letteratura italiana* 56 (1910): 107–20.

Oculus pastoralis. Edited by Dora Franceschi. Memorie dell'Accademia delle Scienze di Torino, ser. 4a, no. 11. Turin: Accademia delle Scienze, 1966.

Olivieri degli Abbati, Annibale. *Orazioni in morte di alcuni signori di Pesaro della casa Malatesta*. Pesaro: Casa Gavelli, 1784.
O'Malley, John W. "Egidio da Viterbo and Renaissance Rome." In *Egidio da Viterbo, O.S.A. e il suo tempo*, pp. 67–84. Rome: ed. Analecta Augustiniana, 1983.

———. "Erasmus and Luther: Continuity and Discontinuity as Key to Their Conflict." *Sixteenth Century Journal* 5, no. 2 (1974): 47–65.

———. "Erasmus and the History of Sacred Rhetoric: The *Ecclesiastes* of 1535." *Erasmus of Rotterdam Society Yearbook* 5 (1985): 1–29.

———. "The Feast of Thomas Aquinas in Renaissance Rome: A Neglected Document and Its Import." *Rivista di storia della Chiesa in Italia* 35 (1981): 1–27.

———. *Giles of Viterbo on Church and Reform: A Study in Renaissance Thought*. Studies in Medieval and Reformation Thought 5. Leiden: Brill, 1968.

———. "Grammar and Rhetoric in the *Pietas* of Erasmus." *Journal of Medieval and Renaissance Studies* 18 (1988): 81–98.

———. "Historical Thought and the Reform Crisis of the Early Sixteenth Century." *Theological Studies* 28 (1967): 531–48.

———. "The Jesuits, St. Ignatius, and the Counter Reformation: Some Recent Studies and Their Implications." *Studies in the Spirituality of Jesuits* 14, no. 1 (January 1982): 1–28.

———. *Praise and Blame in Renaissance Rome: Rhetoric, Doctrine, and Reform in the Sacred Orators of the Papal Court, c. 1450–1521*. Duke Monographs in Medieval and Renaissance Studies 3. Durham: Duke University Press, 1979.

———. "Some Renaissance Panegyrics of Aquinas." *Renaissance Quarterly* 27 (1974): 174–92.

———. "The Vatican Library and the Schools of Athens: A Text of Battista Casali, 1508." *Journal of Medieval and Renaissance Studies* 7 (1977): 271–87.

Onofri, Laura. "Sacralità, immaginazione e proposte politiche: la *Vita* di Niccolò V di Giannozzo Manetti." *Humanistica Lovaniensia* 28 (1979): 27–77.

———. "*Sicut fremitus leonis ita et regis ira*: Temi neoplatonici e culto solare nell'orazione funebre per Niccolò V di Jean Jouffroy." *Humanistica Lovaniensia* 31 (1982): 1–28.

Oppel, John W. "Peace vs. Liberty in the Quattrocento: Poggio, Guarino, and the Scipio-Caesar Controversy." *Journal of Medieval and Renaissance Studies* 4 (1974): 221–65.

———. "Poggio, San Bernardino of Siena, and the Dialogue *On Avarice*." *Renaissance Quarterly* 30 (1977): 564–87.

Orationes clarorum hominum, vel honoris officiique causa ad principes, vel in funere de virtutibus eorum habitae. Cologne: I. Quentel and G. Calenius, 1560.

Orationes funebres in morte pontificum, imperatorum, regum, principum, etc. Hanau: apud haeredes I. Aburii, 1613.
Oravec, Christine. "'Observation' in Aristotle's Theory of Epideictic." *Philosophy and Rhetoric* 9 (1976): 162–74.
Orazioni, elogi e vite scritte da letterati veneti patrizi . . . . Edited by G. A. Molin. 2nd ed. 2 vols. Venice: A. Curti, 1798.
Orlando, Saverio. "L'ideologia umanistica negli *Apologi* di P. Collenuccio." In *Civiltà dell'umanesimo*, edited by Giovannagiola Tarugi, pp. 225–40. Florence: L. Olschki, 1972.
Pagello, Bartolomeo. ". . . oratio habita in senatu de duobus rhetoribus post mortem Omniboni publico salario conducendis ac de laude ipsius Omniboni." Vicenza, Bibl. Comunale Bertoliana, MS G.7.1.79, fols. 55–58.
Palaeologus, Manuel II. *The Letters of Manuel II Palaeologus*. Edited and translated by George T. Dennis. Dumbarton Oaks Texts 4. Washington, D.C.: Dumbarton Oaks, 1977.
Panella, Emilio. "Per lo studio di Fra Remigio dei Girolami (†1319)." *Memorie Domenicane*, n.s. 10 (1979).
———. "Un sermone in morte della moglie di Guido Novello o di Beatrice d'Angiò?" *Memorie Domenicane*, n.s. 12 (1981): 294–301.
Panofsky, Erwin. "*Mors vitae testimonium*: The Positive Aspect of Death in Renaissance and Baroque Iconography." In *Studien zur Toskanischen Kunst: Festschrift für Ludwig Heinrich Heydenreich zum 23. März 1963*, edited by Wolfgang Lotz and Lise Lotte Möller, pp. 221–36. Munich: Prestel, 1964.
———. *Renaissance and Renascences in Western Art*. Figura 10. Stockholm: Almquist & Wiksell, 1960.
Paris de Grassis. *Tractatus de funeribus et exsequiis in Romana curia peragendis*. BAV, MS Vat. lat. 5944.
Pastor, Ludwig. *The History of the Popes*. Translated by F. I. Antrobus et al. Vols. 1–7. St. Louis: B. Herder, 1923.
Patrinelis, C. G. "An Unknown Discourse of Chrysoloras Addressed to Manuel II Palaeologus." *Greek, Roman, and Byzantine Studies* 13 (1972): 497–502.
Patterson, Annabel. *Hermogenes and the Renaissance: Seven Ideas of Style*. Princeton: Princeton University Press, 1970.
Paul, G. M. "*Urbs Capta*: Sketch of an Ancient Literary Motif." *Phoenix* 36 (1982): 144–55.
Percival, W. Keith. "Grammar and Rhetoric in the Renaissance." In *Renaissance Eloquence: Studies in the Theory and Practice of Renaissance Rhetoric*, edited by James J. Murphy, pp. 303–30. Berkeley, Los Angeles, and London: University of California Press, 1983.
Peri, Vittorio. "Tre lettere inedite a Fantino Valaresso ed un suo catechismo

attribuito a Fantino Dandolo." In *Miscellanea di studi in onore di Vittore Branca*, part 3, *Umanesimo e Rinascimento a Firenze e Venezia*, 2 vols., 1:41–67. Biblioteca dell'*Archivum romanicum* 180. Florence: L. Olschki, 1983.

Perreiah, Alan R. "A Biographical Introduction to Paul of Venice." *Augustiniana* 17 (1967): 450–61.

———. "Humanistic Critiques of Scholastic Dialectic." *Sixteenth Century Journal* 13, no. 3 (1982): 3–22.

Perry, Marilyn. "Cardinal Domenico Grimani's Legacy of Ancient Art to Venice." *Journal of the Warburg and Courtauld Institutes* 41 (1978): 215–44.

Pertusi, Agostino. "L'umanesimo greco dalla fine del secolo XIV agli inizi del secolo XVI." In *Storia della cultura veneta: dal primo Quattrocento al Concilio di Trento*, 3:part 1:177–264. Vicenza: Neri Pozza, 1980.

Petrarca, Francesco. *Le familiari*. Edited by Vittorio Rossi. 4 vols. Florence: G. Sansoni, 1933–42.

———. *Scritti inediti di Francesco Petrarca*. Edited by A. Hortis. Trieste: Lloyd Austro-Ungarico, 1874.

Poliziano, Angelo. *Opera omnia*. Edited by Ida Maïer. 3 vols. Basel, 1553. Reprinted Turin: Bottega d'Erasmo, 1970–71.

Porzi, Alfonso. *Umanesimo e francescanesimo nel Quattrocento*. Rome: Libreria Sant'Antonio, 1973.

Pratt, Kenneth J. "Rome as Eternal." *Journal of the History of Ideas* 26 (1965): 25–44.

Prodi, Paolo. *Il sovrano pontefice, un corpo e due anime: la monarchia papale nella prima età moderna*. Saggi 228. Bologna: Il Mulino, 1982.

Pullan, Brian. *Rich and Poor in Renaissance Venice*. Cambridge: Harvard University Press, 1971.

Quint, David. "Humanism and Modernity: A Reconsideration of Bruni's *Dialogues*." *Renaissance Quarterly* 38 (1985): 423–45.

Rabil, Albert, Jr. *Laura Cereta: Quattrocento Humanist*. Medieval and Renaissance Texts and Studies, 3. Binghamton, N.Y.: Center for Medieval and Early Renaissance Studies, 1981.

Raith, Werner. *Die Macht des Bildes: ein humanistisches Problem bei Gianfrancesco Pico della Mirandola*. Humanistische Bibliothek, Reihe 1, Abhandlungen 3. Munich: W. Fink, 1967.

Ramage, Edwin. "Velleius Paterculus 2.126.2–3 and the Panegyric Tradition." *Classical Antiquity* 1 (1982): 266–71.

Reden und Briefe Italienischer Humanisten. Edited by Karl Müllner. Vienna, 1899; reprinted Munich: W. Fink, 1970.

Renaissance Eloquence: Studies in the Theory and Practice of Renaissance Rhetoric. Edited by James J. Murphy. Berkeley, Los Angeles, and London: University of California Press, 1983.

Resta, Gianvito. *Le epitomi di Plutarco nel Quattrocento.* Miscellanea erudita 5. Padua: Antenore, 1962.
Reuterswärd, Patrik. "The Dog in the Humanist's Study." *Konsthistorisk tidskrift* 50 (1981): 53–69.
Reynolds, B. "Bruni and Perotti Present a Greek Historian." *Bibliothèque d'humanisme et Renaissance* 16 (1954): 108–18.
Ricci, Maria Lisa. "Definizione della *prudentia* in Sant'Ambrogio (a proposito di *De excessu fratris* 44–48)." *Studi italiani di filologia classica*, n.s. 41 (1969): 247–62.
Rice, Eugene. *Saint Jerome in the Renaissance.* Baltimore: The Johns Hopkins University Press, 1985.
Riess, Jonathan B. "The Civic View of Sculpture in Alberti's *De re aedificatoria.*" *Renaissance Quarterly* 32 (1979): 1–17.
Rinuccini, Alamanno. *Lettere ed orazioni.* Edited by Vito R. Giustiniani. Nuova collezione di testi umanistici inediti o rari 9. Florence: L. Olschki, 1953.
Robey, David. "Humanism and Education in the Early Quattrocento: The *De ingenuis moribus* of P. P. Vergerio." *Bibliothèque d'humanisme et Renaissance* 42 (1980): 27–58.
———. "Virgil's Statue at Mantua and the Defence of Poetry: An Unpublished Letter of 1397." *Rinascimento*, n.s. 9 (1969): 183–203.
———. "Vittorino da Feltre e Vergerio." In *Vittorino da Feltre e la sua scuola: umanesimo, pedagogia, arti*, edited by Nella Giannetto, pp. 241–53. Civiltà Veneziana: Saggi 31. Florence: L. Olschki, 1981.
———, and Law, John. "The Venetian Myth and the *De republica veneta* of Pier Paolo Vergerio." *Rinascimento*, n.s. 15 (1975): 3–59.
Roger, Pierre. "Sermo factus . . . in sepultura domini Neapoleonis Ursini." Venice, Bibl. Naz. Marciana, MS 2293 (Marc. lat. III 79), fols. 53v–54v.
Rosa, Lucia Gualdo. "Ciceroniano o cristiano? A proposito dell'orazione *De morte Christi* di Tommaso Fedra Inghirami." *Humanistica Lovaniensia* 34A (1985): 52–64.
———. *La fede nella "Paideia": aspetti della fortuna europea di Isocrate nei secoli XV e XVI.* Studi storici fasc. 140–42. Rome: Istituto storico italiano per il Medio Evo, 1984.
Rose, Paul Lawrence. "Bartolomeo Zamberti's Funeral Oration for the Humanist Encyclopaedist Giorgio Valla." In *Cultural Aspects of the Italian Renaissance: Essays in Honour of Paul Oskar Kristeller*, edited by Cecil Clough, pp. 299–310. Manchester: Manchester University Press; New York: A. Zambelli, 1976.
———. *The Italian Renaissance of Mathematics: Studies on Humanists and Mathematicians from Petrarch to Galileo.* Geneva: Droz, 1975.

Rosenberg, Charles. "'Per il bene di . . . nostra cipta': Borso d'Este and the *Certosa* of Ferrara." *Renaissance Quarterly* 29 (1976): 329–40.
Ross, James Bruce. "Venetian Scholars and Teachers Fourteenth to Early Sixteenth Century: A Survey and a Study of Giovanni Battista Egnazio." *Renaissance Quarterly* 29 (1976): 521–66.
Rossi, Vittorio. *Il Quattrocento*. Milan: F. Vallardi, 1933.
Rubinstein, Nicolai. *The Government of Florence under the Medici (1434 to 1494)*. Oxford: Clarendon Press, 1966.
———. "Political Ideas in Sienese Art: The Frescoes by Ambrogio Lorenzetti and Taddeo di Bartolo in the Palazzo Pubblico." *Journal of the Warburg and Courtauld Institutes* 21 (1958): 179–207.
Ruether, Rosemary R. *Gregory of Nazianzus: Rhetor and Philosopher*. Oxford: Clarendon Press, 1969.
Rugiadi, Annamaria. *Tommaso Fedra Inghirami: umanista volterrano (1470–1516)*. Amatrice: Scuola Orfanotrofio, 1933.
Ruiz, Santiago. *Investigationes historicae et litterariae in Sancti Ambrosii De obitu Valentiniani et De obitu Theodosii imperatorum orationes funebres*. Munich: Facultas Theologiae Catholicae, 1971.
Runciman, Steven. *Mistra: Byzantine Capital of the Peloponnese*. London: Thames & Hudson, 1980.
Russell, D. A. *Plutarch*. London: Duckworth, 1972.
———, and N. G. Wilson, eds. *Menander Rhetor*. Oxford: Clarendon Press, 1981.
Sabbadini, Remigio. "Guarino Veronese e la polemica sul Carmagnola." *Nuovo archivio veneto* 22 (1896): 327–61.
———. "Lettere e orazioni edite e inedite di Gasparino Barzizza." *Archivio storico lombardo* 13 (1886): 363–78, 563–83, 825–36.
———. *Il metodo degli umanisti*. Florence: F. Le Monnier, [1920].
———. *Le scoperte dei codici latini e greci ne' secoli XIV e XV*. 2 vols. Biblioteca storica del Rinascimento 4. 1905–14. Reprinted Florence: G. Sansoni, 1967.
———. *La scuola e gli studi di Guarino Guarini Veronese*. Catania: F. Galati, 1896.
———. *Vita di Guarino Veronese*. Genua: Tipografia del R. Istituto Sordo-Muti, 1891.
Salutati, Coluccio. *Epistolario*. Edited by Francesco Novati. 4 vols. Rome: Tipografia del Senato, 1891–1911.
Salvadori, G., and V. Federici. "I sermoni d'occasione, le sequenze e i ritmi di Remigio Girolami fiorentino." In *Scritti vari di filologia a Ernesto Monaci*, pp. 455–508. Rome: Forzani, 1901.
Sambin, Paolo. "Ricerche per la storia della cultura nel secolo XV: la biblio-

teca di Pietro Donato (1380–1447)." *Bollettino del Museo Civico di Padova* 48 (1959): 53–98.

———. "Su Giacomo della Torre (†1414)." *Quaderni per la storia dell'Università di Padova* 6 (1973): 149–61.

Santini, Emilio. *Firenze e i suoi "oratori" nel Quattrocento*. Biblioteca Sandron di scienze e lettere 77. Milan: R. Sandron, 1922.

———. "Leonardo Bruni Aretino e i suoi *Historiarum Florentini Populi Libri XII*." *Annali della R. Scuola Normale Superiore di Pisa* 22, no. 4 (1910).

Schnaubelt, Joseph Cletus, O.S.A. "Andrea Biglia (c. 1394–1435) Augustinian Friar and Renaissance Humanist: A Critical Edition of Four Orations with Introduction, Translations, Commentary, and Appendices." Ph.D. dissertation, Catholic University, 1976.

Schröter, Elisabeth. "Der Vatikan als Hügel Apollons und der Musen: Kunst und Panegyrik von Nikolaus V. bis Julius II." *Römische Quartalschrift für christliche Altertumskunde und Kirchengeschichte* 75 (1980): 208–40.

Schulz, Anne Markham. *The Sculpture of Bernardo Rossellino and His Workshop*. Princeton: Princeton University Press, 1977.

Schweyen, Renate. *Guarino Veronese: Philosophie und humanistische Pädagogik*. Humanistische Bibliothek, Reihe 3, Band 3. Munich: W. Fink, 1973.

Seigel, Jerrold E. *Rhetoric and Philosophy in Renaissance Humanism*. Princeton: Princeton University Press, 1968.

Setton, Kenneth M. "The Byzantine Background to the Italian Renaissance." *Proceedings of the American Philosophical Society* 100 (1956): 1–76.

Sinding-Larsen, Staale. *Christ in the Council Hall: Studies in the Religious Iconography of the Venetian Republic*. Institutum Romanum Norvegiae: Acta et archaeologiam et artium historiam pertinentia 5. Rome: "L'Erma" di Bretschneider, 1974.

Siraisi, Nancy. *Arts and Sciences at Padua: The "Studium" of Padua before 1350*. Pontifical Institute of Mediaeval Studies: Studies and Texts 25. Toronto: Mediaeval Institute, 1973.

Skinner, Quentin. *The Foundations of Modern Political Thought*, vol. 1, *The Renaissance*. Cambridge: Cambridge University Press, 1978.

Škunca, Stanislaus. *Aelius Lampridius Cervinus poeta Ragusinus (saec. XV)*. Rome: Ed. Francescane, 1971.

Sorbelli, Albano. "I teorici del reggimento comunale." *Bullettino dell'Istituto storico italiano per il Medio Evo e Archivio Muratoriano* 59 (1944): 31–136.

Sottili, Agostino. *Studenti tedeschi e umanesimo italiano nell'Università di Padova durante il Quattrocento*, vol. 1, *Pietro del Monte nella società accademica padovana (1430–1433)*. Contributi alla storia dell'Università di Padova 7. Padua: Antenore, 1971.

Soudek, Josef. "The Genesis and Tradition of Leonardo Bruni's Annotated

Latin Version of the (Pseudo-) Aristotelian *Economics.*" *Scriptorium* 12 (1958): 260–68.

———. "Leonardo Bruni and His Public: A Statistical and Interpretative Study of His Annotated Latin Version of the (Pseudo-) Aristotelian *Economics.*" *Studies in Medieval and Renaissance History* 5 (1968): 49–136.

Spencer, John R. "*Ut rhetorica pictura*: A Study in Quattrocento Theory of Painting." *Journal of the Warburg and Courtauld Institutes* 20 (1957): 26–44.

Stäuble, Antonio. "Due panegirici di città tra Medioevo e Rinascimento." *Bibliothèque d'humanisme et Renaissance* 38 (1976): 157–64.

Stinger, Charles L. *The Renaissance in Rome.* Bloomington: Indiana University Press, 1985.

———. "*Roma Triumphans*: Triumphs in the Thought and Ceremonies of Renaissance Rome." *Medievalia et humanistica* 10 (1981): 189–201.

Stornajolo, Cosimus. *Codices Urbinates latini.* 3 vols. Rome: Typis Vaticanis, 1902–21.

Strasburger, H. "Thukydides und die politische Selbstdarstellung der Athener." *Hermes* 86 (1958): 17–40.

Strnad, Alfred. "Francesco Todeschini Piccolomini: Politik und Mäzenatentum im Quattrocento." *Römische historische Mitteilungen* 8–9 (1964–66): 101–425.

Strocchia, Sharon Therese. "Burials in Renaissance Florence, 1350–1500." Ph.D. dissertation, University of California, Berkeley, 1981.

Thomson, Ian. "Manuel Chrysoloras and the Early Italian Renaissance." *Greek, Roman, and Byzantine Studies* 7 (1966): 63–82.

Tierney, Brian. *Foundations of the Conciliar Theory.* Cambridge: Cambridge University Press, 1955.

Tiraboschi, Girolamo. *Storia della letteratura italiana.* 9 vols. Rome: L. P. Salvioni, 1782–97.

Tomasi, Gioacchino Lanza. *Ritratto del condottiero.* Turin: Edizioni RAI, 1967.

Töth, Paolo de. *Il Beato Cardinale Nicolò Albergati e i suoi tempi.* 2 vols. Acquapendente [Viterbo]: La Commerciale, 1934.

Tournoy, Gilbert. "Francesco Diedo, Venetian Humanist and Politician of the Quattrocento." *Humanistica Lovaniensia* 19 (1970): 201–34.

Trapp, J. B. "The Poet Laureate: Rome, *Renovatio* and *Translatio Imperii.*" In *Rome in the Renaissance: The City and the Myth*, edited by P. A. Ramsey, pp. 93–130. Medieval and Renaissance Texts and Studies 18. Binghamton, N.Y.: Center for Medieval and Early Renaissance Studies, 1982.

Traversari, Guido. "Di Mattia Lupi (1380–1486) e de' suoi *Annales Geminianenses.*" *Miscellanea storica della Valdelsa* 11 (1903): 10–28, 108–28; 12 (1904): 117–36.

Trebizond (Trapezuntius), George of. *Collectanea Trapezuntiana: Texts, Docu-*

ments, and Bibliographies of George of Trebizond. Edited by John Monfasani. Medieval and Renaissance Texts and Studies, 25. Binghamton, N.Y.: Center for Medieval and Early Renaissance Studies, 1984.

Trinkaus, Charles. *In Our Image and Likeness: Humanity and Divinity in Italian Humanist Thought*. 2 vols. Chicago and London: University of Chicago Press, 1970.

———. "The Question of Truth in Renaissance Rhetoric and Anthropology." In *Renaissance Eloquence: Studies in the Theory and Practice of Renaissance Rhetoric*, edited by James J. Murphy, pp. 207–20. Berkeley, Los Angeles, and London: University of California Press, 1983.

Troilo, Sigfrido. *Andrea Giuliano, politico e letterato veneziano del Quattrocento*. Biblioteca dell'*Archivum Romanicum* 18. Geneva and Florence: L. Olschki, 1932.

Ullman, B. L. "Leonardo Bruni and Humanistic Historiography." In *Studies in the Italian Renaissance*, pp. 321–44. Raccolta di studi e testi 51. Rome: Storia e letteratura, 1955.

Valier, Agostino. *De cautione adhibenda in edendis libris* . . . . Padua: I. Cominus, 1719.

Vasaly, Ann. "The Spirit of Place: The Rhetorical Use of *Locus* in Cicero's Speeches." Ph.D. dissertation, Indiana University, 1983.

Vasoli, Cesare. "Considerazioni sulla *Laudatio urbis florentinae* di Leonardo Bruni." In *Studi sulla cultura del Rinascimento*, pp. 48–68. Manduria: P. Lacaita, 1968.

———. "Poggio Bracciolini e la polemica antimonastica." In *Poggio Bracciolini 1380–1980 (nel VI centenario della nascita)*, pp. 163–205. Istituto nazionale di studi sul Rinascimento, Studi e testi 8. Florence: Sansoni, 1982.

Vauchez, André. "Assistance et charité en Occident, XIIIe–XVe siècles." In *Domanda e consumi: livelli e strutture (nei secoli XIII–XVIII)*, edited by V. Barbagli Bagnoli, pp. 151–62. Florence: L. Olschki, 1978.

Verani, Tommaso. "Notizie del P. M. Giovacchino Castiglioni Milanese dell'Ordine de' PP. Predicatori tratte da due codici del secolo XV." *Nuovo giornale de' letterati d'Italia* 43 (1790): 74–176.

Vergerio, Pier Paolo. "De dignissimo funebri apparatu in exsequiis clarissimi omnium principis Francisci Senioris de Carraria." In *RIS*, 16:cols. 189A–94A.

———. *De ingenuis moribus*. Edited by Attilio Gnesotto. *Atti e memorie della R. Accademia di scienze, lettere ed arti in Padova*, n.s. 34 (1917–18): 75–157.

———. *Epistolario*. Edited by L. Smith. Rome: Tipografia del Senato, 1934.

Vermiglioli, G. B. *Memorie per servire alla vita di Franc. Maturanzio oratore e poeta Perugino*. Perugia: Carlo Baduel and son, 1807.

Vescovini, Graziella Federici. "Medicina e filosofia a Padova tra XIV e XV secolo: Iacopo da Forlì e Ugo Benzi da Siena (1380–1450)." In *"Arti" e filosofia nel secolo XIV: studi sulla tradizione aristotelica e i "moderni,"* pp. 231–78. Florence: E. Vallecchi, 1983.

Vespasiano da Bisticci. *Le vite.* Edited by Aulo Greco. 2 vols. Florence: Istituto nazionale di studi sul Rinascimento, 1970–76.

Vollmer, Fridericus. "Laudationum funebrium Romanorum historia et reliquiarum editio." *Jahrbucher für classische Philologie, Supplementband* 18 (1892): 445–528.

Walters, K. R. " 'We Fought Alone at Marathon': Historical Falsification in the Attic Funeral Oration." *Rheinisches Museum für Philologie* 124 (1981): 204–11.

Ward, John O. "Renaissance Commentators on Ciceronian Rhetoric." In *Renaissance Eloquence: Studies in the Theory and Practice of Renaissance Rhetoric*, edited by James J. Murphy, pp. 126–73. Berkeley, Los Angeles, and London: University of California Press, 1983.

Wardman, A. E. "Plutarch's Methods in the *Lives.*" *Classical Quarterly*, n.s. 21 (1971): 254–61.

Way, Sr. Agnes Clare. "Gregory Nazianzenus." *CTC*, 2:43–192, 3:413–25.

Weinstein, Donald. "In Whose Image and Likeness? Interpretations of Renaissance Humanism." *Journal of the History of Ideas* 33 (1972): 165–76.

———. "The Myth of Florence." In *Florentine Studies: Politics and Society in Renaissance Florence*, edited by Nicolai Rubinstein, pp. 15–44. London: Faber & Faber, 1968.

Weisinger, Herbert. "Renaissance Accounts of the Revival of Learning." *Studies in Philology* 45 (1948): 105–18.

Weiss, Roberto. *Medieval and Humanist Greek: Collected Essays.* Medioevo e umanesimo 8. Padua: Antenore, 1977.

Weissman, Ronald F. E. *Ritual Brotherhood in Renaissance Florence.* New York: Academic Press, 1982.

Westfall, Carroll William. "Biblical Typology in the *Vita Nicolai V* by Giannozzo Manetti." In *Acta Conventus Neo-Latini Lovaniensis*, edited by J. IJsewijn and E. Kessler, pp. 701–9. [Leuven]: Leuven University Press; Munich: W. Fink, 1973.

———. *In This Most Perfect Paradise: Alberti, Nicholas V, and the Invention of Conscious Urban Planning in Rome, 1447–55.* University Park: Pennsylvania State University Press, 1974.

———. "Painting and the Liberal Arts: Alberti's View." *Journal of the History of Ideas* 30 (1969): 487–506.

Wicks, Jared. "Thomism between Renaissance and Reformation: The Case of Cajetan." *Archiv für Reformationsgeschichte* 68 (1977): 9–32.

Wilcox, Donald. *The Development of Florentine Humanist Historiography in the*

Fifteenth Century. Harvard Historical Studies 82. Cambridge: Harvard University Press, 1969.
Wilkins, Ernest Hatch. *Studies in the Life and Works of Petrarch*. The Mediaeval Academy: Publication 63. Cambridge, Mass.: The Mediaeval Academy, 1955.
Witt, Ronald. *Coluccio Salutati and His Public Letters*. Travaux d'humanisme et Renaissance 151. Geneva: Droz, 1976.
―――. "Coluccio Salutati and the Origins of Florence." *Pensiero politico* 2 (1969): 161–72.
―――. *Hercules at the Crossroads: The Life, Works, and Thought of Coluccio Salutati*. Duke Monographs in Medieval and Renaissance Studies 6. Durham: Duke University Press, 1983.
―――. "Medieval *Ars dictaminis* and the Beginnings of Humanism: A New Construction of the Problem." *Renaissance Quarterly* 35 (1982): 1–35.
―――. "Salutati and Plutarch." In *Essays Presented to Myron P. Gilmore*, edited by Sergio Bertelli and Gloria Ramakus, 3 vols., 1:335–46. Florence: La Nuova Italia, 1978.
Wittschier, Heinz Willi. *Giannozzo Manetti: das Corpus der Orationes*. Studi italiani 10. Cologne and Graz: Böhlau, 1968.
Zappacosta, G. *Francesco Maturanzio umanista perugino*. Saggi e ricerche di lingua e letteratura italiana 1. Bergamo: Minerva Italica, 1970.
―――, ed. *Studi e ricerche sull'umanesimo italiano (testi inediti del XV e XVI secolo)*. Saggi e ricerche di lingua e letteratura italiana 5. Bergamo: Minerva Italica, 1972.
Zonta, Gasparo. *Francesco Zabarella (1360–1417)*. Padua: Tipografia del Seminario, 1915.

INDEX OF MANUSCRIPTS

Bergamo, Biblioteca Civica
   MS Delta IV 40 (MA 273): 252, 275
Bologna, Biblioteca Universitaria
   MS Lat. 741: 272
   MS Lat. 742: 273
   MS Lat. 746: 273
   MS Lat. 1622: 272
   MS Lat. 1896: 271–72
Casale Monferrato, Seminario
   Vescovile
   MS 1 b 20: 253, 289
Coburg, Landesbibliothek
   MS S IV 2, 41: 262
Cortona, Biblioteca Comunale
   MS 162 (243): 292
Cremona, Biblioteca Governativa
   MS Civico BB 2.5.2: 285–86
Dubrovnik, Biblioteca Male Braće
   MS 1247: 266
Florence, Biblioteca Laurenziana
   MS Ashb. 270: 263
   MS Ashb. 271: 283
   MS Conventi Soppressi 449: 251, 253
   MS Plut. 54.10: 250
Florence, Biblioteca Nazionale
   MS Conventi Soppressi G IV 936: 168 (n. 20), 301
   MS Conventi Soppressi J VII 5: 251, 253, 288
   MS Landau Finaly 152: 283
   MS Magl. VII 1095: 281
   MS Magl. VIII 1390: 276
   MS Magl. IX 123: 249
   MS Naz. II IV 34: 264–65
   MS Rossi-Cassigoli 372: 258
Florence, Biblioteca Riccardiana
   MS 149: 174 (n. 67)
   MS 660: 284
   MS 771: 288
   MS 784: 251, 254, 261, 277
   MS 811: 250
   MS 911: 289
   MS 928: 283
   MS 3903: 278
Fulda, Landesbibliothek
   MS C 10: 276
Leningrad, Archive of the Institute of the Academy of Sciences (LOII)
   MS 1/614: 289
London, British Library
   MS Add. 15406: 260
   MS Arundel 138: 286
Lucca, Biblioteca Governativa
   MS 762: 273
Mantua, Archivio di Stato
   MS Archivio Gonzaga 85 (B XXXIII 10): 292
Mantua, Biblioteca Comunale
   MS F II 6: 290
Milan, Biblioteca Ambrosiana
   MS B 124 sup.: 254, 264
   MS C 145 inf.: 252, 253
   MS E 124 sup.: 264
   MS F 55 sup.: 257
   MS G 33 inf.: 257, 262–63
   MS L 69 sup.: 289
   MS N 165 sup.: 269
   MS N 339 sup.: 275

MS P 259 sup.: 252
MS R 93 sup.: 266
MS & 179 sup.: 251
Milan, Biblioteca Nazionale
  Braidense
  MS A D XIV 27: 263
  MS A E XII 10: 251, 253–54
Milan, Biblioteca Trivulziana
  MS 783: 289
Modena, Biblioteca Estense
  MS Alpha J 9, 43 (Est. lat. 1269): 275
  MS Alpha O 6, 15 (Est. lat. 174): 262, 284
  MS Gamma G 1, 12 (Campori 55): 251
  MS Gamma G 7, 18 (Campori 1365): 283
  MS Gamma I 1, 48 (Campori app. 1614): 250
Munich, Staatsbibliothek
  MS Clm 766: 253
  MS Clm 24837: 266
Munich, Universitätsbibliothek
  MS 2/607: 278
Naples, Biblioteca Governativa dei Gerolamini
  MS M.C.F. 2, 12 (cart. 163): 252
Naples, Biblioteca Nazionale
  MS V E 40: 292
  MS V F 2: 286
  MS VIII A A 6: 255
  MS IX F 49: 250, 270
  MS XII E 7: 283
Padua, Biblioteca Capitolare
  MS B 62: 289
Padua, Biblioteca del Seminario
  MS 84: 270
  MS 116: 287
  MS 692: 275
Padua, Biblioteca Universitaria
  MS provv. 197: 271

Palermo, Biblioteca Comunale
  MS 4 Qq A 8 n. XI: 252
Paris, Bibliothèque Nationale
  MS Lat. 6802: 238 (n. 43)
  MS Lat. 7843: 264
  MS Lat. 8642: 251, 253
Parma, Archivio di Stato
  MS 90 bis: 264
Perugia, Biblioteca Comunale Augusta
  MS Fondo Vecchio C 61 (178): 173 (n. 63), 293
  MS Fondo Vecchio F 73 (399): 280
Rimini, Biblioteca Civica Gambalunga
  MS SC-157 (4 B I 43): 274
  MS SC-415 (4 D II 38): 281
  MS SC-1251 (4 H IV 2): 291
Rome, Biblioteca Angelica
  MS 1139: 200 (n. 14), 253, 255
  MS 1503: 258
Rome, Biblioteca Casanatense
  MS 1861: 270
Rome, Biblioteca Corsiniana
  MS 33 E 27 (Nic. Rossi 229): 168 (n. 19), 251
San Daniele del Friuli, Biblioteca Civica Guarneriana
  MS 183: 271
Sarzana, Biblioteca Comunale
  MS XXVI F 175: 276
Siena, Biblioteca Comunale degli Intronati
  MS H VI 26: 200 (n. 14), 289
Stresa, Centro di Studi Rosminiani
  MS 22: 260
Taggia, Convento Domenicano
  MS Arch. 2: 267
Trent, Biblioteca Comunale
  MS 4964: 253
Treviso, Biblioteca Comunale
  MS 38: 262

Trieste, Biblioteca Civica
 MS Sez. Petrar. I 4: 283
Turin, Archivio di Stato (Sezione 1)
 MS Bibl. Antica H II 25: 290
Turin, Biblioteca Nazionale
 MS J III 13: 290
Udine, Biblioteca Arcivescovile
 MS 70: 200 (n. 14)
Udine, Biblioteca Capitolare
 MS Bini 21.1: 271
 MS Bini 21.3: 250
Vatican City, BAV
 MS Barb. lat. 1868: 259
 MS Barb. lat. 1880: 252
 MS Barb. lat. 1952: 290
 MS Capponiani 3: 253, 260
 MS Chigi. I VI 215: 174 (n. 66, n. 67), 274, 293
 MS Ottob. lat. 489: 309
 MS Ottob. lat. 1153: 261
 MS Ottob. lat. 1834: 253, 275, 287
 MS Ottob. lat. 2854: 252
 MS Palat. lat. 327: 252–53
 MS Palat. lat. 607: 257
 MS Palat. lat. 1364: 254
 MS Palat. lat. 1592: 286–87
 MS Palat. lat. 1606: 307
 MS Regin. lat. 1370: 254
 MS Regin. lat. 1555: 295
 MS Urb. lat. 1023: 291–92
 MS Urb. lat. 1233: 282
 MS Vat. lat. 2694: 281
 MS Vat. lat. 2850: 291
 MS Vat. lat. 2906: 251
 MS Vat. lat. 2918: 273
 MS Vat. lat. 2939: 265–66
 MS Vat. lat. 3567: 209 (n. 89)
 MS Vat. lat. 3675: 276
 MS Vat. lat. 4376: 277
 MS Vat. lat. 4380: 267
 MS Vat. lat. 4872: 281, 283
 MS Vat. lat. 4912: 270
 MS Vat. lat. 5223: 281
 MS Vat. lat. 5336: 284
 MS Vat. lat. 5358: 280
 MS Vat. lat. 5815: 177 (n. 89), 284
 MS Vat. lat. 5891: 288
 MS Vat. lat. 5944: 311
 MS Vat. lat. 6835: 174–75 (n. 72), 284–85
 MS Vat. lat. 6850: 277
 MS Vat. lat. 6855: 174 (n. 67)
 MS Vat. lat. 7179: 269
 MS Vat. lat. 8106: 263, 285, 290
 MS Vat. lat. 8750: 252, 285
 MS Vat. lat. 8761: 174 (n. 67), 251, 269
 MS Vat. lat. 8919: 165 (n. 6), 271
 MS Vat. lat. 11761: 275
 MS Vat. lat. 13679: 277
 MS Vat. lat. 13709: 256
Venice, Biblioteca del Conte Alessandro Marcello del Maino
 MS ser. A I, Busta 4: 279
Venice, Biblioteca del Museo Civico Correr
 MS Cicogna 797 (1048): 256
 MS Cicogna 2755: 218 (n. 35), 267
 MS Correr 225: 281
Venice, Biblioteca Nazionale Marciana
 MS 2293 (Marc. lat. III 79), 168 (n. 22), 313
 MS 3788 (Marc. lat. X 254): 253
 MS 4002 (Marc. lat. XIV 12): 277
 MS 4296 (Marc. lat. XIV 264): 279
 MS 4351 (Marc. lat. XI 3): 257
 MS 4451 (Marc. lat. XII 137): 261
 MS 4499 (Marc. lat. XIV 236): 298
 MS 4679 (Marc. lat. XIV 229): 261
 MS 4717 (Marc. lat. XIV 250): 270
 MS 4736 (Marc. lat. XIV 230): 269
Vicenza, Biblioteca Comunale Bertoliana

MS G.7.1.79: 311
Vienna, Nationalbibliothek
  MS Lat. 4292: 254
  MS Lat. 4300: 268
  MS Lat. 4710: 270

MS Lat. 5513: 292
West Berlin, Staatsbibliothek
  MS Lat. fol. 486: 262
  MS Lat. fol. 613: 251, 252

GENERAL INDEX

Abimelech, 71
Acciaiuoli, Angelo, Cardinal, 128
Acciaiuoli, Donato, 24, 106, 118–19, 120–21, 249, 277
Accord (*convenientia*), 127–28
Acerbo, Tommaso, 249
d'Acqui, Tommaso, 280
Active and contemplative lives, 13, 86, 121, 147, 157
Adolescence, 58, 61, 125, 156
Adrian VI, Pope, 69, 149, 291
Adriani, Marcello Virgilio, 41–42, 50, 51, 79–80, 249–50
Adrian of Utrecht. *See* Adrian VI, Pope
Aeneas, 46, 110
A fortiori logic, 19–20, 128, 157
Agriculture, 124–25
Alamanno, Andrea, 51, 58, 250
Alatus, Petrus Simon, 250
Albergati, Niccolò, Cardinal, 69, 72–73, 79, 258, 289
Alberti, Leon Battista, 5–6, 21, 250, 293
Alberto da Castelfranco, 25–26, 140, 141–42, 250
Albornoz, Gil, Cardinal, 71, 279
Alexander III, Pope, 41, 100
Alexander VI, Pope, 48, 63, 64
Alexander III of Macedonia ("the Great"), 47, 99, 103
Alfonso I of Naples, King, 106, 110–11, 134, 309
Aliotti, Girolamo, 250

Almerici, Giovanni, 271
Alps, 48, 98–99
Altaflores Pamphilus, Ioannes Hercules, 250
d'Alviano, Bartolomeo, 281
Amanseur, Jeán, 261
Ambition, 67, 92–93, 103, 158
Ambrose, Saint, Bishop of Milan, 15, 18, 19
Anagni, 48
Andrea da Modena, 147, 265–66
Angeli, Iacopo, da Scarperia, 26
Angelo dalla Pergola, 250
Anglus, 46
Annales ecclesiastici, 2
Antenor, 43
Anthony, Mark (Marcus Antonius), 17
Anthropology, 61
Anticlericalism, 67, 72
Antonio da Rho, 26–27, 254
Apostolis, Michael, 24, 254
Aquinas, Thomas. *See* Thomas Aquinas, Saint
Aragon, Alfonso V of. *See* Alfonso I of Naples, King
Aragon, Aloysius of, Cardinal, 76, 263
Aragon, Beatrice of, 120, 260
Aragon, Eleanor of, 29, 85, 113, 256, 275
Aragon, Ferdinand I of, 254
Aragon, Ferdinand II of, 278
Aragon, Juan of, 267

Archimbaldus de Fuxo, 251
Arezzo: praise of in funeral oratory, 43–44
Argyropulos, Giovanni, 121, 143–44
Aringhieri, Francesco, 268
Aristides, Aelius, 7, 110; *Panathenaicus*, 23, 127
Aristotle, xi, 15–16, 54, 59, 60, 61, 97, 113, 115, 125, 130, 139, 142, 143–44, 150, 151, 156, 160; *Economics*, 130; *Politics*, 130; *Ethics*, 130, 151; *Poetics*, 151
Arno River, 94, 130
Arquá, 9
Arrigoni, Giacomo, 254
Arsendi, Raniero, 251
Ars poetriae, 7
Artes praedicandi. *See* Preaching
Art of good and holy living. *See* Cicero
Arts (*artes*): 53–54, 57–58, 120, 160; liberal, 44, 51, 54, 58, 61, 66, 75, 81, 90, 92, 96, 103, 124, 131, 139, 152, 153, 155; visual, 30–33, 58; good (*bonae*), 54, 57–58, 61, 92, 96, 125, 136, 159; mechanical, 58
Athens, 5–6, 39, 41, 42, 51, 89, 91, 102, 110, 124, 127. *See also* Funeral oratory
Augustine, Saint, Bishop of Hippo, 15, 140, 150
Augustinian hermits, 11, 28, 53, 70
Augustus, Emperor, 18, 81, 83, 110, 118
Avarice, 14, 83, 103, 114, 117, 124, 125, 158
d'Avenza, Gian Pietro, 136, 274
Avignon, 8, 9, 65

Badoer, Bonaventura, 9–10, 123, 254
Baglioni, Braccio, 108, 109, 119, 280
Baglioni, Galeotto, 108, 109
Baglioni, Grifo, 279
Baglioni, Nello, 108–9, 119, 260
Baglioni, Orazio I, 280
Baglioni, Pandolfo, 108, 109
Baglioni (family), 108–9
Baldini, Giusto, 254
Bandini, Bartolo, 86, 147, 268
Barbaro, Ermolao, 254
Barbaro, Francesco, 17, 22, 146, 147, 155, 254–55, 270
Barbaro, Zaccaria, 287
Baron, Hans, 23, 93–94
Barozzi, Giovanni, Patriarch of Venice, 78, 255
Barozzi, Pietro, Bishop of Padua, 43, 44, 46–47, 78, 144–45, 151, 255, 278–79
Barzizza, Cristoforo, 77, 143, 255
Barzizza, Gasparino, 97, 104, 132, 146, 255, 260, 294; popularity of funeral oration for Iacopo da Forlì, 11, 24; authorship of oration for Francesco Zabarella questioned, 200 (n. 14), 253
Barzizza, Guiniforte, 255, 294
Basil, Saint, 7, 69, 127
Basilli, Paolo, 265
Battista Mantovano, 85, 113, 149, 255–56
Battle of Fornovo, 117
Battle of Marathon, 102
Battle of Tau, 78
Battle of Varna, 84
Becci, Lazzaro, 119, 251
Becichemo, Marino, 256
Bembo, Bernardo, 256
Bembo, Bonifazio, 294
Benigno Salviati, Giorgio, 256
Bentivoglio, Andrea, 273
Benzo d'Alessandria, 38
Bergamo, 106
Bessarion, Cardinal, 24, 58, 72, 74,

75, 148, 254, 261
Bianchi, Apollonio, 256
Bibbiena, Pietro da, 269
Bible, 33, 73, 82, 98, 149, 150; 1 Corinthians, 14–16; 1 Thessalonians, 16; Vulgate Psalms used for grammatical instruction, 53; theme of "Good Shepherd," 73; poor, widows, and orphans in, 84, 85, 86, 114, 157–58; Gospel of John, 84, 158; Gospel of Matthew, 86, 114, 157; Letter of James, 86, 157–58; Wisdom, 98; Ecclesiasticus, 132; Proverbs, 132; Books of Samuel, 150
Bienato, Aurelio, 41, 42–43, 256
Biglia, Andrea, 11, 48, 97, 98, 105, 256–57
Bigolini, Paolo, 144, 257
Boccaccio, Giovanni, 130, 142
Boldú, Giacomo, 40, 257
Bologna, 69, 72, 75, 79, 104; Council of Six Hundred, 69. *See also* University of Bologna
Bolzanio, Urbano, 25, 140, 141–42, 250
Bondina Roccabonella, Agnesina, 282
Boniface VIII, Pope, 47–48
Bonisoli, Ognibene, 40, 58, 137, 258, 295, 311
Borghi, Giovanni Antonio, 251
Borgia, Alfonso. *See* Calixtus III, Pope
Borgia, Cesare, 137
Borgia, Giacobino, 262
Borgia, Pietro, 263
Borgia, Rodrigo. *See* Alexander VI, Pope
Borgognone d'Asti, 77, 258
Borromeo, Filippo, 270
Bracciolini, Poggio, 2–3, 22, 25, 31, 32, 33, 42, 43–44, 58, 62, 69, 75, 77, 84, 86, 122, 126, 129, 130, 133, 136, 139, 141, 142, 155, 258, 295; funeral oration for Francesco Zabarella, 11–14, 20–21, 24, 66–68; oration to Council of Constance, 12, 65–66, 83; date of final redaction of funeral oration for Leonardo Bruni, 230 (n. 101)
Brancaleoni, Gentile, 270
Brandolini, Aurelio, 258
Brandolini, Raffaele, 52, 70, 76, 87, 148, 258–59; funeral oration for Mariano da Genazzano, 36–37
Brembati, Pier Francesco, 289
Brescia, 102
Bribery, 118, 120, 146
Britannico, Giovanni, 259
Britannico, Gregorio, 259, 296
Brolo, Mosé del: *Liber pergaminus*, 38
Brown, Peter, 65
Brugnoli, Benedetto, 286
Bruni, Leonardo, 17, 20, 21, 22, 23, 29, 31, 33–34, 35, 41, 42, 43, 44, 49, 57, 60, 93–97, 101, 103–4, 113–14, 120, 121, 122, 127–31, 132, 135, 137, 154, 155, 251, 258, 259, 278, 296; his panegyric of Florence, 21, 23, 39, 94–95, 96, 127; funeral oration for Nanni Strozzi, 23, 24, 95–97; abandoned law for the humanities, 58, 128–29, 132; Greek translations, 60, 127–28, 130; his "Journal," 128; *Dialogi ad Petrum Histrum*, 130; scholarship of, 130; *De interpretatione recta*, 131; *Isagogicon moralis disciplinae*, 131
Bruno, Ludovico, 28, 259
Brutus, Lucius Iunius, 18, 110, 112
Bucci, Gabriele, 260, 296
Bufalini, Niccolò, 262
Buglioni, Santi, 114

Burchard, Iohann, 25, 28, 296
Burckhardt, Jacob, 25, 94
Bussi, Giannandrea, 82
Buzzacarini, Arcoano, 118, 292
Byzantium, 21–24, 35, 40, 46, 55, 106–7, 124, 125, 126, 129. *See also* Greece

Cabala, 150
Cabrini, Cabrino, 132, 260
Caccia, Tommaso, 251
Caccialupi, Ludovico, 256
Caesar, Gaius Iulius, 17, 18, 44, 46, 47, 89, 90, 103, 108, 110, 118
Cajetan, Cardinal (Tommaso da Vio), 2, 148–49, 270
Calcagnini, Celio, 112, 119, 151, 260
Caldiera, Giovanni, 260
Caligula (Gaius Iulius, Emperor), 82
Calixtus III, Pope, 72, 281, 283
Camici, Agostino, 260
Camillus, Marcus Furius, 118
Campano, Giannantonio, 52–53, 70, 75, 108–9, 113–14, 133, 160, 260–61, 268
Canonici, Pietro, 145–46, 289
Capitani, Battista, 251
Capodilista, Giovan Francesco, 279
Capogallo, Giovanni, 261
Cappello, Carlo, 115, 261
Capra, Bartolomeo della, Archbishop, 97
Capranica, Angelo, Cardinal, 36–37
Capranica, Domenico, Cardinal, 28, 71, 81, 284
Capranica, Domenico (the younger), 262
Capranica, Niccolò, Bishop, 24, 31, 72, 74, 75, 148, 250, 261
Carafa, Oliviero, Cardinal, 287
Carbone, Ludovico, 30–31, 32, 58, 80, 137, 147, 160–61, 261–62; funeral oration for Guarino, 55–56
Cardinals, 74, 81–82
Cardoni, Alfonso, 288
Cardulo, Francesco, 262
Carmagnola, Gregorio, 262
Carrara, Francesco il Vecchio da, 10–11, 92, 276–77, 291, 292
Carrara, Francesco Novello da, 92, 101
Carrara, Giovanni Michele Alberto, 262
Carrara, Niccolò da, 292
Carrara (family), 88
Casa, Angelo, 262
Casali, Antonio, 262
Casali, Battista, 26, 47–48, 49–51, 58, 69, 76, 81, 82, 86, 138, 139, 142, 144, 257, 262–63
Casciotti, Bartolomeo, 263
Casella, Ludovico, 119, 262, 275
Cassandra, Gian Battista, 291
Cassinari, Bartolomeo, 291
Cassinari, Girolamo, 291
Castanea, 263
Castelleto, Pietro, 11, 263
Castiglioni, Baldassare (d. 1444), 269
Castiglioni, Branda, Cardinal, 81, 264
Castiglioni, Dorotea, 264
Castiglioni, Giovacchino, 26, 264
Castiglioni, Guarniero, 264
Cato, Marcus Porcius (234–149 B.C.), 125, 126; his definition of the ideal orator, 26, 57, 126, 132, 158–59
Cattanei, Giovanni Lucido, 43, 85, 264
Cattanei, Marco, 287
Cattani, Francesco, 143–44, 264–65
Catullus, Gaius Valerius, 43
Catulus, Quintus Lutatius: funeral oration for his mother Popilia, 17
Cavalcanti, Otto, 24, 128, 259

Celani, Pietro, 255
Centori, Caterina, 256
Cereta, Laura, 265
Cerva, Elio "Lampridio," 141, 147, 265–66
Cesarini, Giuliano, Cardinal, 19, 31, 45, 77–78, 84, 258, 292
Character, 68, 125; excellence of, 131, 136. *See also* Ethos; Moral living; Virtue
Charity, 18, 19, 68, 84, 85, 86, 87, 110, 112, 114, 115, 117, 124, 134, 136, 147–48, 161
Charlemagne, 41, 46
Charles VIII of France, King, 117
Chiaramonte, Isabella di, 26
Chiericati, Giovanni, 280
Chiericati, Leonello, 71, 266
Chiericati, Niccolò, 280
Chrysoloras, Manuel, 11, 22, 23–24, 25, 26, 54, 55, 58, 123–26, 128, 129, 132, 151, 274
Church, 19, 50, 63–87, 104, 158–59; liberty of, 40–41, 74, 78–79; reform of, 64, 65, 79, 126, 158–59; art of good and holy living for the, 76–84; and wealth, 83–84; ideal proposed by humanist orators, 86–87
Churches, 94, 103; building or rebuilding, 74, 83–84, 85, 97, 109, 159
Church offices, 68–84, 158–59; criteria for selection to, 68–72; humanist emphasis on pastoral character of, 72–74, 158; criteria for evaluating performance in, 72–84. *See also* Cardinals; Papacy
Cibó, Lorenzo, Cardinal, 52, 76, 259
Cicero, Marcus Tullius, 17, 32, 34, 39, 50, 54, 56, 59, 61, 62, 67, 82, 84, 86, 89, 118, 121, 127, 129, 130, 132, 133, 138, 140, 143, 144, 146, 150, 157–58, 160–61; *Orator*, 1, 21, 31; *De oratore*, 2, 6, 21, 23, 89, 91, 135, 137, 144; *De lege Manilia*, 2–3, 90; *De republica*, 19, 141, 157; *De inventione*, 20; *Partitiones oratoriae*, 32; humanist adaptation of his art of good and holy living, 32, 54, 61, 76–84, 87, 90, 125, 131, 140, 144, 156, 160–61; letters to Atticus, 34; *Brutus*, 42, 91, 105, 158; *Pro Archia*, 59–60; *De legibus*, 71, 160; *Pro Marcello*, 89, 110; *De officiis*, 106, 157, 158; *De amicitia*, 124; *De senectute*, 124, 125, 126; *De finibus bonorum et malorum*, 157; *Tusculan Disputations*, 160. *See also Rhetorica ad Herennium*
Ciriaco d'Ancona, 266
Clemency, 99, 100, 102, 106, 107, 110, 111, 112, 116, 124, 161. *See also* Mercy
Clement VII, Pope, 1, 2, 51, 274–75
Cleofilo, Francesco Ottavio, 136–37, 140, 266
Collenuccio, Pandolfo, 266
Colleoni, Bartolomeo, 106, 262, 283
Colonna, Giovanni, Cardinal, 48, 263
Colonna, Oddone. *See* Martin V, Pope
Colonna, Prospero, Cardinal, 28, 72, 284
Colonna, Sciarra, 48
Colonna (family), 47–48
Colucci, Benedetto, 266
Comino, Bartolomeo, 267
Communes, 8, 38, 91
Compari, Luigi, 268
Conciliarism, 12, 68
Concord. *See* Harmony
Constantinople. *See* Byzantium

Contarini, Antonio, 267
Contarini, Gasparo, 40, 100
Contarini, Pietro, 41, 115, 267
Copiousness (*copia*), 133–35; in learning, 59–60, 124–25, 135, 150–51, 156
Cornelius Parisiensis, 267
Corner, Caterina, Queen of Cyprus, 115
Corner, Francesco, 114–15, 289
Corner, Giorgio, 115, 261
Corner, Marco, 267
Corner, Marco, Cardinal, 76, 269, 278
Corner (family): supposed descent from *gens Cornelia*, 46
Corradini, Giovanni, 17, 146, 147, 254–55
Cortasmeno, Ignazio, Metropolitan of Selimbria, 58
Corvino, Mattia, King of Hungary, 120, 265, 272, 286
Cossa, Baldassare, 252
Costa, Domenico, 279
Costabili, Antonio, 260
Costanzi, Antonio, 136–37, 140, 266, 267
Council of Basel, 47, 77–78, 97
Council of Constance, 65–68, 83, 123, 124; funeral orations for Francesco Zabarella at the, 11–16
Council of Florence, 129, 148
Crassus, Lucius Licinius, 59, 133
Crete, 24, 73, 148
Cristoforo da Milano, 267
Crivelli, Girolamo, 267
Crotti, Gian Giacomo, 133, 267
Crucius, Georgius, 265
Crusades, 46, 78, 80, 107, 134
Culture: harmonization of pagan with Christian, 18–20, 98, 114, 127, 128, 157–58

Curro, Carlo, 267

Dal Lino, Antonio, 273
Dal Lino, Giacomo, 30–31, 261
Dalmatia, 111, 141
Damian, Peter, 15, 69
Dante Alighieri, 130
Dardani, Luigi, 269, 287
Dati, Agostino, 86, 145, 147, 150, 268
Dati, Leonardo (d. 1425), 268
Decembrio, Pier Candido, 98, 99, 268, 298; panegyric of Milan, 39, 97
Decorum, 121, 133
De Grassis, Paris. *See* Paris de Grassis
Deliberative oratory. *See* Rhetoric: deliberative
Della Porta, Ardicino II, Cardinal, 262
Della Ratta, Giovanni, 261
Della Rovere, Cristoforo, 274
Della Rovere, Domenico, 259
Della Rovere, Giuliano. *See* Julius II, Pope
Della Rovere, Leonardo, 25, 47, 271
Della Torre, Girolamo, 110, 143, 147, 284, 291
Demosthenes, 23, 125
Diakonia. *See* Service
Dialectic, 59, 143, 145. *See also* Logic
Dictamen, 7, 8
Diedo, Francesco, 26, 298
Dio Chrysostom, 7
Dionysius of Halicarnassus, 17, 32
Diplomacy, 40, 66, 74–75, 105, 118–19, 120–21, 134, 146, 159
Discord, 67, 78–79, 91, 93, 107, 108, 109, 110, 118, 145, 158
Disjunction: stylistic, 9, 33–35
Docci, Tommaso, 268

Dolfin, Pietro, 286
Dominican order, 8, 17
Dominici, Giovanni, 127
Dominicus de Furno, 268
Donato, Pietro, 66–68, 268–69
Donato, Tommaso, 40, 257
"Dream of Scipio," 19, 45, 157
Duodo, Niccolò, 259

Eclecticism, 143, 155. *See also* Copiousness
Ecphrasis (vivid description), 14, 30–31, 76, 78–79, 121, 134–35; as one of the *progymnasmata*, 22; of Florence by Leonardo Bruni, 94
Education, 42, 53–61, 90, 131–52; parents' role in, 53; methods in, 58; teacher's role in, 58–59; of clerics, 81; and the environment, 139, 156. *See also* Humanist education
Egnazio, Giovanni Battista, 26, 269
Elegantia (refinement), 42, 55, 60, 139, 144
Eloquence, 44, 54, 55, 57, 58, 59, 60, 61, 66, 68, 70, 74–76, 90, 91, 103, 105, 113–14, 119, 120, 121, 124, 126, 130, 132–36, 141, 144, 146, 147, 148, 154, 155, 156, 158, 159–60; ideally conjoined with wisdom, 44, 54, 60, 91, 121, 129, 132, 148, 152
Emigli, Pietro, 258
Encomium: schema, 20; as one of the *progymnasmata*, 22. *See also* Panegyric
Epideictic oratory. *See* Rhetoric: epideictic
Epitaphs, 30, 57
Equity, 98, 108, 111, 112, 113, 145–46
Erasmus, Desiderius, 82, 149, 154
Ercole, Giovanni, 147, 160–61, 261
Eroli, Bernardo, Cardinal, 84, 252

d'Este, Alfonso I, Duke, 112, 119, 260
d'Este, Bertoldo, 256, 262
d'Este, Borso, Duke, 29, 112, 119, 261
d'Este, Ercole I, Duke, 29, 112–13, 282, 284
d'Este, Ippolito I, Cardinal, 260, 275, 284
d'Este, Leonello, 29, 85, 86, 105, 112, 119–20, 138, 275
d'Este, Niccolò III, 55
d'Este, Niccolò di Leonello, 29
d'Este, Sigismondo, 19, 269
d'Este (family), 55, 112–13, 119
Ethics. *See* Moral philosophy
Ethos, 4, 13–14, 58–59, 61, 64, 66, 67, 71, 80, 83–84, 87, 91, 102–3, 117–18, 120, 129, 136, 138, 146, 158–60; and ecclesiastical reform, 158–59; and political reform, 159; and humanist education, 159–60
Etruscans, 41, 43, 45
Eugene IV, Pope, 100, 146
Europe, 39, 40
External goods, 12–13, 36–62, 68, 128; ancestry, 37, 45–52; birthplace, 38–45; omens, 52–53; education, 53–61

Faccino, Gian Luigi, 269
Factional violence. *See* Discord
Fasoli, Gina, 38
Fasolo, Francesco, 286
Fausto, Vettore, 269
Federigo da Montefeltro. *See* Montefeltro, Federigo da, Duke of Urbino
Ferrante I of Naples, King, 51
Ferrante II of Naples, King, 256
Ferrara, 29, 55–56, 86, 96, 103, 105, 112–13, 119, 137, 151

Ferrici, Pietro, Cardinal, 278
Ferry de Clugny, Cardinal, 18, 287
Ficino, Marsilio, 121, 142, 144
Filelfo, Francesco, 22, 23, 106, 107–8, 269–70
Filelfo, Giovanni Mario, 270
Filetico, Martino, 270
Filippo da Lucca, 270
Filippo da Rimini, 270
Flavi, Giovanni Battista, 148–49, 270
Flemmyng, Henry, 270; thematic sermon for Francesco Zabarella, 11, 14–16
Florence, 13, 23, 29, 33, 39, 49–51, 56–57, 58, 59, 67, 93–97, 99, 103–4, 106, 115, 118, 120–22, 127, 129, 130, 131, 142, 153; humanist funerals and laurel crowning, 27, 29, 120–22, 135–36; the Signoria of, 27, 118; praise of in funeral oratory, 41–43; leadership in rebirth of letters, 44, 96; Palazzo Vecchio, 94; catasto of 1427, 104; convent of Santo Spirito, 142. *See also* Council of Florence
Forlí, 115–16
Forlimpopoli, 115–16
Fortebracci, Braccio, 109, 251
Forteguerri, Niccoló, Cardinal, 81, 281
Foscari, Francesco, Doge, 27–28, 40, 100–101, 104–5, 106, 134, 274
Foscari, Pietro, 40, 295
Foscarina, Marina, 283
Fracanziani, Antonio, 148, 284
France, 41, 44, 75
Francesco da Grado, 271
Francesco da Toledo, Bishop, 47, 271, 286; printing of funeral oration for Leonardo della Rovere, 25
Francesco da Vellate, 2, 271
Franciotti, Galeotto, Cardinal, 276

Franciscan order, 25–26
Frederick I Barbarossa, Emperor, 41, 99, 100
Frederick III, Emperor, 77, 110
Fregoso, Federigo, Cardinal, 287
Frezzi, Federigo, Bishop, 268
Funeral oratory, ix, 1–35; humanist, 2–3, 12–14; at Athens in antiquity, 5–6, 17, 38, 49, 63; at Rome in antiquity, 5–7, 17–18, 30, 37, 46; history of to the Renaissance, 5–9; Egyptian, 17; monody as a form of, 22–23, 24; diffusion of Renaissance funeral speeches, 24–25; and the visual arts, 30–33
Funeral rites, 3, 28–30, 32–33, 47; variety of literary commemorations by humanists for, 29–30

Gabrielli, Angelo, 72, 271
Gabrielli, Gabriello, Cardinal, 81, 263
Gaetani, Daniele, 271
Galen of Pergamum, 147, 151
Galeota, Silvestro, 286
Gandulfi, Giacomo, 272
Garzoni, Giovanni, 271–73
Gaspar de Sancto Ioanne. *See* Sighicelli, Gaspare
Gattamelata, Erasmo, 24, 31, 85, 102, 285, 286
Gatti, Giovanni, 273
Gauls, 45
Generosity, 66, 74, 85, 86, 100, 110–11, 114–16, 124
Genoa, 88, 89, 151
Georgius, Iunius, 256
Gerardo da Lucca, 273
Ghislieri, Giovanni, 257
Giacomo da Alessandria, 73, 148, 273
Giacomo da Bologna, 257

Giacomo da Pesaro, 273
Giberto da Correggio, 252
Gigli, Silvestro de', 273
Giles of Viterbo, Cardinal, 70, 77, 150, 275
Gioia, Girolamo, 21, 69, 274
Giovanni da Lucca, 254
Giovanni da Roma, 288
Giovanni da San Miniato, 127
Giovanni da Vecchiano, 274
Giovio, Paolo, 27
Girolami, Remigio de', 8, 301
Giudici, Battista de', 274
Giuliano, Andrea: funeral oration for Manuel Chrysoloras, 11, 24, 25, 54, 123–26, 274
Giustini, Lorenzo, 258
Giustiniani, Antonio, 63
Giustiniani, Bernardo, 32, 40, 41, 134, 274; funeral oration for Francesco Foscari, 27–28, 100–101, 104–5
Giustiniani, Leonardo, 22, 39, 99–100, 155, 274; funeral oration for Carlo Zeno, 11, 24, 27, 88–91, 101
God, 14, 36–37, 48, 52, 69, 84, 86, 98, 106, 128, 157, 161
Godly feast, 82, 139
Golden Age, 76, 79, 105, 106, 116, 119, 130
Gonzaga, Antonio, 252
Gonzaga, Barbara, 85, 264
Gonzaga, Federigo I, 264
Gonzaga, Francesco, Cardinal, 58, 264
Gonzaga, Francesco II, 117, 292
Gonzaga, Margherita, 53, 55, 60, 113, 270, 275
Gonzaga (family), 29
Good Shepherd. *See* Bible
Gotius, Bartholomaeus, 265
Gotius, Damianus, 265
Gotius, Ioannes, 141, 265
Gotius, Nicolaus, 265
Gotius, Orsatus, 265
Gradaeus, Marinus, 265
Grammar, 13, 53, 54, 55, 59, 136, 154
Grammarians, 136–37, 141
Grana, Lorenzo, 51, 70, 77, 150, 274–75
Gravitas (seriousness), 55, 133
Great Western Schism. *See* Schism
Greece, 57, 125, 137, 141–43, 153
Greed. *See* Avarice
Greek language, 23, 57, 58, 125, 127–31, 137, 139, 151
Gregory VII, Pope, 71, 78
Gregory of Nazianzus, Saint, 7, 23, 69
Gregory of Nyssa, Saint, 23
Grifi, Girolamo, 291
Grifi, Leonardo, 277
Grimani, Domenico, Cardinal, 26, 82, 139, 142, 263
Gritti, Andrea, Doge, 160, 309
Guarini, Alessandro, 275
Guarini, Battista, 85, 113, 119, 275; *De ordine docendi et studendi*, 56, 302
Guarini, Guarino, 19, 22, 25, 32, 33, 43, 53, 54–56, 58–59, 60, 85, 86, 90, 105–6, 112, 113, 119, 123, 125–26, 137, 138, 159, 261, 275, 302; popularity of funeral oration for Giannicola Salerno, 24
Guid'Ubaldo I, Duke of Urbino. *See* Montefeltro, Guid'Ubaldo I da, Duke of Urbino

Halm, Karl: *Rhetores latini minores*, 38
Harmony, 57–58, 91, 94, 105, 107, 108, 109–10, 116, 120, 124, 127–28,

132, 145, 148, 152, 156–58, 160
Hermogenes of Tarsus: *progymnasmata*, 22, 38
Hildebrand. *See* Gregory VII, Pope
Hippocrates of Cos, 140, 147
History, 13, 54, 55, 56, 57, 59, 103, 130, 131, 137, 139, 155; its relationship to panegyric, 21
Holy Thursday: ritual washing of feet, 112, 114
Hospitals, 114, 147
Hugonet, Philibert, 277
Humanism, 1–4, 13, 125, 135, 142, 148, 149, 154–61; harmonization of Christian and pagan cultures, 18–20, 98, 114, 127–28, 156–58; grammatical and rhetorical currents, 33–34, 154–56; truth related to conduct of life, 61, 122, 144, 152, 156; and the Church, 67, 74–87; subdital, 91; and scholarship, 140–42; positive view of humankind, 160. *See also* Church; Humanist education; *Humanitas*; Humanities; Rhetoric
Humanist education, 37, 53–61, 67–68, 70, 96, 102–3, 119, 124–26, 131–42, 152, 159–60; preferred disciplines, 13, 54, 57, 59, 130–31
Humanitas (humanity), 54, 66, 67, 75, 101, 116, 124, 136, 143, 160–61
Humanities (*studia humanitatis*), 42, 53–57, 59, 60, 66, 86, 114, 119, 121, 123, 126, 127, 128–31, 136, 137, 150–51, 153, 154–56
Hungary, 101, 120, 149
Hunting, 76, 107
Hunyadi, Ioannes, 249
Hussites, 77–78

Iacopo da Bologna, 276
Iacopo da Forlì, 11, 24, 143, 146, 255

Imitation, 32, 60, 127
Immortality of the soul, 127, 151
Imola, 115–16
Imperialism, 39–40, 42, 93–101
Inghirami, Tommaso "Fedra," 17, 28, 276; funeral oration for Pietro Menzi da Vicenza, 63–64; funeral oration for Ludovico Podocataro, 70–71; funeral oration for Pope Julius II, 78–79
Innocent VII, Pope, 26, 127
Innocent VIII, Pope, 71, 115, 266
Integrity. *See* Ethos
Invective, 63–64, 133, 156
Ioannes Germanicus, 252
Isabella of Castile, Queen, 28, 259, 283
Isocrates, 23, 32, 137–38, 159; support for a pan-Hellenic alliance, 138
Italy, 35, 36, 42, 44, 48, 50, 58, 81, 86, 93, 98–99, 104, 108, 114, 116–17, 119, 129, 135, 137, 140, 141, 147, 153, 154; liberty of, 50, 97
Ivani, Antonio, 276

James of Portugal, Cardinal, 71
Jean de Broniac, Cardinal, 2, 271
Jeremiah: lament for Josiah, 18
Jerome, Saint (Eusebius Hieronymus), 55, 69, 150
Jerusalem, 46, 50
Jesus Christ, 19, 73, 77, 106, 112, 158, 160, 161
Jews, 73, 77, 98, 150
Josephus, Flavius: *The Jewish War*, 55
Jouffroy, Jean, 80–81, 276
Judicial oratory. *See* Rhetoric: judicial
Julius II, Pope, 28, 40, 45, 47, 48, 52, 64, 69, 78–79, 81, 149, 276; and the Golden Age, 79

Justice, 91, 93, 95, 100, 102, 107, 108, 110–12, 116, 118, 120, 145–46. *See also* Clemency; Equity; Generosity
Justinian I, Emperor: legal code of, 132, 144

Kohl, Benjamin, 91
Kristeller, Paul Oskar, ix, 1, 33; *Iter Italicum*, x

Lactantius Firmanius, Lucius Caelius, 15, 55
Ladislas V of Poland, King, 146
Ladislas of Naples, King, 93
Lagraulas, Jean de Bilhères, Cardinal, 263
Lambertazzi, Cassandra, 272, 273
Lambertazzi, Francesca, 272
Lambertazzi, Giovanni Ludovico, 10, 276–77, 292
Lampugnano, Giovanni, 104, 277
Landino, Cristoforo, 62, 120–21, 277; popularity of funeral oration for Donato Acciaiuoli, 24
Lando, Vitale, 281
Landulphus, 277
Lascaris, Constantine, 151
Last Judgment: scene in Gospel of Matthew, 86, 114, 157
Law, 13–14, 58, 59, 66, 128–29, 132, 144–46; civic value of, 14; and eloquence, 59, 144; and humanist scholarship, 144–45
Lay piety, 84–86
Leo I, Pope, 71
Leo X, Pope, 49, 51, 70, 76, 79–80, 149
Leonardi, Niccolò, 277
Leto, Pomponio, 17, 20, 25, 137–38, 139, 277, 279
Letters (*litterae*), 51, 53, 55, 57, 70, 74, 90, 129, 136, 137, 141, 146, 151, 153, 156; rebirth of, 51, 152; sacred, 124, 136, 149; Greek, 57, 125, 129–31; Latin, 57, 126
Libanius, 7
Liberal arts. *See* Arts: liberal
Liberty, 99, 136–37, 146
Libidinous desire (*libido*), 61, 125, 156
Libraries, 82, 142, 153
Ligurni, Polonia, 264
Lion, Paolo da, 101, 281
Literature. *See* Letters
Livy (Titus Livius), 43, 44, 47, 56, 130
Logic, 13, 121; subordinated by humanists to rhetoric, 144
Lollio, Antonio, 277
Loredan, Giorgio, 274
Loredan, Leonardo, Doge, 47, 281–82
Lorenzo da Bologna, 257
Louvain, 149
Luca a Ripa, 281
Lucaro, Niccolò, 133, 139, 267, 278
Lucca, 96–97, 99; public funeral for Gian Pietro d'Avenza, 136
Lucullus, Lucius Licinius: Roman commander against Parthians, 102
Ludovico da Ferrara, 75, 290
Ludovico da Imola, 278
Lupi, Mattia, 136, 282
Luther, Martin, 149, 151
Luxemburg, Francis of, 263
Lysias, 23

Macer, Aemilius, 43
Macrobius, Ambrosius Theodosius: *Saturnalia*, 135
Maggi, Antonio, 39, 76, 278
Magliana: villa of Pope Leo X, 76
Magnanimity, 47, 116
Magnificence, 97, 112, 114, 119. *See*

also Charity; Generosity
Magno, Marcantonio, 44, 278
Maino, Giasone del, 19, 133, 144, 145, 278, 288
Malatesta, Carlo, 273
Malatesta, Elisabetta, 113, 252
Malatesta, Galeotto Roberto, 252, 282
Malatesta, Pandolfo II, 85, 252
Malatesta, Roberto, 274
Malatesta (family), 136
Malvezzi, Virgilio, 271
Manetti, Giannozzo, 17, 57, 58, 106, 120, 130, 134, 135, 141, 278, 307
Mansueti, Leonardo, 17, 59, 280
Mantua, 29, 43, 117
Manzoli, Battista, 273
Manzoli, Giorgio, 272
Maramaldi, Landolfo, 254
Marcello, Cristoforo, 151, 278–79
Marcello, Niccolò, Doge, 254
Marcello, Pietro, 41, 111–12, 279
Marcellus, Marcus Claudius: funeral oration for his father Quintus Claudius, 18
Marciano di Tortona Ligure, 255
Marco da Verona, 279
Mariano da Genazzano, 36–37, 52, 75, 148, 258
Marimeni, Bernardino, 252
Marini, Giovanni, 279
Marius, Gaius, 64
Marsi, Pietro, 115–16, 137–38, 139, 279
Marsili, Luigi, 58, 129, 142
Marsuppini, Carlo, 42, 44, 58, 284
Martin V, Pope, 12, 48, 69, 120
Mary, 19, 52
Mascarelli, Montorio, 279
Mathematics, 59, 151
Maturanzio, Francesco, 17, 57, 59, 109, 279–80, 288

Mauro, Gabriele, 280–81
Maximus, Quintus Fabius, 18, 33, 47, 50
Maxine, Countess, 290
Medici, Cosimo de', 49–50, 51–52, 54, 95, 153, 249; awarded title *pater patriae* posthumously, 49–50, 106, 118–19, 153
Medici, Giovanni di Cosimo de', 58, 250
Medici, Giovanni di Lorenzo de'. *See* Leo X, Pope
Medici, Giuliano de', Duke of Nemours, 41–42, 49, 249–50, 263
Medici, Giuliano di Piero de', 115, 121
Medici, Giulio de'. *See* Clement VII, Pope
Medici, Lorenzo de', Duke of Urbino, 49, 264–65, 289
Medici, Lorenzo di Giovanni de', 56–57, 95, 118, 258, 283
Medici, Lorenzo di Piero de', 41, 50–51, 115, 119–20, 120–21, 256; known as "the Magnificent," 50
Medici (family), 42, 49–52, 153
Medicine, 59, 143, 146–48, 151
Mellini, Celso, 275
Menander Rhetor (of Laodicea), 22–23; *Peri epideiktikon*, 7
Mendicant friars: criticized by humanists, 83–84
Menzi, Pietro, Bishop, 63–64, 70, 276
Merchione da Vizzano, 264
Mercy, 102, 124; works of, 114, 147, 157
Metaphysics, 121, 124
Metellus, Quintus Caecilius: funeral oration for his father Lucius Caecilius, 17
Micheli, Ugolino de', 283

Michiel, Domenico, 46
Michiel, Fantino, 24, 27, 99, 102, 117–18, 290
Milan, 9, 11, 26–27, 48–49, 50, 91–92, 94, 96, 97–99, 104, 105, 106, 107–8, 117, 119, 151; Castello Sforzesco, 108
Milani, Andromaco, 271
Miltiades: Athenian commander at Marathon, 102
Minutolo, Francesco, 286
Mirror, 71, 73
Mocenigo, Tommaso, Doge, 88
Modesti, Giannantonio, 281
Modesty (*pudicitia*), 113
Monaci, Lorenzo de', 281
Montaldo, Adamo di, 106, 110–11, 309
Montano, Giovanni, 107, 281
Montano, Roberto, 281
Monte, Pietro del, 47, 54, 281
Montecatini, Antonio da, 281
Montefeltro, Battista Malatesta da, 113
Montefeltro, Federigo da, Duke of Urbino, 119–20, 282
Montefeltro, Guid'Ubaldo I da, Duke of Urbino, 60, 283
Moral living, 54, 66, 92, 106, 131, 143, 156, 159, 160. *See also* Ethos; Virtue
Moral philosophy, 54, 57, 59, 129–30, 131, 143, 147, 155–56
Morandi, Nestore, 271
Morelli, Niccolò, 265
Muret, Marc Antoine, 134
Muses, 18, 57, 82, 138, 144
Music, 57–58, 89
Myths: fostered by humanist praise, 153

Naldi, Pietro, 27, 283

Naples, 44, 50, 69, 106, 110–11, 148; memorial service for Lorenzo de' Medici, 41
Nasi, Gabriele, 268
Navagero, Andrea, 47, 58, 281–82
Navagero, Bernardo, 160, 309
Negro, Pescennio Francesco, 282
Neoplatonism, 142, 150
Nepotism, 69
Nerucci, Bartolo, 282
Niccoli, Niccolò, 58, 129, 136, 139, 141, 142, 153, 258
Niccolò da Modrussa, 82, 83, 282; printing of funeral oration for Pietro Riario, 25
Niccolò da Rimini, 282
Nicholas V, Pope, 8, 16, 54, 57, 72, 73–74, 75, 76, 80–81, 106, 141, 153, 159, 276, 284
Nobility, 62, 123–24
Nogarola, Elisabetta, 258

Obizzo da Polenta, 275, 281
Odassi, Ludovico, 60, 282–83
Oliva, Alessandro, Cardinal, 52–53, 70, 261, 283
Oliviero, 283
O'Malley, John W., ix, 18, 82
Omens. *See* External goods
"Orator and poet," 58, 119, 135–36
Oratory, 90, 124, 130, 131, 132, 134, 137; conflicting evidence whether humanists revised orations before publication, 176 (n. 85). *See also* Rhetoric
Orphans and widows. *See* Bible
Orsini, Giordano (orator), 60, 68, 283
Orsini, Giordano (papal condottiere, d. 1483), 277
Orsini, Latino, 273
Orsini, Napoleone, Cardinal, 9, 313

Orsini, Niccolò, 269
Ovid (Publius Ovidius Naso), 34, 140, 160

Pacini, Antonio, 118, 283
Padovano, Bartolomeo, 103, 252–53
Padovano, Francesco, 27, 283
Padua, 12, 40, 43, 88, 92, 101, 110, 118, 151. *See also* University of Padua
Pagello, Bartolomeo, 137, 311
Pagello, Guglielmo, 283
Pagliarini, Bartolomeo, 26, 298
Pagliello, Girolamo, 280
Painting, 31, 58
Palaeologa, Medea, 255
Palaeologus, Manuel II, Emperor, 23–24, 311
Paleotti, Vincenzo, 272
Pallavicini, Rolando, 264
Palmeri, Niccolò, 28, 32, 73–74, 77, 80–81, 141, 284
Palmieri, Matteo, 27, 120, 121, 135, 284, 287; praise for his *La città di vita*, 140–41
Pandolfini, Giannozzo, 106, 278
Panegyric, 21, 75, 123, 130, 154; Greek tradition of, 23, 35, 39, 63. *See also* Encomium; Rhetoric: epideictic
Pannizzati, Niccolò Mario, 284
Papacy, 71–72, 73–74, 80–81, 158–59; diplomatic missions, 74–75, 80
Papal court, 16, 25, 27, 28, 63–64, 128
Papal State, 71, 78–79, 137
Parentucelli, Tommaso. *See* Nicholas V, Pope
Paris de Grassis, 16, 17, 18–19, 25, 26, 27, 28, 31, 311
Partenio, Pietro, 147, 148, 284
Partini, Antonio, 266

Pastor, Ludwig, 115
Patela, Giannantonio, 262
Pater patriae, 49, 50, 118–19, 135–36, 153; Roman origins of title, 118
Patronage, 90, 93, 119, 138, 159; by ecclesiastics, 80–84
Paul, Saint, 10, 16, 74
Pavia, 81, 97
Pazzi, Cosimo de', 250
Pazzi conspiracy, 50–51, 115, 120–21
Peace, 91, 92, 99, 104–6, 107, 116–17, 119, 132, 135, 148, 158; and concord, 57–58, 67, 75, 79–80, 120, 145, 158, 159; as an evangelical imperative, 80, 158. *See also* Harmony
Peace of Lodi, 50, 106, 118–19, 120
Pendaglia, Bartolomeo, 261
Penzo, Antonio, 272
Pérès, Guillaume, 70, 258–59
Pericles of Athens: funeral speech of, 23
Perleone, Pietro, 284
Perotti, Niccolò, 24, 82, 284–85
Perotti, Severo, 284–85
Persia, 89, 99, 138
Perugia, 43, 108–9, 119; codex of Biblioteca Comunale Augusta, 22–23; *See also* University of Perugia
Peruzzi, Antonio, 267
Pesaro, Benedetto, 280–81
Peter, Saint, 19, 71, 74
Petrarch (Petrarca, Francesco), 1–2, 9–10, 31, 32, 33–34, 35, 44, 65, 91–92, 123, 128, 130, 131, 135, 142, 146, 154, 155, 254, 285, 312
Petrus de Lonato, 267
Philosophy, 13, 54, 59, 90, 121, 123–24, 143–44, 149; Greek, 124–25. *See also* Dialectic; Logic; Metaphysics; Moral Philosophy; Physics

General Index

Physics, 121, 124, 151
Piasi, Battista, 278
Piccinino, Niccolò, 26, 96, 99, 102, 254, 268
Piccolomini, Enea Silvio. *See* Pius II, Pope
Piccolomini, Laudomia, 277
Pico della Mirandola, Giovanni, 82, 142
Pisa, 96
Pistoia, 81, 120; Hospital of the Ceppo, 114
Pius II, Pope, 52, 75, 113–14, 260
Platina, Bartolomeo, 82
Plato, 19, 20, 40, 60, 61, 71, 98, 99, 124, 128, 143–44, 146, 157, 160; *Phaedo*, 127
Platonism, 140, 142, 150
Plethon, Gemisthos, 24
Pliny the Elder (Gaius Plinius Secundus), 43
Pliny the Younger (Gaius Plinius Caecilius Secundus), 43
Plutarch, 22, 125
Podestà: manuals of instruction for, 8, 91
Podiani, Luca Alberto, 146, 288
Podocataro, Ludovico, 70–71, 276
Poetry, 13, 53, 54, 55, 56, 57, 59, 135, 137, 154. See also *Ars poetriae*
Poggio Bracciolini. *See* Bracciolini, Poggio
Politics, 87–122, 159
Poliziano, Angelo, 75, 141, 154, 312
Polybius, 30, 32, 37
Pompey (Gnaeus Pompeius), 3, 90, 103
Pontano, Giovanni (d. 1446), 60, 283, 285
Pontano, Giovanni Gioviano (d. 1503), 75
Pontico Virunio, Ludovico, 285

Porcari, Camillo, 285
Porto, Dorotea da, 280
Porto, Francesco da, 280
Porto, Isotta da, 280
Pozzo, Francesco Dal, 285–86
Pozzo, Gianniacopo Dal, 282
Preaching, 7, 8, 65–66, 75–76, 154, 159; *artes praedicandi*, 7, 8–9, 34; thematic sermons, 8–10, 11, 21, 33, 65–66, 75, 123, 154
Printing: of funeral orations, 24–25
Priscian: *Praeexercitamina*, 22, 38
Priuli, Eusebio, 40–41, 286
Progymnasmata, 6–7, 22, 30, 38
Prosopopoeia, 32, 69
Prudence, 55, 113
Pseudo-Dionysius the Areopagite: *Divine Names*, 19
Publicola, Publius Valerius: funeral oration for L. Iunius Brutus, 18
Public service, 59, 66, 87, 90, 92, 123, 124, 131, 132, 155, 157–58; as an ideal for the orator, 18–19, 86
Pucci, Alessandro, 161, 289
Pucci, Francesco, 286
Pucci, Lorenzo, Cardinal, 37, 290
Punic Wars: the second, 44, 89

Questenberg, Jakob, 25
Quintilian (Marcus Fabius Quintilianus), 2, 4, 15, 26, 56, 158
Quirini, Giovanni, 131, 286
Quirini, Lauro, 286
Quirini, Taddeo, 293

Ragusa (Dubrovnik), 141
Ramusio, Giovanni Battista, 286
Ranuzzi, Girolamo, 271
Ranzano, Pietro, 286
Rasini, Baldassare, 20, 31, 108, 286–87
Rebirth, renaissance, revival, 42, 43,

44, 45, 51, 55–56, 78–79, 80–81, 127, 129–30, 138, 152, 153–54
Reform, 61, 76, 116, 118, 124, 149, 158–59; tie between aesthetic and moral dimensions, 83, 93. *See also* Church
Reformation, 148–49
Remolino, Francesco, 263
Resti, Bartolomeo, 265
Rhetoric, 1, 13, 54, 55, 56, 57, 59, 67–68, 75, 92, 113–14, 129, 133, 140, 144, 146, 150, 151, 153, 155, 158; epideictic, 2, 6, 10, 32–33, 76, 91, 121, 127, 130, 134, 135, 136, 152, 154, 155–56; handbooks and treatises, 6–7, 12, 34–35, 123; medieval, 7; Byzantine, 7, 21–24; deliberative, 10, 32, 34, 134, 135; judicial, 10, 34, 134, 135, 144; importance of the situation for, 27–28; triad of nature, training, and practice, 58; stasis theory, 134. *See also* Eloquence; External goods; Invective; Oratory; Panegyric; Preaching; Style; Topics
Rhetorica ad Herennium, 7, 20, 23, 37; schema for an encomium, 20
Riario, Girolamo, 115–16, 279
Riario, Pietro, Cardinal, 25, 82, 282, 285
Ricoveri, Niccolò, 147, 268
Rinuccini, Alamanno, 27, 121, 140–41, 287
Rocca, Lorenzo, 287
Roger, Pierre, 9, 313
Romagna, 40, 115
Rome, 24, 26, 31, 36, 39, 41, 42, 43, 44, 45, 47, 48, 51, 57, 63–64, 65, 72, 78, 81, 83, 94, 96, 98, 99, 102, 105, 108, 110, 116, 118, 124, 132, 133, 139, 140, 153, 158; ancient funeral customs, 18, 47; Forum, 31; Roman Republic, 31, 43–44, 94, 118; Roman Empire, 41, 79, 99, 118; image of in Renaissance funeral oratory, 45; Castel Sant'-Angelo, 63; Santa Maria in Aracoeli, 63; churches rebuilt by Nicholas V, 81; Saint Peter's basilica, 81, 83; Capitoline Hill, 135; wages at the *studium*, 138–39; center for Thomism in Renaissance, 150
Roscius, Lucius, 31
Roselli, Antonio, 19, 43, 46–47, 144, 146, 255
Rossellino, Bernardo, 135
Rossi, Pietro, 150, 268
Rosso, Francesco, 269
Ruffo, Matteo, 287
Rugio, Benedetto, 69, 274, 287
Rustici, Cencio, 126

Sabellico, 57, 287
Sadoleto, Iacopo, Cardinal, 287
Sailing, 58, 90
Salerno, Giannicola, 19, 24, 54–55, 275
Salerno, 43
Sallust (Gaius Sallustius Crispus), 32–33, 47, 56, 103
Salutati, Coluccio, 41, 97, 127, 129, 135, 142, 146, 314
San Bonifacio, Ludovico di, 261
San Gimignano, 119; public funeral for Mattia Lupi, 136
Sangiorgi, Giovanni Antonio, 18, 287
Sapia, Sebastiano, 144, 145, 288
Sassi, Cristoforo, 146, 288
Saturnino, Niccolò, 263
Savelli, Leonardo, 27, 283

Savorgnan, Niccolò, 289
Savoy, Amadeus VIII of, Duke, 47, 77, 255
Savoy, Louise of, 47, 252
Scarpa, Caterina, 291
Scevola, Niccolò, 288
Schism, 77; Great Western, 13, 65, 67, 93; Greek, 124
Scholasticism, 9, 10, 11, 20, 123, 143–44, 145, 150, 153; scholastic methods, 34, 143, 145; and theology, 149–50. See also Aristotle; Logic; Preaching: artes praedicandi, thematic sermons
Scipio Africanus Maior, Publius Cornelius, 33, 44, 45, 47, 89, 90, 102
Sclarici dal Gambaro, Tommaso, 288
Scripture. See Bible
Sculpture, 31
Scyllacius, Nicolaus, 288
Second Sophistic, 7, 21
Seneca, Lucius Annaeus (the elder): Controversiae, 26, 158
Seneca, Lucius Annaeus (the younger), 15, 118, 141
Seratti, Giovanni Peregrino, 288
Service (diakonia), 72–73, 114. See also Public service
Servius, 56
Seyssel, Claude de, Archbishop, 149, 290
Sforza, Battista, 113, 261, 266
Sforza, Beatrice, 278
Sforza, Francesco, Duke, 85, 102, 106, 107–8, 260, 269, 287
Sforza, Galeazzo Maria, Duke, 107
Sforza, Ippolita Maria, 282, 288
Sforza, Ludovico Maria, Duke, 294
Sforza, Sforza Maria, 285–86
Sforza (family), 48–49, 50
Sibilla, Bartolomeo, 288

Sighicelli, Gaspare, 69, 79, 289
Sigismund, Emperor, King of Hungary, 100, 101, 146
Simonetta, Margherita, 264
Simony, 69
Sixtus IV, Pope, 45, 48, 50, 70, 82, 83, 115, 291–92
Soardi, Armachide, 289
Socrates, 55, 125, 143
Soderini, Francesco, Cardinal, 263
Solerio, Antonio, 86, 145–46, 289
Solon of Athens, 17, 99
Sorgius, Iunius, 266
Sozzini, Mariano, 145, 268
Spagnoli, Pietro, 290
Spain, 44
Sparta, 41, 105
Squarciafici, Bartolomea, 279
Statues, 31, 101
Stefano da Borgo, 253
Stella, Girolamo, 289
Sterponi, Stefano, 161, 289
Strassoldo, Ludovico, 114, 289
Strozzi, Ercole, 135, 260
Strozzi, Nanni, 23, 24, 41, 95–97, 103–4, 259
Studia humanitatis. See Humanities
Style, 12, 133; figures of speech, 14; three kinds of, 133, 134
Suarez de la Vega, Lorenzo, 269
Sulla Felix, Lucius Cornelius, 17, 41, 52
Superchi, Giovanni Francesco, 289
Suriani, Antonio, 279
Syllogism, 10, 16

Tacitus, Cornelius, 56
Telesio, Antonio, 290
Thaddeus of Lyon, 149, 290
Themistocles of Athens, 89, 91, 98, 103

Theodosius I, Emperor, 18
Theology, 13, 44, 59, 66, 148–50
Theon, Aelius, of Alexandria: *progymnasmata*, 38
Thomas Aquinas, Saint, 149–50
Thomism, 149–50
Thucydides: his account of funeral speech by Pericles, 23
Tiberius, Emperor (Tiberius Iulius Caesar Augustus): funeral oration for Augustus, 18
Timoteo da Modena, 290
Tizzone, Ludovico, 290
Todeschini, Stefano Federigo, 270
Tolerance, 2, 148; religious, 77–78
Topics, xi, 71–72, 82
Tortelli, Giovanni, 44, 147, 290
Torti, Girolamo, 133, 145, 278
Traversagni, Lorenzo: *Epitome Margaritae eloquentiae*, 134
Traversari, Ambrogio, 23
Traversini, Pietro, 290
Trebizond, George of, 22, 23, 24, 27, 46, 99, 102, 117–18, 290, 316–17
Trevisan, Ludovico, Cardinal, 290
Trinkaus, Charles, 18
Triumphs, 101, 107–8
Trivulzi, Gian Giacomo, 290
Tron, Paolo, 253
Truth, 78, 134, 142, 144, 148, 150, 152, 156; related by humanists to conduct of life, 61, 122, 144, 156
Turks, 41, 80, 84, 106–7, 125, 138
Tyranny, 95, 98, 136

Ubaldino, 290
Uberti, Francesco, 291
Universities, 59, 137, 139, 142
University of Bologna, 46–47
University of Padua, 143, 147
University of Paris, 44, 153
University of Perugia, 57, 133

Valaresso, Fantino, Archbishop, 73, 148, 273
Valeriano, Piero, 147, 291
Valla, Giorgio, 143, 150–51, 292
Valla, Lorenzo, 77, 134, 154
Varano Sforza, Costanza, 273
Varini, Gian Francesco, 291
Vaucluse, 135
Vegerius, Conradus, 69, 149, 291
Vendramin, Andrea, Doge, 111–12, 279
Veneto, Paolo, 77, 143, 255
Venice, 24, 27, 28–29, 31, 39, 46, 54, 58, 78, 88–91, 99–101, 104–5, 106, 111–12, 114–15, 123, 124, 131, 147, 151; praise of in funeral oratory, 39–41; office of Doge, 40, 100, 111–12; convent of Sant'Antonio, 82; Santa Maria Celeste, 88; Council of Ten, 88, 89, 111; spirit of cohesion (*unanimitas*), 89, 99–100, 110; ritual wedding with the sea, 100; procurator of San Marco, 100, 111; public attorney (*avogador di comun*), 100, 111; conquest and defense of Brescia, 102
Vergerio, Pier Paolo, the elder, 10, 20, 22, 33–35, 57, 59, 66, 68, 75, 131, 134, 154, 155, 291, 317; *De ingenuis moribus*, 10, 131, 155; funeral oration for Francesco il Vecchio da Carrara, 10–11, 92; *De republica veneta*, 39
Verona, 40, 43
Vigerio, Marco, 83, 285, 291–92
Vigilio, Francesco, 117, 292
Virgil (Publius Vergilius Maro), 53, 135; *Aeneid*, 110
Virtue, 67, 68, 70, 74, 90, 95, 96, 99, 121, 122, 125, 126, 128, 132, 136, 138, 139, 142, 146, 147, 152, 155, 156, 158–59, 160; in warfare, 101–3

Visconti, Bernabò, 92
Visconti, Bianca Maria, 107, 267, 269–70
Visconti, Caterina, 97, 253; date of anniversary funeral oration for, 217 (n. 29)
Visconti, Filippo Maria, Duke, 40, 96, 97, 99, 101, 102, 107, 260, 281; his scruple, 104
Visconti, Galeazzo, 92, 98
Visconti, Giangaleazzo, Duke, 11, 19, 48, 90, 93, 97–98, 99, 127, 253, 255, 257, 261, 263, 277
Visconti, Giovanni, Archbishop, 9, 10, 91–92, 285
Visconti, Matteo, 92
Visconti (family), 46, 48–49, 91–92, 96, 97–99, 107, 137
Visdomini, Elisabetta, 285
Visual evidence, 92, 97, 112, 134–35, 156. *See also* Ecphrasis
Vitelleschi, Giovanni, Cardinal, 71
Viterbo, 43, 128
Vitrè, Robert, Cardinal, 69, 263
Vittorino da Feltre, 53, 55, 59

War, 51, 79–80, 85–86, 92, 93, 98–99, 101, 107, 116–17, 118–19, 120, 138, 158; humanist ambivalence toward, 103–6; defense of wars as just, 105
War of Chioggia, 88, 90

Wealth, 68, 114–15, 118; ecclesiastical, 83–84
Wisdom and eloquence. *See* Eloquence
Women: praise of in funeral oratory, 113–14, 160

Xenophon: panegyric for Agesilaus, 23

Zabarella, Bartolomeo, Bishop, 47, 250
Zabarella, Francesco, Cardinal, 11–16, 19, 20–21, 24, 31, 47, 66–68, 72, 80, 118, 126, 133, 146, 159, 258, 268–69, 270, 292; question whether subject of funeral oration attributed to Gasparino Barzizza, 200 (n. 14), 253
Zabarella, Giovanni, 47, 54, 281
Zamagna, Martullus, 265
Zamagna, Paula, 265
Zambeccari, Giovanni, 272
Zambeccari, Peregrino, 271
Zamberti, Bartolomeo, 150–51, 292
Zane, Lorenzo, 280
Zeno, Battista, Cardinal, 72, 271
Zeno, Carlo, 11, 24, 27, 88–91, 101, 103, 274
Zeno, Iacopo, 45, 77–78, 292
Zilioli, Teodora, 275

OF DAVIDSON COLLEGE